Customer Service on the Internet

SECOND EDITION

Building Relationships, Increasing Loyalty, and Staying Competitive

Customer Service on the Internet

SECOND EDITION

Building Relationships, Increasing Loyalty, and Staying Competitive

Jim Sterne

Wiley Computer Publishing

John Wiley & Sons, Inc.

NEW YORK · CHICHESTER · WEINHEIM · BRISBANE · SINGAPORE · TORONTO

Publisher: Robert Ipsen
Editor: Cary Sullivan
Managing Editor: Michelene Frederick
Text Design & Composition: North Market Street Graphics

Designations used by companies to distinguish their products are often claimed as trademarks. In all instances where John Wiley & Sons, Inc., is aware of a claim, the product names appear in initial capital or ALL CAPITAL LETTERS. Readers, however, should contact the appropriate companies for more complete information regarding trademarks and registration.

This book is printed on acid-free paper. ∞

Published by John Wiley & Sons, Inc.

Published simultaneously in Canada.

This publication is designed to provide accurate and authoritative information in regard to the subject matter covered. It is sold with the understanding that the publisher is not engaged in professional services. If professional advice or other expert assistance is required, the services of a competent professional person should be sought.

Library of Congress Cataloging-in-Publication Data:

Sterne, Jim, 1955–
    Customer Service on the Internet : building relationships, increasing loyalty, and staying competitive / Jim Sterne.—2nd ed.
        p.cm.
    Includes index.
    ISBN 0-471-38258-2 (pbk. : alk. paper)
    1. Customer services—Communication systems.   2. Internet marketing.
3. World Wide Web.   4. Internet (Computer network)   I. Title.

HF5415.5 .S737 2000
658.8'12'02854678—dc21   00-028213

Printed in the United States of America.

10 9 8 7 6 5 4 3 2

This book is dedicated to Colleen.

CONTENTS

Chapter 6   Measuring Your Success   183

The Customer Service Bar Is Raised

The companies that have had the foresight, the resources, and the necessity to tackle the difficult aspects of electronic customer service took an early lead. These companies did the unexpected. They stretched the envelope. They broke the mold. They took one step beyond.

It took serious competitive pressure, vision, and a unique understanding of client/server networking for these companies to pull ahead of the pack.

You'll always have serious competitive pressure. You can have vision. But today, everybody has been handed the World Wide Web. Now everybody has a way for their customers to reach them. Everybody has a new tool in their arsenal. Everybody is going to use it in different ways.

The bar has been raised again.

We thought the motor car had changed the world, and we were right. We thought the telephone had changed the world, and we were right. We thought the computer had changed the world, and we were right. Now, it's time for the Internet to alter the way we work and how we interact with our trading partners.

You have the need, you have the connectivity, you have the competitors snapping at your heels. But most of all, you have customers demanding nothing short of the very best.

Ode to a Customer Service Web Site

I have a little problem, so I call you on the phone
I'm given numbered options—to punch them each by tone.
After hitting number 7, then 2, 8, 6 and pound

A short recording tells me that no operators can be found
They're busy helping others and would I hold this once?
Because my call is SO important. What am I? A dunce?

My call's not so important that I'll spend an hour on hold,
While my shoulder aches, my patience bakes and my coffee grows green mold.
Nothing your recording says can cause me to believe
That my call will be taken in the order it was received.

So down I put the telephone and up I pick the modem
To find solutions on your site, and once found, download 'em.
I calmly wait while DNS looks up your URL
Until your server answers your home page front door bell.

I wait for frames to paint themselves, my solution to begin.
And then I wait for plug-ins so I can see your logo spin.
I wait to get an audio file—greetings from your CEO
He doesn't get the Internet, but he loves the radio.

I wait until a picture of your building is on my screen
And I realize there are things that should not be heard nor seen.
Finally, there's a menu and I poise my mouse to click . . .
But first, a Java applet! "Starting Java." I know that won't be quick.

The menu choices indicate you know yourselves full well.
You know all about your company and that's what you want to tell.
But where's the button I can push, that takes me to the page
That solves my problem? Feels my pain? And soothes my mounting rage?

There, in the lower corner, down by the copyright
There's a little tiny icon that looks as if it might
Be a link to customer service. My troubles soon will quit!
I click upon it and I get . . .
a 404.
Oh, sugar.

And when I finally reach that page that promises relief.
I'm staring at a document that's far beyond belief.
For where there should be answers to frequently asked questions
And online help and knowledge-bases, is naught but indigestion.

For there in type italics, underlined and bold
Is the number for your help desk phone
I should have stayed on hold.

DILBERT reprinted by permission of United Feature Syndicate, Inc.

CHAPTER 1

The Web Was Made for Customer Service

I f you have any doubts about the importance, value, and potential of the Internet, go pick up another book. There are enough titles out there to convince you that the Web is changing the face of the planet. It's true. Enough said.

This book does not set out to convince you that the world has changed. We take that for granted and look for ways to leverage that knowledge while our competitors are still wondering why they're losing business.

The only questions that remain are: How can I use the Web better? How can I provide an interactive experience that increases customer satisfaction? How can I put up a barrier to competition and bond my customers to me so they'll want to buy from me now and forever?

If you're asking those questions, you're on the right track.

If you're looking for an academic treatise on the rigors of creating data systems that will let you track all of your customer data, you might want to pick up Michael Cusak's *Online Customer Care* (ASQ Quality Press, 1998). Or, at least get a copy of it for the people in your information technology (IT) department.

If you're wondering how e-mail management systems, troubleshooting guides, and artificial intelligence fit into an overall customer care program heading toward full-on customer relationship management, you've come to the right place. And if you're wondering about building a Web site that can provide your company with a competitive edge in treating customers the way they want to be treated, you've come to the right place.

The World Wide Web Grows from Infant to Toddler

The commercial use of the World Wide Web didn't appear fully-formed as a customer service tool. It started off as a marketing medium.

Phase One: The Product Page

A few farsighted marketing people discovered the Web and created the corporate equivalent of the personal home page. This is our brochure! You can click on this brochure instead of turning pages! See the pretty pictures of our headquarters! Read the exciting hype! Aren't we clever?

Phase Two: The Corporate Web Site

Upper management decided that its Web site should properly represent the whole company. Here's everything you would ever want to know about us and our products and our policies and our opinions and our white papers and our press releases and our trade show schedules. It's online, all the time, right here, read it while it's hot! Aren't we hip? Click here to download this important message: "Hello, I'm Lou Gerstner, chairman of IBM. On behalf of all of us at IBM, I'd like to welcome you to our World Wide Web server."

Promising Lou that his photo and voice would be on the home page secured the funding John Patrick needed in 1994 to move the company from grass roots into the tall bushes. But it would still be a few years before those bushes grew into fruit-bearing trees.

Phase Three: The Participatory Web Site

Then site visitors started to expect more. They knew that the Internet and the World Wide Web would support interaction. They didn't have to settle for static ads from the advertising department; they could manipulate the Web site, interact with it, play with it. They could track an overnight package at Federal Express (www.fedex.com, Figure 1.1). They could rent a car from Alamo (www.freeways.com), buy an airline ticket at PCTravel (www.pctravel.com), and bid on coins from their desks at Numismatists Online (www.bonsai.com/qnu/hobby/index.html).

Until this point, the excitement of the Web was in how many hits could you generate—how much attention could you garner? Get enough attention and

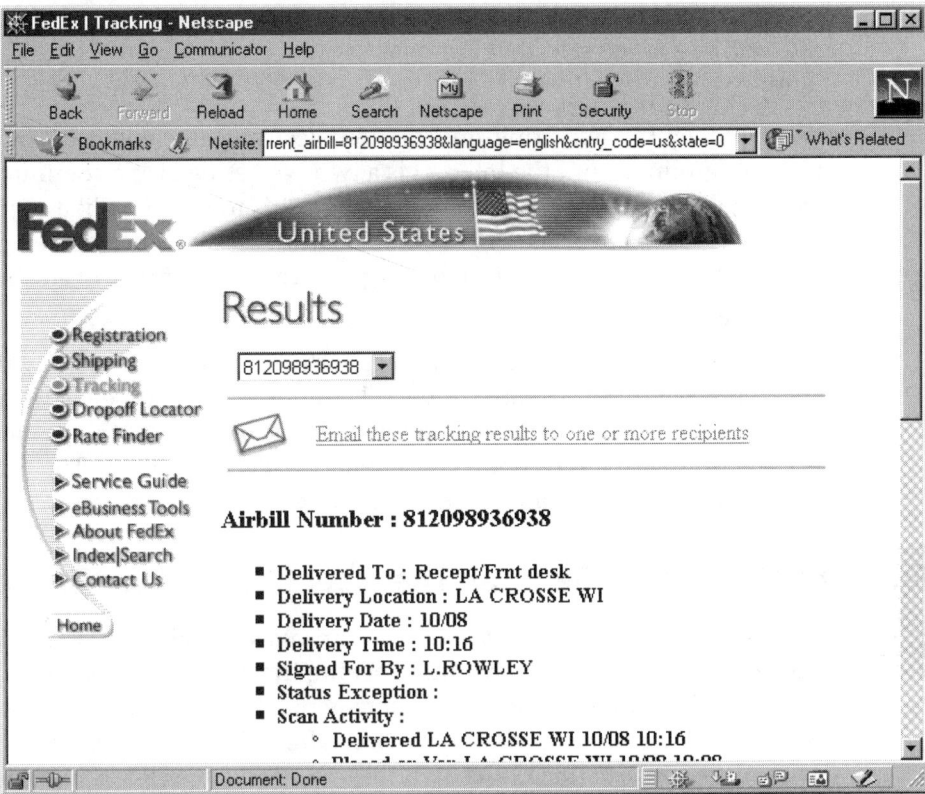

Figure 1.1   Want to know where your package is at the moment? Federal Express knows you do.

you could sell ads on your site. Since nobody seemed to be buying things in droves at the moment, you could defray the cost of your site with link-ads. It was easy to convince others that their message would be seen by the millions who came to your directory, search engine, or soap opera.

Then a small number of people began talking about the serious financial benefits they were reaping from their customer service applications on the World Wide Web. The results made everybody happy.

Customer Service Online: The Early Days

In 1995 Jerry Neece, then Sun Microsystems' senior product manager for Internet product marketing, announced that putting customer service on the Web had saved Sun an estimated $1.3 million—in January of that year alone. Approximately one third of that was in human resources. The majority was saved by delivering software fixes over the Internet, instead of having to create magnetic tapes and installation documents and then stuffing them into postal packaging. Not to mention the associated shipping costs. By January of 1996, one employee said that Sun was showing a savings of $12 million each month.

Saving money by delivering information electronically might be enough for most bottom-liners. But the Internet is a two-way street. It's a communications medium. It's not a TV, a radio, or a magazine. It's much more like a telephone, with the ability to hear as well as to be heard. You don't use the telephone to deliver a radio message and then hang up. You use it for conversation, be it chitchat, problem solving, or transaction processing.

Like the telephone, the Web also allows for conversation. Yesterday that conversation was written. Today it's verbal. Tomorrow it will be visual. The verbal and visual tools are helping and will help us take care of things on the Web that we previously did with our telephone 800 numbers. The complaint department is simply available in a new way.

Customer Service in General: The New Competitive Battlefield

Tom Peters keeps proving that he's not an old dog. He keeps learning new tricks and then turning around and teaching them to us. In *Circle of Innovation* (Knopf, 1997), Tom hails the end of incremental improvements, rallies around the Do Anything As Long As You Do Something flag, and calls for a corporate CDO—Chief Destruction Officer.

Peters also says to focus on customer lust. Forget customer satisfaction. You can even forget customer delight. Delight is temporary. Lust is visceral.

Your customers should not want your goods and services because those products are delightful for the moment or are satisfactory (as damning with faint praise as you can get). Lust is getting the customer to the point past recommending your company to others. Lust moves that customer into becoming an apostle for the company. Such customers become your best salespeople.

> If you make customers unhappy in the physical world, they might each tell six friends. If you make customers unhappy on the Internet, they can each tell 6,000 friends with one message to a newsgroup. If you make them really happy, they can tell 6,000 people about you. You want every customer to become an evangelist for you.
> Jeff Bezos, Amazon.com
> *Customer Service Management* magazine, November/December 1999

You can't create customer lust unless you have a service organization/process/ethos/Web site that can sustain customers through all of their inquiries, problems, needs, hopes, and dreams. Surprise the customer, says Tom Peters. Brand your customer care organization.

Bill Floyd is senior vice president and chief information officer with Novus, the issuer of the Discover Card. He knows that a credit card is a commodity.

But he also knows that he can stand out from the crowd by offering better service: "Our customer service can distinguish us from others. That's where we want to be."

According to the same *Information Week* article that Bill was quoted in (October 5, 1999):

> The customer-service imperative is spreading across industries. The Chlor-Alkali & Derivatives division of chemicals company PPG Industries Inc. is using a new interactive inventory-management system to keep its customers informed about supply levels. American Airlines and British Airways are teaming with Canadian Airlines, Cathay Pacific Airways, and Qantas Airways to link their customer-service and frequent flier–operations. Chase Bank of Texas is using customer-management software from Siebel Systems to transform bankers into what it calls "relationship managers."

You want the short course? Look to Patricia Seybold's book *Customers.com* (Times Books, 1998). She spells out eight critical success factors:

1. Target the right customers.
2. Own the customer's total experience.
3. Streamline business processes that impact the customer.
4. Provide a 360° view of the customer relationship.
5. Let customers help themselves.
6. Help customers do their jobs.
7. Deliver personalized service.
8. Foster community.

A dedication to customer service is needed to pull it off. Fortunately, the Web is finally living up to the promise. Real companies are seeing real returns on their customer care investments.

Customer Service on the Web Grows Up

Cisco Systems estimates that in 1999 it achieved a savings of more than half a billion dollars by putting customer service on the Internet. In that year, 77 percent of all questions were handled online, and customer satisfaction levels were up by 20 percent over 1995. Customers also enjoyed 98 percent accuracy and timely repair shipments.

Cisco had four goals in mind when it started the online services:

1. Make it easier to do business with the company.
2. Improve customer satisfaction and productivity.
3. Reduce the time required to make decisions.
4. Develop stronger relationships with customers and business partners.

That $500 million savings was gravy. Companies are overcoming data silos, production-focused mentalities, and old white guys who still have their secretaries print out their e-mail and leave it in the In box, to get the most out of customer interaction on the Web.

Jeff Rumburg is a Meta Group analyst who calculates that the typical cost of a customer service transaction over the phone is about $5; that the same service costs about 50 cents through a voice-response system ("Press 4 to listen to sixteen more choices . . ."); and that it costs around three cents over the Web.

FedEx figured that calls to 1-800-Go FedEx to track a package cost the company about $7 each. When people track their packages on www.fedex.com, it costs about 7¢.

Forrester Research says that companies' call center labor costs were slashed by 43 percent by the end of the last century. Companies like Siebel Systems have added Web interfaces to their call center and customer contact management systems that not only provide call center representatives with the ability to get a 360° view of the customer relationship, but allow the customer to directly access the legacy customer care system and do it themselves.

Jupiter Communications (www.jup.com) found that the percentage of customers saying they were "largely satisfied" with their online shopping experience dropped from 88 percent in the summer of 1998 to 74 percent in January 1999.

Jupiter published its "Customer Service Online" report in September 1998. Among the key findings: "Proactive customer service is emerging as a key customer conversion tool. Fully 90 percent of online merchants surveyed plan significant changes and associated investment in customer service operations in the next 12 months."

Customer Service Is the Next Wave on the World Wide Web

You still find three-quarters of IT budgets are put towards transactions and engagement. But that's wrong. I think that 75% of budgets need to go to E-service.
Tom Harmon, VP retail and distribution information strategies, Meta Group

Why is customer service suddenly becoming so important? Because people are demanding it.

Information Week magazine conducted a survey in the summer of 1999 asking consumers what mattered most when buying a personal computer. Sixty-nine percent said positive past experiences helped them make up their minds, while 73 percent said availability and on-time delivery made the difference.

But fully 80 percent agreed that service and support were the biggest reasons for making a buying decision. Then, 89 percent said that online technical support should be a standard feature with all computers.

Why is the Web *the* place to put your customer service efforts at the moment? Because it offers customers more of what they need:

- 24×7 availability
- Limitless depth of knowledge
- Ability to remember customers as individuals

During the summer of 1999, *Information Week* asked 300 information technology executives about their key strategic technology and business priorities. In 1998, the number-one answer had been "improve customer service." In 1999, that answer took second place, right after "understand and meet customer needs."

When those IT execs were asked in 1998 how they would characterize their companies' efforts to satisfy the needs of their external customers, 42 percent said "very committed," and 52 percent said "somewhat committed." But when asked the same question in 1999, 69 percent said "very," and only 29 percent said "somewhat."

Just as lots of products are becoming commoditized on the Web, customer satisfaction is becoming visible on the Web:

> BizRate.com is an unbiased, independent guide built on the continual feedback of millions of actual online buyers. BizRate.com does not accept money to feature or include an online store. Our program is free to e-commerce retailers. All customer-certified online stores are listed because they have opted to participate in our program by inviting their customers to provide input on every transaction. These stores appear in our recommended lists solely on the basis of their performance and your selection criteria.

One quick glance at the BizRate rating for shop.theglobe.com (Figure 1.2) is enough to keep anybody from shopping there.

In the middle of 1999, The Yankee Group (www.yankeegroup.com) asked 100 customer care executives if they used the Web for customer service. Fifty-seven percent said yes. When pressed about using the Web to "strategically augment" their support efforts, they all said they intended to. And most intended to do so soon:

Within the next 6 months	26 percent
Within 7 to 12 months	17 percent
Within 13 to 18 months	31 percent
More than 18 months	13 percent
Don't know	13 percent

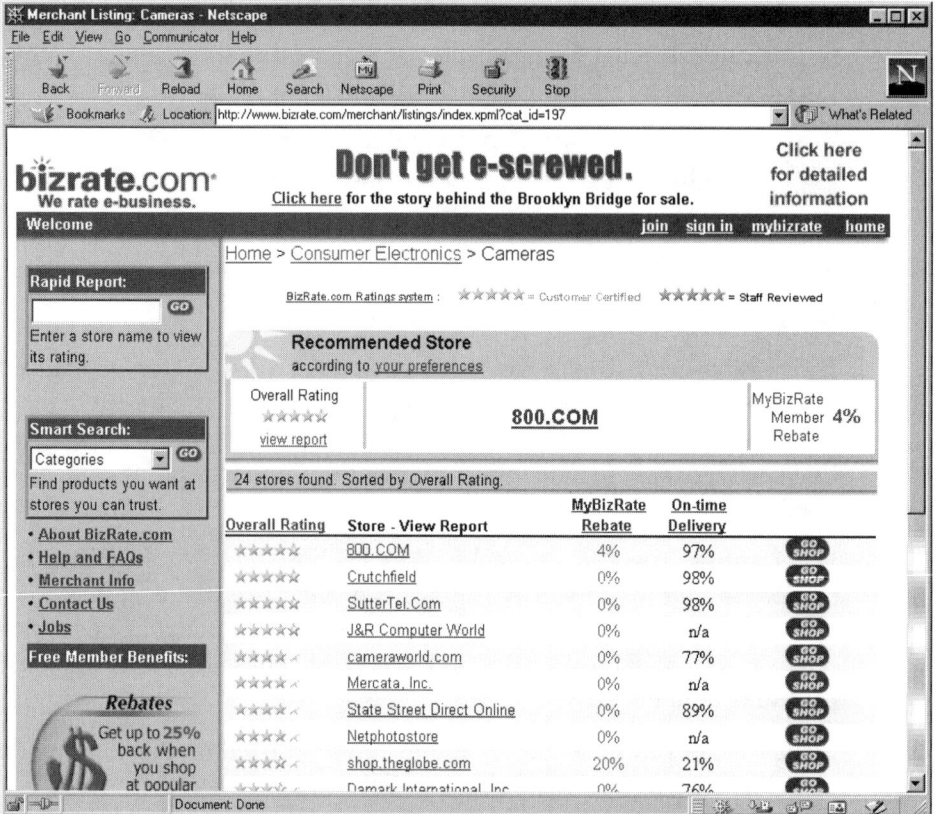

Figure 1.2   BizRate shows that shop.theglobe.com may be offering a 20 percent rebate—but that 21 percent on-time delivery rating will keep customers away.

Why are companies around the world putting more time, energy, and money into Web-based customer service projects? Because the payoff is a given. If you do it right.

The magic of a well-constructed Web site is that it can provide the information a customer wants, when the customer wants it, and in as much detail as the customer wants. Customers can answer their own questions, in their own time, and to their hearts' content. At first, this sounds wonderful merely because of the cost savings. You don't have to pay for the call to the 800 number. You don't have to pay for the person to answer the phone. You don't have to pay for printing, storing, picking, packing, and posting brochures and specification documents.

But the true wonder comes from the heightened sense of satisfaction felt by the customer. Giving your customers the ability to get an answer to a problem, in sufficient detail and in minimal time, is a gift they will receive gladly. A stronger bond of loyalty will be created, ensuring you a larger share of that customer's commerce.

Deliver on the Promise—Or Get Left Behind

With the advent of the telegraph, the world began getting exponentially smaller. When news could travel across the country in a matter of hours or minutes instead of months, expectations grew explosively. Now, with instantaneous communications, I want to hear about it *as* it happens. I want to see it televised live, and I don't want to be told I have to wait for anything.

I was asked the other day if I wanted the new battery for my laptop sent regular ground, two-day express, or overnight. My first reaction was surprise. If I wanted it delivered the day *after* tomorrow, I wouldn't be ordering it so soon. When clicking on a link and waiting forever for the page to download, you're usually thinking, "Come on, come on. I don't have all minute!" (Thank you, JoAnna Brandi, www.customerretention.com.)

Keeping up with this constant rise in expectations is no easy task. The goal is to make it easier for your customers to do business with you. If you can create a Web site that is useful to your customers, you can build loyalty very fast. Faster and stronger than any other means known, aside from having pleasant, helpful, and omniscient people constantly available to answer your 800 number.

If your Web site is *very* good, it becomes a source of pride and a rallying cry for your sales force to take into battle. After all, good service adds value to any product, and automated service is hard to beat. Brand your service.

Unfortunately, as you read this book, your competitors are dreaming up new ways to serve their clients and, hopefully, yours. And they are dreaming 24 hours a day. The business world went global during the Age of Discovery, when Portuguese ships plied the seven seas. Now it is global and on a continuous basis. Sunset out your office window is sunrise out your competitors' window.

Your competitors know that customers are expecting more access to information about products, order status, and their specific business dealings between trading partners. Customers don't want to be told "no" or "the day after tomorrow" anymore.

If you can view your company through the eyes of one of your customers, you will quickly see what's required of your Web site. You will understand that the true value you can electronically offer customers is high-speed information.

If you can get your whole organization to constantly look through customer-colored glasses at every Web page you create, every process you initiate, and every customer interaction opportunity you have, you can grab the brass ring. Because it all comes down to winning customers once and keeping them forever.

The Lifetime Value of a Customer

The One to One Future (Bantam Doubleday, 1997), *Enterprise One to One* (Doubleday, 1999), *The One to One Fieldbook* (Bantam Books, 1999), and *The One to One Manager* (Doubleday, 1999) are all by Don Peppers and Martha Rogers with some help from Bob Dorf (www.1to1.com). These are books that drive home one lesson: Since it's less expensive to sell something to a current customer than to drum up a new one, spend your time and effort getting as close as possible to your current customers.

This is a slap-on-the-forehead, D'oh!, tell-me-something-I-didn't-know sort of pronouncement. What makes these books must-reads is that you know it, but you're not doing anything about it. Even more important, today's technology lets us get closer to our customers than ever before. The competitive advantage to treating customers on a one-to-one basis is enormous.

It boils down to recognizing that customers mean more than momentary profitability. Momentary profitability means spending as little time with customers as possible. Call-management systems are being sold as call-avoidance systems. Phone representatives are measured on how many calls they can take a day.

There's something obviously insincere about a customer service rep who finishes a call with, "Thank you for calling Acme Rent-A-Pencil. Have a nice . . ." and then hits the disconnect button before the word "day" is uttered.

Instead, Don and Martha beg us to see how a little more care with each customer can turn each customer into a lifelong customer.

The lifetime value (LTV) of a customer is based on the premise that the most expensive part of the relationship is starting it in the first place. Field sales reps in the business-to-business world; advertising in the consumer marketplace; direct mail, print, and broadcast advertising; all around—it adds up. It can cost hundreds or even thousands of dollars to find a suspect, qualify him or her as a prospect, and close him or her as a customer.

Measuring LTV

The first step is thinking of your customers as assets. Just as you would want to spend more of your energy on building maintenance than on buying a new building every year, you want to focus on customer relationships as something of value that needs to be preserved. You want to calculate the net present value of the profit a single customer will generate over time. This is the sort of thinking that allows stores to sell loss leaders. If they can get customers into the shop and show them what a nice store they have, those customers will become return customers.

The questions that need numerical answers are easy to ask, but not easy to answer. Some creative accounting may be in order to give you some idea of the LTV of your customers:

- New customers per year (or month, or quarter)
- Customer loss per year
- Revenue per customer per year
- Cost per customer per year (acquisition)
- Cost per customer per year (service)
- Cost per customer per year (production and distribution)
- Cost per customer per year (G and A)

A net present-value calculation is thrown in as a discount you apply, based on the time value of money and a rate you apply for risk. If 2 percent of your receivables end up as bad debt, that needs to be part of the equation.

In an ideal spreadsheet, the numbers apply to a specific market segment. If it costs three times as much to sell something to a teenager in the Northeast who is five times more likely to leave the fold within months, then advertising on MTV is not your best move.

You're going to use the resulting LTV to give you a compass. Should you spend more on customer retention—such as a frequent buyers program? More on upselling and cross-selling? Changes in distribution channels? Changes in customer complaint management systems?

Let's say that you run up the calculations on a loyalty program and determine that you can increase retention by X, if you spend Y. A run through the spreadsheet might show that the cost of the program will be recovered in three years, but you've only extended the average customer life by two years and eight months. Not a wise move.

On the other hand, you might spend a great deal less on an internal campaign to get employees to come up with ideas on improving the customer experience in your company. Give a $500 prize every month to the employee who comes up with the best idea.

There's a wonderful old story told about a factory worker who suggested they change the fluorescent warning stripes surrounding automated equipment on the factory floor. His suggestion was that they paint them half as wide as before since the stripes could still be seen from a safe distance. The result of this change across the entire company ended up saving hundreds of thousands of dollars a year in paint.

Five hundred dollars for good ideas isn't much. The suggestion box can fill with little gems. How about adding a handwritten thank-you note every time a customer makes his or her 10th purchase? Why not have a customer appreciation day and invite them all to the factory for a picnic? How about assigning a single service plus one backup to each account, so whenever customers from that company call or e-mail, they get the same person? Will those things make a difference to customer retention? Oh yes.

The only problem comes when you don't live up to the promise.

Being Held Up to Ridicule

A friend of mine recently tried to buy a computer for her parents from Gateway's Web site. She was initially pleased with the many configuration options available through Gateway's slick order form. But after she placed the order, there was no confirmation about the total price or the expected delivery date, and she found no way to get the critical information from the site.

   Concerned, she called Gateway. But she ran into a scenario that's all too common among companies just starting out in Internet commerce: The ordinary phone service representative couldn't help her with her Internet orders. Instead, she had to speak with a special Internet order division.

   After she finally got connected to the right person, the harried representative told her that systems requested through the Internet were on back order for three weeks and that she'd be better off canceling her order, then placing a new one the traditional way: by phone.

   Dylan Tweney
   Infoworld, November 9, 1998

Stories like this are all too common, indeed. And while it's one thing to upset your customers, it's another to be vilified in print. Some say bad press is better than no press at all. Those people live in Hollywood.

The Industry Standard and *Information Week* magazines both published articles entitled "Customer Disservice" within a month of each other (May and June, 1999). They weren't playing copycat—it takes too long to create these articles for one to have inspired the other. They were simply reporting on a common theme: Customers are being treated rather shabbily online, and the miscreants are due to get their comeuppance in print.

The *Information Week* article described the dissatisfaction E*Trade (www.etrade .com) caused when its servers went down several times in February. That was the tip of the iceberg. The disaster came when customers tried to e-mail and call the company and found that the 300 new call-center agents were still in the process of being added—not up and running yet. The article also pointed out that a Web outage at eBay (www.ebay.com) caused that company's stock to nose-dive.

The Industry Standard published a chart it called "Service Without A Smile."

> The *Standard* played secret shopper and e-mailed a typical customer support question—"Do you have [x] in stock?"—to the online customer help desks at the country's top 10 e-commerce sites, according to March (1999) traffic figures from Media Metrix.

While some of the sites came out smelling more like roses than fertilizer, others did not fare as well. bluemountainarts.com sent back an automated "robo-mail" that didn't answer the question. And it took 26 hours to do it. eBay only took 1 hour and 37 minutes to send *two* robo-mails, but neither answered the question. Download.com (CNET) took *8 days and 20 hours* to send a personal message—and didn't answer the question.

Charles Wesley Orton went to some of the top pharmaceutical Web sites for an article on customer support in *Web Merchant* magazine (Summer 1999). At Parke-Davis, he couldn't find an address or a phone number. The feedback form asked for name and address and your feedback, but once submitted, it tells you your answer will take three business days to reach you. Prozac maker Eli Lilly had no contact information at all.

You don't want your company's foul-ups to end up in a magazine. Or in a book. All customers have bad service stories, and I've been on the Web as a customer long enough to have acquired some of my own.

The most frustrating instances are those that cause you to just give up. I got annoyed at my new Dell computer and went to the company's Web site. I found the form to fill out to describe my problem and did so at once. Then I realized I didn't have a record of the communication. Had I sent in an e-mail, I would at least have had my copy. So there *is* a good reason for autoresponders—tell me you got the message and show me the message you got.

In due course I got a reply. How long did it take? I don't know—I didn't have a record. The response did, however, include my original problem:

```
Name: Jim Sterne
Email: jsterne@targeting.com
Service Tag: HTBQS
System Label: Inspiron 7000
Problem: Computer

Problem Description: Howdy—Love my Inspiron, but I'm baffled as to why
it freezes up for about 5 seconds every now and then. I usually notice
it while doing e-mail or word processing.
```

```
The cursor freezes on the text screen and won't display keyboard input.
The mouse still moves the cursor around the screen. After the five-
second freeze—the screen displays all the text I've written during the
pause.

It seems the keyboard buffer is still working, but the results just
don't show up on the screen.

What gives?
```

In reply, the helpful agent wrote:

```
Jim,

The hard drive of the Inspiron 7000 goes to sleep every 3-4 minutes
despite the settings in the system BIOS & Windows 98. This is part of
the temperature management of the unit (a firmware setting of the drive
itself) and unfortunately cannot be changed. This is true on the
Inspiron 3000, 3200, and 3500 as well.
```

I thought this was an excellent first effort, but I also didn't think it was the right answer. So I wrote back:

```
I've been watching it and it seems to do it even when the drive is
running. I'm in a very quiet room this morning and can easily hear the
hard drive doing its thing. Yes, it spins down every now and then, but
the problem I'm having isn't concurrent with a sound-change in the
drive.

Any further thoughts?
```

This kind of give and take is what makes for good customer service. It's a conversation. It's a chance to let the customer have his say so the company can better address the customer's problem. The reply, however, left me flat:

```
Jim,

As it is a firmware setting of the drive, it cannot be completely
disabled. However, you can download the latest BIOS release for your
system and install it—this will lengthen the amount of time between
spin-downs and should cause it to be less of an interruption. You can
find these files in the Dell File Library (http://support.dell.com/
filelib)—input your service tag and it will give you a list for you to
pick what you need.
```

A nice, detailed description. Dell hadn't overwhelmed me with information the first time around. It was only when I wanted to dig deeper that the customer support agent switched from a general answer to a more technical one. The rep even pointed to a possible solution. Wonderful. Too bad he or she simply wasn't listening.

While offering a fix to the problem Dell thought I had, the rep didn't notice that I had explained that that problem was different from the one I was experiencing. The damage is threefold. First, it was a rather innocuous problem. It's not going to get me to yell and complain. It's not going to get me to stop using the product. But it left a bad taste in my mouth regarding what is considered by most to be one of the best support organizations in the world.

The next damage done was that I have lost interest in having a relationship with this support organization. Rather than acquiesce to their desire for improvement . . .

```
* Tell us what you think of our service.
* Take our online customer support survey at:
* http://support.dell.com/support/ssurvey_e.asp?svctag=
```

. . . I'm not going to bother. It's not worth the trouble.

The third, of course, is that you have now heard my sob story. Dell Computers had one agent who read my message just a little too fast and didn't quite answer my question—and now thousands of readers know about my dissatisfaction. If I were just a little more miffed, I might have taken my attitude to a couple of sites designed for letting off steam—professional, independent complaint departments online.

Web Ridicule as a Business

Now, there are a handful of Web sites that are built for customer complaints. You really don't want your company to become the target of sites like www.complain.com (Figure 1.3) or www.EllensPoisonPen.com (Figure 1.4).

These sites are the Internet version of consumer advocates. They'll take on your customers' complaints and, with pens mightier (or at least more poisoned) than swords, they will charge after you until the wronged party gets satisfaction. These are professional complainers—people who have made an art of telling you just how lowly your level of service is and why you should grovel to get back into your customers' good graces.

Complain.com figures that it has the clout to make something happen. "We record your complaints in our database, analyze and report on trends and the details of cases here and in other media. . . . You get extra attention when your letter carries our 'via Complain!com' logo."

Ellen's Poison Pen takes on the same role.

Ellen's Poison Pen ® L.L.C. is a fee-based service that acts as a consultant and advocate for aggrieved consumers. People who have experienced problems with defective products, shoddy service, or uncooperative companies or who find a petition, an appeal, or another type of specialized correspondence to be necessary sometimes simply need another person's voice to make their predicament heard by those at the top of the chain of command. Ellen's Poison Pen ® L.L.C. becomes that voice. By writing clear, concise, well-documented and professional letters and adding a personal

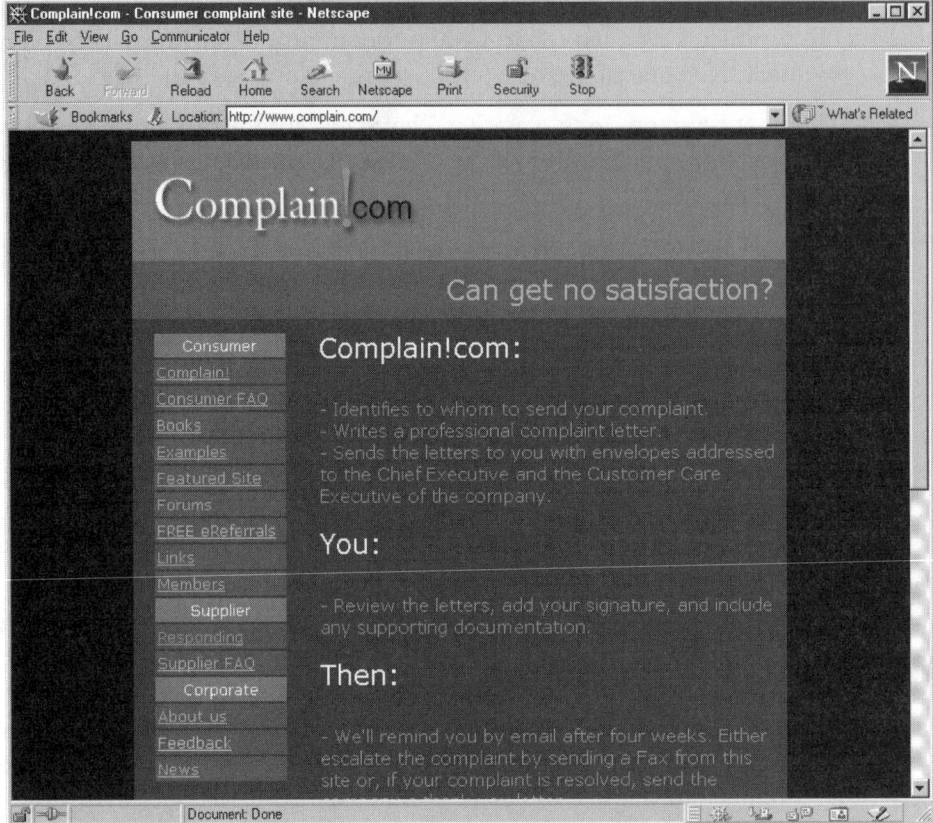

Figure 1.3 Complain.com aggregates complaints to try and shame the offenders into remunerative action.

touch to each, the service helps consumers to gain a 75–90 percent successful resolution to their problems.

The Better Business Bureau had 138 customer complaints on file for Shopping.com about unanswered e-mail and busy telephones. *Information Week* magazine made that fact public in a very pointed way.

Are there worse things than being held up for ridicule by members of the press or complaint aggregators? How about by your own customers?

Customers Taking Up Arms

Get a customer mad enough and find your company the target of a grudge site.

Beginning on June 13, 1996, Jeremy Cooperstock decided to get satisfaction from United Airlines: "Following a series of unpleasant incidents during a trip to Japan and Hawaii, taken on United Airlines, I sent a polite letter to United

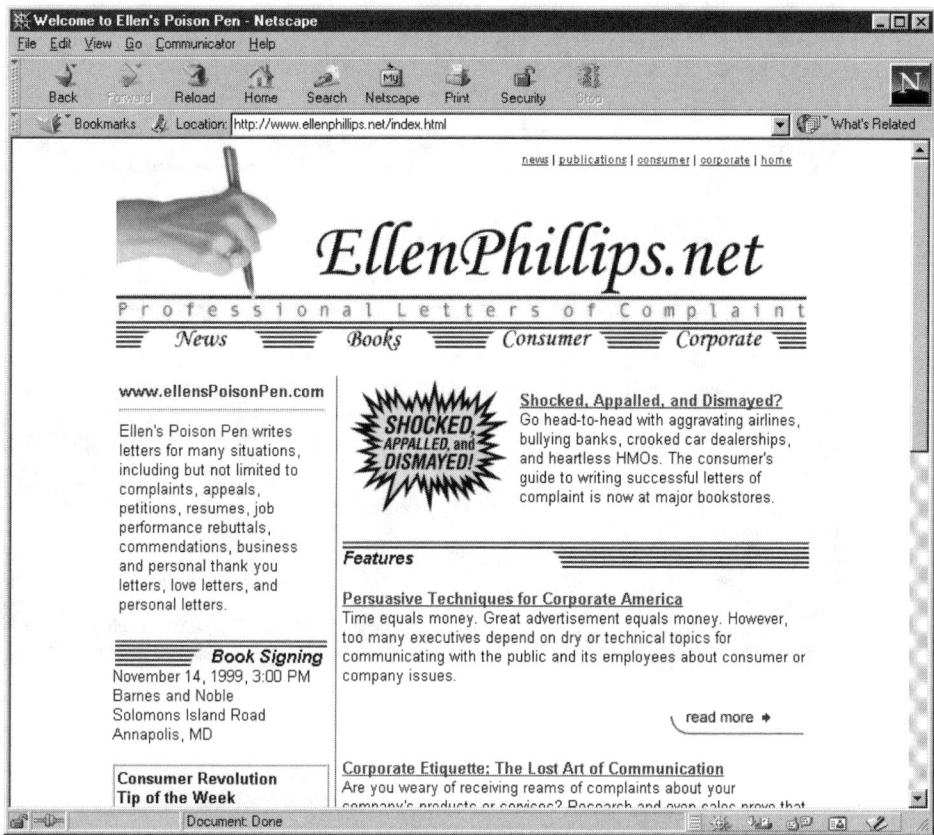

Figure 1.4 Ellen's Poison Pen is a little gentler in approach, but along the same vein.

Airlines' president, Mr. Gerald Greenwald, with a copy to the director of Customer Relations, simply asking for a reply to a number of complaints relating to their service."

After being ignored for weeks, Jeremy received a form letter from an individual in United Airlines' customer relations department, which essentially ignored his problem. That prompted him to create his anti-United Web site, called Untied, on servers at the University of Toronto.

Over time, Jeremy's Untied site started receiving gripes from other unhappy customers. By April, 1997, United Airlines had made enough ugly noises to the University of Toronto to cause Jeremy to create a new off-campus site located at www.untied.com (Figure 1.5), which looked eerily like the official United site at www.ual.com (Figure 1.6)

After fourteen months, Jeremy finally received an apology from a United Airlines official. They were sorry their responses had been so unresponsive. In the

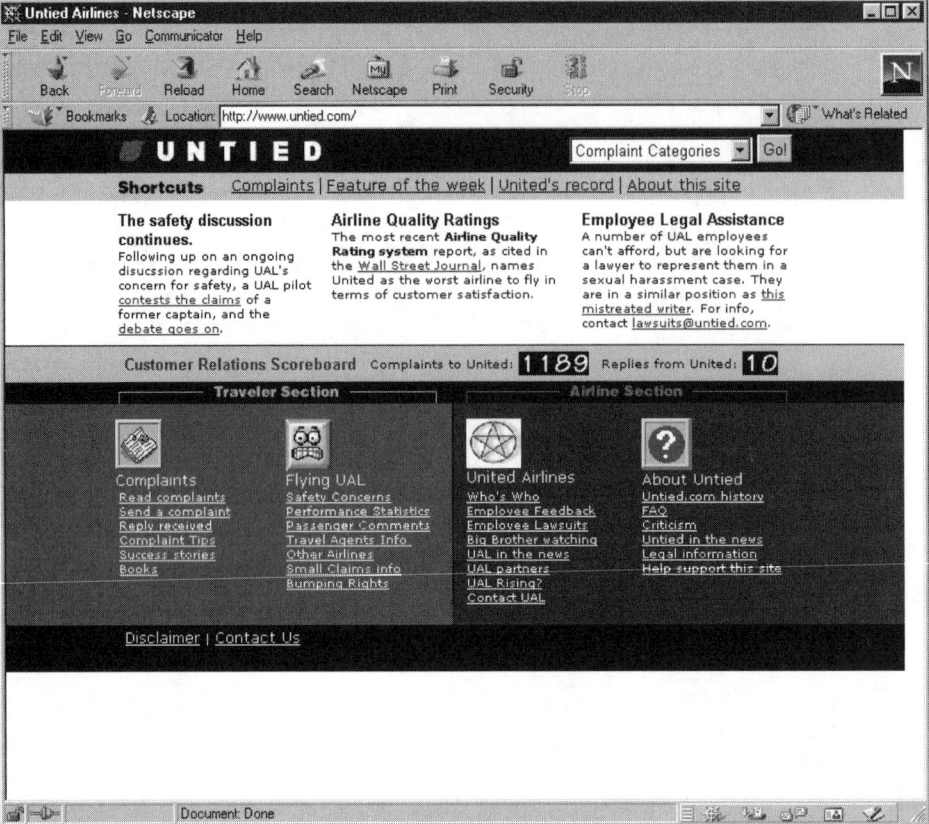

Figure 1.5   The Untied site is a magnet for United Airlines frequent gripers.

meantime, www.untied.com had taken on a life of its own. In October, 1998, with financial contributions from readers, Jeremy put up a new complaints form, "with the ability to copy complaints directly to Denise Harvill, United's Director of Customer Relations, and James Goodwin, President and Chief Operating Officer of UAL."

In February, 1999, Jeremy hosted a database of thousands of complaints. A few samples follow:

> If they don't want to bother being nice, then they should pick a profession that doesn't require people skills.

> The flight crew had flown its FAA mandatory maximum 14 hours of flying in one day and a back-up crew wasn't available so I had to sleep at the airport.

> My unaccompanied minor was put at risk by changes in schedules that nobody told me about.

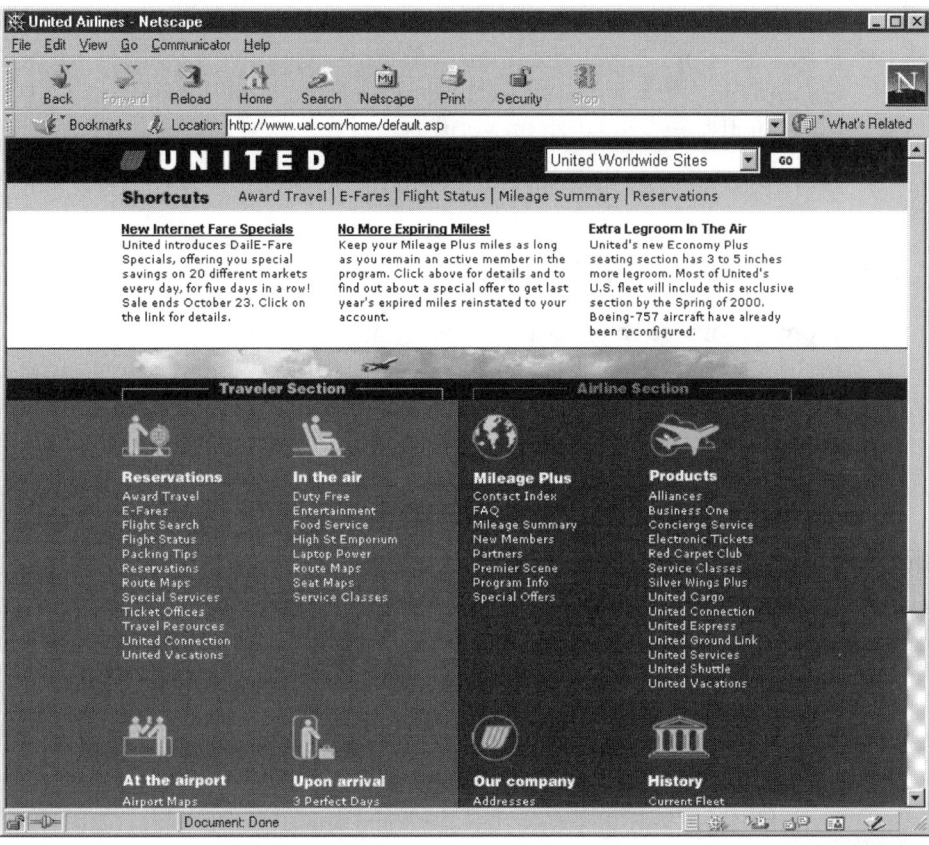

Figure 1.6 Untied copied United Airlines' look and feel.

> I did not know that our company agent was not logging my miles when booking my tickets. I mailed in copies of all my airline tickets and receipts to get credit. Since it was a year past the mentioned miles, I was told that it was too late and too bad.

This site is not a pretty sight if you're a United employee/owner.

In the October 5, 1999, issue of his monthly e-zine *Digital Strategies*, Mel Bergstein, chairman and CEO of Diamond Technology Partners, allowed as how, "At least half of the Fortune 1000 companies now face complaint sites developed by disgruntled customers."

Mel cited a trademark infringement and libel suit over "The U-Hell Website: Misadventures in Moving" (the case is pending). In self-defense, as a sort of preemptive strike, Chase Manhattan Bank registered a bunch of unflattering domain names such as IhateChase.com, ChaseStinks.com, and ChaseSucks .com, but missed chasebanksucks.com. According to Mel, that site is thriving.

The solution? Mel says to kill them with kindness. "In the spirit of 'Living well is the best revenge,' the most effective response of all is to make your e-commerce Web site so friendly that customers with problems will deal with you quietly, on your turf, on your terms."

Have you gone on an e-hunt for unhappy customers yet?

Customers Taking Up Lawyers

From an Iomega sales letter I received in early 1998:

> Dear Valued Customer:
>
> More than 12 million people—just like you—depend on a Zip drive to back-up, store, transport and share computer files . . . easily, quickly, and securely.
>   But as good as it is, we wanted to make the Zip drive even better. To do it right, we listened to feedback from our customers. Then we went to work.

From the notification from the State of Delaware Civil (class) Action 15809, I received on the same day:

> The plaintiffs brought this lawsuit on behalf of themselves and all others similarly situated, claiming, among other things, that the warranties on Iomega's Zip, Jaz and Ditto drives implied that Iomega would provide technical support at no charge to customers with technical questions or problems. The plaintiffs also claimed that where customers with Zip, Jaz and Ditto drives called Iomega's customer or technical support lines for help, they were put on hold for unreasonably long periods.

The proposed settlement asked Iomega to create a "virtual consultant" on the Web, "based upon case-based reasoning technology capable of responding to customer technical support inquiries (1) a basic single question/single answer format, (2) a more advanced multiple question/multiple answer format, (3) a decision tree format, and (4) generated case queries using fuzzy logic."

The suit also called for an online tutorial, technical illustrations, and that these be made available to 250 concurrent users.

The lesson? You can be sued for bad customer service. The solution? The World Wide Web. Was Iomega an especially bad provider of service? Not especially. But then, even the best of them can be subject to public ridicule. Even Amazon.

No Site Is Sacred

In the June 7, 1999, issue of *Network World* magazine, columnist Mark Gibbs took on the one true paragon of e-commerce—Amazon.com:

E-comm: Love, Trust and Doing Wrong

"Love all. Trust a few. Do wrong to none."—William Shakespeare

I loved Amazon.com. I trusted it. And it did me wrong.

I was going to continue with last week's topic of talking to refrigerators but this, this . . . this betrayal demanded attention.

I've placed numerous orders with the company and had been happy with the interactions and service. But Amazon.com just blew it.

It all started a few months ago when I ordered a book from Amazon.com in advance of the publication date. A couple of hours ago, I received notification that the book had been shipped, and I was delighted. The e-mail notification was brief, and it didn't say whether the book I'd ordered was a hardcover or a paperback, so I thought I'd check.

I went to Amazon.com and found the book's listing straight away (the company has always had excellent response times). There were two versions listed as I expected: the hardcover for $17.50 and the paperback for $11.20. Which was I about to receive?

Well, the price quoted on my order confirmation was $14 so I figured maybe it was a hybrid . . . a hardpaper coverback perhaps?

I checked my order history (another excellent response time) and found that I had ordered the paperback. I called Amazon.com's customer service department.

A pleasant young man answered quickly (these guys are fast) and checked my order (the speed made tears come to my eyes). He didn't know what to do and handed me over (very quickly) to an "order specialist," a charming young lady who (in short order) determined I hadn't been given the discounted price but rather the original publisher's price.

No problem—the company would credit my American Express card with the difference. Great, problem solved. Except . . .

It leaves the enormous problem that I no longer completely trust Amazon.com. Why? Because I wonder what other "mistakes" the company has made in my orders.

I pointed this out to the young lady who said she understood (I got the impression that she would rather I just said "thanks" and buzzed off—quickly—but I got the impression only fleetingly).

She said that perhaps she ought to report it as a problem to be fixed. "You're kidding," I said. "You mean that there was a chance that you might not have reported it if I hadn't questioned it?"

She (quickly) denied it, but I'm afraid I'm not convinced. After all, how often have customers spotted this kind of problem? Rarely, I suspect.

How often, when the problem has been reported, has the problem been escalated? I have no idea, but I have my suspicions that "none" is the answer. Now you might say this error was not a big deal, but I would have to disagree. In fact, the issue is not much different from the problem with telephone billing I discussed a few columns ago that got a lot of you fired up [*Network World,* March 1, page 62].

Our online world is becoming increasingly friction-free. We are offered the carrot of warp-speed transactions and equally high-speed service to counter the stick of wasting our time on unimportant "stuff" and, therefore, we tend to accept these Teflon transactions as reliable.

As consumers, we have to keep a keen eye on every transaction because those little errors happen, I suspect, more often than we know. And they can cost us money—sometimes a lot of it.

As vendors, we need to examine our systems very carefully because mistakes such as this profoundly undermine our credibility. We want to have our customers love and trust us. Doing wrong like Amazon.com is all too easy, and once you've lost your customer's trust, well, that's the beginning of the end.

Mark got a lot of feedback on that article, and a surprisingly healthy number of those who wrote to him were outraged that he was nitpicking a true-blue Internet legend.

The next week, Mark wrote the wrap-up:

One of the (supportive) readers wrote to say the same thing had happened to her and to a coworker. The lady had copied the message to Susan Robinson, Amazon.com's customer care and QA manager, and I followed the message with a copy of the column.

Robinson replied with a perfect response: Yes, they had a problem, she thought they had fixed it, she was now on a mission to boldly go, to seek, to destroy and, to . . . well, get it fixed. Excellent. No whining that I was subjecting them to cruel and unusual treatment, no blaming the dark side, no calling me a loser [as one of Mark's readers had].

Now those of you who complained that I was holding Amazon.com to higher standards than their real-world counterparts were absolutely right. And so should you. A couple of you asked if I would complain if I were overcharged at the supermarket? What do you think? Of course, I would!

And if I found myself being overcharged frequently, I might well write to the store management. Unfortunately, in the real world, I can be overlooked. I can get shuffled into the circular file and there's not much I can do. But online, things are different. I, and you, can complain in a dozen different forums and lists.

Online, we can get action that can't be achieved in the real world and in doing so, we're doing vendors a favor: We're helping them to be better vendors—to provide better service, give better value and do more efficient business. And they need to be as good as they can be because the competitive pressures are far greater online.

My proof of this pressure, at least in the bookseller's world, can be found at http://isbn.nu. On this site, you can enter an ISBN number and get a list of the prices offered by a number of book vendors. I just checked this site for the book that started the whole thing (*Suits Me: The Double Life of Billy Tipton* by Diane Wood Middlebrook, a unique, amazing and very well-written biography).

I found that Amazon.com's price ($11.20) is matched by Barnes and Noble and Books-A-Million (although you can get it at a 10 percent discount there if you join their Millionaire's Club for $5 per year), and beaten by Bookstreet.com if you take shipping cost into account (currently Bookstreet.com has a free standard domestic shipping promotion).

Under this kind of pressure—which is unlike anything in the real world—only the efficient, the accurate and the competitive survive.

And let us be clear: I think Amazon.com runs a terrific operation and despite my comments in the previous column, I will still be buying books from the company (price comparisons not withstanding).

And I will continue to buy products computers from Dell. But Mark's point is well made. We hold companies up to a higher standard online. Why? Because it's possible to deliver truly great service. If you provide service beyond expectations, you can earn the recognition you so richly deserve.

Becoming a Legend

The goal as a company is to have customer service that is not just the best, but legendary.
Sam Walton, Wal-Mart

Visiting the National Semiconductor Web site (www.national.com) one afternoon, I spotted a couple of typographical errors. I was deeply surprised. National Semi is one of the leaders on the Web, and I thought the company would be deeply embarrassed to see such a flaw. I quickly found the feedback form and wrote a little note.

Before the end of the day, I received a reply:

```
Date: 24 Aug 1999 19:04:52 -0700
From: SCDEVSFA01 <SCDEVSFA01@nsc.notes.nsc.com>
To: jsterne <jsterne@targeting.com>
Subject: Regarding Your Feedback

Hello,

Thank you for visiting National Semiconductor's Web Site We have
corrected the spelling mistake. Thank you for informing us. If at any
time, you have another suggestion for the National Site, please contact
us at http://wwwd.national.com/feedback/

Regards,

InterActive Marketing at National
```

Why might this sort of response be legendary? Because it was not a robotic response from a computer; they thanked me for my efforts; and they fixed the problem immediately.

National Semiconductor deals with thousands of feedback comments a day. What happens when your company deals with tens of thousands?

United Airlines has discovered that it's cheaper to have customers book their own tickets at www.ual.com than to have them call the 800 number and ask a phone representative to do it for them. To encourage this behavior, United took to handing out extra frequent flier miles with every Web-booked ticket. But I didn't get my miles.

The seat-selection feature had a glitch that produced an error message. I had to call the 800 number and book the flights the old fashioned (and expensive for them) way. Then I decided to write to United and let them know of my efforts to earn extra miles, of their failure to credit the miles to me, and of my disappointment. The next morning, I received an e-mail asking for a couple of details, and that afternoon I was assured that my miles would be credited to my account.

Why is that legendary? United could have denied my request outright. The company could have waited so long to answer my inquiry that I gave up hope and stopped caring. Or, the airline could have done what so many do—not answer at all. But then, they have Jeremy Cooperstock at www.untied.com looking over their shoulder. You should act as if you did, too.

In his book *Batteries Included! Creative Legendary Service* (Century/Arrow, 1999), Nigel Barlow defines *legendary service:*

> Redefining the customer's expectations in your industry or sector—as, for example, McDonald's originally did with food retailing and Virgin Atlantic has started to do with airlines.
>
> Generating passionate customer loyalty—beyond the temporary pull of loyalty cards.
>
> Becoming famous for service—where the service legend is spread by your customers. Ninety-five percent of owners of Saturn cars in the USA become passionate advocates of the product to others.

If there is one story I've heard over and over, it's the one where a book buyer has gone to Amazon.com and found the book that he or she wants is out of print. They click-to-purchase and get an e-mail within days that offers a specific copy of the book in a specific condition at a specific price.

The first time I heard that story, it was from my wife. Amazon had tracked down and offered her an autographed first edition for $85. She declined. One day later, they offered her a "slightly water damaged" version of the same book for $4.50. She was delighted. She told me, her colleagues, her friends, and about 2,000 people on an e-mail discussion list about her experience and how she thought Amazon.com was the best.

Customer lust, indeed.

Getting Started

The tools of the Internet trade are the tools of the database administrator and the tools of the librarian. But first you have to be willing to help your customers in any way you can. Having a fully automated droid handle all customer inquiries would be wonderful and is a goal well worth pursuing. However, infinitely intelligent droids aren't available this year, so you'll have to start from the beginning.

Contrary to the way most companies have gone about setting up Web sites, you *can* plan your work and then work your plan. From e-mail to FAQs (frequently asked questions) to search tools to databases, there are minimum requirements and significant returns.

Your task will be to start with something meaningful and move up the value chain. You will continue to move up this chain as your customers demand more, your competitors offer it, and you have to keep up. You will find that you must openly publish customer criticism, you must engage your clients in public discussions, and you must be willing to give them access to information that lives at the very center of your company's electronic nervous system.

At the same time, your customers will reveal information about their likes and dislikes, and their needs and their habits, like never before. They will tell you what they think, and the knowledge you glean from your customers will be unprecedented.

The winners in the new world order will not just publish and publish until there are no secrets left. The winners will be those who know how to interpret what their customers are telling them via e-mail, via discussion groups, and via mouse clicks.

The real winners are those who will tune into their customers as a way of life, and not an occasional exercise.

CHAPTER 2

Customer Service in a Modern World

Albert Einstein was cautioned about a physics exam he was giving because it contained the same questions as the previous year. "Yes," he replied, "but the answers are different this year."

The formula used to be simple. You produced goods and services. Your customers gave you money for them. If you made things that customers liked, they continued to buy. But the formula has shifted over time. Today's successful company finds out what customers want and makes it—rather than making something the company wants and hopes that people will buy.

Changing Consumer Needs

To say we are living in a fast-paced world is to understate the painfully obvious. Taster's Choice coffee commercials showing quiet, contemplative chats between friends over steaming cups of Swiss-almond-mocha coffee seem like something our parents may have done before we were born. Nobody has that kind of luxury of time anymore.

If you feel that people are getting more and more picky, more and more demanding, and that their level of expectation is getting higher and higher, you're right. Manufacturers and sellers are seeing to it with mass customization and instant gratification. Want it to spell out the name of your loved one? We can ship it overnight. Would you like these glasses tinted? Come back in an hour. Time for a tune up and oil change? We'll wash your car as well.

Vendors have made it their goal in life to offer better, faster, more prestigious service than their competition. They have to because the bar is constantly raised higher and higher. How do you compete? Watch what your customers do, how they live, how they work—then figure out a way to make their lives a little easier.

Expectation Inflation

When asked for examples of truly great customer service, one seminar attendee told the story of a recent visit to Amazon.com. He recounted how easy it was to find the book he wanted. How easy it was to make the purchase. How delighted he was when the item actually showed up on his doorstep the very next day.

Another audience member pointed out how sad it was that he was delighted when a company he was doing business with made a promise and actually stuck with it. The rest of us chuckled, but we realized our level of expectation in most stores is rather low. Our expectations online are considerably higher.

When you walk into your local dry cleaner's, you're greeted like an old friend because you've been going there for years. Saunter into Nordstrom's and get treated like the most important customer they have, because they are trained within an inch of their lives to do so. Walk into a fast-food joint and you'll get very efficient, very impersonal service. Head over to the video rental store and be waited on by a nose-ringed, orange-haired individual who didn't pass the test to work behind the counter at the fast-food place.

We have very different expectations of the various retail venues we frequent. But not of Web sites. We have very low expectations of the sort of help we can find in a Big Box warehouse store. But not so with Web sites. The fact is that with their high standards CDnow and Amazon.com and FedEx have set the level of expectation for all surfers on all sites.

I have spent 20 minutes in a major department store looking for a human to whom I might give my money. I have been stared at with bovine indifference while complaining about a troublesome home appliance. I have been studiously ignored in a national consumer electronics store. I have accepted each of these slights with a sigh and written them off as the slow but sure degradation of the work ethic in America.

But show me one 404—File Not Found and I'm livid.

There's a problem with the login routine? The .cgi script doesn't work? Out of stock on an item? Server not responding? 'Scuze me while I take a moment to flame the Webmaster.

It doesn't matter what industry you're in—if you're on the Internet you're competing with the best and the brightest. If you sell macramé drink coasters,

Figure 2.1 With the advent of stores like the Amazon.com zShops, *anybody* can sell *anything* online.

goat-hair earmuffs, home-made French-lavender-honey-flavored nail polish, or festive foil embossed holiday cards (Figure 2.1), you are up against service-level expectations set by pure Internet companies that have millions of IPO dollars to spend on sophisticated Web content management and back-end database tools. If you expect to compete on service, get ready to dig in.

It doesn't take long for wonderful service to become normal service. Delivery by the end of the week used to be great service. Now it has to be there overnight.

Today's marketplace offers goods delivered from one end of the nation to the other tomorrow, overseas in the day after tomorrow, and custom-made suits before dinner. Keeping your customers no longer rests in their willingness to stay with you out of blind loyalty or through inertia. Consumers and business buyers are becoming more and more sophisticated and getting used to better and better service. People are also expecting greater access to:

- Product information
- Order status information
- Specific account information

Greater Access to Product Information

In 1994, Silicon Graphics (SGI) posted a letter from a customer extolling the virtues of online product information. He was going to make a presentation to upper management on why they should buy his department more SGI machines. This resourceful manager had surfed over to www.sgi.com and found the product information and visuals he needed to put the finishing touches on his pitch the next day. He got the additional machines he was looking for.

Greater Access to Order Status Information

Customers know that you keep information about them in computers. They know that your World Wide Web site is on a computer. Computers can talk to each other. The expectation is that their and your computers can talk to each other and that the customer can access account information.

- What was the last order I placed?
- Has it shipped yet?
- When will it be delivered?
- When will my back order be filled?
- Are there any alternative products I can get faster?

Greater Access to Specific Account Information

- Who is my sales rep?
- How much have I ordered in the past six months?
- When will I hit the next discount level?
- How many frequent flier miles do I have?
- When will I need my next tune-up?
- When will my membership expire?
- Who is authorized to place an order over $5,000?
- What is my current credit aging?

What do you mean I can't find out on your Web site? What do you mean you haven't linked your Web site to your back-end corporate datacenter? I can get that information 24 hours a day, 7 days a week from your competitor. . . .

Making It Easy to Do Business with You

At the Technopolis '95 conference in Long Beach California, I was on a panel about electronic commerce with three other people. One was there to talk about the Small Manufacturers Institute, and one came from a company that builds Web sites for businesses. The fourth member of the panel was Kevin Donnelly, controller at PlastiColor Corporation, a company that makes plastic car mats.

Before the session started, the first two panelists and I asked each other what on earth Mr. Car Mats was doing there. What could he tell the audience about the brave new world of modern technology?

When it was his turn to speak, Mr. Donnelly told how his small business had been forced into electronic data interchange (EDI) by his customers. His customers were huge retail outlets like Wal-Mart and Kmart. They insisted they would only place orders and accept invoices electronically. Any small business that wanted to sell to these eight-hundred pound gorillas had to play by their rules.

PlastiColor spent months and months getting its PCs to talk to the retailers' systems. The company had to have a different software application for each customer, and in one case had to put in a different operating system. This was not simple. It was not cheap. But when the transition was completed and the systems were working, PlastiColor turned the tables and started looking for vendors who could and would perform commerce electronically. Why had Mr. Donnelly switched from a grumbling seller who suffered through computerized communication chaos into a promoter of the new online lifestyle?

"Because it is easier to do business electronically," said Kevin Donnelly. And when he did, the other two panelists and I knew why he had been asked to be part of our panel. "Doing business manually was more time-consuming and error-prone," he said. "Now, we're encouraging our other customers to work with us electronically, and we offer it as a competitive edge."

Once upon a time it was common practice among larger vendors to give computer terminals to their larger customers. The computer terminals were directly linked to the vendor's order entry system. This made it easier for the customers to place and track orders. It also made it harder for them to go elsewhere with their business.

Objects Are Closer than They Appear

In the May 1, 1994 edition of *Datamation* magazine, Tom McCusker gazed into his crystal ball. "It may be 10 to 15 years off, but visionaries within the EDI community foresee a scenario in which a purchasing person sitting at an EDI screen calls up color pictures of a product and a multimedia presentation on how the product works. The user then places the order, employing all the facilities of today's EDI techniques while encountering none of the restrictions—such as the necessity for some form of prearrangement with the trading companies."

Guessing at the future gets harder and harder due to the accelerating rate of change. But 20/20 hindsight spots this scenario as yesterday's news.

In October 1998, the Ford Motor Company put out a memo to its suppliers that was pure *Back to the Future.* Allow us to buy supplies and raw materials over the Internet by June 1999, said the memo, or we will take our business elsewhere. Companies like Snap-On, the makers of high-end hand and power tools, woke up and smelled more than 10 percent of their income at risk. It was time to move from curious to serious about the Web.

Today, any company of any size can offer electronic data interchange because the World Wide Web provides the transport medium. Every company can afford a PC with a modem and a link to the Internet. That gives them a link to you. Any company today operating without a PC is the same as operating without a fax machine was 5 years ago or without a telephone 70 years ago.

Making your company easier to do business with is today's great competitive edge. Customers expect the best price. They expect fast service. They expect to get answers instead of being put on hold until dawn. And they will flock to buy from you if you can save them 10 minutes here and 20 minutes there.

We have phones. We have computers. We have MBA degrees. We have budgets that can be shifted to meet our needs. And we have spare change—but we don't have spare time. We don't have a moment to lose. We're working longer hours and having more responsibilities heaped upon us as the pace quickens and the plot thickens. If we can buy it easier from company B, company A will have to go a long way to convince us that its difficult acquisition procedure is worth it.

Ease of Doing Business as a Competitive Edge

One management information system (MIS) manager told me about a choice he was making between two desktop PCs. He was looking at buying 250 computers from either Dell or Compaq, and he was stuck for a decision. He had mapped out the same specifications. Both companies offered the same warranty. He had negotiated prices so similar as to be indistinguishable. Both companies had excellent reputations. How was he to decide?

One evening, he went to look at their respective Web sites. He had seen all of the literature and found it duplicated on the Web. He had seen all of the pictures, read all of the testimonials, and pored over all of the reviews. Having put off his decision as long as possible, he clicked onto the customer service areas of each company. He was surprised. At that point in time, Dell offered a list of telephone numbers that customers could call to get help. On the other hand, Compaq offered a wealth of information, printer drivers, diagnostic software, and advice on configuring new computers.

This buyer thought about the engineers who would be installing these new systems at night. He imagined them running cables through the ceiling and trying to get workgroups of computers to share printers. He realized they would be working after-hours, when the computer users were at home. His decision was clear.

Since then, in order to remain competitive and stay in the race, Dell has implemented a wide variety of information and tools on its site (Figure 2.2), including self-diagnostic tools and instant automated answers to typed-in questions.

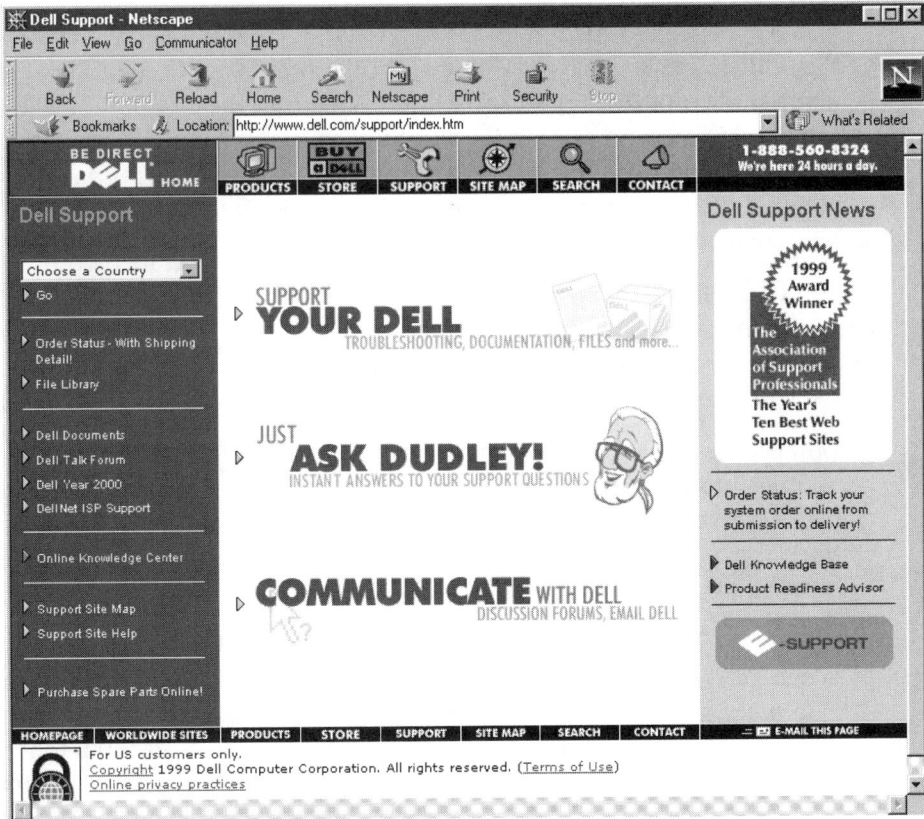

Figure 2.2 Dell won the Association of Support Professionals' second annual "Best Web Support Sites Competition."

When Federal Express put package tracking on its Web site, UPS was quick to follow. When Wal-Mart started selling online, K-Mart had no choice but to follow suit.

Take a moment to look at your competitors' efforts on the Web. Take a moment *every week*. It's the only way you're going to stay ahead of the game. What can you offer that your competitors cannot? If you can't improve your products any more and you can't lower your price any more—improve your service.

A Harris poll commissioned by Dell Computers in the fall of 1999 showed that 43 percent of PC users were planning on shopping online for the winter holidays, compared to just 10 percent in 1998. In a November 16, 1999 article in *Information Week,* Sharon Solfest, manager of interactive distribution for Northwest Airlines, warned that "if customer support is not there, people will try the site once and never come back."

The Race Is Getting Vaster and the Pace Is Getting Faster

When prospective customers can see what it's like to be a real customer, and they like it, this turns them into a real customer faster than can a large advertising budget or the largest sales force. Now that the quality of customer care can be viewed from around the world in seconds, you no longer have to provide better service than your competitor did yesterday. You have to provide better service than your competitor did *this morning.*

A torrent of tools is coming onto the market to help you help your customers online. Tools for e-mail management, for database access, for Web-based order processing, or for Web page personalization. These are not just neat new toys for your IT department to play with; they are weapons of mass destruction in the war for your customers.

Don't forget that your competitor isn't necessarily who you thought he was. You used to compete with the company across town. As you grew, you competed with companies across the country. You knew who they were and could track them. But today, somebody in Holland, Switzerland, or Beijing could become a competitor overnight. It's up to you to watch the Internet for new arrivals.

When Peter Granoff and Robert Olson founded Virtual Vineyards (Figure 2.3) in January of 1995, it was not in addition to their winery business. It was not in addition to their wine brokering business. It was not in addition to their wine retailing business. They saw an opportunity and went into the virtual retail wine business from scratch. The opportunity was online, and there are high-end retail wine merchants out there to this day who cannot figure out what happened to their best customers.

Figure 2.3 Virtual Vineyards (now wine.com) offers customer service one would only expect in the tasting room of an exclusive winery.

Virtual Vineyards was established with the realization that its unique advantage could be duplicated by anyone, anywhere in the world. Established corporations that don't understand this competitive threat will not be able to maneuver fast enough when their fortunes change due to slightly better service offered on the Web.

We live in a world where the words "dot-com" follow the word "Amazon" more often than not. We live in a world where the word "Amazon" has become a verb. You want to try to amazon your competition before it amazons you.

Living in a 24-Hour World

The most important reason for Web-based customer service is the feasibility of proffering full-time availability. New trends in business call for 24-hour accessibility. Providing meaningful service around the clock is very expensive if it depends entirely on humans. Really good humans not only know how to find the answers; they know if the found answer is actually useful. These people are quickly promoted into positions where they don't answer the phone during the graveyard shift.

Why do your customers need service 24 hours a day, 7 days a week? Because that's when they're working. Engineers, operations managers, human resource workers, marketing executives, and others have always burned the midnight oil to finish projects. More and more virtual corporation partners are working at home and getting on-line after the kids are asleep. These people need answers at all hours. Not just from nine to five, and certainly not just in your time zone.

The steamship, the airplane, and the telephone have all done wonders to make the world smaller. But their efforts pale in comparison to the Internet. This network of networks makes it possible for a company's staff to be located almost anywhere. As a result, project team members may be spread around the world. Virgol Serviços de Convencia, S.A., is located in Portugal; makes use of a consultant in California; and has confidentiality agreements written up by its American attorney in Delaware. Sun Microsystems has a team of software developers in Russia. How do they manage? Over the Internet. What does that mean to your company?

It means that people all over the world need access to your information. All over the world means all around the clock. The printed circuit board designer in Egypt needs specifications from the chip manufacturer in the Silicon Valley right now. Sending a fax and waiting until the next morning for a response the next day is no longer fast enough for the designer to maintain a necessary time-to-market advantage. The designer needs answers right now.

Reg Hargrove at Decision Support, Inc., in Mathew, North Carolina, discovered that one of the company's marketing partners, OCTUS Software in Brazil, was closing its offices in the United States to cut costs. Octus provides mainframe compression software to Decision Support. But Hargrove wasn't upset. He knew that he can still get service and software updates from the vendor through the Internet (Figure 2.4).

As technology spreads around the world and into our homes, location for knowledge workers becomes less and less important. In the blizzard of 1996 that had the U.S. East Coast at a standstill for almost two weeks, corporate network managers observed that high-speed corporate network traffic was below half the usual concentration. People were unable to reach their desktop com-

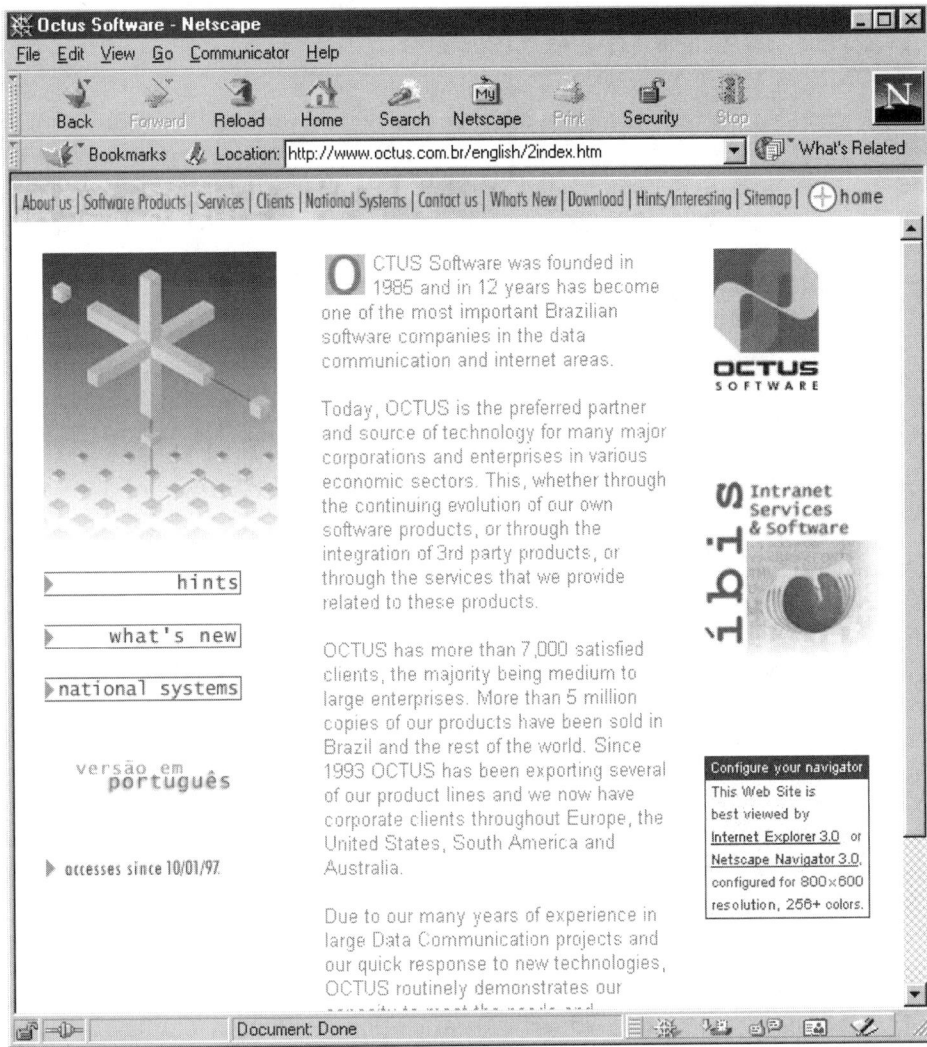

Figure 2.4 OCTUS Software can support its marketing partners online without local offices all over the world.

puters, which are connected to the Internet via the corporate local area network. At the same time, Internet access companies reported a 40 percent *increase* in dial-up traffic. People were continuing to work from home.

These trends make the case to provide customer service 24 hours a day and 7 days a week on your Web site. It's not just that you should do it because you can. It's not just that you should do it because your competitors will. You should also do it because your customers are going to expect it.

There's Money to Be Saved

Sun Microsystems has an obvious reason to promote the World Wide Web as a customer service medium. More Sun computers were used as Web servers in 1994 and 1995 than those of all other manufacturers combined. As the company that promoted itself for years with the tag line, "The network *is* the computer," Sun was in the best position to profit from the growth of the Web. If the Internet grows, so does Sun. But the company's figures are so compelling and its savings so enormous that it doesn't matter if it's a little self-serving. In the words of Neil Knox, general manager and vice president of network computing at Sun:

> Our Web-based SunSolve service lets customers retrieve product documentation, query a 1.2GB technical database, exchange information with other users in online forums and download the latest software updates. They can also get fast answers to technical questions and obtain up-to-the-minute advisories without the intervention of Sun support staff. This self-serve approach saves an estimated $250,000 in telephone support and $13,000 in literature request processing per quarter. Online delivery of software has made an even bigger impact, reducing by roughly $1.5 million each quarter the amount we spend sending out updates via magnetic tape.
> *Webmaster* Magazine, November 1995

Yes, it sounds idyllic, if not hyperbolic. Saving more than $7 million per year would be enough to cost-justify any tool, facility, project, or Web site. But it turns out that these numbers are soft-peddled by Sun. As a senior staff engineer at Sun Microsystems, Will Snow managed sunsolve.sun.com, which he said was "the server with all the cool stuff. The other one, www.sun.com, is the one with all the marketing hype."

When asked about cost savings to the organization, Will liked to put the number at about $1.5 million per quarter. "Otherwise, there's too much attention from the media and from the organization. I just hate getting all those awards. Besides, the more visibility we get, the less time we have to implement some really interesting new technologies.

"If you do the math, you could say we're saving $12 mil a month! So I usually divide by four or five before I hand out numbers. I think lots of people are pulling down software patches who wouldn't bother to get them by phone and mail. But it's free, it's easy, so they do." As a result, more customers are running computers with current bug fixes than ever before.

Sun has a head start on the rest of us. The company had already been in the networking business for years when the Internet hit the cover of *Time* on July 25, 1994 (Figure 2.5). Its customers are online sort of people. It sells an online-type product. Even so, Sun's success was so breathtaking that it pointed the way for the rest of us.

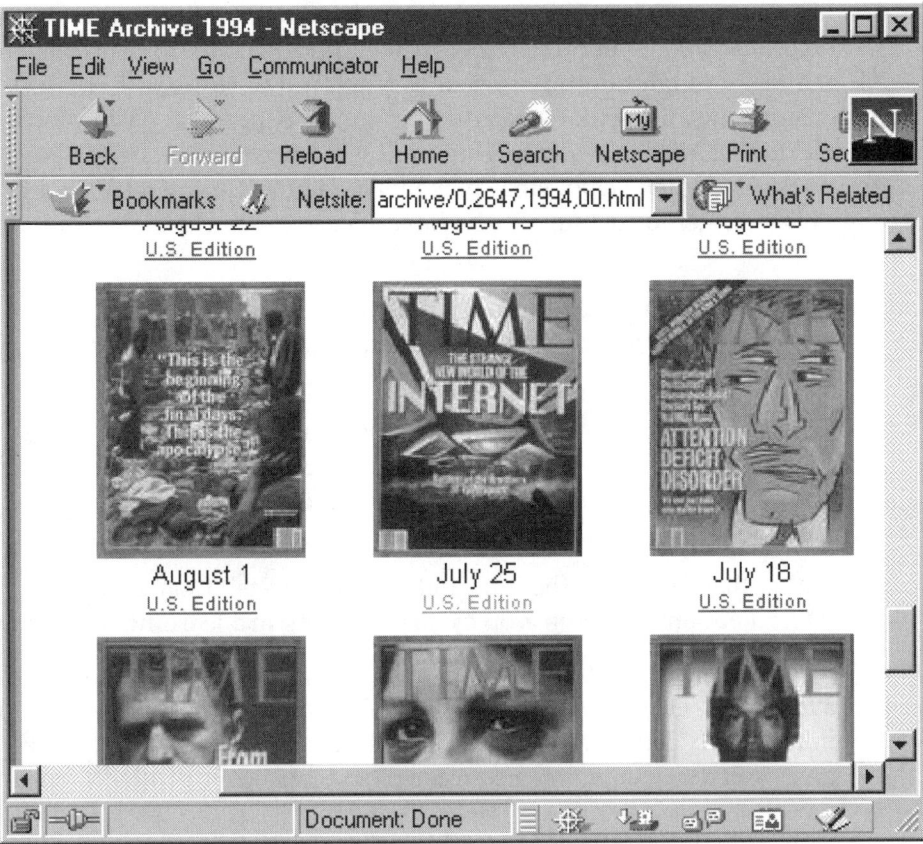

Figure 2.5 *Time* magazine reported on the value of the Internet to business.

The savings come from call avoidance tools and technologies. If customers can find the answers, they don't have to call you. If they don't call you, you don't have to pay for the call, or for the person who would have to be hired to answer all those calls. But this advantage comes with a twist.

Providing exceptional online customer service is not going to make those pesky customers go away and not bother you any more. But it will change the kinds of questions they ask when they do call. They'll ask harder questions.

Julia King follows the changes the Internet has been making to business and writes about it in *Computerworld* (www.computerworld.com). For an article published on August 16, 1999, she spoke to several customer-service-immersed companies. Mike Anderson, vice president of information systems at Home Depot, told her that people coming into the stores now have a lot more knowledge than they did before.

"If you're giving more information to customers online and educating them before they come into the store," Mike told Julia, "that means they're asking the really tough questions when they get to the store." At HomeDepot.com customers can calculate exactly how much paper and paste they'll need to tackle that kitchen wallpapering project. They can view step-by-step instructions. But Home Depot store personnel are now getting advanced training in order to cater to customers who have clicked every calculator and tried every tutorial.

So is there no middle ground? Will there be no real savings in the future because people will be asking harder questions? The real savings will be not losing customers.

When you listen to the Don Peppers and Martha Rogers' 1to1 story (www.1to1.com) you learn of the growing need to talk to your customers *more*. You want to know more about their complaints and their desires. You want to know what you can do to get them to buy more of your goods and services.

Rather than spending the time and resources to tell them things they can easily find out on their own, you can be engaging in a learning relationship.

Rather than asking about speeds and feeds, sizes and colors, and prices and availability, customers are going to ask about alternative uses and applications. When people start asking about how to use your product better, that gives you the opening to encourage them to use your products more.

There's Money to Be Made

You've always heard how inexpensive it is to keep a customer compared to finding a new one. It is easily argued that selling something to somebody you know is easier than turning a prospect into a customer. Yet so many sales organizations are geared toward the new client. So many compensation plans pay better for new sales than repeat sales. This hurts the organization by falsely focusing the sales people in the field. The attitude of catering to would-be customers and ignoring those already sold quickly permeates an organization. But a little spent on current customers goes much further than a lot spent on prospects.

Customer loyalty programs can pay off quickly. A quick review of the figures bears this out:

Suppose you spend $2 million on average each year to add 2,000 new customers to your installed base. Over time, your installed base has grown to 10,000 customers. Unfortunately, attrition can be expected to knock 1,667 customers off each year. Net, you are up only 333 customers. The net cost of acquiring each new customer is an astounding $6,300!

Now suppose you put a loyalty program in place that costs you $200,000 but reduces attrition by a modest 2 percentage points, from 16 percent to 14 percent. Is it worth it? Absolutely. You'll still need to spend $2 million on new customer acquisition to gain another 2,000 customers, but now your yield after attrition is 600 customers. The net cost of acquiring each new customer is $3,300, a savings of almost 50 percent.

Marcia Kadanoff
Marketing Computers magazine, December 1995

But there's a more direct way to make money with a strong customer service ethic. It's called sales.

When a sales rep calls a prospect, the prospect listens to the sales rep the same way a young woman listens to a young man in a singles bar. There's little question about the desired outcome. That sales rep is there to make a sale.

But what happens when the customer calls on the company to ask a question or solve a problem? This changes the singles-bar scenario into a damsel-in-distress situation. Whether calling on the phone or clicking on a Web site, the customer is looking for solutions. If the helpful customer service rep or the informative Web page replies to the query with a useful suggestion, it's going to be well-received.

From the customer perspective, this is known as *helpful hints and suitable suggestions*. From the company perspective, this is known as *cross-selling and up-selling*.

Such customer service must be provided with the utmost of care. The second that the damsel in distress suspects that the knight in shining armor is really Lounge Lizard Larry in shining amour, the whole thing goes sour. That means your cross-selling and up-selling must be prudently designed to offer the customer real value and serious advice.

They're looking for new speakers? Ask them about their amplifier so that you can suggest the best pair to fit the output range of the equipment they already own. They're looking to refinance their home? Find out more about their long-term plans to see if a 15-year loan might not be a better choice. They have a question about that sweater that's on sale? Make sure they're aware of the matching blouse that's also on sale.

A well-designed Web site can serve up suggestions like those just as well as a well-trained customer service representative. The secret to making your customers feel that you're looking out for their better interests is to, well, look out for their better interests. Look at the world from their side of the screen. Every day.

Seeing the World through Customer-Colored Glasses

Successful customer service always means looking at your products, your company, and your customer service methods through your customers' eyes. The customer doesn't care if your company is organized by product line, business unit, or spheres of political influence. The customer just wants his or her question answered or problem solved.

The most important task for a customer service Web builder to undertake is figuring out what the customer will want to see, want to ask, and want to get out of the experience. It may be well worth the effort to ask customers directly, "As you do business with us via our Web site, what additional information would you like us to show? What functionality would you like us to add?"

Once your Web site is up, offer incentives to customers to comment on their experience. Give them ample opportunity to click on a button that lets you know if they really like the service, somewhat like the service, dislike the service, or hate the service. Give them lots of chances to express a written opinion. Your customers will be forthright, and they will come up with good ideas—which is good because you're going to need those ideas.

As your Web site grows and your competitors' Web sites grow, your customers are going to develop higher and higher expectations. So the first question is, where do you start? The next chapter takes an incremental approach to putting your customer service on the Web.

CHAPTER 3

Publishing on the Web

Taking the bull by the horns, you decide the to make some basic information available on your Web site. This will show your customers you're paying attention to a changing world and your heart is in the right place. But how much information do you supply? What information do you provide first?

With the available technology, it's possible to let your imagination run wild while brainstorming great customer service features for a Web site. Separating the possibilities into manageable chunks is the only way to get a handle on a reasonable and manageable implementation.

From the Beginning—Lend an Ear

It doesn't take fancy graphics or big budgets or sophisticated systems to produce results. It just takes an understanding that customer support is important. Good customer support doesn't have to be expensive—just good.

What Are They Looking For?

In the land of the 80/20 rule, 80 percent of your Web site visitors are looking for the same 20 percent of your information. There are three ways to figure out what people are looking for on your site; two of these should be used when creating Web pages, and two should be used continuously once the pages are up and running.

First of all, scratch your head, look up at the ceiling, and pull some answers out of thin air. What do customers ask when they call on the phone? What is your most popular piece of marketing literature? Which PowerPoint slide do your prospects refer back to the most? Put yourself in your prospects' and customers' shoes and try to imagine what information will help them learn what they need to learn to choose, buy, and use your products. This method is the single most popular—and least effective—course of action. Nevertheless, it's a place to start.

Next up: Ask Your Customers. Before uttering, "D'oh!" and slapping your forehead in that Homer Simpson way, be advised that this method of learning about customers is woefully lacking in business today. Nobody has time. And if some hotshot insists on asking customers, which customers get asked? The friendliest ones? Nonsense. Instigate a whole Customer Research and Feedback Technique (with or without a fancy acronym) that makes a point of including customer opinion in everything you do. After the new section of your site is live, ask the customers for their opinion.

In my collection of Favorite Buttons on the Internet is a short-lived item that was found on Sun Microsystem's home page during part of 1996 (Figure 3.1).

Like most good sites, Sun has a "Feedback" button on every page. But this flagrant taunting of Sun's prospects and customers on the home page gave the company the input it needed to make its Web site a better place.

Okay, you've scratched your head, and then you asked your customers. Now try following them around. Sift through your log file to see what people are looking for *and how they are looking*. I'll go into more detail about log files on Chapter 6, "Improving Your Value." At the moment, I want you to think in terms of bread crumbs.

Some people come to your home page just to look around. Those are the same sort of people who pull into your parking lot, saunter in the front door and strike up a conversation with the receptionist. "Nice building. I always wondered what SuperMegaTech does for a living. You got a brochure?"

Everybody else is on a mission. They are looking for something in particular and it's up to you to figure out what they want and make it as easy as possible for them to find it. You do that by following the breadcrumbs they leave as they click from page to page. Your server logs will reveal what pages people are most interested in and give you a clue as to what they want.

Figure 3.1 Sun wanted to know what you thought of its handiwork.

What Do They Need?

No Web site can publish everything a prospect or a customer *might* want to find. But if they can't always get what they want, maybe they can get what they need. It's time to put on the psychologist's hat and try to second-guess them.

Some people come to your site just to complain. As with the phone, sometimes getting it off their chest is all they need. They want somebody to listen. You can create sections of your site that offer up a variety of shoulders to cry on. That's what Hewlett-Packard did with the technical support section of its LaserJet 3100 printer pages (Figure 3.2).

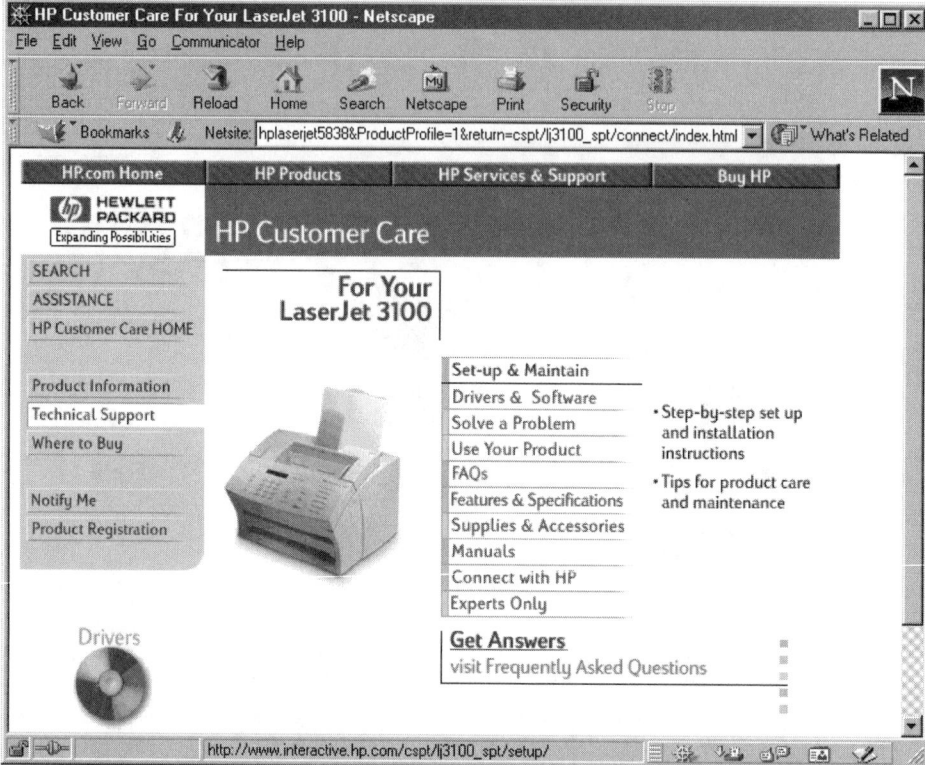

Figure 3.2 Hewlett-Packard offers a myriad of ears to lend to its customers.

In Figure 3.2, you can see the results of rolling your mouse over the "Set-up & Maintain" button. Rolling over the other buttons reveals other descriptions (see Table 3.1).

HP is offering up a wide variety of ways to tackle a problem or find an answer. Does the customer have a problem, need a part number, wish to talk to a representative, or want to learn more about how to make the most of their printer? HP decided to set up its page to provide the right kind of ear for the right situation: a technician to help fix things, a coach to help train the user, a shoulder to cry on if you just want to rant. Whatever site visitors *need*, they can find, even if they can't always find what they *want*.

In a software package, we look for the Help button. At airports, we look for the big Information sign. At a nice hotel, we scope out the lobby for the Concierge desk. On the Web, we've been conditioned to hunt for the Customer Service button and once there, we're fairly likely to click on the Frequently Asked Questions link. After all, if we need to know, surely everybody else does as well.

Table 3.1 Mouse Rollover Results

BY ROLLING THE MOUSE OVER THIS BUTTON:	YOU GET THIS DESCRIPTION:
Set-up & Maintain	Step-by-step set up and installation instructions
	Tips for product care and maintenance
Drivers & Software	Instructions on downloading and installing printer drivers
	Access to the HP drivers library
Solve a Problem	Step-by-step instructions for solving problems
	Troubleshooting
	Help with error messages
Use Your Product	Instructions for all the HP product features . . . with tips on printing
FAQs	Get answers to frequently asked questions
Features & Specifications	Product Facts
	Technical Specifications
	Warranty Info
Supplies & Accessories	Information on complementary HP products
	Order supplies
	Find resellers
Manuals	Users Manual and Guide
	Manual Updates
Connect with HP	The HP product, service and technical news, and information via e-mail
	Personal assistance from HP
	Online user forums
	Register your product
Experts Only	Technical information for advanced users

Organizing Your Information—First Step: The FAQ

The very first step and the document most often expected by the Internet aficionado is the frequently asked questions (FAQ) page. The FAQ is a place of introduction. It provides the fundamentals and lets the casually curious as well as the intent hunter-seeker come up to speed as quickly as possible.

A FAQ Is Born

FAQs were engendered on the Usenet newsgroups as a tool to keep the conversation threads from repeating. On a newsgroup, one person posts a question, another posts an answer, and yet another posts an opinion on the question and a rebuttal to the answer. The ensuing conversation is known as a thread. After several months of sharing technical tidbits, newsgroup denizens self-educate to higher levels of knowledge. Thus, when a new participant posts an elementary question, the other members are disinclined to discuss something they covered in great detail months before. They can even be abusive. But helping others is part and parcel of the Internet culture, so FAQs were born.

Most newsgroups have a FAQ and post it periodically. Some generous newsgroupie takes it upon him- or herself to compile a handful of questions and answers and becomes the FAQ moderator. The initial FAQ is posted for all to see and comment upon. Over time, it is expanded to include the information the group feels is important to pass along and the items that have been most frequently asked and answered.

If you wish to post a message, it's expected that you will have read the FAQ first. Chances are excellent that the answer to your question (and a great deal of other useful information) will be in the FAQ. These documents are well worth perusing as they represent the culmination of many heated debates and pearls of wisdom. If your particular problem is not found in the FAQ, your question will be welcome, as it gives the assembled group of self-styled experts a bone to chew on. It gives the participants a chance to explore a new twist and engage in some friendly, intellectual rivalry.

To see the handiwork that goes into a good FAQ, take a look at the well-known Usenet Periodic Informational Postings Archive at the Massachusetts Institute of Technology (ftp://rtfm.mit.edu/pub/usenet). You'll find all sorts of FAQs there, including the Haying FAQ with such questions as:

1. Why Grow Hay?
2. Mowing Hay.
3. Adjusting Mowers.
4. Drying Hay.
5. Gathering Hay.
6. Small Hay Fields.
7. Custom Operators.
8. Equipment Costs.
9. Annual Costs.
10. Making Hayfields.

11. Hays.

12. Fertilizing Hay.

13. When to Cut Hay.

14. Haying Weather.

15. Identifying Good Hay.

16. Hay Feeders.

17. Haying Alternatives.

18. Weeds and Pests.

19. The Value of Haying.

To really study up, you can find FAQ FAQs at Ohio State University (www.cis .ohiostate.edu/hypertext/faq/usenet/FAQ-List.html).

A FAQ of Your Own

Determining which questions to place in your FAQ should be very straight-forward because your customer service people deal in frequently asked questions for a living. They know which questions are the asked most often. They also know the answers. More important, they understand that a person asking "Does it weigh more than 100 pounds?" is usually asking about delivery methods and costs. When somebody asks about delivery, he or she is also asking how long it will take to make the product useful. When somebody asks about warranties, they're also asking about reliability.

Spend some time with the people who make service calls in the field. Spend some time with your frontline sales people. Spend some time with the people who answer your phone. Give your receptionists pads of paper and ask them to write down all those questions they've heard a million times before. These folks aren't responsible for the answers, but they can give you two very important pieces of information: They can tell you exactly what language the customer used, and they can tell you who has the answer.

Spelling out your questions and answers in customer-speak, rather than product manager-speak is critical. I want to know why my laptop seems to freeze up for several seconds at a time. I don't know enough to click on the question that reads, "Tell me more about the temperature control management system."

Knowing how your customers ask questions is key. When somebody walks into your store or calls on the phone, what do they ask first, and how do they ask?

The FAQ at Subject Wills & Company (www.swc.com) about its Produce Pro software for those in the perishable foods industry is clearly geared toward prospects (Figure 3.3). Why do I need this software? What will it do for me? How does it stack up against the competition? Inquiring minds want to know.

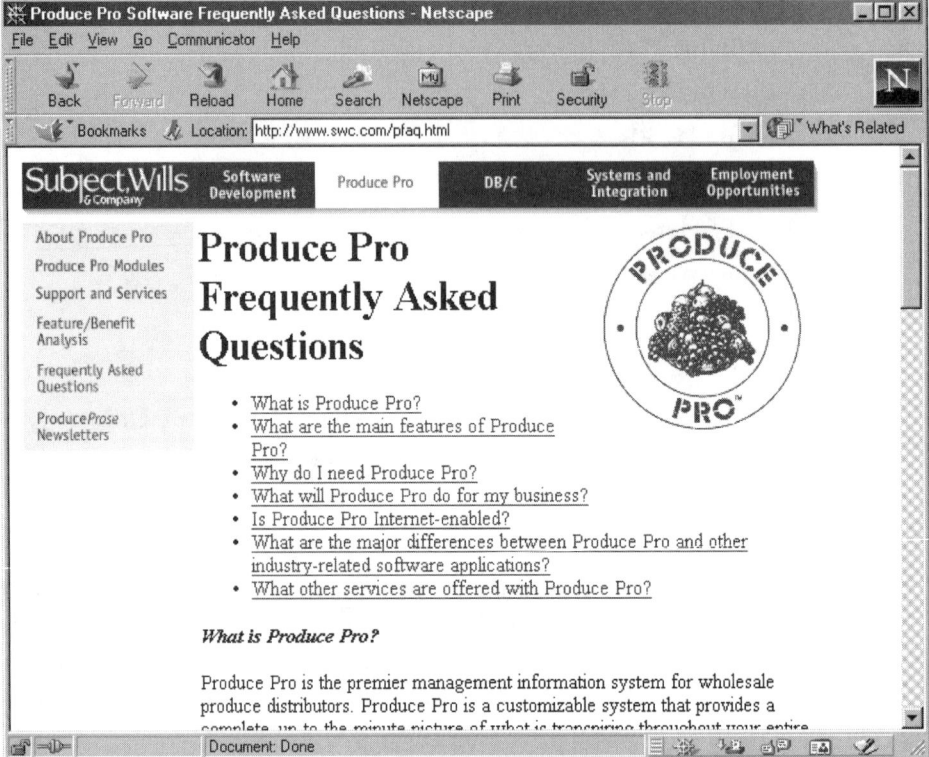

Figure 3.3 The Produce Pro FAQ asks the questions a buyer has in mind when looking for software.

But for those who have already purchased and installed the software, these questions have no value at all. What to do?

The Customer-Only FAQ

Consider following the advice of Denes Bartakovich, manager of Internet marketing at Cognos, a public company that makes software tools for business computing. Denes suggests having two levels of FAQ—one for targeted prospects and newer customers with somewhat basic questions, and one for registered customers who know their way around your products and services. This helps your prospects get a better feel for how you do business and will turn them into customers faster. They will be even more enticed by the fact that there is another FAQ for registered users only.

Prospects will realize that your company is serious about supporting them, and authorized customers can feel like they are getting special attention. In the customer-only area, the questions are a bit more detailed and not for public consumption. When will the product include a specific feature? When will a software bug be corrected? Whom do I contact in case of a major meltdown?

The second FAQ can also provide Qs and As that assume the customer knows more. When a particular client logs in, the customer database can determine which set of frequently asked questions to display based on how long the visitor has been a customer, what level of training that person has completed, what has changed since the last visit, and how often he or she calls the support desk to talk to humans. Experienced customers may only need the short-and-sweet answer, while newcomers will probably be looking for more detailed explanations with a little more background information thrown in.

Structuring FAQ Pages

The organization of a FAQ page deserves some attention to the finer points of Web page design. Those that are well organized will be well-used and will save you and your customers a great deal of telephone time.

Your FAQ must be easy to read, like all of your Web documents. It must be easy to navigate, and you must set the proper expectations so that customers don't spend their time looking and looking, only to be disappointed.

Many FAQ areas on Web sites are simply long text documents. They do, indeed, have the most frequently asked questions, but not necessarily in the most frequently asked order. Some firms can get away with this if the FAQ is short. But the shorter the FAQ, the less potential help it will be, and the lower its value will be.

The Swiss Banking FAQ (www.swconsult.ch/chbanks/faq.htm, Figure 3.4), created by SW Consulting, is one such short-and-simple FAQ. SW Consulting provides computer consulting services to the banking and financial community and offers the FAQ as a gesture of goodwill. This is the company's way of giving back to the Net. It is not of much use to clients or potential clients, because the questions and answers are too simple and high level. Instead it is geared toward the casual browser.

As a marketing device, the SW Consulting FAQ is ill-aimed. As a customer service device, it is a complete waste of time and bandwidth. There are only five questions. Each has only the briefest of answers. Sporting a copyright mark of 1995, the page had not been updated for more than two years the last time I looked. Just how frequently are those questions being asked today?

The initial lessons are obvious. First, if you must create a tool like this, and you don't plan on keeping it fresh, do *not* publish the date it was last updated. On the other hand, don't create a customer service FAQ like this at all. Create something of real value instead.

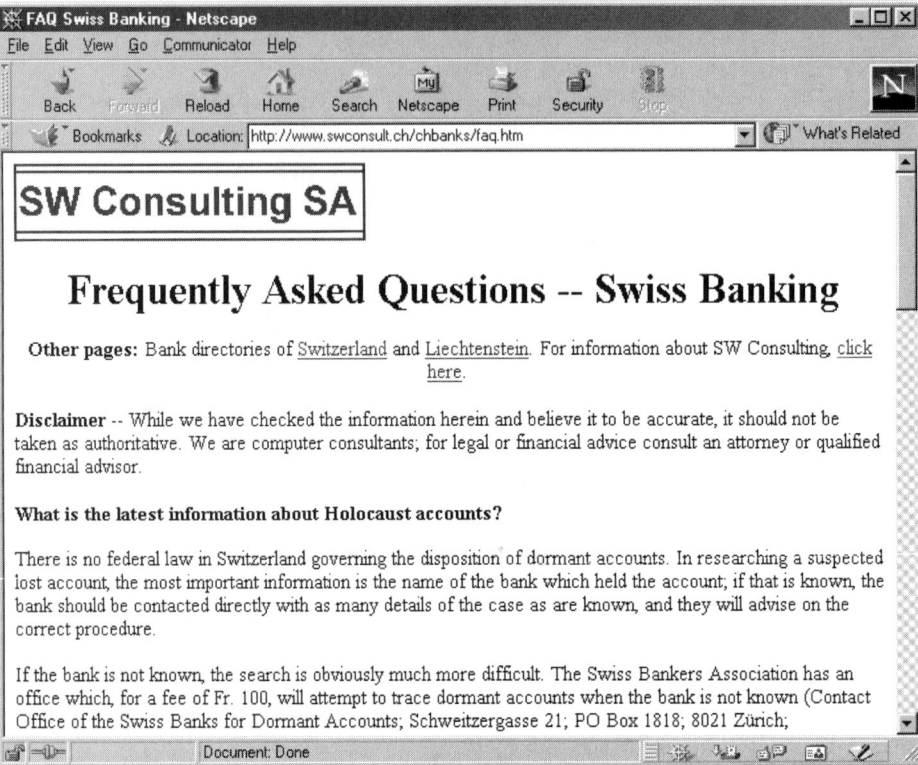

Figure 3.4 SW Consulting maintains a short FAQ on Swiss banking.

Give your FAQ some depth. Answer the questions in as much detail as will help 80 percent of the people who come to read it and provide links for the next 5 percent. I promise that 15 percent of the people who come to most Web sites will have questions that you've never heard before, or are likely to hear again.

Making It Easy to Find

It's a common problem for all Web site designers: How do you offer a sufficient amount of information to make the site truly worthwhile, while making everything easy to find?

Some Web builders create hard-and-fast rules: Nothing should be more than four clicks away from the home page; one visual metaphor will satisfy all navigational needs; no menu will be longer than seven items. Hard-and-fast rules are just that—hard to justify and fast to disappoint. But, do you need overall look-and-feel rules for your site? Absolutely. You want to make sure that your visitors don't get confused because different departments like different button bars and colors. Just don't get carried away by rule enforcement.

The pointer to the FAQ may be on the home page as a stand-alone button. Thereafter, it might be one of the items on the button bar on every page. It should easily available from many pages on your site, so that people can find the FAQ when they drill down into product information.

A description of your products and services helps visitors satisfy their interests, their curiosity, and their need for decision-making detail. If the product descriptions you publish point back to the detail found in your FAQ, you can concentrate on keeping the FAQ up to date. That should save you a good deal of time rewriting all of your pages.

Pointing back to your FAQ is also useful for showing visitors just how comprehensive your site is. If these pages are well organized, people looking in one area will find corresponding information above and below the specific item they're investigating. Your job is to organize the FAQ in the most logical manner possible.

A simple FAQ is a joy to behold, but make it too simple and you create more work for the visitor than necessary. The Haley & Steele FAQ (www.haleysteele .com) has good questions and good answers, but they're one solid block of text (Figure 3.5).

NEC Computers goes one better by listing the questions as hyperlinks (Figure 3.6).

By keeping the questions short and the links blue, NEC gives customers an easy-to-browse, quick-to-choose road to resolution. You can quickly scan the questions for the one that's keeping you up at night and then click to your salvation.

It's very strange, however, that this page is totally devoid of identifying marks. If it weren't for the support.neccsd.com URL, there would be no way to tell what sort of help you're getting, nor from whom. How could this have happened?

Frames.

While this is hardly the right place to delve into the fine points of Web page design, I will strike a blow against the use of frames. Figure 3.6 is the FAQ frame without the surrounding frameset. The designers had intended the page to look like Figure 3.7. For more on the evils of frames, check out Jakob Nielsen's Website (www.useit.com).

Multiple FAQs

The most significant rallying cry you can incorporate into your FAQ formatting endeavor is, "Think like a customer." Maybe even like a prospective customer. The customer doesn't care whether your company is organized by product line, business unit, or spheres of political influence. The customer

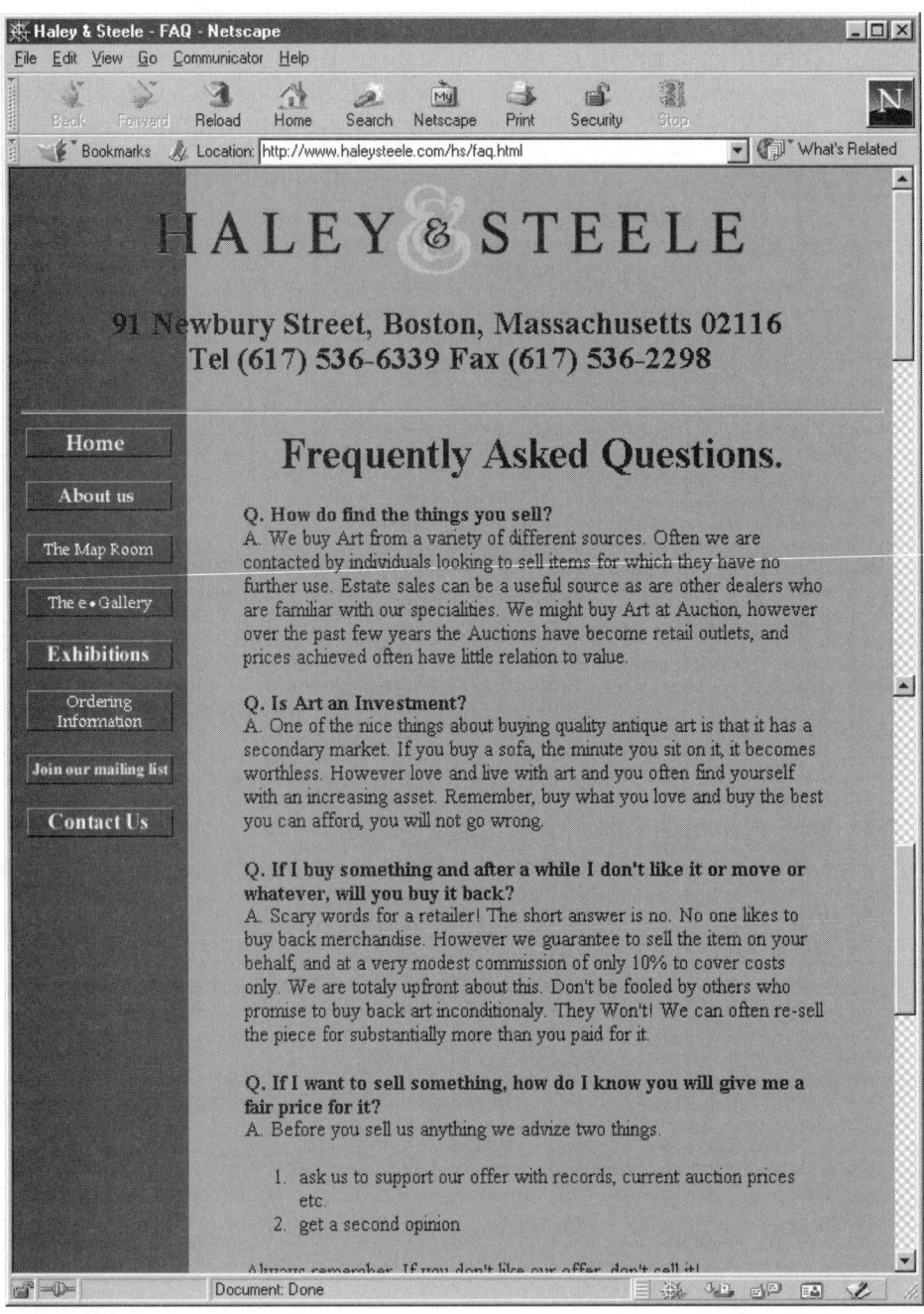

Figure 3.5 The Haley & Steele FAQ asks and answers but doesn't offer decent navigation.

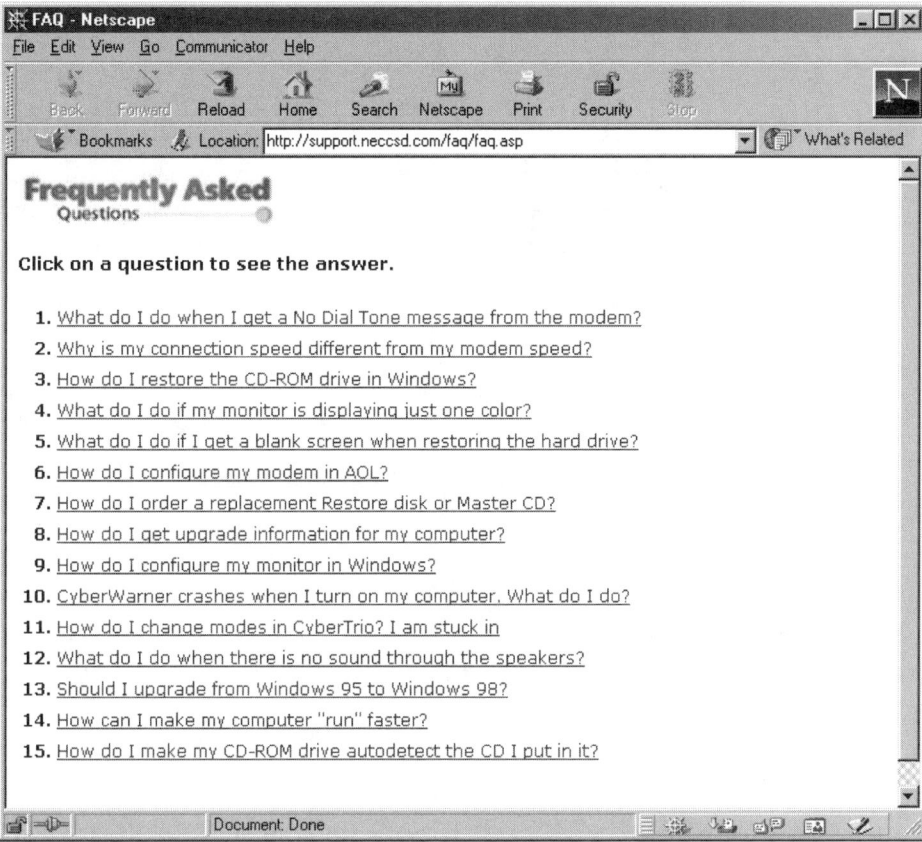

Figure 3.6 NEC lets the customer decide which question is the most important one at the moment.

wants his or her question answered. Let your FAQ reflect how customers think of your company.

One of the most common ways to divide up a FAQ is by subject area. The following listed areas are general enough that most folks would know where to look for that which interests them:

FAQ about product A

FAQ about product B

FAQ about product C

FAQ about upgrades

FAQ about ordering, shipping, and returns

FAQ about getting individual help

FAQ about the company

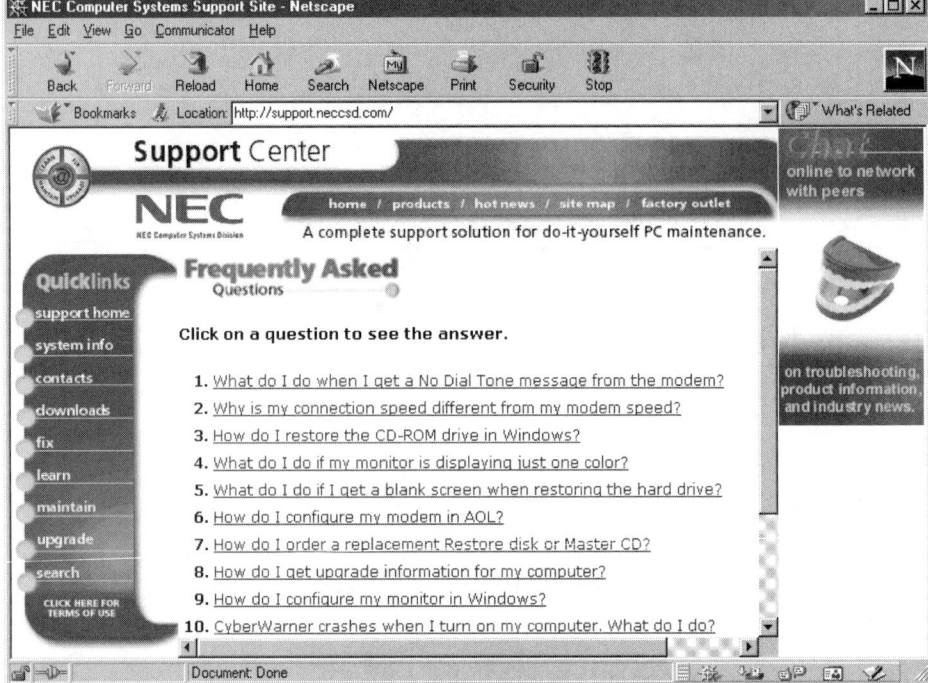

Figure 3.7 The FAQ page as intended. Lesson? Don't use frames.

The folks at ezenia! (www.ezenia!com) sell multimedia communications servers for intranet conferences. With nine products to choose from, they decided that a drop-down menu was the best way to let people select from their list of FAQs (Figure 3.8).

The double-drop-down menu lets you choose the product, but it also lets you choose a subsection of FAQs about each product. Choices include General, Purchasing, Troubleshooting, and Unspecified. The result is 36 different FAQ pages, so customers don't get bogged down in one long document.

Nested Answers

The brilliance of hypertext is that it allows information to be navigated rather than plowed through. It allows the use of discovery as an aid to learning. It also lets people find the key bit of data they're after instead of being subjected to an entire treatise.

Don't try to explain everything on the first pass. An effort to describe calculus without first offering some insights into algebra will be a wasted effort. The

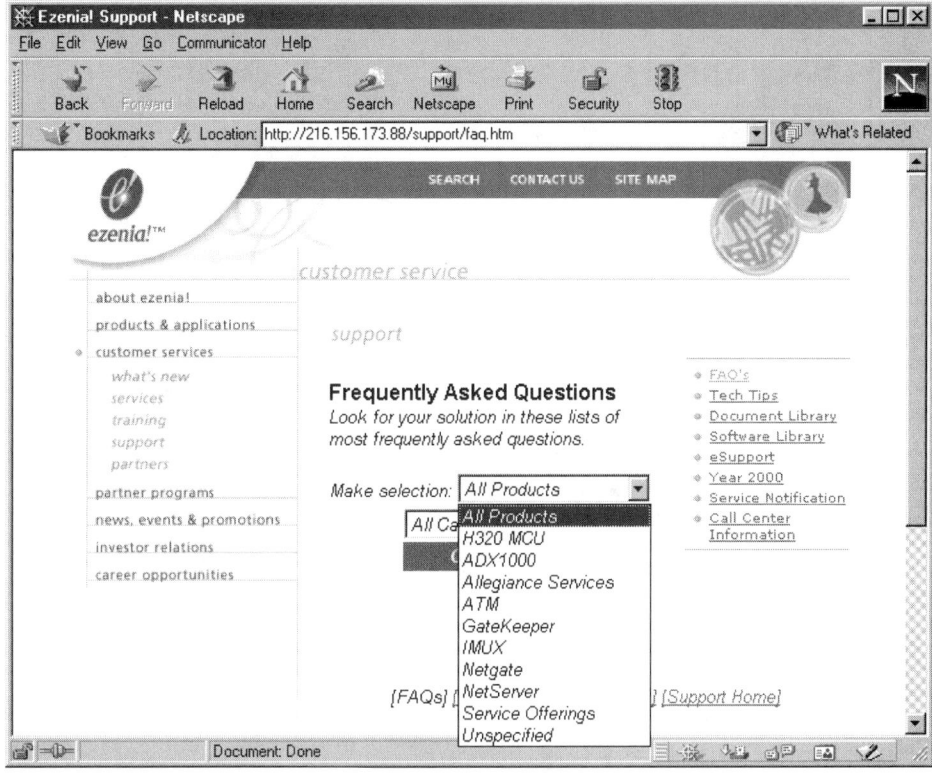

Figure 3.8 ezenia! saves on page real estate by offering a double-drop-down menu of FAQ choices.

calculus descriptions should be a click away to those who need to know. But FAQ readers will run away, never to read again, if the answer they need can only be found after reading long and laborious documents. Let them quickly click through the information. Give them clear and concise indexes and tables of contents of your FAQ.

Take a lesson from the U.S. Postal Service, which sprinkles its answers with pointers to more in-depth information (Figure 3.9).

Putting It All Together

The 15 Seconds Web site (www.15seconds.com), one of the many properties of Internet.com, is "a free resource for developers and administrators working with Microsoft Internet Solutions, with a focus on server side solutions like Active Server." One of the ways the 15 Seconds people keep their market niche informed is through a fairly sophisticated set of FAQs (Figure 3.10).

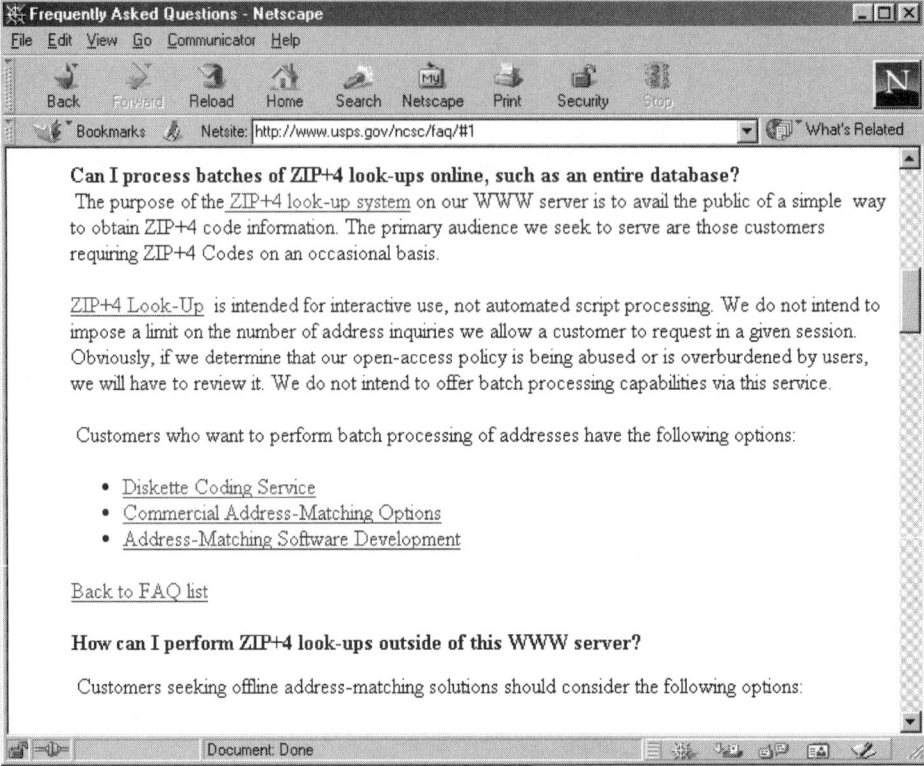

Figure 3.9   Your Postal Service understands that one answer just isn't enough.

"All the Frequently Asked Questions are divided into categories listed below," notes the 15 Seconds FAQ introduction. "For a description of each category click here." When you do, the result is a list of more than 35 FAQs, with a short paragraph describing each one. The first time you come to this site, these descriptions make for great reading. Every time after that you don't really need them; you just need the quick links.

Notice that each of the links in Figure 3.11 has a number in parentheses next to it. For instance, the Cookies link shows (13). That's indicates how many questions there are. This is a very useful tool if you are interested in a specific area and want to know if any new questions have been added since the last time you looked. That's important here, because frequently asked questions are added as they are asked by fellow Web site builders.

In the case of the Cookies FAQ (Figure 3.11), 15 Seconds has labeled the question for quick scanning; written out the long question for full understanding; dated the question so you'll know how fresh the information really is; and pro-

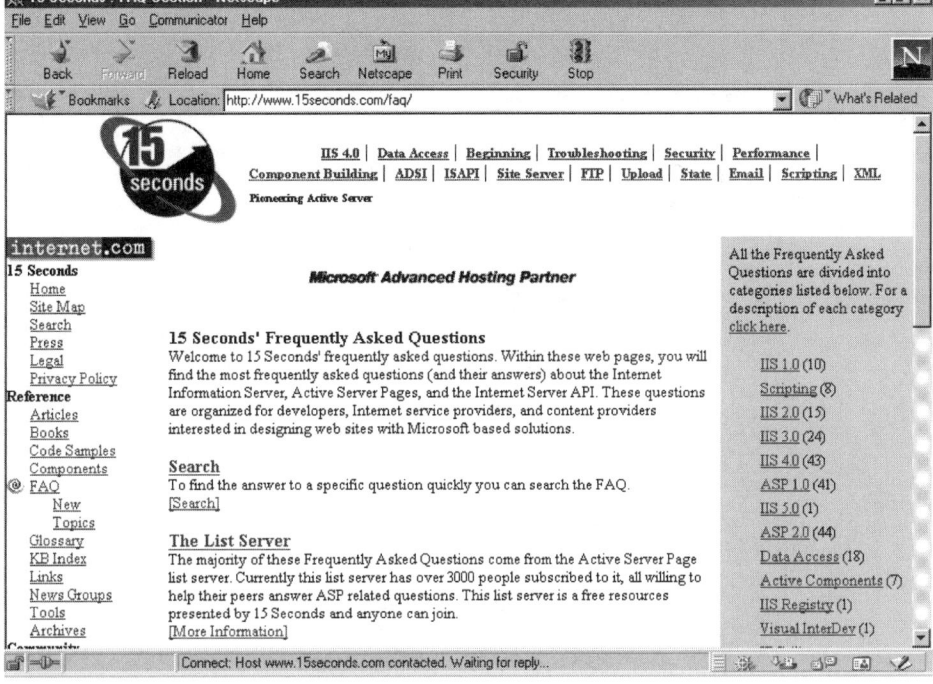

Figure 3.10   15 Seconds has a long list of FAQs, with some navigational clues appearing next to each one.

vided a link to the answer, rather than try to squeeze all of the questions and all of the answers onto one page.

Once you decide which question meets your needs, 15 Seconds takes you to the pot of gold at the end of the rainbow (Figure 3.12). It starts with a straightforward answer. The answer includes the e-mail address of the person who answered the question so that you can ask a question about the answer. This is a wonderful technique to make the visitor feel that the answer is backed by an individual's reputation, and to hook up the visitor to the right person to ask a follow-on question. As a result, your staff isn't wasting time filtering questions to the right person—that person is listed, front and center.

Next up? A list of articles about the topic. Additional, in-depth information that's been previously published on your site—or even pointing to other sites. News, opinion, detailed technical specifications—all of it adds depth to the quick-and-simple answer already given.

15 Seconds then has links to code samples for programmers (Creating a Unique Cookie with SQL Server and Check Cookie Assignment), followed by a list of related topics, some of which are other FAQs.

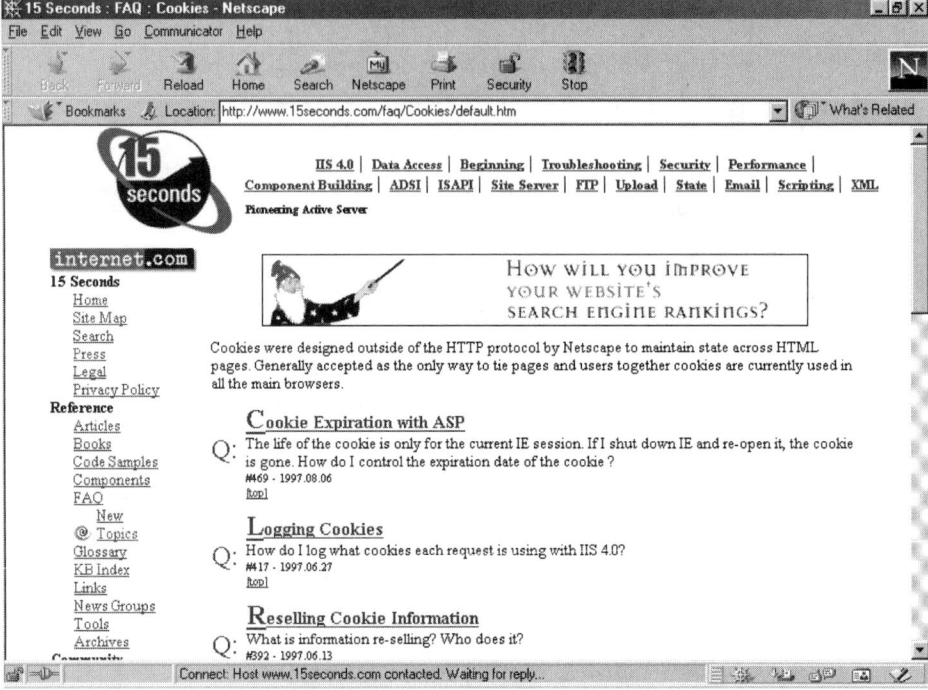

Figure 3.11   The 15 Seconds Questions page offers lots of useful meta information to help you decide where to click.

This blending of information about the questions, information about the answers, and pointers to more detailed information makes for an ideal FAQ. Somebody with a question in mind is going to find some answers, some background, and somebody to ask for help.

If your FAQ is well architected, your customers are going to be able to find the answers they need in a hurry. That will save them time and frustration, and save you from answering another phone call.

The Telltale FAQ

Turning back to your server logs, it's time to ascertain your single *most* frequently asked question. Your MFAQ is a red flag. It's a flare shooting through the night sky. It's a warning that what you have is a failure to communicate.

If 80 percent of the people who read your FAQ pages are looking at the same question, then you have dropped the ball somewhere along the way. If 80 percent of the people *have* to read the FAQ to learn that one piece of information, then it's time to rewrite the user manual. Maybe it's time to put the answer on

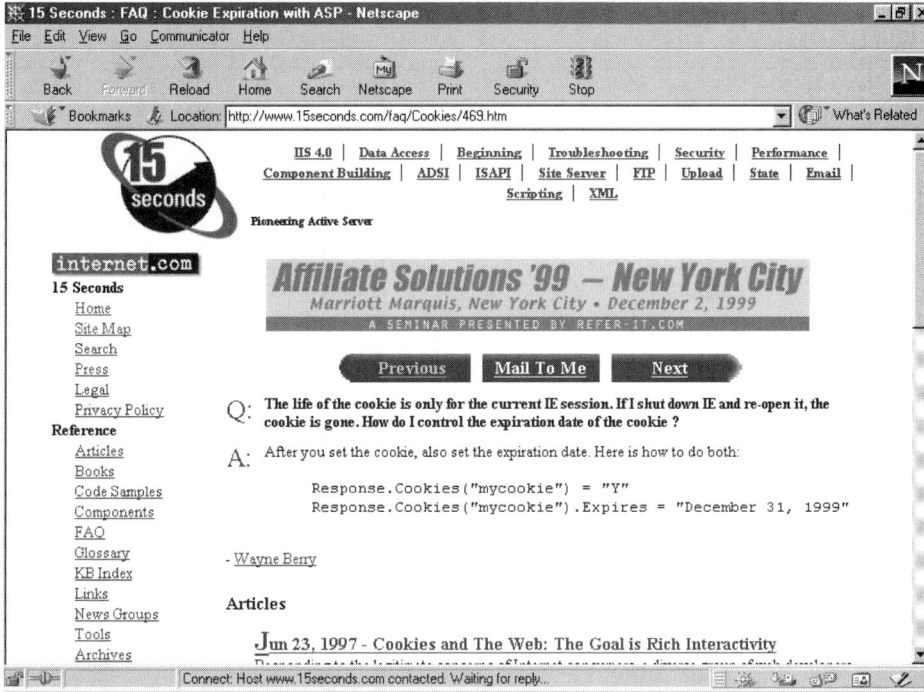

Figure 3.12 15 Seconds shows the world how to answer a frequently asked question in full.

your home page or rewrite the copy on your packaging, or rewrite the bright orange sticker that customers have to peel off in order to put the batteries in. Maybe it's time to change your ads to alter people's expectations of your product.

Some page design consideration comes into play if you want to rely on your FAQs to reveal the depths of your customers' confusion. Rather than providing an index of linked questions at the top of the page that point to paragraphs further down the same page, have them point to different pages.

An anchor on the same page may show up in your logs as www.company .com/faq.html#Q9, but it may not. Customers can just as easily scroll down the list to look at the answer to the MFAQ—and you won't learn a thing. Better to have each link point to another page that has the answer. That will force a click which will be duly recorded in your log file for further analysis.

But don't place all your trust in the power of FAQ pages. Even the best-designed document will scare off some customers and frustrate others. Some products call out for a troubleshooting guide.

Knowledge Base

What happens when your frequently asked questions are not so much frequent as they are plentiful? When lots of people are asking lots of questions that are all phrased differently, it may be time for a knowledge base. This is pretty easy to describe. You just take all the questions that have come in, and all the answers that have gone out, and drop them into a database. Customers can then rummage around in the database with keyword searches to see if their question has already been asked and answered.

Easy to describe—but not so easy to do.

Step one: Find the answers that are properly sanitized to go along with those questions. Remember going to the receptionist to get the questions? Now we have to turn to various players inside the company to get the various answers we need in order to create the best answer.

Sales will give you the answers that will satisfy the customer the fastest.

Marketing will explain how that problem is a product feature.

Product management will tell you how the problem will be solved in the next version.

Engineering will tell you how dumb your customer is.

Customer service will give you the answer that will soothe your customer's frazzled nerves.

Now that you have the whole panoply of answers, it's time to mold them into coherent, generic responses. Make sure that the responses are complete. Make sure they include pointers to additional information. Do not try, however, to come up with the definitive answer that will take care of every single question a person could ask about a topic. Customers are desperate for specific, on-target, and *short* solutions to their problems. Sprinkling your answer with links to pages and pages of info is fine, as long as you clearly explain what they'll get if they click.

If you have the right kind of products, and a staff with a real desire to help customers, consider adding pointers to individuals who can personally be of assistance. "If you have a question about how to install your new Brain-Wave-Scanner, please get in touch with PlumberNorton@brain!s.com. If you have problems communicating with your Brain-Wave-Scanner, try PsychicSylvia@brain!s.com. If you're concerned about the readouts from your Brain-Wave-Scanner Personality Analyzer, try contacting FreudJung@brain!s.com."

Don't forget formatting. Straight blocks of text are hard to read. Use paragraphs, indents, lists, bullet points, or whatever else comes to hand in breaking up your messages' otherwise tedious visual appearance.

Don't forget to follow up with your customers. Implement a periodic check to determine whether people are getting the answers they need when they need them. "You recently checked our Brain-Wave-Knowledge base. Did it do the trick? Did it help?"

If you need some help and/or want to learn more about making a knowledge base work for you, check out Right Now Technologies (www.rightnowtech .com). Right Now Web (RNW), their product, is designed to create a knowledge base as you communicate with your clients.

> With RNW you are able to establish a knowledge base on your server that provides targeted information, via automated, frequently asked questions, a keyword searchable knowledge base and support for personal assistance requests.
>
> Delivers consistent, accurate service on a 24×7 basis
>
> Empowers your customers to find their own answers quickly, thus reducing phone, email and Web support time
>
> "Learns" as it is used. Customers may rate the effectiveness of the answers they receive enabling the knowledge base to "learn" as it is used

Shooting Trouble Right between the Eyes

A troubleshooting guide (which is not a FAQ, and not a knowledge base) tackles a whole host of predefined potential problems and their solutions. A troubleshooting guide is predicated on knowing how customers approach a problem and what clues they might have in front of them at the moment. This is where PsychicSylvia is your best friend.

The only way you're really going to succeed with a troubleshooting guide is to get real dumb. You have to approach this task with the Zen beginner's mind and forget everything you know about your products. Empty your mind of all the intuitive things you'd try if you were having trouble with the product.

Real-life customers don't look for the link that says, "I'm having trouble with the primary domain name server in my Windows 98 dial-up networking control program." They click on the one that says, "The screechy sound that comes out of my modem sounds funny and I can't get to Yahoo!"

As for the format, you might go as simple as the table that San Diego Rain Gutters decided on (Figure 3.13). It's simple. It's straightforward. It's usable. And it can answer a bunch of questions right off the top.

If you want to walk people through the step-by-step process, you can take a page from the Leading Edge Airfoil Web site (www.leadingedge-airfoils.com). Leading Edge makes Rotax aircraft engines. Troubleshooting a recalcitrant aircraft engine is very serious business, and Leading Edge makes sure that things are laid out very simply (Figure 3.14).

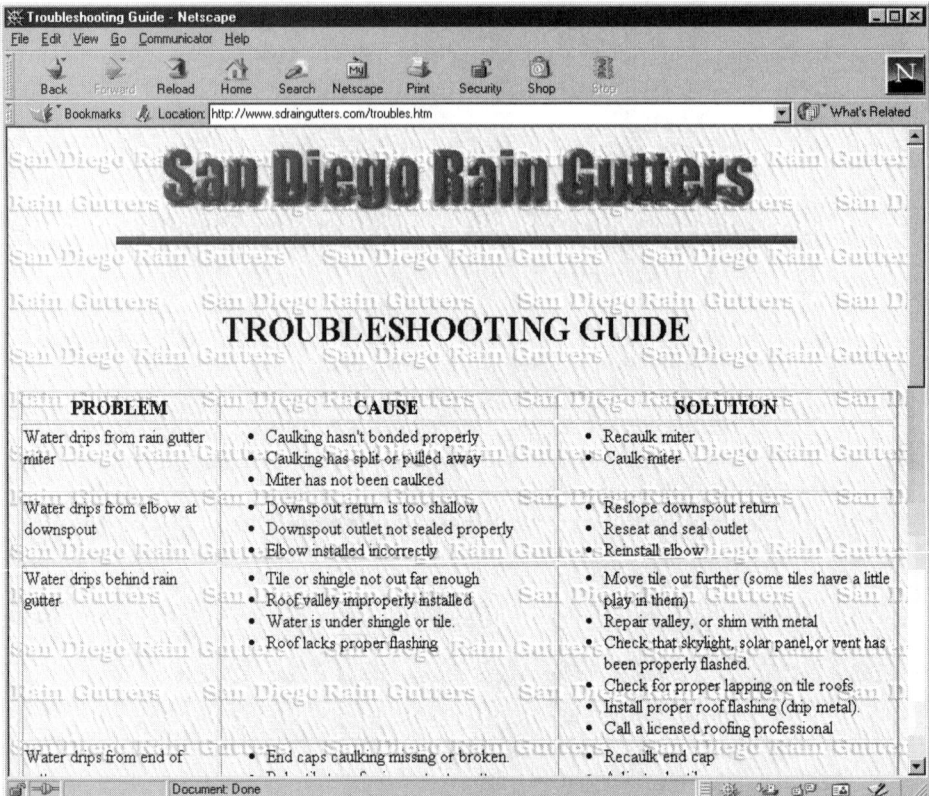

Figure 3.13 San Diego Rain Gutters found a very elegant troubleshooting guide layout.

If you follow Leading Edge's step-by-step instructions, you get some very basic advice. If you click on "Engine will not start," they ask, "Does gas reach the carburetor?" If you click "No," they suggest the following Probable Faults:

- Gas tank empty
- Blockage in tank cap
- Blockage in fuel cock
- Blockage in fuel line
- Needle valve blocked
- Blockage in fuel filter
- Broken or improperly installed fuel pump

Looking at that first entry elicits a chuckle. Sort of along the lines of, "Is it plugged in?" But this kind of steadfast adherence to procedure is what keeps airplanes up in the sky.

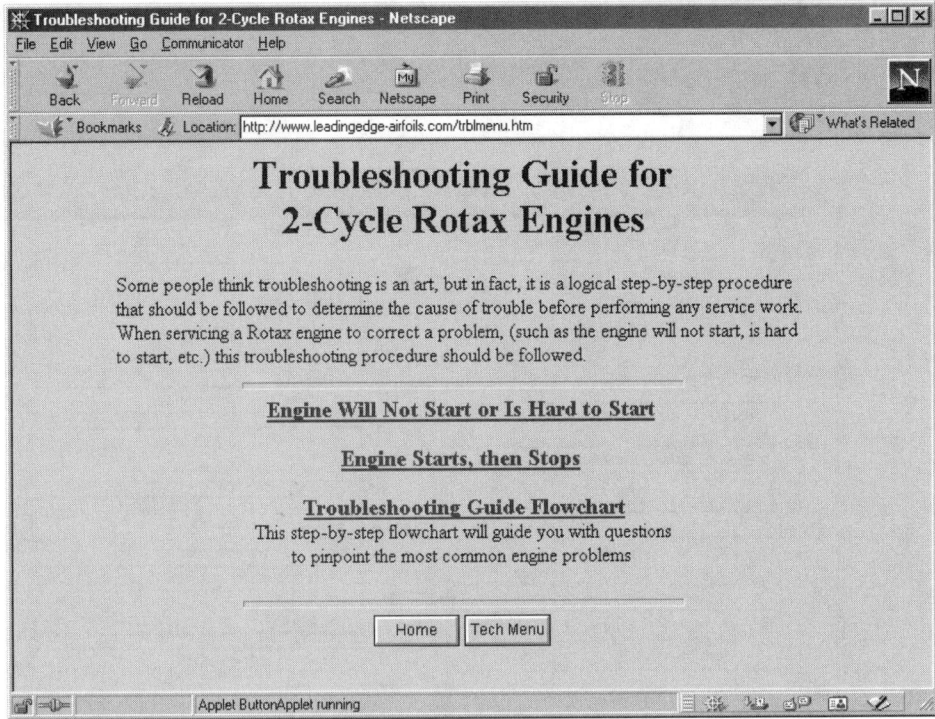

Figure 3.14   There is more emphasis on procedure than intuition when troubleshooting an aircraft engine.

There are several alternative paths you can take when analyzing your Rotax engine and you might click several layers deep into more and more complex questions and answers. In late 1999, the powers that be at Leading Edge decided that their simple HTML approach to the Q&A process was too simplistic, so they published their guide in PDF files. (Figure 3.15).

Aside from publishing the riveting monograph, "Evolution of the Septic System," the good people at the Rural Home Technology Web site (www .frontrunnercorp.com) deliver a thorough troubleshooting flowchart (appropriately enough) for figuring out what's wrong with your septic tank (Figure 3.16).

Just a couple of final hints for troubleshooting guides. Please answer completely. Nothing is more aggravating than walking through a 25-click step-by-step guide and finding that the branches peter out before *your* particular problem is identified. Also, give the customer a way to contact a human who can explain just how far we go in the guide. That way your support rep can pick up the thread as if the customer had been talking with him or her from the start.

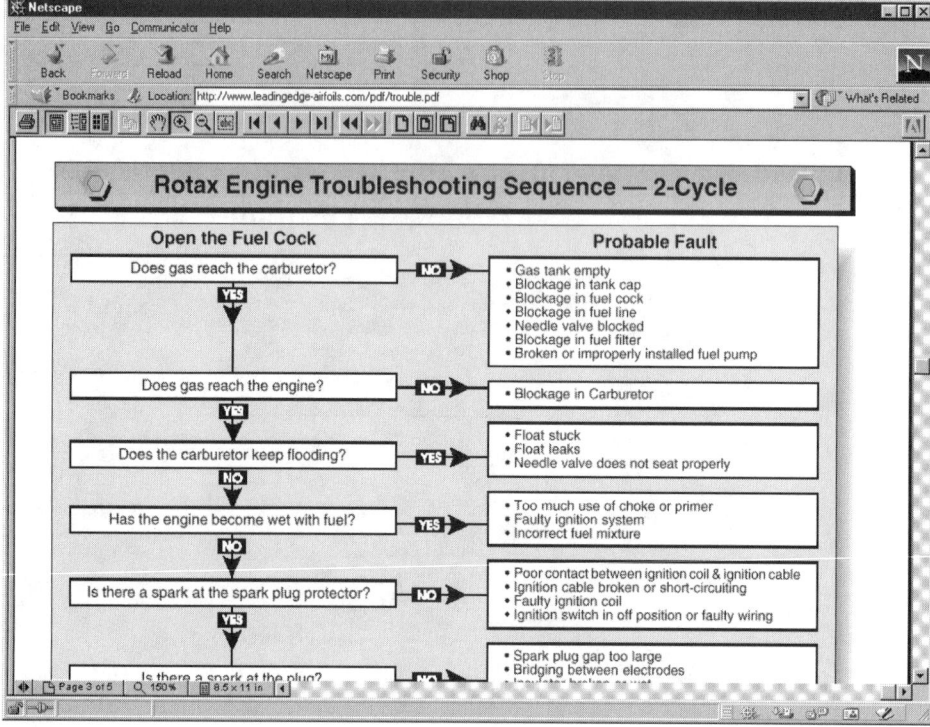

Figure 3.15 The PDF version is easier to read all at once, but still should have been created in HTML.

With all that you've done to lead people to the end of their troubles, some answers will inevitably be locked up in large documents: long pages of white papers or product descriptions or installation manuals. Granted, you were kind enough to put these up on your site, but if I don't know what I don't know, then I don't know how to find the answer either. In these cases (and they will outnumber all the rest), it's best to let people search your entire site.

PDF: Good for You, Not for Your Customer

PDF stands for *portable document format*. It means you can take a document ready for printing and slap it onto the Web in no time. There's a problem, however: Your customer has to have the Adobe Acrobat reader downloaded and installed on their machine, and PDF creates a whole bunch of navigational headaches.

So why do people use it? First, it has a lot of appeal to graphic arts types. "PDF is a universal file format that preserves all of the fonts, formatting, colors, and graphics of any source document, regardless of the application and platform used to create it," says Adobe on its Web site. And it's true. But Acrobat, the free Adobe PDF reader, weighs in at 5.5MB. You're imposing a great deal on your customer just so that you can avoid converting a print document to HTML.

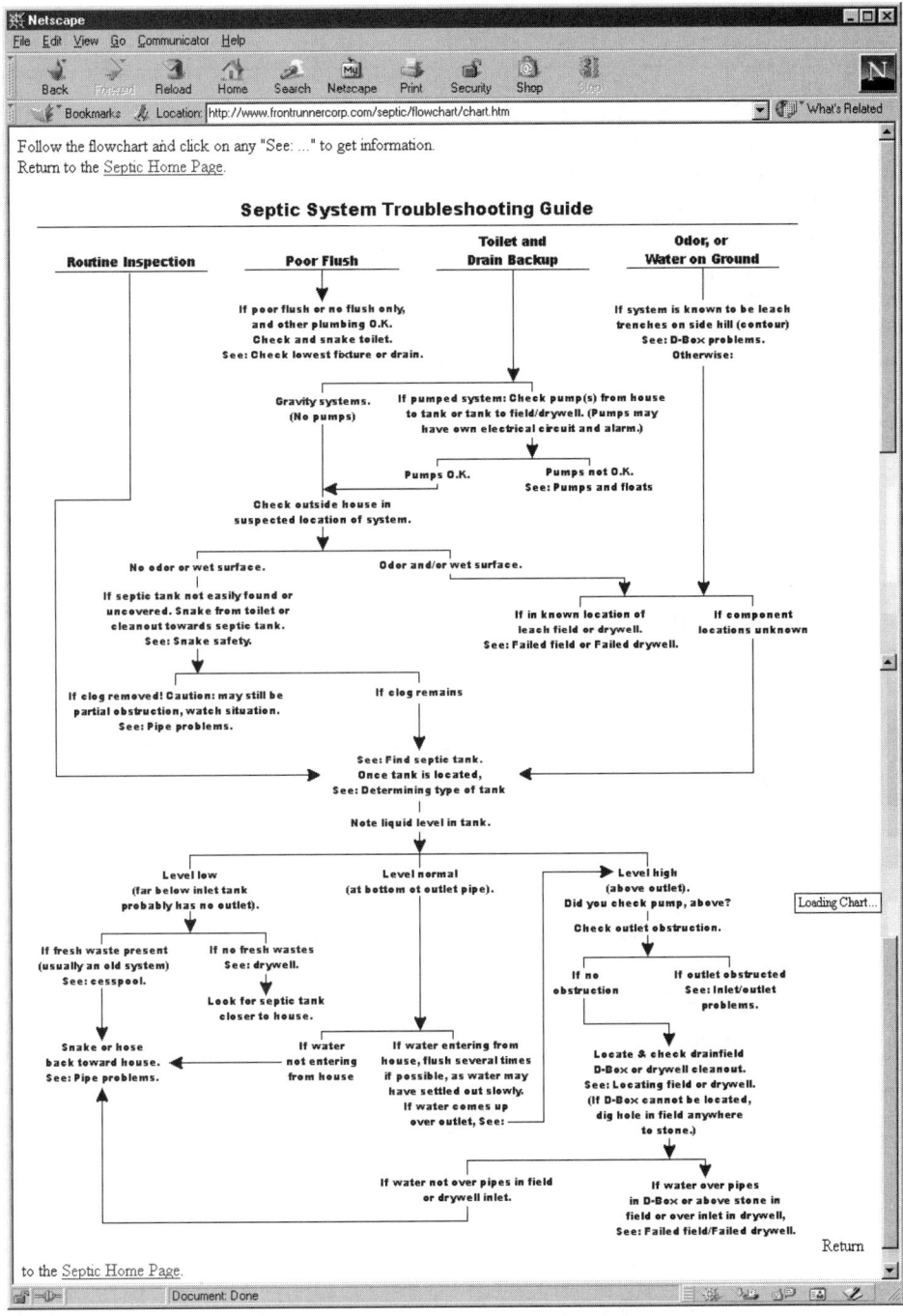

Figure 3.16 A troubleshooting flowchart can graphically indicate the choices and resolutions to your more malodorous problems.

Next Step—Let Them Search

The first time somebody comes to your Web site, they're going to poke around and see what you've got. They might familiarize themselves with your site by clicking around to see what you have to offer—what they can expect from you. They're going to find some interesting things, some of which they can use at the moment and some of which they will file away in that part of the brain where interesting things are kept—briefly.

And sure enough, the very next day, Jack in accounting is going to ask them if they know anything about how to hook up a computer with a DVD drive to a television set and they'll access that brain location and smile and respond that, yes, they can remember they saw that very information on your Web site just yesterday. With a few keystrokes, they're back on your home page—and have absolutely no clue about how to get to the page that has the information that will answer Jack's question.

Do a favor for those of us with an insufficient cranial capacity for remembering things like 37-character-long URLs—give us a search button.

After that first visit, every time a visitor comes to your site he or she will be looking for something in particular. It really doesn't take long to tire of playing Web site hunt and click. Either you help customers find it fast, or they'll stop thinking of your company's Web site as a resource. Then they'll stop thinking of your company as a resource. Then they'll stop thinking of your company altogether, and they'll stop being a customer.

All larger Web sites should offer a search tool. It should be accessible from the home page. If you find the traffic to your search page is high, skip the search page altogether and give visitors a search box and button on every page of your site. Why make them click to get to a page where they can enter their query, when you could just give them the ability to enter their query whenever the impulse strikes?

The search engine itself should be powerful, and it should be easy to use. Your technical team can find a wide variety of available tools. Your budget-minded manager can come up with several that are free. You have to pick the one that will give your customers the answers they want.

Some tools only report back a minimum amount of information, such as file name, file size, and the first line or two of text. Minimal information makes for minimal help. It's much better to find a search tool that reports back with more information. This should include the document title (which is very different from the file name), the document date, a few keywords from the file, and a cogent description of what's in it. Anybody who has used the major search engines to find Web sites knows how hard it is to get information that's good enough to help you click.

Search tools can only do so much. You can help them.

Context

When creating each page on your site, create some meta data to go with them. Yes, that means more corporate standards and rules and regulations. But as annoying as these may be, they end up helping the customer.

Meta data includes subject, date, author, product category, information on who is allowed to see the page, and who can modify it. Customers searching for a starter cord for a new lawn mower don't end up with a power cord for an antique toaster.

Creating software that helps keep things in context is newsworthy, as exemplified by this tidbit from Edupage (www.educause.edu/pub/edupage) on a *Los Angeles Times* article:

> *Meaningful Searches with Watson Software*
>
> Computer scientists at Northwestern University have come up with software they've dubbed Watson (after Sherlock Holmes' helpful sidekick) that links the browser software and the word processing program and uses information gleaned from the document being typed to fine-tune Web searches. "Essentially, it just sits there in the background, and it does an analysis of the document you are working on," says Kristian Hammond, director of the university's Intelligent Information Laboratory. "It figures out the content of the document and then goes and does searches on the Internet to find other documents that would be useful to you. Then it tosses those up in its little window. At any point, you can click on those documents to see what it has suggested. . . . If you are writing a paper on construction equipment and you ask Watson to find documents related to "Caterpillar," it will never return pages related to fuzzy insects. . . . It looks for whatever it believes your current context is." (*Los Angeles Times*, October 28, 1999)
> www.latimes.com/business/19991028/t00009750.html

Think like a Customer

After thinking about the power of a search tool—how fast it can scan terabytes of data—remember that your customer is much more interested in finding the right information within a reasonable time frame than in finding the wrong information fast. There are other methods that allow access to information that don't involve complex engines. They just require you to think like a customer. Beginner's mind.

Limit Their Choices

North Iowa Realty (www.niowarealty.com) is a home-finding site. Because homes come in so many shapes and sizes, North Iowa had to come up with a way to help people find what they need even when they don't know what they want. The solution? Drop-down menus (Figure 3.17).

North Iowa Realty offers a choice of 19 different real estate companies, 6 price ranges, 27 locations, 9 types, 8 styles, from 1 to 6 bedrooms, and from 1 to 6 bathrooms, thereby enabling customers to choose from over one million possible permutations. That's not to say there are that many homes in that many varieties to choose from, but directing a customer's thinking this way helps them analyze their situation, their desires, and their problems before hitting the Submit button.

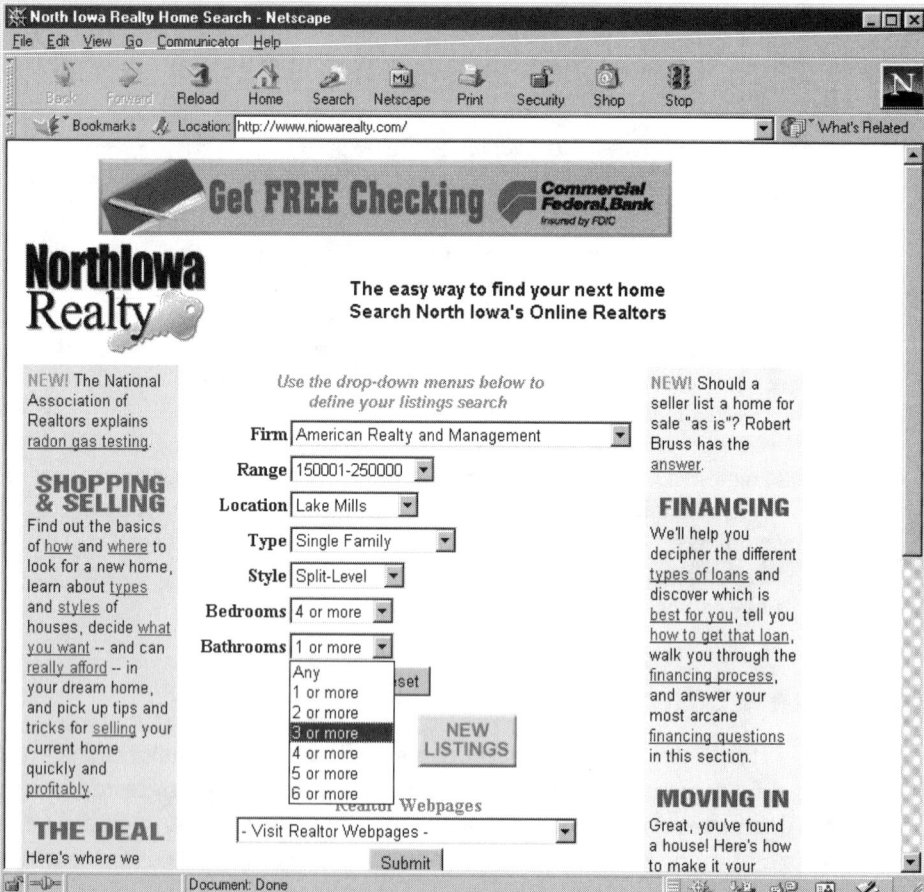

Figure 3.17 North Iowa Realty channels a visitor's thoughts though set menu choices.

North Iowa Realty also benefits from this sort of sorting. Its agents get to see what people are looking for. In your case, it's the same as watching to see which are the most frequently asked questions.

Drilling Data

Another way to help people find things is by giving them a visual clue. Sifting through a lot of textual information is hard work. But recognizing patterns or colors is far easier. That's why Peter Sklar came up with the Data Drill (www.datadrill.com). Imagine a search engine front end that uses visualization capabilities to paint a picture. No, not some 3-D multifaceted hybrid of bar charts and virtual Venn diagrams, but simply the use of color and location to impart meaning as much as text (Figure 3.18).

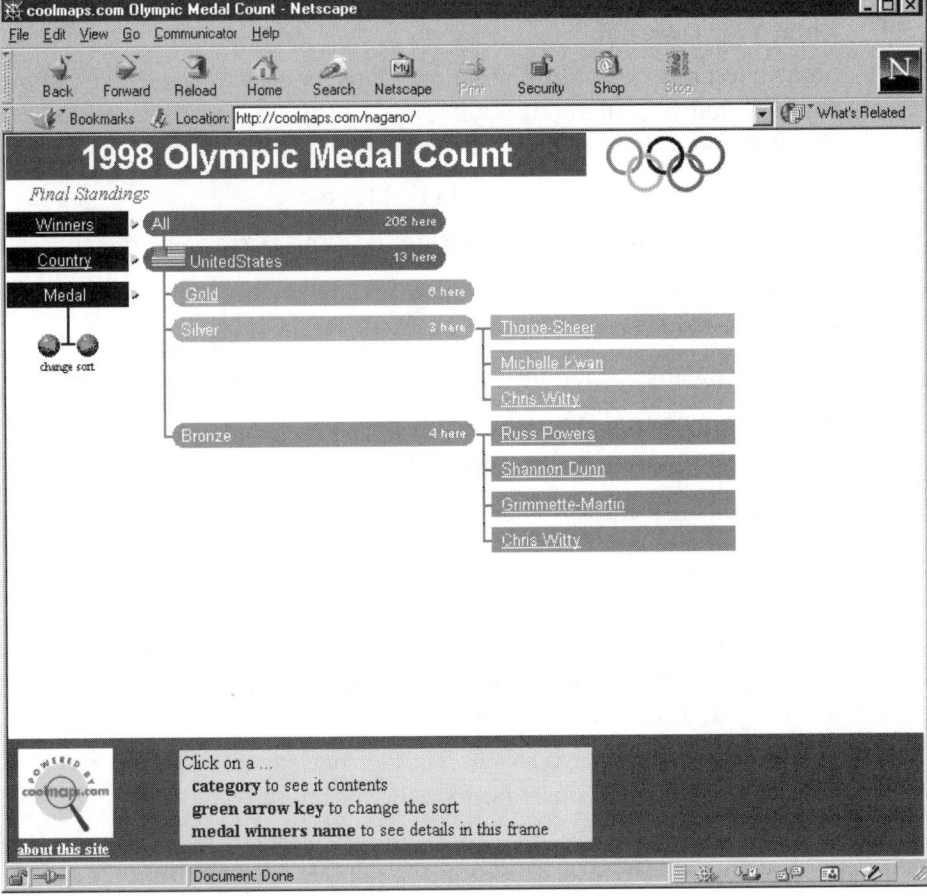

Figure 3.18 Data Drill lets you drill down six ways to Sunday based on the number of items found in each category.

Data Drill decides that there is not enough room on the screen to show the contents of a category with six items or more in it, so it makes the Gold Medal group clickable. The result is the Gold Medal winners categorized by gender.

Think about applying that sort of interface on top of your knowledge base or your vast reservoir of detailed product documentation.

But what if your customers *still* can't get to the answer they're looking for? Before you turn them over to your call center, turn them on to your answerbot.

Answerbots

Today's answerbots have the mental ability and the social agility of a three-year-old—a three-year-old savant, that is. If they grasp what your customer is after, they are brilliant at delivering the answers. If they don't—well, what the heck, they're only human.

Build Your Own Bot

Neuromedia (www.neuromedia.com) has a virtual representative named Red. Red will tell you all about buying and building your own virtual representative (vReps). What's a vRep? It's an answerbot that can:

- Answer customer questions in real time.
- Proactively gather key marketing data and perform suggestive selling.
- Improve customer service and reduce operating costs.
- Rapidly build new content to handle dynamic information.
- Instantly answer requests and supply supporting information.
- Conduct natural language conversations.
- Require only a web browser, no "plug-ins".
- Reward customers for using an automated system by providing a natural, direct response.

Further, these automata will:

- *Provide significant, rapid return on investment (ROI).* They decrease demand for both staffing and infrastructure in any enterprise where rich two-way communications are needed.
- *Enhance customer satisfaction.* They provide instantaneous, consistent, and accurate information 24 hours a day, 7 days a week.
- *Capture customer feedback.* They offer valuable input back to product development, marketing, brand management, etc.
- *Provide an efficient first line of defense.* They create an automated mechanism for level-one problem resolution and seamlessly integrate with existing systems for escalation.

- *Offer instant answers for customer questions.* They can answer many of the simple questions your customers ask, thus freeing up key customer service representatives to focus on more critical issues.

- *Can be built by nonprogrammers.* The authoring and server tools for developing and deploying vReps are designed for use by content and subject matter experts who know how your business really operates.

Before getting all excited, running out and buying a vRep and heaving a great sigh of relief that you don't have to personally be at the ready to answer customer questions, there's a bit of implementation to endure. A quick look at the tool kit that comes with this software gives you an idea of what it's going to take.

- *Complete array of vRep scripting tools:* Aids developers in creating sophisticated vReps for deployment in enterprise environments.

- *Integrated conversation analyzer:* Helps vRep developers and testers analyze the performance of their projects and immediately fix conversation errors.

- *Complete online help:* Includes an extensive tutorial and context-sensitive help for dialogs and scripting commands.

- *Topic creation wizard:* Creates scripts automatically from questions and answers, with built-in thesaurus to extend the range of questions answered by the script.

Want more than just a chatterbot to textually converse with your customer?

Putting a Good Face On It

Big Science (www.bigscience.com) has a Klone named Eve that's more than just an answerbot. She's a pretty face as well (Figures 3.19–3.21).

And yes, she smiles every now and then. Like when you express interest in letting Eve take you on a tour of their product offerings.

I couldn't resist putting these fresh-from-the-graduate-student brainstorm bit-puppies to the test. Today's question: What time is it in Brazil?

Red: "The correct time and date here in San Francisco is now: 15:08."

Eve: (along with a slightly puzzled look on her face): It's 6:27 PM EDT in Atlanta, GA. I don't know the time in Brazil."

The winner: Eve! Not only did she exhibit verbal *and* facial concern over her lack of South American temporal knowledge, she was more accurate by 19 minutes.

It may sound disparaging to call these technological wonders bit-puppies, but they are still wet behind the ears and exhibit more enthusiasm than skill. Still, they don't need newspapers on the kitchen floor. But a less ambitious approach is getting more play. A search engine with a personality—Jeeves.

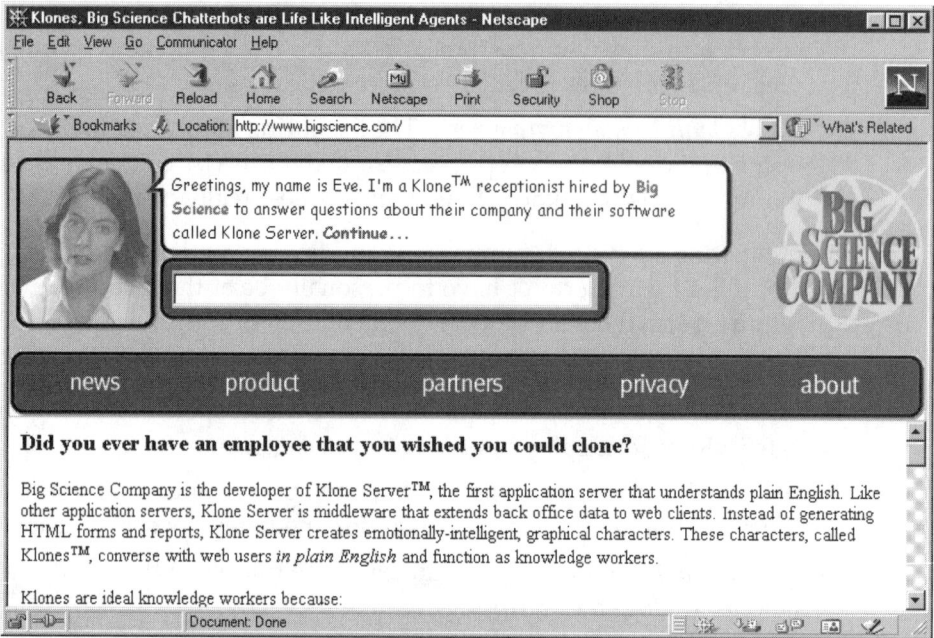

Figure 3.19 Eve looks attentive when she's poised for a question . . .

Ask Jeeves

If you haven't read any of the P.G. Wodehouse books about the adventures of the bungling Bertie Wooster and his able manservant Jeeves, then you've missed a wonderful period piece, humorous social satire, and just plain fun. Bertie is forever getting into hair-raising scrapes by sheer intellectual incompetence, and Jeeves is forever bailing Bertie out with the wisdom of years of observation and an innate sense of human motivations. Bertie's a sop and Jeeves is a wizard. What better a role model for a search engine that's a little smarter than the rest?

If Michael Ovitz has had his way, Jeeves has been promoted from a 1920s literary butler to a 1990s Internet search engine to a Roaring Zeros cartoon action figure. You'll know soon enough. In the meantime, a quick look at how this tool works will give you an idea as to why Dell Computer and Microsoft have both opted to use the Ask Jeeves (www.aj.com) technology on their sites.

The premise is that people ask questions in English better than they do in Boolean strings. So, the Ask Jeeves engine spends more time analyzing the question than its rivals. In response to a question like, "What is the state flower of Idaho?" Jeeves will announce, "I know the answer to these questions: Where can I find government information of the type: an official Web page, or government information, or office of the governor, or the capital and state facts." (Figure 3.22). Clearly, the right answer is only a click or two away.

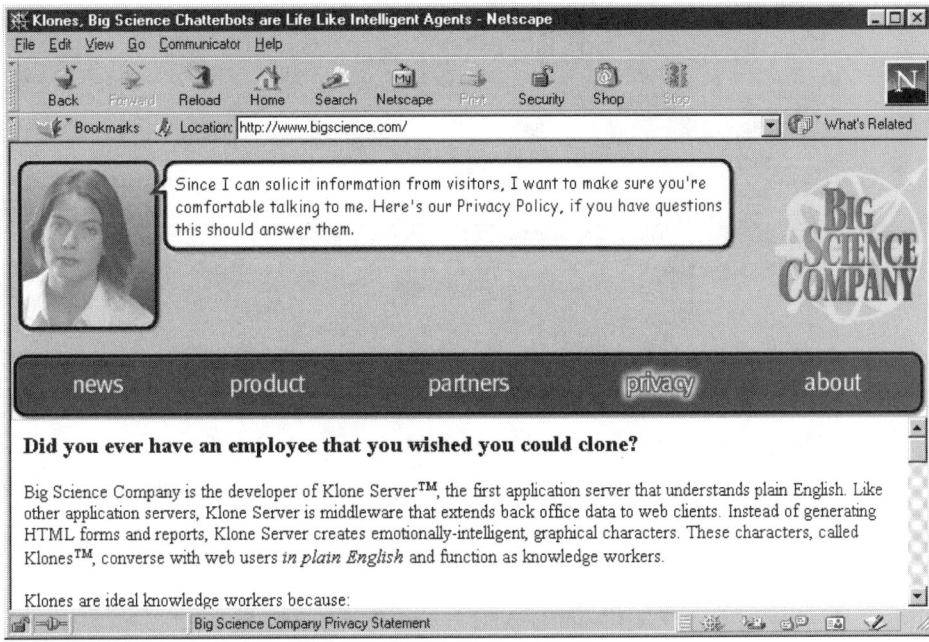

Figure 3.20 . . . sincere when she makes a point on privacy . . .

Dell Computer decided this sort of interface was just the ticket to help people with their technical questions. The result is Ask Dudley—a different character than the one Ovitz wants to make famous. Dell added a seemingly voyeuristic feature to its implementation: "Take a peek at what customers are asking Dudley right now!" A series of perfectly spelled questions flickers by and soon repeats, proving that the real-time promise is a sham. Nevertheless, the examples are wonderful in helping the user understand what sort of questions are possible:

- How will Dell address the Western Digital recall of their 6.4 GB and 13.6 GB 5400 hard drives, and will Dell notify me if my system shipped with one?

- How do I install Microsoft Office 2000?

- Why does Windows show my Pentium III processor as a Pentium II when I view the General tab of System tools?

When asked, "How do I get S-Video/DVD from my Inspiron 7000 onto my TV?" Dudley replies with Figure 3.23.

The drop-down choices under, "Where can I read the most recent . . ." include:

- AGP capabilities in OptiPlex computers . . .

- Dell announces new Dell Dimension computers . . .

- Dell extends Inspiron product line . . .

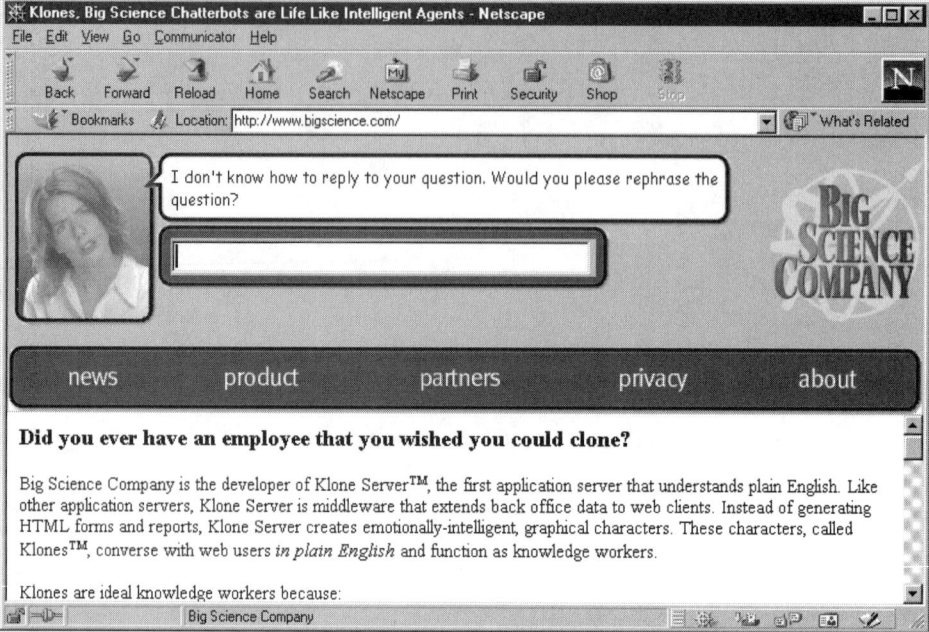

Figure 3.21 ... and downright perplexed if she can't quite understand what you're after.

- Dell launches Inspiron portables with Pentium II processors . . .
- Dell launches Intel Pentium II-Based workstations . . .
- Dell new workgroup server: PowerEdge 2300 . . .
- Dell OpenManage provides standards-based system management . . .
- Dell server quality assurance . . .
- Dell state-of-the-art acoustics lab . . .
- Dell Year 2000 readiness program . . .
- Dell's new Enterprise server—the PowerEdge 6300 . . .
- Latitude CP portable computer . . .
- Memory protection on Dell OptiPlex systems . . .
- Mobile-optimized CD-ROM drives . . .
- New OptiFrame chassis . . .
- OptiPlex Net PC . . .
- Portable computers and industrial design . . .
- PowerEdge 6100 best transaction processing performance . . .
- PowerEdge cluster 6100 . . .

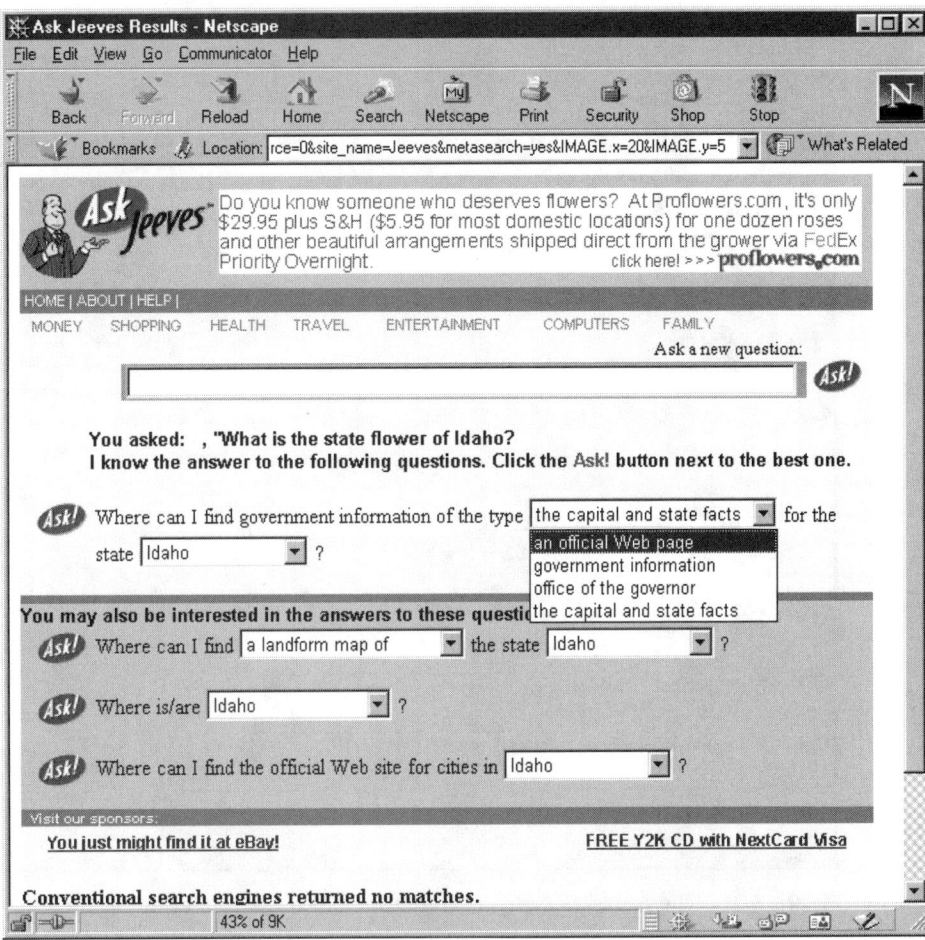

Figure 3.22 Ask Jeeves responds with a variety of possible answers.

- SMP servers . . .
- SMP WorkStations . . .
- Transition to IA/NT personal workstations gains momentum . . .
- Wired for management . . .
- WorkStation 400 . . .
- Product highlight from *"Vectors: A Dell Technology Newsletter"*

If you get a lot of questions, this might be the tool for you. Microsoft says that it gets a quarter of a million inquiries every day. That's why it has implemented the Ask Jeeves technology. Microsoft has playfully named its answer-bot the "Automated Personal Support Assistant." Nontechnical companies like Office Depot, E*Trade, and Oxygen Media are trying it out as well.

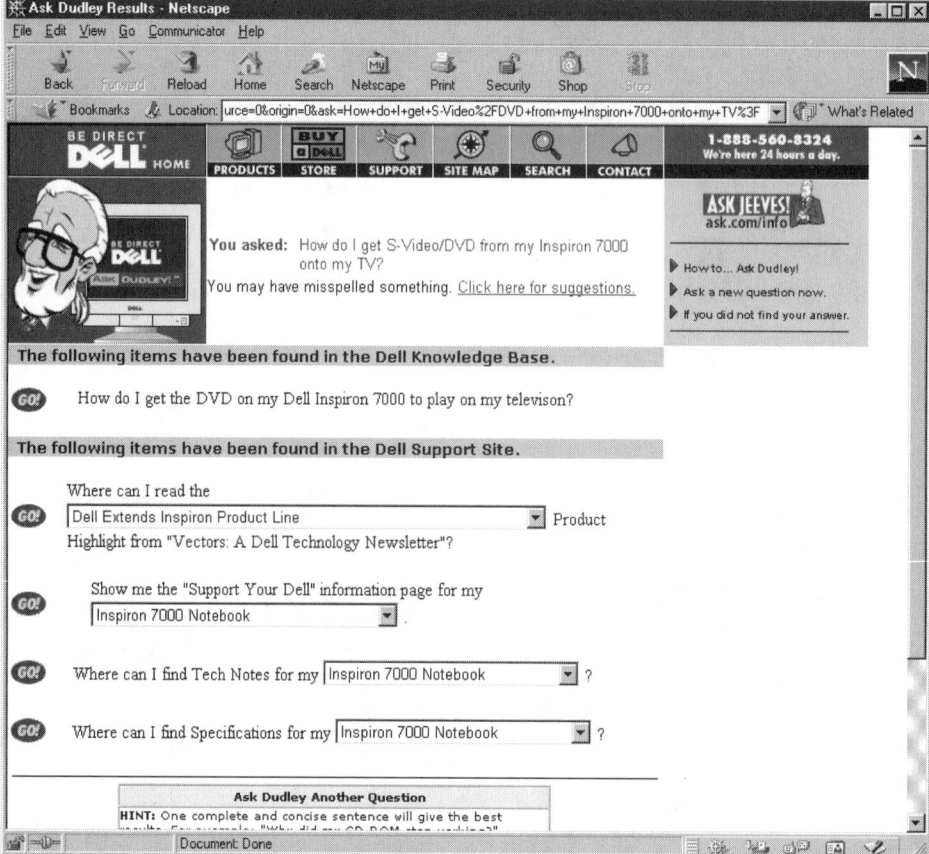

Figure 3.23 The Ask Jeeves engine is morphed into Ask Dudley at the Dell Web site.

Setting Expectations

As a rule, people can get used to anything. If the chances of winning the lottery are a gazillion to one, they don't expect to win—they hope to win. But if their overnight package doesn't arrive, they are seriously aggravated. If the milk they just bought at the store is sour, they're up in arms. If you lead them to believe that they can expect full-on, full-time, no-holds-barred customer service on your Web site—and they can't—you will have made an enemy where you could have made a friend.

The Time It Takes

This is a serious issue on any Web site because of the time it takes to find something and the kind of time it takes.

The time it takes is measurable with a stopwatch. A customer fires up a browser, dials into an access provider (or opens their LAN connection), types in your address (after a quick check of stock quotes, sports scores, and the daily look at Dilbert) and looks around your site for 3, 4, 5, maybe even 10 minutes.

If your customer can't find the voltage output of your secondary power supply, or the nutritional content of your breakfast cereal when consumed with a half a banana, or the average life expectancy of your all-terrain traction-rated tires, he or she would have been better off listening to your 800 number music-on-hold while doing other work.

The Perception of the Time It Takes

The *type* of time your customer spends is even more important. Browsing through a catalog or a manual is very different than browsing a Web site. Paper documents do not require a person to be in a specific chair at a specific location in a specific position. Catalogs can be read at any time and any place. They have superb random access with instant data retrieval speeds and are very easy to use. They have standard methods for organizing and indexing information.

A computer terminal, on the other hand, is *work*. It's not casual browsing while sitting in front of the fire or the television. It's work. A customer service Web site is always browsed at work. If not actually in the office, then certainly while working.

Working time is pressure time. Working time comes with the constant question of the useful use of one's time. Ten minutes at your Web site feels like a lot more. During 10 minutes of flipping paper pages, the browser's mind is fully engaged. The turn of a page occurs in the blink of an eye. After that blink, the information is immediately available for analysis.

The World Wide Web doesn't offer that sort of instant response. During 10 minutes of browsing your site, more than half of the time might be spent waiting for the next page to arrive, depending on the speed of the connection. Five minutes of waiting coupled with five minutes of analysis is worth the effort if the payoff value is very high. If not, the experience will be perceived as a waste of time. That brands your company as incompetent.

Give Them Fair Warning

Your best bet is to be clear about what is available on your Web site and what is not. Your customers are wondering how hard it will be and how long it will take to find the information they're after. They're worrying about the most efficient use of their time. They're wondering about the value of the information when they finally find it.

Be as clear as you can up front, and nobody will have wasted their time at your site.

Lend Them a Hand

Even with FAQs to read and databases to search, the most savvy customer cannot always solve a problem—even one that's been solved before and is clearly described in the FAQ. Sometimes the best and the brightest go looking to solve the wrong problem. And a bright individual with a powerful search engine can spend a long time looking in the wrong places. Running up against a series of dead ends is not conducive to building confidence in the database, the service, or the company. Sometimes it takes a good customer service person to get the customer to ask the right questions.

Consider implementing a search tool watcher that can keep an eye on the number of searches an individual makes, the number of pages they click on, the iterations of drop-down menus they try. Then, based on averages for your site, you can serve up an offer of personal service through e-mail or phone should the visitor go well beyond the norm. Keep it short and keep it out of the way of the person who *is* finding what he or she wants, but make it apparent that their usage is unusual and assistance is available.

Even without being told, everybody knows they can send you e-mail. And, just as there are people who walk up to the Information desk and ask where they can find the Information desk, there will always be those who will send e-mail to you before bothering to read a simple FAQ. So it's up to you to be ready for them.

CHAPTER 4

Managing E-Mail:
When Customers Come Calling

E-mail is the glue that cements the Internet together. Unless you're surfing from a friend's computer or at a public access terminal, you have an e-mail account. As wonderful as file transfers are and as great as the Web is, it is e-mail that is the common denominator and the most powerful tool we have.

The true joy of e-mail is that it blows away time constraints. When I have a question, I don't have to wait until 8:30 in the morning the next day to try to catch you at your desk. If I call earlier, you're going to be in traffic or at the coffee machine. If I call later you're going to be in meeting after meeting. I'll be stuck with voice-mail.

If I'm calling your customer service desk I don't want to hear the recording that says you're not open yet, and if I wait too long I'll get the message that says, "Thank you for calling the support line. Your call is very important to us. Due to the popularity of our new products we're receiving a wonderful response. You are caller number FIFTY SEVEN in the queue and we estimate the waiting time to be THIRTY-FIVE minutes. Please hold while we tell you about our other exciting offers. And remember, your call is very important to us. Due to the popularity of our new products . . ."

Consider instead, the power of e-mail. When I have a question, I don't have to wait at all. I can get the entire problem off my chest and on your desk where you can review it when you are ready, willing, and able. You can see all of them at a glance and prioritize which should be read first, which can wait, and which should be forwarded to others.

These are the reasons the Gartner Group's Donna Fluss (www.gartner.com) forecast that "By 2001 enterprises will receive 25 percent of all customer contacts and inquiries through Internet e-mail messages and Web forms." Are you ready?

Warning—It's a Different Communication Tool

The critical importance of e-mail is it's your customer's voice. The rest of your Web site is looking from the inside out, trying to give customers what they need. Electronic mail is from the outside, coming in. It's your connection to the outside world. Be sure to give it the attention it deserves.

E-mail provides a wonderfully frictionless way to communicate. A message comes to the desktop. The reply is written on the same screen, and out it goes at the speed of light. No paper trays to fill, no fax machine to run out of paper, and the response is delivered directly instead of sitting in interoffice mail. An e-mail can contain more detailed, specific information than can be written on a "while you were out" note or left in voice mail. Answers to questions that come up again and again can be stored for quick retrieval.

Arming your customer service department with e-mail is giving your customers one more method of corresponding with your firm. More sociable people like speaking on the phone. More formal people prefer writing letters or sending faxes. Some prefer e-mail. With so many people using e-mail in their homes and offices, it behooves you to cater to them.

In a report released at the beginning of 1998, Forrester Research predicted that 50 percent of the people in the United States would be using e-mail in five years. No surprise. Students are given e-mail accounts the moment they enter a university. When these people enter the workforce, e-mail is going to be a requirement.

You wouldn't consider running your company without a fax machine. Customers won't consider doing business with a company without an e-mail address—and the skills to use it wisely.

Responding to a customer comment, question, or complaint via e-mail requires the same care that is used when responding over the phone and in writing. Over the phone, inflection and attitude are critical to maintaining a happy and healthy customer/vendor relationship. The correct answer, spoken in the wrong manner, can have a very negative effect. On paper, the wrong words can return to haunt the well-meaning customer service representative over and over again.

Keep in mind that people react to the written word differently than the spoken word. I listen carefully on the phone when my supplier says "Gosh, Jim, I'm sorry. I'll get it out just as soon as I can. Really. We've got a backup here, but it looks like a couple of days to get it to you." I listen carefully to the level of confidence expressed in the tone of voice used. If confidence is not high (perhaps overt emphasis on the word "couple"), then I make my plans knowing he's probably not going to come through.

If the statement, "It looks like it'll take a couple of days to get it to you," shows up in e-mail or in a letter, I expect two or three days to delivery and plan accordingly. If the company doesn't deliver, I'm in a tight spot and I lay blame squarely on the guy who lied to me. If you're going to work in the modern world, you'll have to treat your e-mail with the respect it deserves.

E-mail falls between the spoken word and the written word. It is fast. It is spontaneous. When an e-mail beeps onto you desk, there is a feeling of instant communication—somebody wants to tell you something right now. The natural reaction is to respond at once, with the same informal manner used when passed a note in school. This casual regard for the written word is creating a middle layer of communications. Companies will have to protect themselves from employees being overly informal. But not to the point of not using e-mail altogether.

Damned If You Don't

While many firms find using e-mail daunting, the people at Volvo (www.volvocars.com, Figure 4.1) found it terrifying. They had a feedback area on their Web site where they asked people to comment. Unfortunately, they got more than they bargained for.

After the usual series of missives about spelling mistakes and broken links, Volvo started getting customer service type complaints about their cars. People would ask questions like:

> My 94 model Volvo 850 Turbo sedan started to have an engine stalling problem within the first year and the Volvo dealership attempted to fix it five times without any success. What are you going to do about it?

The problem for Volvo is that the vehicle in question may be subject to the lemon laws of certain states. As the Executive Office of Consumer Affairs in Boston puts it:

> The Massachusetts Lemon Law, M.G.L. c. 90, sec. 7N1/2, protects consumers who have serious defects in their new cars. The law defines a lemon as a new motor vehicle that has a defect that substantially impairs the use, market value, or safety of the

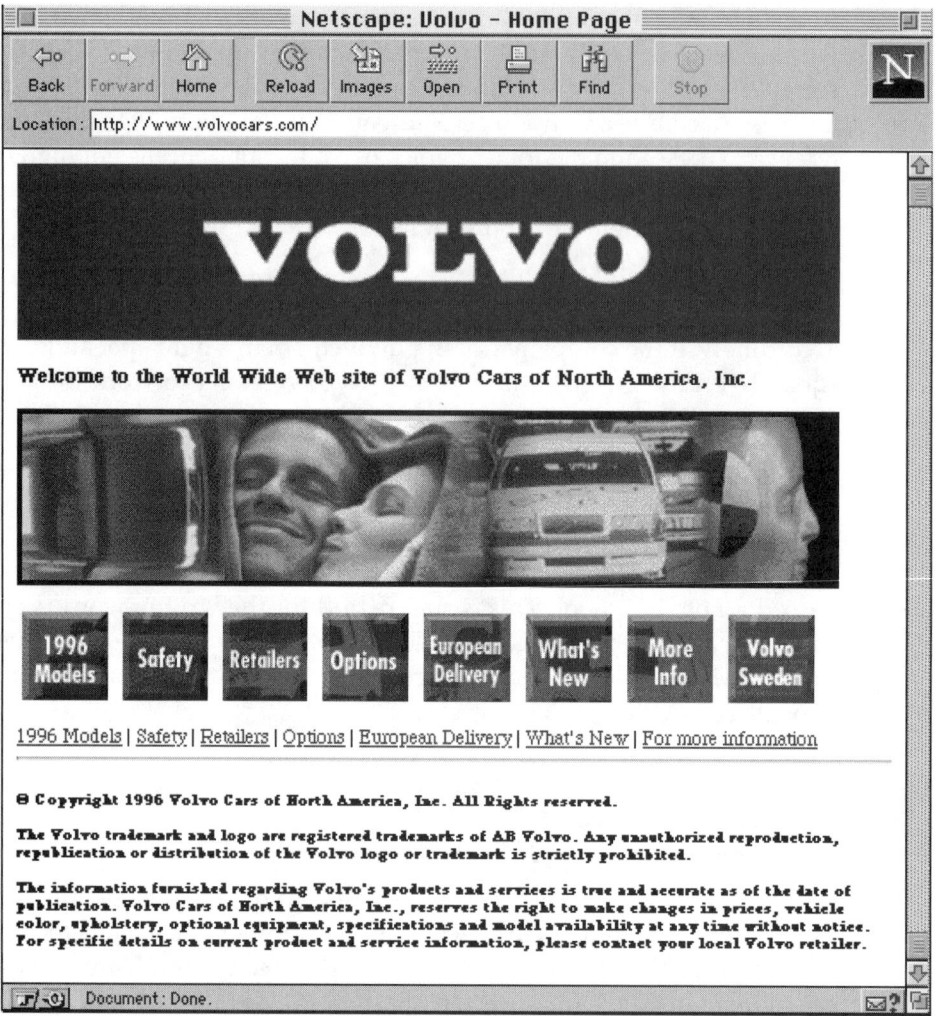

Figure 4.1 Volvo Cars of North America has had a series of false-starts using e-mail to communicate.

vehicle, and which has not been repaired after a reasonable number of attempts. If a substantial defect still exists or recurs after a reasonable number of repair attempts, the consumer has the right to a refund or a replacement vehicle. Keep in mind that not all car problems are serious enough to qualify under the Lemon Law.

The lawyers at Volvo Cars of North America lost no time in telling their Webmaster that e-mail complaints could constitute legal notification under many states' lemon laws. Their advice: Don't accept the complaints. Why? Because no procedure was in place to receive them, catalog them, and reply to them. Afraid that incoming grievances might be ignored, it was decided that closing the door on them was the better alternative.

A subsequent visit to Volvo's "For More Info" page revealed a questionnaire asking for name, street address, city, state, zip, country, phone number, and e-mail address. But no place for comment or complaint.

When economist Assar Gabrielsson and engineer Gustaf Larson joined forces in 1924 to build Volvo cars, they weren't reflecting on the Internet and e-mail. But we can assume they gave some thought to their eventual customers and the need to provide service for them. In the 1994 Volvo annual report, Sören Gyll, president and chief executive officer, gave a nod to the idea:

> The Volvo brand name represents values that are becoming increasingly important in today's society, notably where quality, safety and concern for the environment are concerned. We will consistently and uncompromisingly safeguard and enhance the Volvo brand name as one of the Group's primary assets. To an increasing degree, Volvo as a company must also come to represent customer orientation, the ability to adapt, and flexibility.

That desired ability to adapt to changing modes of communication never really materialized.

In the 1996 Volvo Annual Report, posted in February 1997, Sören Gyll announced that he was stepping down and leaving the driving to Leif Johansson. In February of 1998, Leif told of the need for company growth and operating cost efficiencies. That's the latest we've heard, and there's no longer any mention about the importance of communicating with the customer.

In the meantime, Volvo has tried to open a receptive ear to the public, but it forgot the Q-Tips. In 1997, the site sported an offer to an 800 number, a postal address, and the statement, "We are planning to implement an e-mail function in the United States in the future." (Figure 4.2.)

Volvo did indeed update its site in 1998, adding a form to fill out that actually allowed you to send a message. The Web page was complete with a picture of an antique telephone to let you know that the folks at Volvo really wanted you to talk to them. The site didn't, however, actually allow the message to be *received*. "Mailbox.cgi was not found on this server" was the reply for several weeks.

After a full Madison Avenue–style face-lift, the site once again sported the catchy phrase, "We are planning to implement an e-mail function in the United States in the future."

In 1999, after yet another Madison Avenue face-lift for the home page, a Site Feedback feature offered a series of drop-down menus, radio buttons, and check boxes to choose from to tell Volvo what you think. (As long as what you think is directly in synch with the offered choices.)

Figure 4.2 Volvo suggests an interest in customer communication.

There was also a Contact Us button that led to a text entry box that the visitor could fill in after selecting the appropriate subject line. Finally, at the end of 1999, Volvo added a link to a real, live e-mail address.

Being the curious type, I filled out the form inquiring about Volvo's success in answering e-mail from Web site visitors (Figure 4.3). The response I got was not heartening.

Mind you, I was delighted to get a response, and astonished that it came from a human. You can tell a return e-mail is not from an automated system when they misspell your name.

```
Date: Mon, 19 Jul 1999 14:18:50 -0400
From: "Volvo Volvo" <Volvo@vsi-hq.com>
To: jsterne@targeting.com, Alexis Hohnholt <AHohnholt@vsi-hq.com>
Subject: Re: Your Story
Dear Mr. Strerne,

Thank you for writing Volvo Cars. Thank you for writing Volvo Cars of
North America. We appreciate concern regarding our website and are sorry
for any inconvenience. We want to assure you that your concerns have
```

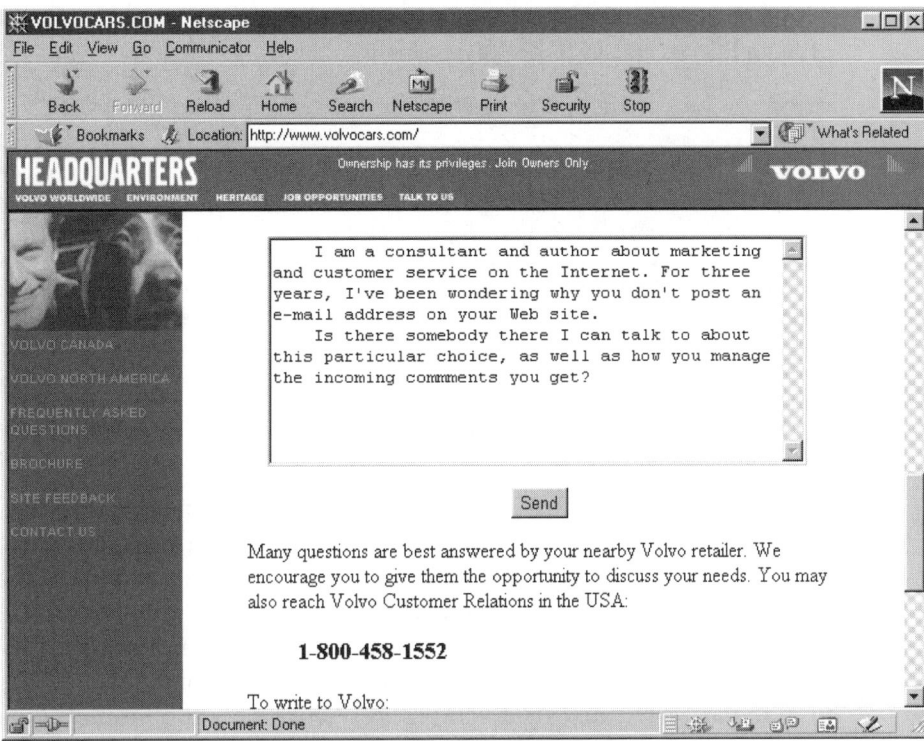

Figure 4.3 Volvo's "Contact Us" provided a chance to actually reach out and touch the company.

```
been brought to the attention of those in the decision-making process.
They will contact you in regards to your request. If, you have any
further questions, please don't hesitate to call us at 1-800-550-5658.

Drive Safely
```

Out of curiosity as to why such an august organization would contract with a company without a spell checker or a grammar checker, I went in search of the infamous Volvo Volvo who sent me this promissory note. Alas, my efforts to get to www.vsi-hq.com were foiled by a request that I log in.

Those in the decision-making process never deemed my inquiry for an interview worthy. Either they couldn't process the decision on who was responsible for the decision to not post an e-mail address, or they simply didn't want to get involved with a consultant who had been holding them up to ridicule in public for the previous three years.

After I had done just that before a gathering of the American Electronics Association in mid-September 1999, Thomas Dannemiller from The Chip Merchant wrote to tell me that he had found a Volvo e-mail address the night after my presentation. He even got an answer within 24 hours! Unfortunately, it advised him to call Volvo's 800 number.

I tried my luck with an e-mail with the subject, "You've Got Mail!"

```
Hello Volvo!

I am a consultant and author about marketing and customer service on the
Internet. For three years, I've been wondering why you didn't post an
e-mail address on your Web site. Now that you *are* accepting e-mail:
How is it going? Is there somebody there I can talk to about Volvo's e-
mail experiences for the new edition of my customer service book?
```

I have yet to receive an answer.

But at least they have been trying. At least they are miles ahead of Southwest Airlines.

Southwest Airlines is a winner. It has consistently won prizes for its superior levels of service—on the ground, on the phone, and in the air. The company's mission statement reads, "Southwest Airlines is dedicated to the highest quality of Customer Service delivered with a sense of warmth, friendliness, individual pride, and Company Spirit." Its credo is, "We're not an airline with great Customer Service, but a Customer Service organization that happens to be in the airline industry." Even on the Web, it was the first to take reservations, and one of the first to sell tickets online.

But Southwest Airlines doesn't accept e-mail.

A statement to that effect used to be on the company's home page. Right at the bottom. Now, you have to dig for a little while to find it, but there it is in all its glory: "Why we don't accept e-mail" (Figure 4.4).

"At the moment, our ability to support e-mail in a manner consistent with our service expectations is not fully in place," has been Southwest Airlines' excuse for over three and-a-half years. This does not sound like an award-winning approach to providing service to customers.

Damned If You Don't in a Hurry

Sometimes a phone call takes a couple of days to return. Why? Meetings. Travel. Other work. Remember, phone calls require both parties to be at their desks and not on the other line. E-mail isn't like that. People know that e-mail will sit patiently and wait for the recipient to read it. But the sender isn't as patient as the mail sent. There is an expectation that an e-mail will secure a reply within 24 hours.

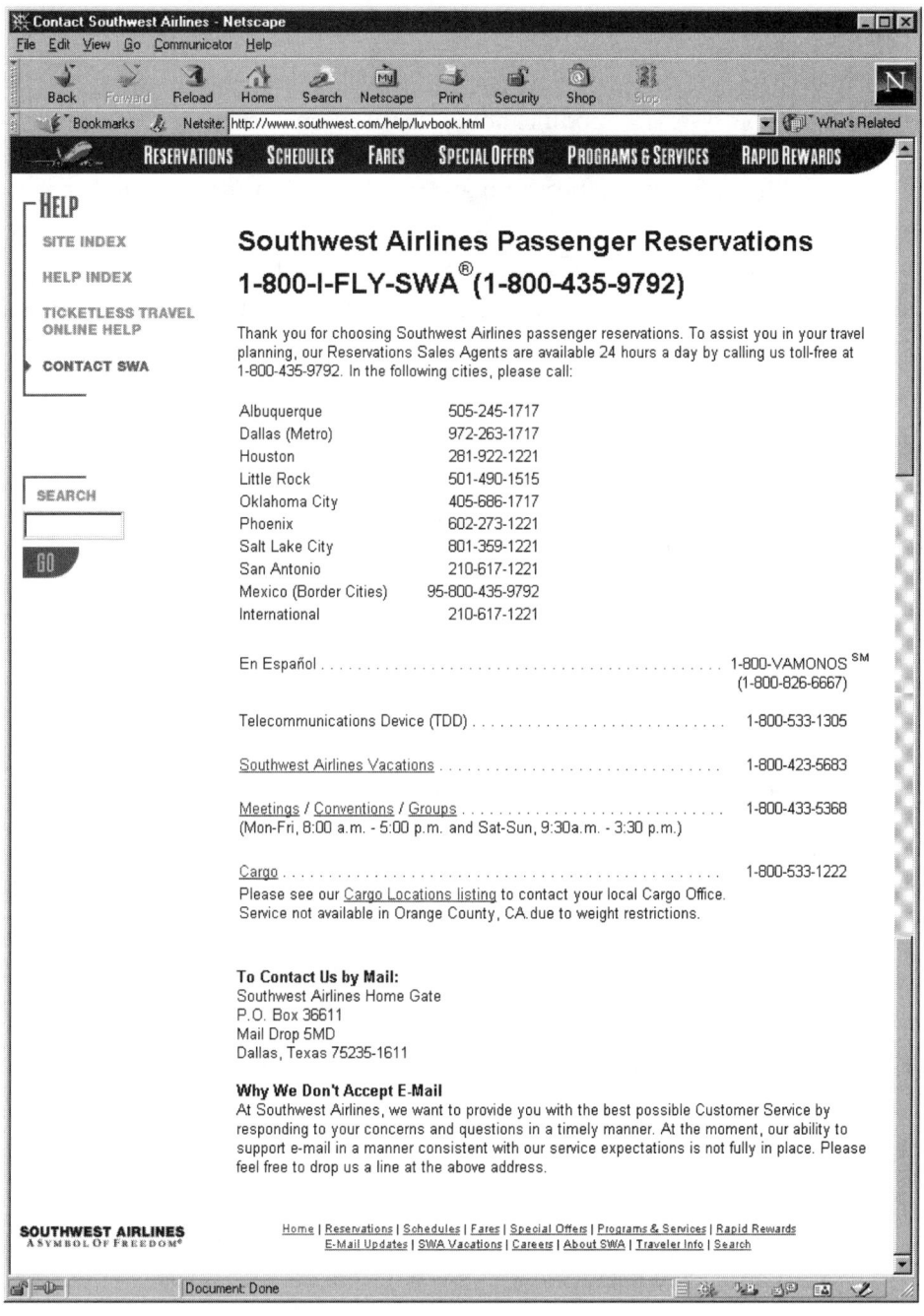

Figure 4.4 Southwest Airlines can't seem to find the Reply button.

If it's critical, a customer will usually call. If it's a contractual issue, they'll send a fax with its inherent status as a legal document. (Expect that to change any minute with the advent of digital signatures.) But if it's merely important—a product question, a service modification, a clarification of some kind—they'll send an e-mail. They don't need an immediate answer, but they're not doing it for their health, either. They expect an answer, and the ball is in your court to get it for them.

You have a policy (or should) that dictates that your company's main phone line will be answered within three rings. When it hits four rings, it's time to hire another operator to field the calls. You even went out of your way to install a voice mail attendant: "If you know your party's extension, you may enter it at any time. . . ." Why don't you have a policy about how soon e-mails are answered?

Worse than Not at All

A late answer can often be worse than no answer at all. A late answer shows up on the customer's doorstep after she has found an answer through a different means (she got fed up and picked up the phone) or worse, has solved the problem herself. Being ignored means one of several things:

1. The e-mail didn't make it.
2. The reply didn't make it back.
3. The company is too busy.
4. The company doesn't care.

But an e-mail that comes way too late to be useful only means one thing—the company is disorganized beyond help, and buying from you again is not going to be on the top of the customer's list.

One fellow told me he sent an e-mail to the manufacturer about a defective CD-ROM drive. After radio silence, he called the company and was told whom to call about returning it for a new one. He did. It worked. He was happy. Three months later, he got an e-mail that told him whom to call about returning it for a new one.

Is Anybody Home Anywhere?

In September 1998, Jupiter Communications (www.jup.com) did a blind survey of large Web sites. The study found that 42 percent of the sites had no e-mail addresses listed; took more than five days to respond; or simply didn't bother to respond.

In January 1999, Brightware (www.brightware.com), makers of e-mail management systems, sent out an e-mail to the Fortune 100 with one simple question: "What is your corporate address?" Brightware started the clock and received answers from four of the Fortune 100 within 15 minutes. These are companies that understand the importance of having operators standing by.

So hats off to Albertsons, Aetna, Costco, and Texaco. And while our hats are doffed, we can scratch our heads in wonder at Hewlett Packard, which required 23 days, 2 hours, and 37 minutes to figure out its corporate address. HP, however, did better than a full third of the Fortune fat cats, who simply did not reply. That third included 26 who took a page out of the Southwest Airlines site by not having any e-mail contact on offer whatsoever.

In February 1999, *PC World* magazine did a similar study, but with a more serious question. Its editors posed as potential customers interested in buying from these major Web sites. The results were not encouraging. Twenty-one percent of the companies contacted did not respond. One can understand how a giant bureaucracy might not be able to get its act together, but these were major Internet-based companies and they should all know better.

In June 1999, Jupiter ran its survey again and found that 25 percent of the companies contacted responded within one day, and 29 percent within two days, while 34 percent gave no response at all. The remaining 12 percent had no e-mail address on offer. eGain Communications (www.egain.com), Brightware competitors, ran a similar survey of the top 150 companies in the U.K. It found that 31 percent responded within one day, 34% within two days, 25% gave no response at all, and 10% had no e-mail address. The eGain message had asked for literature on current products, and after two weeks only half of the requested brochures showed up.

As Ryan Rosenberg, vice president of marketing at eGain Communications, aptly stated, "Given the current situation, the opportunity is huge for forward-thinking companies to capture market share through outstanding customer service."

In November 1999, Bite-Size Customer Service Management (www.csm-europe.com) ran the following bite-sized item:

> Yet more mystery testing . . . this time of companies' responsiveness to e-mails. Telemarketing and e-service provider IMS sent 882 e-mails to 156 of the largest organisations in Europe and the U.S. Two e-mails were sent, one requesting trivial information and the other expressing mild dissatisfaction with a recent experience. Each was sent in three languages. 36% of the 156 companies totally ignored the e-mails. Only 3% of U.S. companies and just under 20% of European companies responded to all six e-mails. The U.S. was particularly bad at dealing with foreign-language requests.

The best advice is to assign somebody to e-mail duty. Just like the switchboard, somebody should be on the receiving end to ensure that incoming e-mail is received, categorized, and forwarded to the right party.

At the very least, install an autoresponder to let people know that their message is in the queue.

The Autoresponder

An autoresponder is a very powerful little tool that is simply itself. It sends out a canned reply to every incoming message before a human even looks at it. This provides an immediate proof-of-delivery to make your customers know that the ball is firmly in your court. It assures them that neither their e-mail software, the Internet, nor your e-mail software went awry. An autoresponder can therefore be a useful tool, but it is one to be used with care.

First Virtual Alleviates a Stilted Reply with Humor

```
To: jsterne@targeting.com
Subject: Your mail to Nathaniel
From: Nathaniel Borenstein <nsb@nsb.fv.com>

Hello. I am Nathaniel Borenstein's automatic mail robot. It is IMPORTANT
that you read this message, and this is the only time I will send it to
the address on the "To:" field of this message.

Your message is in the highest priority category of mail that was not
received through the "urgent backdoor." Nathaniel reads this category of
mail every day he works. He will probably read it tomorrow morning. THE
"URGENT BACKDOOR": If your message absolutely cannot wait until tomorrow
morning, or possibly even a bit later, please re-send it to the address
"nsb+urgent@nsb.fv.com". YOU WILL NOT GET THIS MESSAGE AGAIN, so please
make note of the special urgent address for future reference. Be warned,
however, that Nathaniel can tell me to override the "urgent" delivery
for anyone who regularly abuses it.

Additionally, if you're someone he doesn't know, Nathaniel will NOT
ANSWER your mail if the answer is contained in the NSB FAQ. The NSB FAQ
contains answers to a lot of the questions that people most frequently
ask Nathaniel, including questions about getting Nathaniel as a speaker,
and relatively basic questions about First Virtual, MIME, metamail,
Safe-Tcl, ATOMICMAIL, Andrew, and the ULPAA conference. If you're
writing to ask about any of those, please read the NSB FAQ because
Nathaniel WILL NOT REPLY if your answer is in there. You can get a copy
of the NSB FAQ by sending mail to nsb+faq@nsb.fv.com.

Nathaniel insists that I apologize to you for being what I am, a mail
robot. Personally, I think being a robot is nothing to be ashamed of—
but then, that's what Nathaniel wants me to think, and I am so stupid
that I don't mind. But Nathaniel still feels bad about sending a robotic
```

response to human beings who correspond with him. When you get 600 messages per day, however, you have to take drastic measures, and that's what Nathaniel has done. Please don't be too hard on him, or I'm afraid he'll get rid of the surge suppressor on his computer. Even robots can have phobias, you know, and for some reason Nathaniel wants me to be deathly afraid of power surges. Please humor me and remember the nsb+urgent and nsb+faq addresses that I gave you, OK? Thanks.

—Nathaniel's robot (just trying to do its job)

This example is right on the border. In the long run, it's a nicely thought-out solution to what might have been a real turn-off. Of course, not all readers will bother reaching the bottom of this long run. They might just be turned off. Hopefully, you will assign staff to your very popular employees to help them manage their mail.

A More Serious Approach

```
Date: Fri, 9 Jul 1999 20:18:48 -0400 (EDT)
To: Jim Sterne <jsterne@targeting.com>
From: "Charles Schwab & Co., Inc." <client.service@Schwab.COM>
Reply-To: client.service@Schwab.COM
Subject: Email Receipt Confirmation

Charles Schwab has received your e-mail inquiry and we thank you for
using this channel to contact us.
Due to unprecedented volume related to unusually high market activity,
we may be unable to meet the normal service commitment you expect of us.
Please be assured that we have received your communication and there is
no need to reply to this message. Your original e-mail will be answered
in as timely a manner as possible.

As always, if you have a time sensitive or urgent issue, please do not
hesitate to contact us via telephone.

Thank you for your continued patience and understanding.
(c)1999 Charles Schwab & Co., Inc., member SIPC/NYSE (0099-0572)
```

Confirm the Order

The most common use of the autoresponder and one that you really *must* implement, is the order acknowledgement. This tiny bit of electronic courtesy is critical in an uncertain world. Did I really place the order? Did you really record it as I intended? Are you still going to honor the price I was quoted?

```
To: jsterne@targeting.com
From: orders@amazon.com
Subject: Your Amazon.com order (#002-6083866-6327405)
Date: Tue, 12 Oct 1999 05:47:23 -0700 (PDT)
```

```
We thought you'd like to know that the following item has been
shipped to:

     Jim Sterne
     1130 Arbolado Road
     Santa Barbara CA 93103

using US Priority (comp. upgrade) (3-7 business days).
Please note that these shipments do not have tracking numbers.
Your order #002-xxxxxxx-6327405 (received October 11 1999 14:50 PDT)

Ordered     Item              Price       Shipped       Subtotal
1           Cryptonomicon     $19.25         1           $19.25
                                         Subtotal:       $19.25
                             Shipping & Handling:         $3.95
                                            Total:       $23.20
                               Paid via Mastercard:       $3.20
                         Paid via Gift Certificate:      $20.00
                                      Balance Due:        0.00

This completes your order.

If you have any questions, please contact us via e-mail
(orders@amazon.com), FAX (1-206-266-2950) or phone (1-800-201-7575 for
US customers or 1-206-266-2992 for international customers).

Thank you for shopping at Amazon.com.

Amazon.com
Earth's Biggest Selection
info@amazon.com      http://www.amazon.com/
```

Of course, the autoresponder is not going to stop people from wanting to communicate with people. The only way you can hope to do that is to send a quick "Got your message" message along with twelve pages of Frequently Asked Questions—and I strongly advise against that.

So what do you do when customers want a real answer to a real question? Give them one.

Directing Traffic—Who Gets the Mail?

Working a switchboard was one of the most harrowing experiences of my (then) young life. I had just been hired, fresh out of college, to do customer service and sales support and they said, "Oh by the way, you'll fill in on the switchboard when the receptionist takes her lunch.

Back before the days of voice-mail, it was hard keeping track of who was on hold for whom and who was getting madder by the moment for having been put on hold. The part that really threw me was when somebody called and didn't know whom they wanted to talk to.

They had a problem, and they didn't care who took the call as long as it was somebody who had the solution and I was quick about it. That made me the answer-man. It meant that I had to know how the business worked in order to know who could solve the problem. Then, of course, was the matter of figuring out who *would* solve the problem.

After a few weeks I started to get the hang of it. I knew who went to lunch and when, and who ate at their desk. I knew who would never answer anything but always knew who would. I knew who would never take a call and who would be annoyed if I didn't find out exactly what the caller wanted before I transferred the call.

It was this task that taught me the most important lesson about dealing with people. I learned what people on the other end of the phone wanted. They wanted me to care. They wanted me to take them under my wing and assume responsibility for them. Either I should solve their problem pronto, or guide them safely to the person who would. They wanted me to have anticipated their call and actively try to help.

At the start, when your site first went up, there was only one person who knew there was e-mail to answer—the Webmaster.

The Webmaster May Not Be the Best Choice

Curious about the series of Xerox printer-fax-copier-scanner machines, I went to www.xerox.com a few of years ago and saw nothing there that indicated I might be able to attach one to my Macintosh. The only contact information was at the bottom of the page, where the usual "webmaster@xerox.com" link could be found. Undaunted, I fired off my question and received the following reply:

```
To: jsterne@targeting.com (Jim Sterne)
From: webmaster@xerox.com (Webmaster for Xerox www.xerox.com)
Subject: Re: WWW comment: Document WorkCenter 250 from
jsterne@targeting.com (Jim Sterne)
Cc: webmaster.PARC@xerox.com
Date: Wed, 25 Oct 1995 11:40:59 PDT

Thank you for your message.

We share your interest in a Document Workcenter for Macintosh users
because we are also a Macintosh user. Unfortunately, Xerox has no plans
at present to produce a Document Workcenter compatible with the
Macintosh.

We're sorry we couldn't be of help.
```

Aside from the use of the editorial "we," there was nothing in this communication that made me feel there was a product marketing manager anywhere on the premises. Surely "no plans" could have been stretched to "but your comments are important to our product managers."

That answer would have been much different had I been communicating with the soon-to-be-legendary Bill McLain.

As the Xerox mail-master starting back in 1996, Bill figured it was his job to answer the e-mail that came into the company. All of it. No matter what the question was.

> Webmaster Bill McLain has become an Internet legend because he answers his e-mail. Yes, you answer your e-mail, too. But Bill's e-mail is defined as anything sent to webmaster@xerox.com. He answers all of it—even the wild and weird questions that have no reason going to Xerox. Questions like, "Do Fish Drink Water?"
>
> That's the name of the book he's published (William Morrow, 1999) about his experiences at the Xerox keyboard which have earned him the title, "The Wise Old Man of the Web." He's been at it for four years and isn't about to stop. Especially now that he has three people on his staff to answer questions like:
>
> How long would it take to vacuum the state of Ohio?
>
> What is the world's fastest roller coaster?
>
> What does the information on a United States penny represent?
>
> What makes peppers so hot?
>
> How did grapefruit get its name?
>
> Did Thomas Crapper really invent the toilet?
>
> What is the book the Statue of Liberty holds?
>
> Why do they drive on the left side of the road in England?
>
> You get the idea. Or do you? Bill and his team have been known to get up to 1,000 messages per day. Are you up to that kind of commitment to your customers? Can it be worth your while to answer every e-mail?
>
> From *Email Marketing: Using Email to Reach Your Target Audience and Build Customer Relationships* by Jim Sterne and Anthony Priore (John Wiley & Sons, 2000)

Perhaps now would be a good time for your company to hire people with a little flair to answer your e-mail. There might just be a book in it.

Hire people the same way you hire for your call center. You want people who are outgoing and genuinely care about customers. Nancy Weichbrod has been a flight attendant for United Airlines for more years than would be gentlemanly of me to mention. One evening, Nancy recounted the interview process. They got a group of would-be employees in a room and asked them to stand up and introduce themselves. Shy? Nervous? Didn't matter. They weren't listening to what you said about yourself, they were watching to see how interested you seemed in your fellow applicants. The ones who expressed a sincere regard for their associates were hired. In your case, you just have to be sure they can type.

Create a Blueprint for E-Mail Success

So where do you start? According to the Jupiter Communications report, "Online Customer Service: Strategies for Improving Satisfaction and Retention" (March 1999), you have six steps to complete in order to turn the problem of e-mail overload into a competitive advantage:

1. Review current support process and service levels.
2. Identify common question categories and relevant business units.
3. Define business rules and resolution process.
4. Map the demand for support to the most effective solution.
5. Develop new centers of expertise and management responsibility.
6. Deploy the solution.

The Jupiter report then spends several pages outlining how to get each of these steps done. It's worth looking into, and no, I don't have a financial stake in Jupiter.

How do you prepare for a plethora of potential questions? Start with the people who answer your technical support hotline. Interview the pre-sales support technicians and the 800-number operators. Take what you learned when you assembled the FAQ and put it to use here.

What will people ask about? Everything. So you have to know who will be responsible for responding to them. Until artificial intelligence can interpret natural language (and there are a number of somewhat expensive products out there that can help a lot), you'll need to assign humans to sort through incoming inquiries and divide them up:

1. *Sales.* Price, availability, product information.
2. *Customer Service.* Product suggestions, product problems, returns, refunds, order tracking, policy questions.
3. *Public Relations.* Reporters, analysts, sponsorships, community affairs, investor relations.
4. *Human Resources.* Resumes, interview requests.
5. *Accounting.* Accounts payable, accounts receivable.

Assign one person to each category to read the messages in detail and perform triage. They must be prioritized, based on the urgency of each message. You might rank them in inverse order, as follows:

6. Suggestion requiring a thank-you (respond and file).
5. Standard queue (respond within 24 hours).

4. Emergent situation (forward to appropriate party).

3. Critical problem (alert department management).

2. Red alert (all hands on deck).

1. Core melt down (run screaming, arms waving overhead).

With this filtering in place, the majority of messages will fall into the standard queue. There should be a prewritten answer in the database to resolve most issues, and they should be sent out with instructions on how the petitioners can find the answer themselves next time.

Emergent situations mean that the answer must be found outside the realm of normal customer service channels. For example, a product manager, a shipping clerk, or a collections individual may be assigned to receive the out-of-bounds e-mails, resolve the issues, and respond to the petitioner, while sending a copy to the customer service department.

Critical problems require the decision-making powers of a department head. Something well beyond the norm has popped over the horizon, setting off mild alarms. These may require telephonic notification until you train your managers to read their e-mail religiously.

Red alerts are reserved for the worst crises. When catastrophe looks imminent, the problem is usually cross-departmental and requires a meeting or two to resolve. The protocol requires that as much documentation as possible be electronically forwarded to all involved, and the alarm announced via telephone, sweaty foreheads, and wringing hands.

If you spend planning time anywhere, spend it on procedures and process management for red alerts. They are the least likely situations to ever occur. But if they do, you'll want to have a clear set of instructions ready, to avoid any confusion in the face of disaster.

Get Your Customers to Direct the Traffic

The people at Geico Direct Auto Insurance (www.geico.com) really want to talk to you. They make it easy. Rather than funneling all of the incoming e-mail through the Webmaster, and rather than leaving it to him or her to look at each message and decide who might be the best person to handle a specific problem, Geico trusts its customers to make that decision.

Customers pick the subject, and they pick the e-mail address (Figure 4.5).

At Geico there are e-mail addresses for:

- Homeowner policyholder correspondence
- Other policyholder correspondence

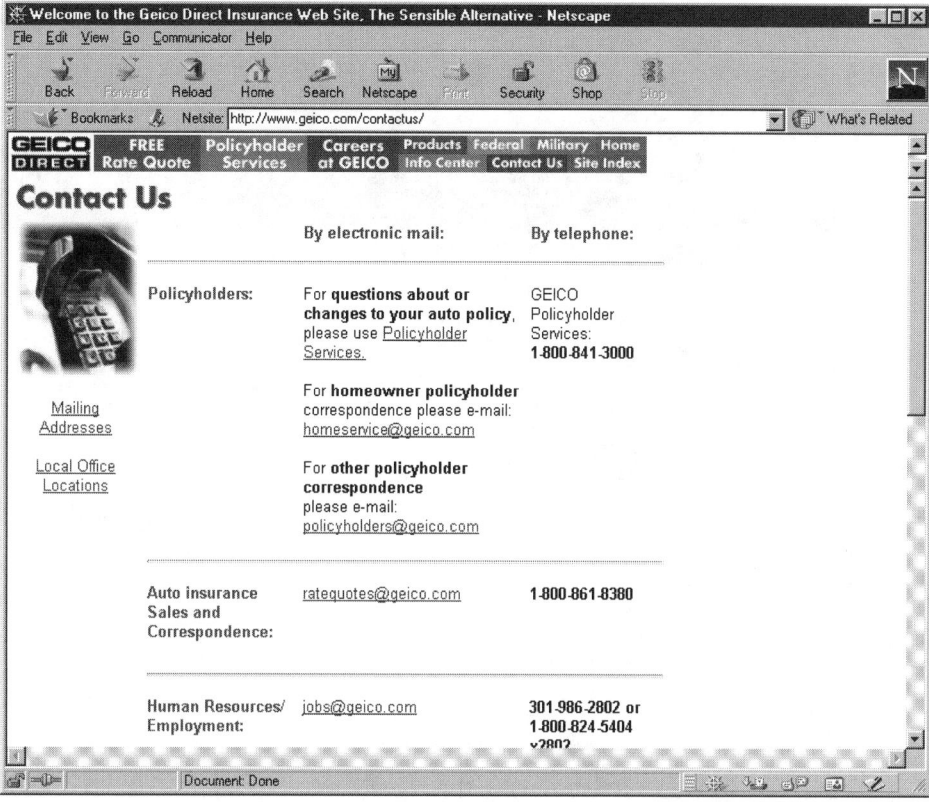

Figure 4.5 Geico offers lots of points of contact.

- Auto insurance sales and correspondence
- Human resources/employment
- Homeowners, condo, and renters sales and service
- Cyclegard motorcycle insurance motorcycle
- Boat insurance
- Overseas insurance

It's easy for the customer, and it makes e-mail management easier for the Webmaster.

Dell Computers decided to go with more descriptive pointers (Figure 4.6).

At Dell there are different links to click on if:

- You need help with basic installation or configuration of Office 2000 subject to Dell's Software Support Policy.
- Your Dell OptiPlex or Dimension Desktop is not functioning properly or you have questions regarding your system's hardware or operation.

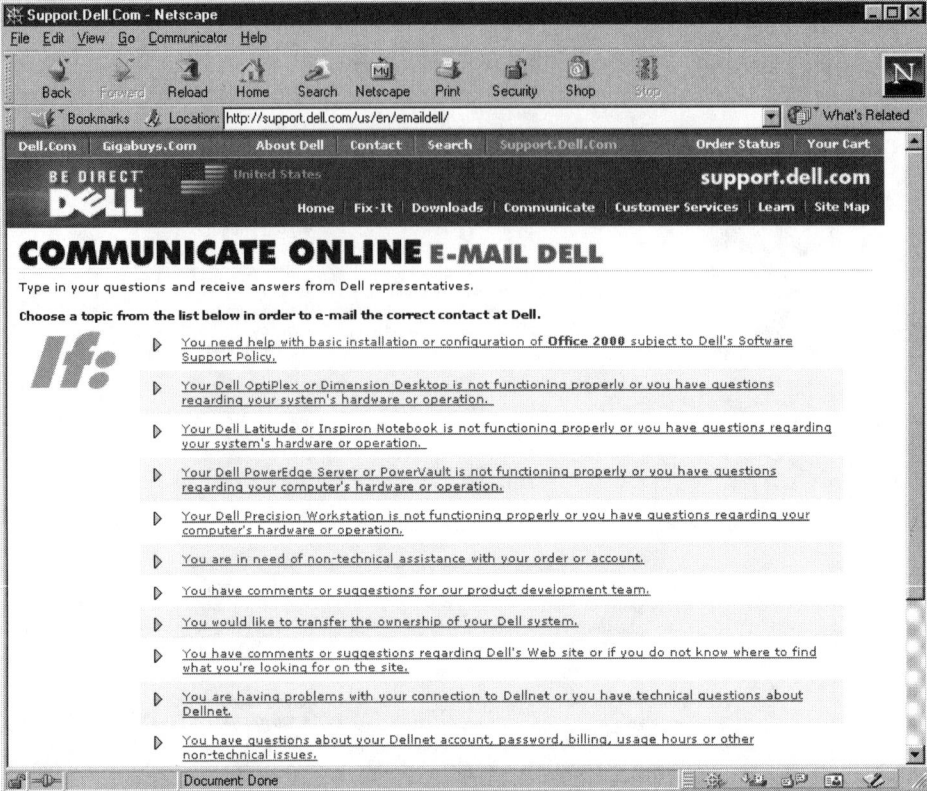

Figure 4.6   Dell sends specific problems to specific groups of service reps.

- Your Dell Latitude or Inspiron Notebook is not functioning properly or you have questions regarding your system's hardware or operation.

- Your Dell PowerEdge Server or PowerVault is not functioning properly or you have questions regarding your computer's hardware or operation.

- Your Dell Precision Workstation is not functioning properly or you have questions regarding your computer's hardware or operation.

And so on.

The folks who run *The Gleaner*, Henderson, Kentucky's, daily newspaper (www.thegleaner.com), have a more personal view of publishing e-mail addresses. They simply publish them all. You can send a message to the publisher, the editor, the general manager, and to the night composing foreman, whoever that is (Figure 4.7).

How much you publish will depend on your corporate culture. Does your company only allow the main switchboard number on your business cards?

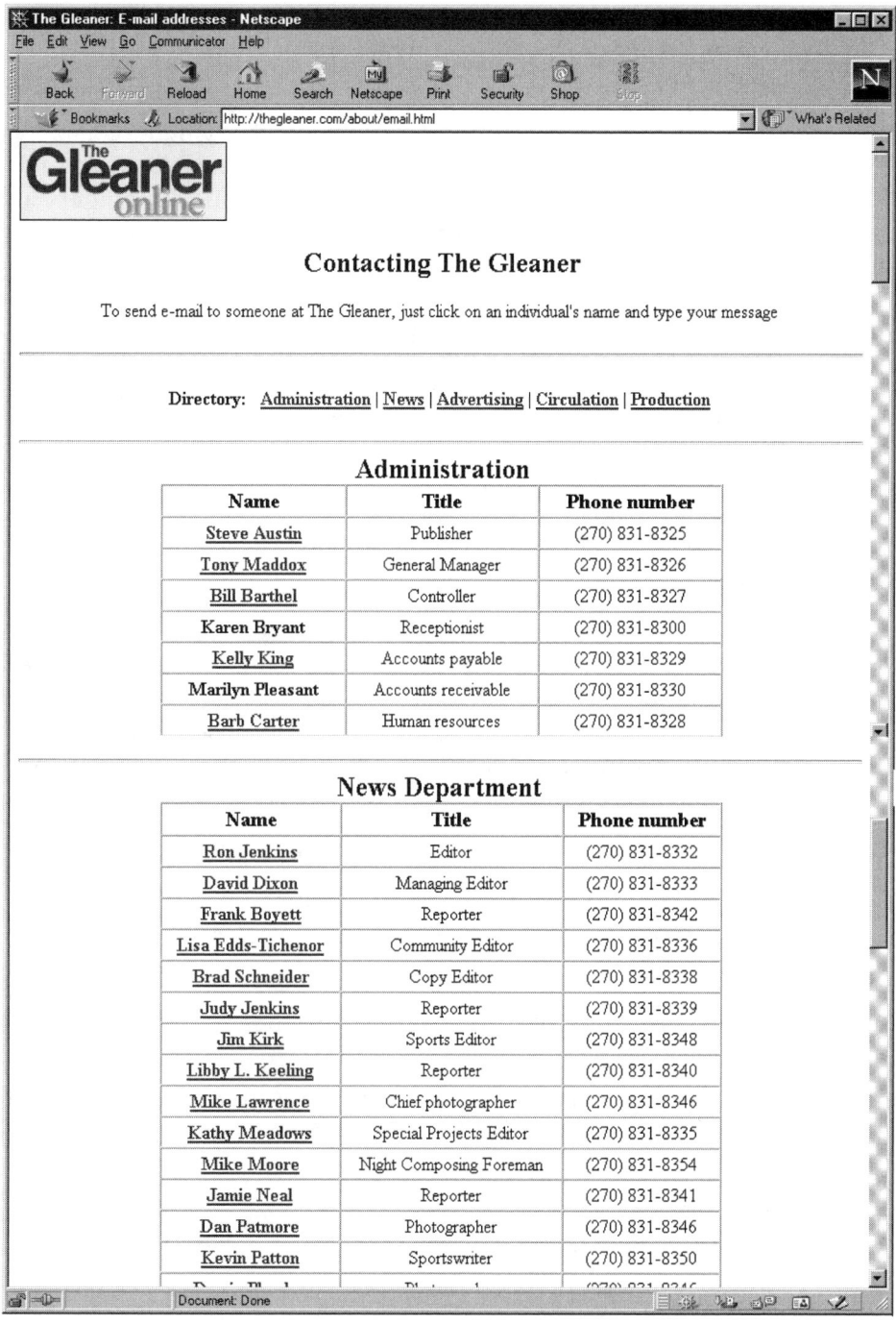

Figure 4.7 If your crew likes to get up close and personal with everybody out there in cyberspace, you might emulate *The Gleaner*.

Or do you work for a firm that encourages you to publish your beeper, car phone, and home number? Is the organizational chart a point of pride or a corporate secret?

You can pour a lot of money into training everybody in the company to be an e-mail maestro, or you can count on a few well-trained people to do the job right. Everybody should get *some* training, but if you spend money anywhere, spend it on the tools that support those processes.

Management Tools to the Rescue

You can write your own software to manage your e-mail. Companies that jumped onto the bandwagon early found that they had to hew the wheels out of blocks of hardwood themselves. That's what J. Crew had to do. The Crew crew decided to build windows in their bandwagon, so that not only customer service managers but their clothing designers as well could peek in and see what customers had to say.

Nowadays, there are plenty of e-mail management tools to choose from, and if you have more than one human answering e-mail, you're a candidate for some of these products. How do you know if you need to buy a tool? According to Jim Harrer, CEO of Mustang Software (www.mustang.com), that time has arrived when you realize having the answers to these questions would help you do your job better:

1. Do you know how many messages come through your Web site every week?
2. Do you know your average message response time, in hours?
3. Can you track down a customer's message in less than 5 minutes?
4. Do you acknowledge every message sent to your Web site?
5. Do you have multiple people responsible for answering messages written to the same generic address?
6. Can you verify that all e-mail messages are answered before you turn off the lights and go home at the end of the day . . . week . . . month?
7. Can you compare message traffic week to week to see if your e-mail traffic is increasing?
8. Can you add a consistent company statement to the bottom of every e-mail response?
9. Can you grade your employees' response times and compare them against companywide averages?

Most e-mail management tools are going to help you answer these sorts of questions. The tools themselves fall into a handful of categories. There are the answerbots (autoresponders, previously discussed), the queuing and routing tools, the boilerplate tools, and artificial intelligence (AI) response tools (much more sophisticated than answerbots).

Queuing and Routing Tools

These are the tools that are going to help you keep track of the Mustang questions. They are going to trap, track, farm out, and keep tabs on the incoming messages. There are several areas of contemplation you'll need to spend some mental energy coming to grips with, like agent management, the business rules for disseminating customer cries for help, and the level of attention each message deserves.

Pull versus Push

This is a simple matter of deciding what's best for your company. Either each service rep reaches up into the common queue and pulls the next e-mail down into his or her workspace, or the system watches to see who's available and pushes it to them.

The decision is going to fall pretty much along the lines of how complex your customers' problems really are. If you sell low-cost, high-volume, easy-to-use items, then it's likely your customers are going to have simple, quick questions that can be answered and problems that can be solved in a trice. As soon as a rep is available, pitch another one.

But if your products are complex and your customers consume their fair share of aspirin trying to use them, it might be better to opt for the pull method. Instead to hitting each pitch out of the ballpark with a single call, your reps are more likely to have to manage ongoing situations with several customers over several days. Just because they do not have a message they are working on at this very moment does not mean that they are ready, willing, and able to take on the next. They may be researching, they may be collaborating, they may simply need to break out of their cubicles and run screaming to the coffee room for a minute or two. Happens all the time.

Routing Rules

When multiple types of messages are being divided up among various groups of agents, you need to create the routing rules that will determine which bucket deserves which message.

The first level simply looks at the address. Is it headed for customerservice@ company.com or techsupport@company.com? Next comes the subject line. If the customer's subject line says "Repairs and tire rotation," it should go to a different rep than the one that says "Test drive on Tuesday?"

Routing requires a few coffee-soaked meetings to nail down the rules that run the show. If one message includes the words "new installation" and another has "replacement parts" in it somewhere, you have to know where to send them and why. You also have to decide what to do if the message says the customer wants help with the new installation of replacement parts.

Routing can also be based on capacity. It might send each repair question to the next qualified repair representative, or simply to the next available rep. These are the rules you're going to have to create in advance, and closely monitor to see how well you could read that crystal ball.

An e-mail message can also be routed to the best person. Brightware's products can include a good number of rules to determine not who is available, but who is actually the best person for the job. That's a little better than straight routing, and a little different from escalation.

Escalation

Countrywide Home Loans uses Brightware (www.brightware.com) software to figure out who comes first in line. If the message is from a current customer with a home in escrow, it gets bumped up higher than the first-time enquiry. You'll also want to be able to have reps easily bump nasty problems upstairs according to your triage blueprint.

Boilerplate Tools

Once the message comes in, what's the fastest way to answer it? Frequently asked questions are not just for customers. Customer service representatives can speed up their responses by rifling through a database of possible cut-and-paste answers. Even in my personal communications, I have a folder of often-used snippets of text. A boilerplate database allows your company to standardize the appropriate verbiage for replication.

There are some tools that will read your e-mail in advance and recommend the potentially proper boilerplate to your service reps. They can even respond without the message's being touched by human hands.

AI Response Tools

The maker of one such tool is eHNC (www.ehnc.com). They call it Select-Response, and its job is to read, analyze, and categorize queries, and make a selection of the best possible answer.

Using neural network techniques (any sufficiently advanced technology is indistinguishable from magic), SelectResponse starts out acting like the previously noted routing tool, but then takes the step into learning as it goes. It

Neural Networks

A neural network is an intelligent computer program, modeled after the human brain, that is able to make decisions and perform complex tasks. Like good employees, neural networks learn from experience and improve their performance. A neural network learns by gathering data and creating relationships between the learned data and all similar pieces of information. —eHNC

doesn't just look for keywords, it looks at context. If it gets a message it can't quite categorize, or it can't quite decide how to answer, it asks a human—and remembers. It learns. But do you trust it?

The people at eHNC will tell you their software can accurately recognize and properly respond to approximately 80 percent of incoming messages. Half of these are no-brainers. Real FAQ-type stuff. But the other half take some serious cognitive skills to decipher and answer, or, if answering is beyond Select-Response's threshold, to route. This is where my third-grade math class comes in handy. If the program answers 40 percent of the queries and routes another 40 percent, what about the 20 percent who get the wrong response? And what about those on the fringes of accurate who get *almost* the right response? That's not good enough for my customers. And that's where human ingenuity takes over.

John Gaffney, general manager for SelectResponse at eHNC, explained that the secret is to limit the automation well before the first sign of diminishing returns. If the software can accurately respond to something like 80 percent of queries, then only let it answer half. Or less. If you're on the receiving end of 10,000 e-mail messages a day like Charles Schwab, wouldn't you want a software system that would cut the number of people you needed to answer the mail by even as little as 30 percent? Thought so. Are you trading at www.schwab.com? Then you may have already been in contact with a neural network.

Primus (www.primus.com) adds something it calls *associative processing* to the mix to help people with problems that they haven't seen before. The Primus system looks at the new problem and tries to associate old problems and solutions to it. Sometimes this leads the customer in the right direction. Sometimes it comes up with the right solution; it's just that the problem was stated in different terms than they had previously seen.

For an even more detailed look at what e-mail can do for you, your customers, and your business, take a look at the "Comparative Evaluation of E-Mail Customer Support Systems" from the Patricia Seybold Group (www.psgroup .com):

In this 100+ page in-depth report, we have examined six high-quality applications that help companies support their customers using e-mail. Each of these products can be used profitably by businesses with needs that match the capabilities of the applications. But not all of the applications will match the needs of any one business. In fact, none of them is a universal solution.

The six represent a cross-section of businesses: Talisma by Aditi, which is best applied to smaller, collaborative businesses; IMC by Mustang, EMS by eGain, and CMS by Kana in the midrange; Brightware by Brightware, aimed at large, low-margin, high-volume businesses; and eMailroom by G2X Software (formerly ErgoTech International), which is tailored to the needs of large, highly compartmentalized businesses.

E-Mail Analysis

You can learn a great deal from your e-mail. Not by reading it, but by having your computers read it. Imagine if you could record every phone conversation with every customer and do a systematic review of what people were talking about? What might you learn?

This is a brand-new area, and one with little practical knowledge available about best practices. If that scares you off, then maybe the Internet is not your strong suit. If it makes your eyes light up with the potential of vastly superior customer service and a serious lead on your competition, then you're in the right place.

Who's the Expert?

In November 1999 Tacit Knowledge Systems (www.tacit.com) rolled out KnowledgeMail (Figure 4.8), a database system that identifies who knows what in your company by reading their e-mail.

You can keep a list of people and what they know a lot about and you can try to get people to keep their lists up to date. But it's a losing battle. Nobody has time to constantly enter a valuable amount of metadata about themselves, and people are either too modest or trying to rise up the ladder of success too fast to be trusted with such a responsibility.

Tacit figured the best way to identify your strengths is to monitor what you write about in your e-mail. KnowledgeMail looks for keywords that are identified as topical for your industry, your company, or your business unit and creates a profile of your supposed wisdom.

Need an expert on making your printer work over a modem? Do a quick search. Need help solving a logistics problem? Query KnowledgeMail. Want to know who has the inside scoop on the big ball game tonight? Well, okay, so it has its limits. Sometimes those who talk the most, know the least. But at least those people can direct you to others who can help.

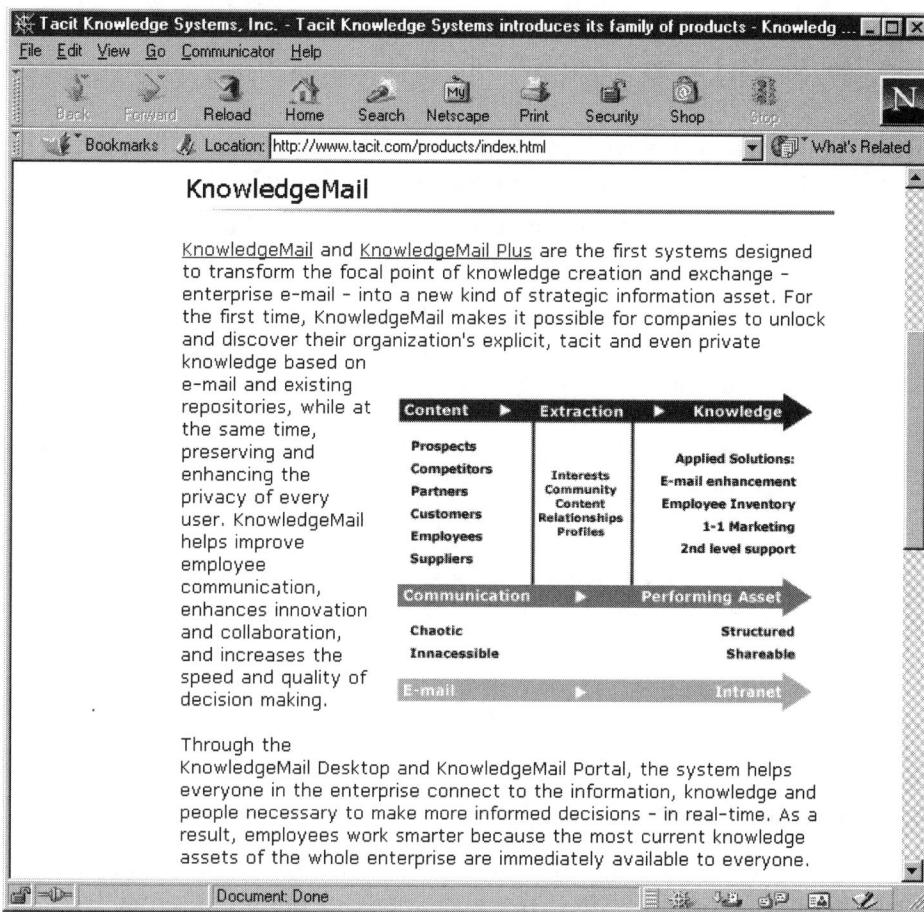

Figure 4.8 According to Tacit Knowledge Systems, you are what you talk about.

What Can You Learn about Your Customers?

Not yet on the horizon are tools to do serious datamining on your customers' e-mail communications. Think of what you could learn from a huge database of messages over a large period of time. Think about the questions you might ask:

- How many customers have asked about a specific problem this week, and how does that number compare to questions on the same topic in the past four weeks? Six weeks? Six months?

- What's the most common problem with product X? How long have our customers complained about it?

- What new features have people been asking about lately?

- How many times do people have to contact us on average before we solve their problem?

- Which customers use the majority of our resources?
- Which customers are most likely to respond to a recommendation for training?
- Is there a way we can encourage our customers to phrase their questions to help us answer them in an automated way?
- What kinds of complaints are we getting about the customer service center, rather than just about our products?

In the long run, the standard statistics about how many questions are answered per day and how long it takes to answer them will be joined by charts and graphs showing customer satisfaction, the types of questions customers ask, and the subjects they ask about. As a result, we'll be much better able to create the FAQs, the knowledgebases, and the troubleshooting guides that can forestall the need to send in an e-mail.

Proactive Customer Service

Customer service isn't just about waiting for people to complain. You can also serve your customers before they ask, and ask your customers what service they need.

Automated Customer Outreach

If you drop all incoming e-mail messages from your customers into a huge database, you can categorize customers for outbound e-mail contact. Divide them up by how often they contact you, how recently they contacted you, what company they're from, and finally, what subjects they brought up.

While the tools you can buy for this are aimed at the people in your marketing department, creating outbound customer service and support messages for different market segments is not a bad idea. Send out a message reminding everybody who bought a specific product from you that it's time for a maintenance checkup. Send a note to your customers who recently had a certain problem, describing other problems they might expect in the future and how to avoid them. Find the customers who haven't contacted you in a while and offer them a rebate on their service contract.

The E-Mail Newsletter

People like to be informed. They like to be kept up-to-date. They welcome information they find interesting—but they are annoyed by junk. If your message isn't meaningful to them, it's junk.

Customers generally like to receive industry news, product promotions, helpful hints, and anything that will help them make better use of your products. Stories told by other customers on unique ways to use your products and suggestions on how to save money and time are also smiled upon.

Proceed with Caution

But first, a word of caution: Do not (I cannot stress this too much), do NOT send any e-mail to them without their permission. Unsolicited e-mail is a crime against nature, a blot on the landscape, and an evil which every man, woman, and child should guard against. Well, okay, maybe I can stress this too much. But the point still stands. There is little you can do on the Web to upset people more or to hurt your brand more than spamming people.

However, once you have confirmation from your customer that he or she is willing to accept the occasional query from you, your path is clear. Just make sure that *every* document you send to an e-mailing list includes easy-to-follow instructions on how one can get *off* that list.

While this quickly becomes a matter for the marketing department, keep in mind that there is plenty of information about your goods and services and your other customers' use of those goods and services that all your customers want to know about.

Do you have a paper newsletter? Save a tree.

Choosing Tools

The Yankee Group put out a report in August 1999 that pegged the e-mail response industry ranking at $400 million dollars in 2002. There's a lot to choose from and a lot more on the way.

The Patricia Seybold Group put out a report in the summer of 1999 on the various vendors and when you might use their products. For example, the report says if you are expecting a lot of questions on a few topics, take a look at Brightware. If you are expecting lots of questions on complex topics, Kana (www.kana.com) or eGain (www.egain.com) might be better solutions.

Keep your eyes on www.personalization.com and www.accelerating.com, as well, for good, detailed reports on the e-mail management software front lines. The former is "your source for news, information and analysis on all aspects of web personalization." The latter "takes Peppers and Rogers Group's core one-to-one strategies—Identify, Differentiate, Interact and Customize—and consistently find[s] new ways to leverage them (and) matches the buyers and sellers of technologies that enable 1to1 relationships." (See Figure 4.9.)

So put in the tools, review the results, and manage from the metrics you collect. But beware of the false productivity improvement problem. Within one month, two IT executives told me about how management-by-example backfired on them.

E-mail managers in these companies were given directives to grind down the e-mail queue and offered bonuses for finishing out each day with an empty e-mail queue. Both achieved their goals almost overnight. A brilliant success of the motivational management method? No, chalk it up to a realization by both that they could collect a bonus by deleting the messages they found too hard

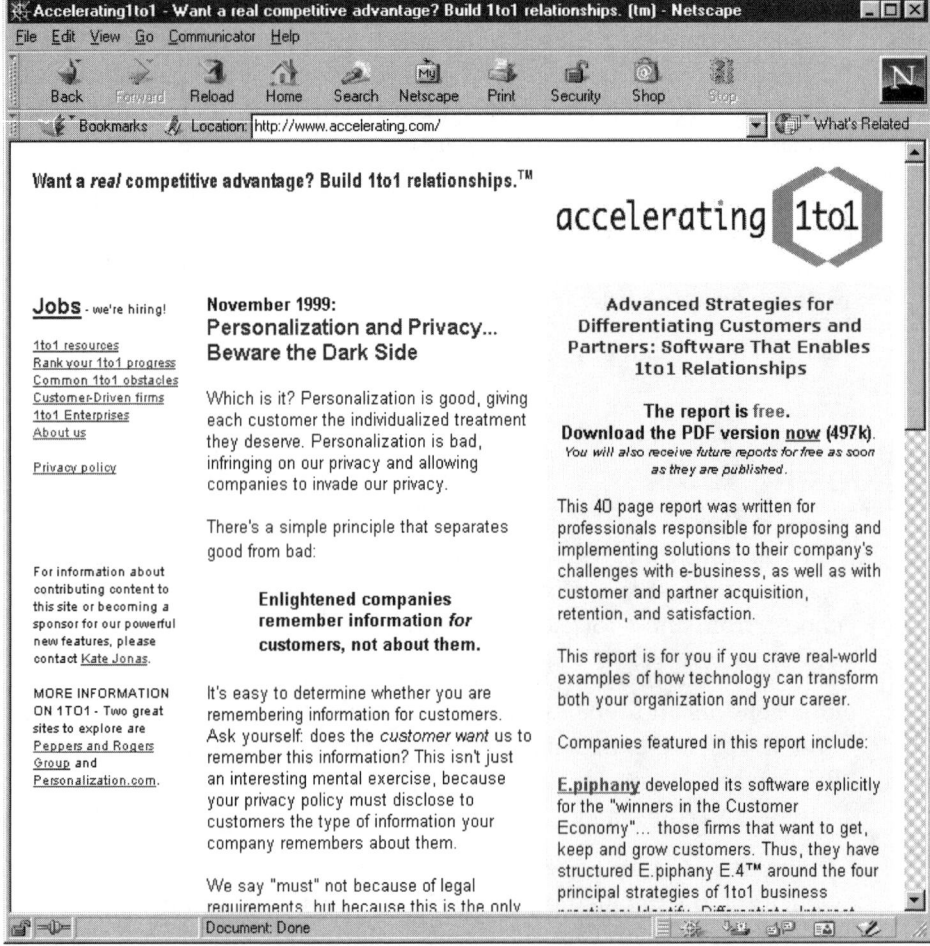

Figure 4.9 The Accelerating1to1 site was designed to take an independent view of the implementation issues surrounding personalization tools on the market.

to answer or just found boring. An empty queue is not necessarily the sign of a successful service agent.

Keep Your Communications Crystal Clear

Some common-sense rules will help keep you, your customers, and your coworkers happy when dealing with e-mail. Especially e-mail in large quantities.

The Subject Line Is Your Friend

Make sure that you always use the Subject portion of each e-mail. All companies have electronic gateways to ensure that no unauthorized traffic, files, or people come into the company network. All firms have such firewalls. I deal with a couple of companies with nasty Internet gateways. Their systems cause e-mail to arrive at my desk with no subject line. I categorize my mail by client or function and end up with directories full of unidentified messages. It makes looking for something in particular especially difficult, as I have to open each one to look at the Subject field that was stored inside.

True aggravation comes in the form of messages that contain no subject at all. The sender simply decided not to include a subject. Then I end up having to open each one and read it until I remember what it was about. Don't do this to your customers. Make each subject as descriptive as possible. Not just for your own files, but for customer service databases that are shared by several representatives. The people who cover the service line in the next shift will have to read the entire message if the subject isn't clear, because they've never seen it before.

If you switch topics in the middle of an e-mail conversation, you can use the Subject line as an indicator. If the Subject started out as "replacement part" and turns into a discussion on dealers in the customer's area, change the Subject line to read: "Local Suppliers (was: replacement part)."

Figure that you only have 25 to 30 characters to play with in the Subject line before the e-mail software on your customer's computer truncates your intended title. And don't forget to leave room for the tracking number. If you're going to make use of the best tools for managing e-mail (more on that later), then you'll want to make use of a trouble-ticket or incident number to help track a particular customer's problem.

Reply with Repetition

When a question comes in, be sure to echo back a sufficient portion of it to the sender when you answer it. An e-mail that goes out on Tuesday is not necessarily fresh in the sender's mind when the answer shows up on Wednesday. E-mails that come back with a simple "Yes" are worthless.

The Answer, the Whole Answer, and Nothing but the Answer

My wife got me an Olympus 320L digital camera for our wedding anniversary. Wonderful toy. I love playing with it and posting family pictures to my personal site. The first time I took it out on the road, I noticed that it beeped every time I changed a setting or took a picture. It was annoying.

I was at the airport at 6:30 in the evening on a Friday night waiting for a plane and decided to take a look at the Olympus Web site. There was my camera, and there was a world of information about how wonderful it would be to own one. But no clues as to how to use it.

I filled out a Web form with a single question: How do I turn off the "beep" on my 320L?

On Saturday, I used the camera and annoyed those around me with its incessant beeping. On Sunday, I left it in my suitcase. On Monday I had meetings, and on Tuesday I got the following response:

```
Date: Tue, 24 Mar 1998 18:14:39 -0500
From: Richard Pellkowski <PELLKR@olympus.com>
To: jsterne@targeting.com
Subject: OLYMPUS DIGITAL Question -Reply

>>> <jsterne@targeting.com> 03/22/98 11:07am >>>
Jim Sterne (jsterne@targeting.com) asked the following question:
   How do I turn off the "beep" on my 320L?
Page 98, owners manual.
```

I was shocked. I was stunned. I resorted to derision. I replied with his message intact and my only addition was, "This is a joke, right?"

He didn't think so.

```
At 5:59 PM -0500 3/27/98, Richard Pellkowski wrote:
Quite seriously sir; page 98, D-320L owners manual explains: "Setting
the Beep Sound". As well, please feel free to contact me directly at:
1-800-622-6372 ext.5256.
```

Shocked and stunned became infuriated and incensed. Pick up the phone and engage this cretin in conversation? Oh no. I was much happier sharpening my wits and proving that the keyboard is mightier than the viper's tongue. I replied:

```
At 07:16 AM 3/27/98, Jim Sterne wrote:

>At 5:59 PM -0500 3/27/98, Richard Pellkowski wrote:
>Quite seriously sir; page 98, D-320L owners manual explains: "Setting
>the Beep Sound". As well, please feel free to contact me directly at:
>1-800-622-6372 ext.5256.

Hi Richard -

My question was not, "What page is it on?" I closely watch how companies
use the Internet for marketing and customer service so I was surprised
by the brevity of your initial response.

Now that it is a weekday and I am back at my desk, I have the manual in
front of me and sure enough, there it is. However, while I was on the
road, over the weekend, when your offices were closed, and I did not
have the manual with me, I was unable to read the manual at all.

I was surprised that you took the time to tell me what page it was on,
without taking an extra couple of seconds to add, "Press and hold the
flash mode button and open the lens barrier at the same time."

Now that I have that off my chest, I was equally surprised that you
thought to pick up the phone and call me directly. That's the mark of
superior customer service.

Was that your doing, or an Olympus policy?
```

Even more surprising than the lack of e-mail sagacity was the fact the Richard had indeed called me and apologized (apologized!) for being less than helpful. At the time, I was so stunned, I was unable to quiz him properly, so I did it in the above message.

Richard wrote back:

```
Date: Fri, 27 Mar 1998 18:46:41 -0500
From: Richard Pellkowski <PELLKR@olympus.com>
To: jsterne@targeting.com
Subject: Re: OLYMPUS DIGITAL Question -Reply -Reply -Reply

It was of my own initiative that I decided to call you.

We take the support of our products very seriously and attempt to do the
best job we can with the resources we have available. I do appreciate
you furnishing me with a phone number to reach you at and the additional
feedback which was certainly constructive. Finally, I will furnish a
copy of our exchanges to my supervisor for his evaluation.

Thanking you again,
                           Richard S. Pelkowski
```

I'm now an Olympus fan. Anybody who is willing to take such abuse from a customer, and then turn around and say *Thank you,* and *I'll pass this along,* and is willing to learn from it rather than just hit the delete key and kick the wall has my vote.

Is your company doing whatever it can to learn from your customers?

Stay on Point

Staying on point sounds simple, but it's not. It's very tempting to cover a couple of topics in one e-mail. If you do, it will be harder to go back and find the right one. Spend as much time as it takes to use as few words as possible to make your point, completely explain your solution, or ask all the right questions. But don't cover multiple topics at once.

The management tools you use will be even more useful if you take a five-subject incoming e-mail and divide it up into five responses. That way, you can track each line of inquiry individually; quickly retire the issues that are quickest to handle; and have multiple, unique subject lines to track the rest.

Practice Clarity

Mark Gibbs, an Internet consultant, writer, and owner of Gibbs & Company in Ventura, California, tells a classic story of electronic miscommunication. He was writing a product review for *Network World* magazine and needed some last-minute information from the manufacturer's marketing VP. With his deadline looming, Mark had called several times and sent numerous e-mails to no avail. He got no response. Finally, in a fit of desperation, he wrote a rather pointed e-mail and sent it to both the VP and his administrative assistant.

Within an hour, the assistant wrote an e-mail back. "Sorry for the delay" she wrote. "VP out of the country this week. I resent your message." Mark was taken aback. How dare a mere secretary pull such an attitude toward his message to her boss! Mark picked up the phone with his ire rising.

"No, no," explained the woman. "I received your message and *re-sent* it to my boss at his other e-mail address."

Mark was properly abashed and swore to read his e-mail more carefully thereafter. Being a new communication medium, e-mail is a little difficult to understand coming *and* going. In *Online Customer Care* (ASQ Quality Press, 1998), Michael Cusak outlines those problems this way:

The customer did not provide enough information.

The customer mentioned several disparate issues.

The receiving agent did not provide an adequate response.

The system did not facilitate the response.

The customer sent the message to the wrong department.

The message was written in a foreign language.

Michael expounds on each of these in detail. With all those kinds of problems waiting for you and your team, you want to be sure that your team is responsible for as few as possible. Often this means teaching members how to communicate clearly in text. Most of making a message clear is in the wording. But sometimes it's in the formatting as well.

Format for Readability

While it may seem like communications one-oh-one, using formatting wisely is critical when it comes to reading text on a computer screen. Feel free to make use of white space to make your message easier to read. Indent, physically separate ideas, and use narrow margins. Newspapers use very narrow columns to good effect. Communicate in bullet points, lists, and tables if you can. Keep your paragraphs and sentences shorter than you would otherwise. This makes it easier for the other person to reply to each thought, individually. Time to reread Strunk & White.

Effective formatting is critical for reading text on a computer:

- Make use of white space to make your message easier to read.
- Indent.
- Physically separate ideas.
- Use narrow margins.
- Use bullet points, lists, and tables.
- Keep paragraphs and sentences short. This makes it easier for others to reply to each thought.
- Reread Strunk & White.

Policies

If the staff members you are going to have answer the e-mail have a penchant for helping people and can type, then you can teach them the rest. The first step is to lay down the law. Or at least to set up some policies.

Company policies serve two purposes. They help employees understand what is expected of them and they protect the company from trouble. Trouble comes in the form of embarrassment and legal issues.

Make it clear, in writing, which employees are allowed to communicate via e-mail. E-mail is letterhead. Sending e-mail to friends from your work computer is the same as writing to them on corporate stationery. It makes the statement that these memorandums are from the company and therefore can be taken as a company-endorsed or approved communication.

Not everybody should be free to send e-mail from the company to anybody. Should employees have access to their own, personal e-mail during lunch and breaks? Sure. Just like the telephone. If they're not using too much time and not abusing company resources, there's nothing wrong with sending a note to hubby reminding him to get milk on the way home. But if they're selling Mary Kay products from their address@company.com, then we have a problem.

E-Mail as a Legal Document

Leo Campbell is the manager of electronic commerce services at the U.S. Postal Service. He's very interested in e-mail. Why? Because the number of e-mail messages is growing and the number of paper letters (with the exception of junk mail) is shrinking. The U.S. Postal Service knows that it has to get into the act, and it has a couple of ideas: authentication and verification.

In a nutshell, authentication of an e-mail message is a digital signature that vouches for you. It says, "Yep, that's him. No doubt about it." Authentication assures me that you really wrote that e-mail. But that's only half the battle. Just because I know it came from you doesn't necessarily mean what it says is really what you said when you sent it in. Maybe it was tampered with along the way. Verification comes into the picture to provide assurance that what you wrote is what I'm reading—that my competitor didn't grab your e-mail order and insert their own message telling me you decided not to buy.

These services can be offered by any third party, and providing them has turned into a competitive little marketplace. The Postal Service believes it can offer some credibility to the market by creating an electronic postmark. Using public/private key encryption technology, the Post Office turns your e-mail into federal e-mail. Just as it's now illegal to tamper with the paper mail, it will be a federal offense to tamper with postmarked e-mail.

With the U.S. Postal Service stamp on it, an e-mail becomes a trusted document. It can be used for legal filings, tax returns, contracts, and purchase orders. The U.S. Postal Service says that it will have a service to make e-mail legal documents. In the meantime, individual states are legislating the validity of electronic signatures.

Until e-signatures come along, your e-mail is still subject to the law of the land. You need to create policies and procedures that will stand up in a court of law, the same as you do for the paper mail that comes in the door, because promises made over the phone, in a fax, or in an e-mail are equally binding.

The best policy on keeping your messages legally acceptable is to make them as clear as possible. The possibilities for misunderstanding e-mail communications are innumerable.

High Touch Is Always More Important than High Tech

With all this automation, don't forget the personal touch. After all, people like working with certain companies because they like the individuals they deal with. It's traumatic to discover the person you've been working with—building a relationship with—has decided to move on. After years of shared experience, years of building rapport, and years of gaining insight into who you are and how you like to work, suddenly you find yourself training a replacement. As a customer, it could spell the beginning of the end. People like to get to know people.

When the Web site for one of my clients (a large telecommunications company) first went up, they got swamped with e-mail. Naturally.

The Webmaster at the time went upstairs to plead for some help, as she was already spending nights and weekends trying to keep her head above keyboard. Of course she could hire some help. It was a good idea. But, of course, it would take some time:

- She would have to write up a job description.
- Have it reviewed by a committee.
- Have it cost-analyzed by human resources.
- Have the new costs added to her budget.
- Send the new job opening out for recruitment.
- Write up the interview plan.
- Write up the training regimen.
- Screen the incoming resumes.
- Schedule the interviews.
- Select potential employees.
- Negotiate employment packages.
- Wait for the new hires to be available.
- Train them.

All told, if they raised the priority to the topmost level and kept this project on the fast track, they might be able to get some e-mail service reps in and functioning in about two months.

Would it be alright then, the Webmaster wanted to know, to bring in a temporary worker to help out until all of the above could happen? That was fine, but where, the GHWMs (gray-haired, white males) wanted to know, would they find somebody who knew how to answer e-mail? After all, this was 1994.

The Webmaster had an answer: Her kid sister, Suzy, who was on summer vacation from the university. All university students were fluent in the ways of e-mail. She would be able to walk in, sit down, and tame the wild e-mail monster.

And so, one warm summer morning, Suzy came to work in her jeans and her ponytail and started putting a serious dent in the pile of e-mail that had been building at an ever increasing rate. She was deft. She was quick. She was mistress of the keys. Everybody was glad to have her there to lighten the load.

But nobody was reading what Suzy was writing.

Suzy didn't know anything about the company. Suzy didn't know anything about the products and services the company sold. Suzy didn't have a clue as to the finer points of formal, corporate communication. The messages she sent out to annoyed or unhappy customers were not the sort they expected from a large, bureaucratic telco.

```
From: Suzy@telcoX.com
To: fred@UnhappyCustomer.com
Subject: Re: This software has bugs

Dear Fred,

That's just terrible! How frustrating that your systems freeze up on you
in the middle of stuff. That'd really fry me.

Let me do a little hunting around here and see who the idiot was that
put hose bugs in that software package.

I'll get back to you this afternoon.

Sigend,
Suzy
```

And, true to her word, that very afternoon would come the next Suzy-gram.

```
From: Suzy@telcoX.com
To: fred@UnhappyCustomer.com
Subject: Re: This software has bugs

Dear Fred,

Nailed it! Looks like Ralph in product management is responsible for the
software on that switch and I told him in no uncertain terms to get in
touch with you by lunchtime tomorrow.

I've never met Ralph before, but he seemed kinda worried, so I'm betting
he'll do it.
```

```
If he doesn't, I found out his boss's name is Penelope (who would name a
new born baby Penelope?) and if you don't hear from Ralph you let me
know and I'll go have a little chat with her about him.

Sigend,
Suzy
```

This sort of thing went on for the remaining two months of summer while the formal, corp-com types were recruited, interviewed, selected, trained, and put in place. With that, Suzy went back to the halls of academe to tackle her junior year.

It only took about three days before e-mails started coming in from customers all over the territory.

```
Where's Suzy?
```

It was not Suzy's expertise in the finer points of voice and data transmission that had enamoured the clients. It was her manner. She was a friend. She was a confidante. She cared.

Shortly thereafter, the company had three people answering e-mail—all named Suzy.

They had a database of frequently asked questions; they had a database of every customer contact with the company (Suzy, do you remember about three months ago when we talked about . . . ?); and they had a one-page description of Suzy pinned to the cubicle wall above each typist.

Suzy is young. Suzy is informal. Suzy is cheerful. Most important, Suzy cares more about the customer than about the company, or the company image. Suzy is the customer's advocate. Along with AOL, which couldn't hide behind a phalanx of telephonic customer service reps named Lee (they got caught because sometimes Lee was male and sometimes female, and if you called to talk to Lee a second time . . .), the Suzy persona had to eventually be promoted off the phones and into the invisible maw of the corporation, never to be seen again.

The point was taken to heart. People like dealing with people.

On a whim, I sent another e-mail message through the Feedback page at National Semiconductor because I spotted another misspelling. The word "information" appeared on a page without the "r." I put it out of my mind until I got an e-mail about two hours later.

"Thanks for the tip, Jim" it read. "Sorry for the typo. I will get it corrected tomorrow."

Just Say No

Sometimes, customers aren't always the type of people we like to deal with. Sometimes you have to tell them, "No." Time Management Systems' founder,

Odette Pollar, advises that sometimes it's kind to be cruel. Sometimes, the fastest way to defuse a tricky situation is to explain why the problem cannot be solved.

Odette says turning a customer down is a four-step process.

1. Listen. Don't assume. Don't jump ahead. Let them get it off their chest.

2. Tell them "No," right up front. Don't get their hopes up. Don't try to protect their feelings.

3. Explain why immediately. Keep it short and sweet, not long and drawn out.

4. Come up with alternatives. Other time-frames, other people, maybe even other companies.

You must also learn to say no to those who glom onto you and your department as their sole source of human contact. These people are almost instantly recognizable. They ask a question, they write, and then they write again. And again. Soon, it's obvious that they have decided to make you their confidant. Be careful that you actually do answer the questions they ask that are work-related, but don't become a shoulder to cry on or a therapist.

Maggie Williams at Bell Advanced Communication in Canada knows just how to handle what they term chronic callers. "The classic was the e-mailer who kept asking question after question. We tried to be patient. We tried to be kind. We started giving more and more terse answers. But we've found people really like to see a phone number at the bottom of these messages in case they just don't understand, and this guy switched from e-mail to the phone. One phone rep reported one conversation that caused us to change our point of view.

"After trying to quickly help him resolve his current problem this gent cut him off with, 'That's okay son, take your time. I'm retired and I have alllll the tiiiiiiiime in the worrrrrld.' It was then we knew we had to stop, and focus all of our attention on him and people like him."

Focus all their attention? On a lonely, gabby, confused, time-wasting old-timer? Yes.

"We realized that if we spent all morning training this person how to find answers in our FAQs, how to use the troubleshooting guide, and how to run some of our self-diagnosis tools," says Ms. Williams, "he'll be able to help himself. Once you focus that much attention on somebody, they start to fend for themselves."

Sometimes the ones who ask the most questions really do need the most help. For them, there's a strong recommendation you can make: education.

Suggest They Get Training

At some point, the types of questions people ask make it clear that they are, indeed, clueless. The following goes down in the annals of computer support as a truly apocryphal tale. I've seen it published many times, with many attributions, and all of them say the same thing: "This is a true story!" So I'll qualify it this way: it probably never really happened, but it *is* a true story:

> This is a true story from the WordPerfect helpline, and was transcribed from a recording monitoring the customer care department. Needless to say, the help-desk employee was fired; however, he/she is currently suing the WordPerfect organization for "termination without cause." This is actual dialogue of a former WordPerfect Customer Support employee:

> "Computer assistance; may I help you?"
> "Yes, well, I'm having trouble with WordPerfect."
> "What sort of trouble?"
> "Well, I was just typing along, and all of a sudden the words went away."
> "Went away?"
> "They disappeared."
> "Hmm. So what does your screen look like now?"
> "Nothing."
> "Nothing?"
> "It's blank; it won't accept anything when I type."
> "Are you still in WordPerfect, or did you get out?"
> "How do I tell?"
> "Can you see the C: prompt on the screen?"
> "What's a sea-prompt?"
> "Never mind, can you move your cursor around the screen?"
> "There isn't any cursor: I told you, it won't accept anything I type."
> "Does your monitor have a power indicator?"
> "What's a monitor?"
> "It's the thing with the screen on it that looks like a TV. Does it have a little light that tells you when it's on?"
> "I don't know."
> "Well, then look on the back of the monitor and find where the power cord goes into it. Can you see that?"
> "Yes, I think so."
> "Great. Follow the cord to the plug, and tell me if it's plugged into the wall."
> ". . . Yes, it is."
> "When you were behind the monitor, did you notice that there are two cables plugged into the back of it, not just one?"
> "No."
> "Well, there are. I need you to look back there again and find the other cable."
> ". . . Okay, here it is."

"Follow it for me, and tell me if it's plugged securely into the back of your computer."

"I can't reach."

"Uh huh. Well, can you *see* if it is?"

"No."

"Even if you maybe put your knee on something and lean way over?"

"Oh, it's not because I don't have the right angle—it's because it's dark."

"Dark?"

"Yes—the office light is off, and the only light I have is coming in from the window."

"Well, turn on the office light then."

"I can't."

"No? Why not?"

"Because there's a power failure."

"A power . . . A power failure? Ah-ha, Okay, we've got it licked now. Do you still have the boxes and manuals and packing stuff your computer came in?"

"Well, yes, I keep them in the closet."

"Good. Go get them, and unplug your system and pack it up just like it was when you got it. Then take it back to the store you bought it from."

"Really? Is it that bad?"

"Yes, I'm afraid it is."

"Well, all right then, I suppose. What do I tell them?"

"Tell them you're too stupid to own a computer."

Instead of taking that satisfying approach, offer your clueless customers a discount on training. Entice them with the excitement of travel to your training center. Pump them up with the promise of advancement as they become more proficient in the use of your products. Maybe you can offer them online training as well.

Those who make Web-based training courses and those who create the courses themselves agree that self-paced tutelage is the best route. The only reason we group children by age is that we cannot offer one-to-one teaching. The Web changes all that. If there are lectures involved, be sure they are prerecorded. If there are discussion groups, be sure they are managed through e-mail or by posting for all to see, rather than chat-based, real-time events which are hard to match up to your customers' schedules.

Real-time presentations are useful if the class size is small and there is a real need for a question-and-answer interaction. Otherwise, stick to the canned course.

You can also record each student's progress and refer back to it when they send in another e-mail question, or use it to suggest follow-on training.

Pick the Right Goal

The goal of most call center managers is to lower costs. You do that by minimizing the number of calls that come in and by minimizing the length of each call. But what if you turned that idea on its head? What if you believed that the way to a customer's heart is through his ear? What if you thought learning more and more about your customers was better than talking to them less and less? Then you and I would be seeing eye to eye.

The question, then, is how do you get customers to talk to you?

CHAPTER 5

Encouraging Customer Conversations

You can try to guess what your customers want. But you're a lot better off finding out directly from them. Isn't it interesting that they are more willing to talk, they are more willing to spend the time, and their expressed opinions are closer to the truth when they are pissed off at you?

An Unhappy Customer Is an Asset

When was the last time you were so disappointed or downright upset that you were compelled to write a letter or pick up the phone to lodge a formal complaint? Most of the time you shrug it off and figure tomorrow will be better. Other times you are actually moved to switch brands or find a different vendor. But rarely do you take the time to place a call or lick a stamp.

I once had a run-in with my business bank. I explained my problem to the bank manager. She explained their policy. I explained that their policy was causing me a problem. She apologized, but said it *was* the policy. I said it made it hard on their customers. She apologized, but said it *was* the policy. I said, "This is a business relationship, and so far it's been just fine. But I would be remiss in my duty as a customer if I did not express my displeasure and my desire that you change your policy. Please record this request as one more datapoint toward improving customer service." Sometimes I actually do talk like that.

Still thinking I expected her to do something about it, she said, "I understand, sir," (it had been "Jim" until then), "but now that you know the policy you won't have this problem again."

I can only assume that my complaint about the bank's corporate rules would reflect badly on her management skills when it came time for review. How sad. It was not my intention. My intention was to help the establishment improve its service.

Burke Customer Satisfaction Associates (www.burke.com, Figure 5.1) looked at almost 1,200 department store shoppers and found that loyal shoppers were much more inclined to complain. The rest just assumed that the poor products and bad service were par for the course. Happy shoppers tended to tell between 5 and 8 people about the store in question, and unhappy shoppers spread the discouraging word to somewhere between 10 and 16.

Technical Research Assistance Programs (TARP) Europe Limited found that 5 percent of people who encountered problems contacted the head office to complain, while 45 percent talked to the frontline staff or the customer service department. According to the study, half of the people who experienced a problem didn't bother to talk to anyone.

Figure 5.1 Burke Customer Satisfaction Associates study customer satisfaction for a living.

Customers who take the time to complain fall into three broad categories: people who are trying to help, people who have gotten a seriously bum deal, and people who are cranks. The folks who are trying to help have your business's best interests at heart. "The soup is too salty," may not necessarily be so much an admonition as it is an offer of advice. "Your service agent was rude," is not always a demand for an apology or an appeal for some payback remedy. It could be a friendly warning that you've got a problem.

Those who have been genuinely wronged deserve to be put right, and in a hurry. As for the cranks, you might be able to learn from them as well.

So why would I suggest you offer a platform for these folks to propagate their displeasure to hundreds and thousands? Because you have a chance to respond—in public. Your first order of business is to see if they are talking about you already.

Customer Service in the Public Eye

The Usenet Newsgroups became a vast resource of technical hints and help early on in the life of the Internet. They started as a means of solving the problems of running the Internet itself. This new computer communication tool was in the process of being invented, and the only people who knew anything about it were the inventors. There were no vendors, no advocacy groups, no training sessions, and, hard as it may be to believe, no *Internet for Dummies*.

The people trying to build the Internet relied on each other. They posted questions that weren't aimed at one vendor about a single product, but about systems and how the different pieces went together. Usually some kind soul who had come across similar problems would respond. This activity is still going strong today. Here's one of my recent favorites:

```
Subject: Simple Caveman needum printer help

Me caveman, simple folk. Want hook-up two printer, two computer. OOG,
let me scratch on cave wall:


   _____  _____    | P5-90 |
  LPT1      | P5-60 |   | Win95 |\
            | Win3.1|   |       | \ |
            |  --------- \ ----|----
       ?  |        \                | LPT1 to 1284D
          |         \               |
    ___?_|_____  \ to 1284C  ____|___
    | Djet      | _____| Ljet  |
    | 855c      |             | 5MP    |
    ------------              ---------
```

```
Gottum 1284C, 1284D cables to Ljet HP 5MP many moons now, work like
bear-bone charm. Two computers talk to HP Ljet, share-share-alike. HP
Ljet 5MP like EPP, like talk to P5-90, P5-60, say "me here! me busy! me
needum paper!"
```

```
Then Djet 855c join home last moon, much powerful magic. Needum make
P5-90 talkum to Djet too. Don't like way me change printers now ...
gottum shut down P5-90, change cables, reboot. Win95 stink like big pile
mammoth dung, many flies, much bad wind.
```

```
Me think me just add new parallel port, LPT2, on little card. But evil
spirits lurk; not many IRQs, caveman afraid change soundcard IRQ from 5,
for evil Win95 never saw soundcard, will kill or hurt soundcard if find
out. Need LPT2 me can assign any IRQ. Me see FarPoint makum extra
Parallel port card, but FarPoint say no good with evil, evil Win95. Me
want EPP port, most card not EPP, or have all manner expensive junk me
no want.
```

```
Or maybe can use fast serial with HP 855c? Gottum extra serial port on
855c, made for funny fruit computer (Appletalk? Me never hear apple talk
in all days as caveman, travel many many lands). Gottum extra unused
16550 serial on P5-90.
```

```
Win95 bad, bad medicine. Stink like ground sloth with mange. MS try make
like fruit computer, computer think it know what caveman want, really
just do random thing it want.
```

```
--- Harlan W. Stockman    hwstock@swcp.com    hwstock@sandia.gov
```

```
Me no really Caveman, me stodgy 41-year-old scientist. Me pretend be OOG
so people actually read story.
```

Asked if I could reprint his OOG post here, Harlan replied,

```
You want put OOG on writing-skin?
```

```
Sure.
```

```
I got lots of good answers—hundreds. This method definitely touched a
gentle nerve, and people from all computational views thanked me for
the humor. Apparently poor OOG was too pitiful and humorous to be
threatening. Intel, Apple, Microsoft employees all sent cheery notes.
```

You can be sure that Microsoft, that maker of bad medicine, mammoth dung, and sloth mange, had a good reason for posting a reply. It knows that people are talking about it out there, and it is paying attention. Chances are, people are talking about you, too.

If you're IBM, they're talking about you a lot. A quick search at Deja.com (www.deja.com, Figure 5.2) revealed 84 newsgroups with IBM in the title. Everything from alt.games.ibmpc to comp.databases.ibm-db2 to comp.sys .ibm.pc.hardware.networking.

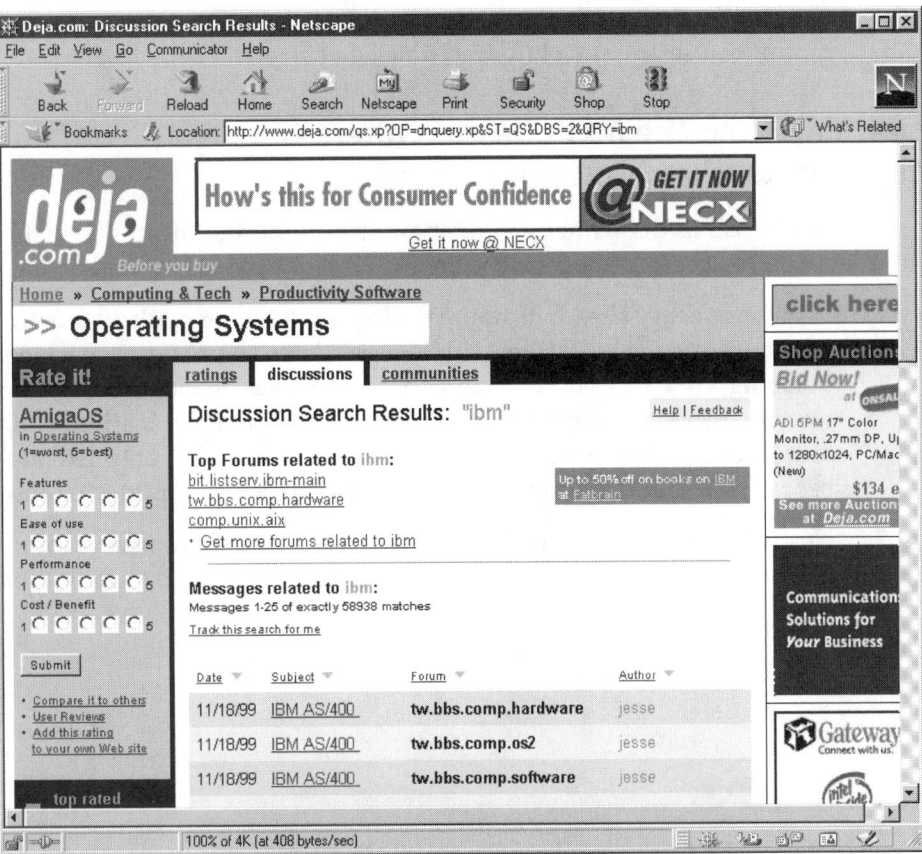

Figure 5.2 Deja.com lets you search for keywords in newsgroup titles.

So, are they already talking about you? Are there discussions about your company out on the newsgroups that you're not paying attention to? Don't you think you should?

What if there was a group that gathered once a week at the local pub to talk about your industry, your company, or your specific products. Wouldn't you like to be a fly on the wall? Wouldn't you like to keep tabs on their conversation? Even more important, wouldn't you like to contribute to and help form public opinion?

Learn to participate in this public forum. Learn to pay attention, and to advise, and to inform, and to never, ever dictate. Each newsgroup is owned by its participants. Just because they're talking about you does not give you the right to turn the conversational gyrations to your own particular spin. People in sufficient numbers have an uncanny way of sniffing out disingenuous behavior and recognizing the truth. That's why there are twelve people on a jury. News-groups can easily run a hundred times that size.

Learning from the Mistakes of Others—
The Pentium Predicament

Just as bad as dissembling in newsgroups is ignoring them. The first harsh lesson in customer service and the public newsgroups was learned by Intel in 1994.

In the summer of 1994, Lynchburg College professor of mathematics Dr. Thomas Nicely discovered a problem with his new Pentium processor machine. He was pursuing a research project in an area of pure mathematics called computational number theory and came across a division error. After eliminating all other likely sources of error (software logic, compiler, chipset, etc.), he contacted Intel in October and was told that no such bug had been previously reported or observed.

He decided to go public and make an inquiry of the CompuServe forums (much like the Internet newsgroups) (http://ftp.mathworks.com/Nicely_1.txt):

```
FROM: Dr. Thomas R. Nicely
      Professor of Mathematics
      Lynchburg College
      1501 Lakeside Drive
      Lynchburg, Virginia 24501-3199

      Phone:    804-522-8374
      Fax:      804-522-8499
      Internet: nicely@acavax.lynchburg.edu

TO:   Whom it may concern

RE:   Bug in the Pentium FPU

DATE: 30 October 1994

It appears that there is a bug in the floating point unit (numeric
coprocessor) of many, and perhaps all, Pentium processors.

In short, the Pentium FPU is returning erroneous values for certain
division operations. For example,

                    1/824633702441.0

is calculated incorrectly (all digits beyond the eighth significant
digit are in error). This can be verified in compiled code, an ordinary
spreadsheet such as Quattro Pro or Excel, or even the Windows calculator
(use the scientific mode), by computing

            (824633702441.0)*(1/824633702441.0),

which should equal 1 exactly (within some extremely small rounding
error; in general, coprocessor results should contain 19 significant
decimal digits). However, the Pentiums tested return
```

```
                        0.999999996274709702
```

```
for this calculation.
```

He finished with a request:

```
I would be interested in hearing of test results from other Pentiums,
and also from 486-DX4s and (if anybody has one yet) the AMD, Cyrix, and
NexGen clones of the Pentium.
```

Dr. Nicely discovered that others shared his finding. Yes, it was the hardware at fault, and not his programming. On November 10, Andreas Kaiser published a list of 23 examples of the bug in comp.sys.intel. He wasn't alone. Turns out lots of people were having problems and that carrying division problems out to the 9th or 10th decimal was pretty important to lots of disciplines.

Individuals became worried about their calculations and started calling Intel. Intel, in a clear misunderstanding of the power of electronic word-of-mouth, treated each individual caller as an individual and not part of a larger community. Intel told each individual that Intel had been aware of the problem for some time and was working on it. They suggested it wasn't as serious a problem as people had been led to believe. Wrong answer.

The image of Intel knowingly shipping a bum product caused an uproar in the newsgroups. So much so, that the story made it to the press. On November 11, 1994, John Markoff wrote in *The New York Times*:

> **Circuit Flaw Causes Pentium Chip to Miscalculate, Intel Admits**
>
> Intel said Wednesday that it did not believe the chip needed to be recalled, asserting that the typical user would have but one chance in more than nine billion of encountering an inaccurate result as a consequence of the error, and thus there was no noticeable consequence to users of business or home computers. Indeed, the company said it was continuing to send computer makers Pentium chips built before the problem was detected.

A full-blown PR nightmare was speedily picking up velocity and mass as it careened down the slope of chip industry dishonor. Still, Intel treated each case as a singular problem to be dealt with and resolved. Finally, Andy Grove, head honcho, buck-stops-here, president and chief executive officer at Intel published his response to the whole brouhaha:

```
www.mathworks.com/Andy_Grove.txt
Date: 27 Nov 1994 19:31:21 GMT
Subject: My Perspective on Pentium-AGS
Newsgroups: comp.sys.intel


.....

We would like to find all users of the Pentium processor who are engaged
in work involving heavy duty scientific/floating point calculations and
```

```
resolve their problem in the most appropriate fashion including, if
necessary, by replacing their chips with new ones. We don't know how to
set precise rules on this so we decided to do it thru individual
discussions between each of you and a technically trained Intel person.
We set up 800# lines for that purpose. It is going to take us time to
work thru the calls we are getting, but we will work thru them. I would
like to ask for your patience here....
```

But Pentium users were not patient. The reaction was not at all pleasant and it was not at all slow. Suggesting what they thought was a reasonable solution, Intel managed to aggravate millions of its clients. Intel was offering to be the judge and jury to determine whether your application was adequately sophisticated to require a chip replacement. Not good enough. The word on the 'net was very negative and very loud. Intel was being greedy. Intel was foisting a shoddy product off onto a public that was being kept in the dark. Intel was being disingenuous.

On December 12, 1994, IBM made an announcement. It was going to halt shipments of its Intel-based computers. It was going to offer a chip replacement to anybody who wanted it. No questions asked.

The New York Times ran the following headline on its front page: IBM HALTS SALES OF ITS COMPUTERS WITH FLAWED CHIP. Intel was so far in the dog house it would take months of promises, apologies, and replacements to recover. To this day you can visit the Canonical List of Pentium Jokes (www .geocities.com/CollegePark/Library/8045/pentium.html, Figure 5.3) which includes 60 Intel zingers including:

Q: How many Pentium designers does it take to screw in a light bulb?
A: 1.99904274017, but that's close enough for nontechnical people.

On the tee-shirt of an inline skater in Mountain View: "I asked for a refund on my Pentium, and all I got was this lousy T-shirt"

Q: What's another name for the "Intel Inside" sticker they put on Pentiums?
A: Warning label.

Make sure that somebody in your organization is responsible for monitoring which way the wind is blowing on the newsgroups. If you don't have the resources to do that, consider having college interns do it for you. While they won't work for peanuts, they *will* work for pizza. If your company policy doesn't allow college interns, consider getting professional help—in the form of an electronic clipping service company that will watch the newsgroups for you.

Watching the Newsgroups

If there are 100 newsgroups with your company name in the title, you're going to have to do some fancy footwork to keep up.

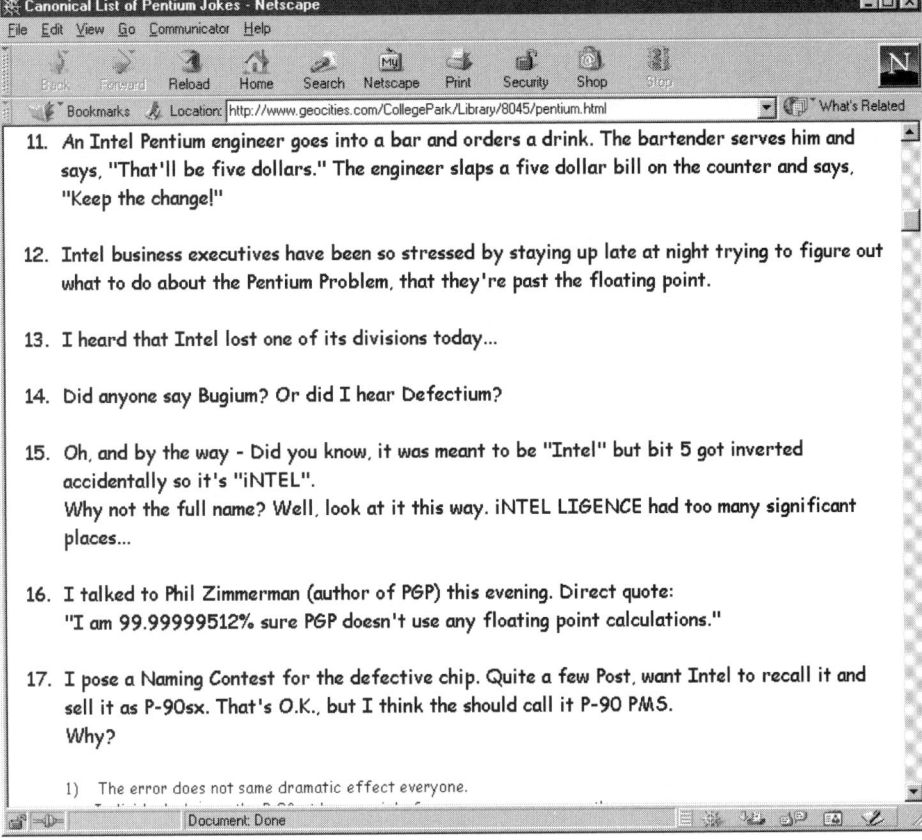

Figure 5.3 The Canonical List of Pentium Jokes remains as a monument to Intel's misreading of the Internet as a word-of-mouth mechanism.

At Remarq (www.remarq.com, Figure 5.4), you can get a list of the different newsgroups about a particular subject. If that subject is your company, getting that list and checking it twice is a good customer-support idea.

The Internet newsgroups hold a wealth of information, including comments you may want to repost on your site. It behooves you to take a continued interest in them. The best way? Try Deja (www.deja.com). This site lets you search the newsgroup postings for instances of specific keywords, including your product, your company—you name it. No, you don't need to hire somebody to scan the postings every day; let the computer do it for you.

Hiring Watchers

If you work for a large enough company, it quickly becomes too labor intensive to keep track of the newsgroups yourself or to manage all those pizza-eaters. Then it's time to turn to a new type of professional—the electronic clipping service. Think of these clipping services as watching your PR back online.

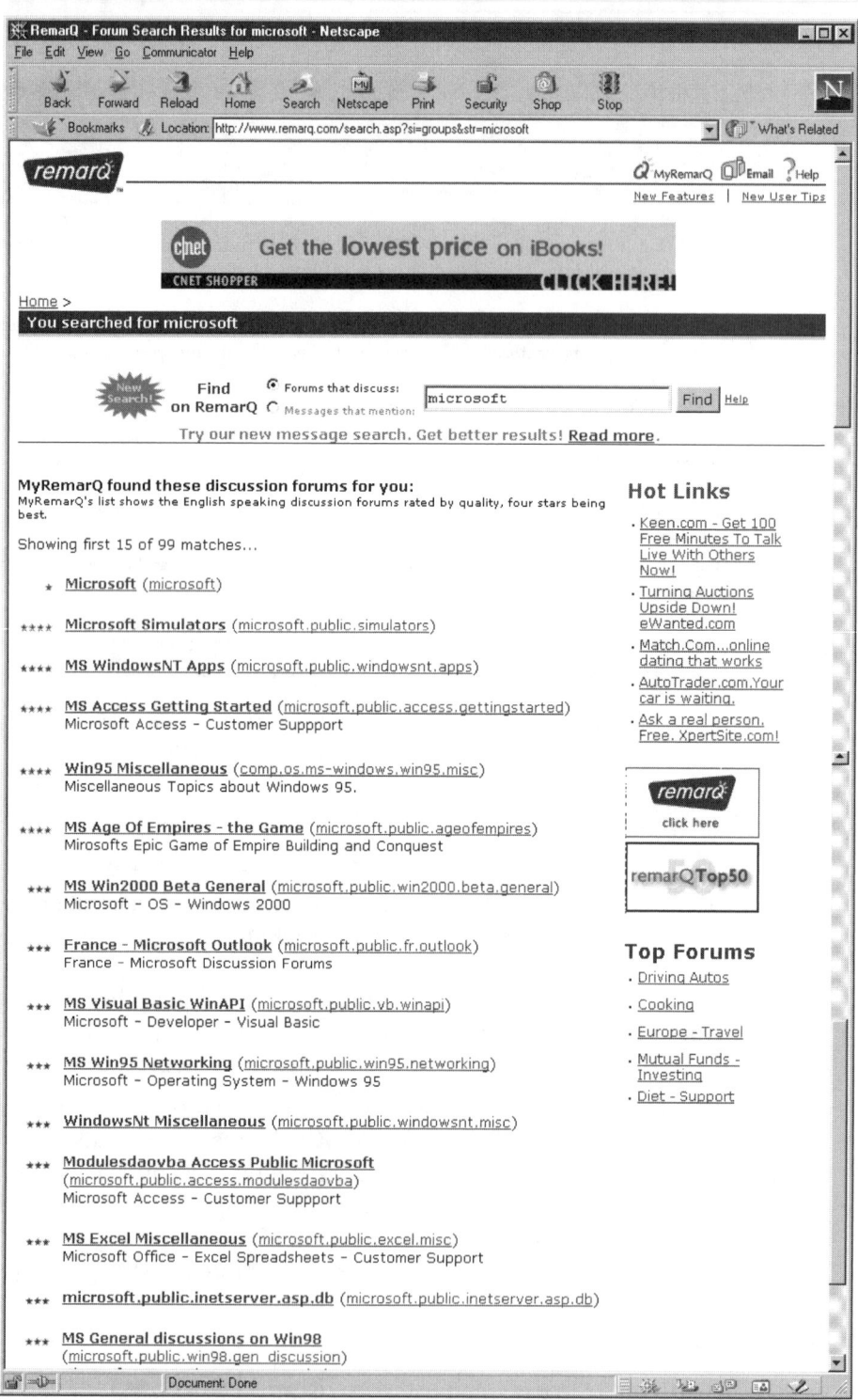

Figure 5.4 Microsoft has its hands full tracking what is said about it in 99 newsgroups.

Heinz has to fight the occasional outcropping of claims that its famous ketchup is made with cow's blood. Northwest Airlines faces the sporadic rumor that its fleet is composed of the oldest and most unsafe airplanes in the sky. The folks at Procter & Gamble have found the Internet to be rife with the old saw about their being devil worshipers, as exemplified by the thirteen stars in their company logo.

None of these imputations are true. None of them will die. But keeping track of where they show up, in order to efficiently quash them, is a challenge. That's why there are companies like eWatch (www.eWatch.com, Figure 5.5).

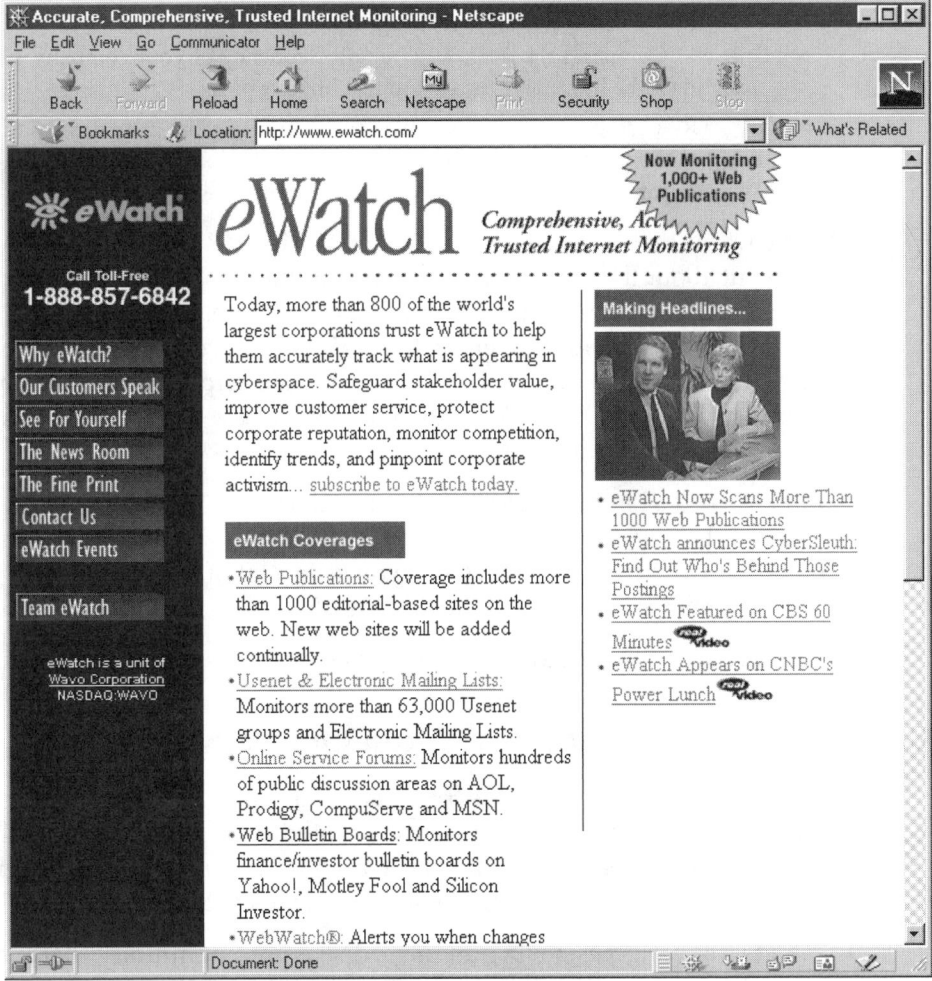

Figure 5.5 eWatch will keep an eye on what people are saying about you online and keep you informed.

Merger rumors, sales figure predictions, stock price warnings. Some are harmless; some can cause irritation; some can kick the legs out from under you. Does spending $13,000 a year sound like a lot of money just to keep tabs on your good name? The people at Dell, Ford, and Mobil Oil are paying $30,000 a year and up—less than half the cost of a full-time employee—to Cyveillance (www.cyveillance.com) for its services. In that company's own words:

> CyVantage is an executive decision support tool designed to provide executive management, Internet strategists and competitive intelligence professionals with valuable competitive data about their company or products on the Internet versus up to four competitors. This unique service provides a bird's-eye view of the Internet's competitive landscape in three key areas:
>
> - *Commerce:* Tracks how your products or content are being distributed over the Net compared to that of your peers.
> - *Exposure:* Compares the overall reach and frequency of your company, product, or brand on the Internet compared to that of your peers.
> - *Image:* Records positive and negative perception of your company, product, or brand on the Internet by tracking the opinion or bias of newsgroup postings and Web sites containing commentary on you and your peers.

Way back in the stone age of the Internet (March 1995), IBM's John Patrick spoke out about the value of newsgroups in *Internet World* magazine. "People on the Internet tend to be more vocal, more accurate, and tend to be a leading indicator of what people are going to conclude. I've seen this many times over the years, where you go out there and you come across people who are really flaming about something. There's a tendency to say, 'Well, these guys are just flaming,' and write them off.

"But I learned a long time ago they are usually right. You may not like the way they said it, or who they said it to, or the extent to which they got emotional about it. If you act on what they say, you save a lot of money and you get a lot more customer satisfaction in the long run."

Just ask Andy Grove about the long-division capabilities of his first Pentium chip.

Understanding the Communication Imperative

The CorelNET Web site (Figure 5.6) was created as a place for open discussion about Corel Software products. It was created for people to share what they knew and to help each other. It was created for people who needed guidance or just wanted to blow off some steam. But it was not created by Corel.

This site was so successful in building a discussion community, that eventually Corel woke up, bought it, and brought the conversation onto their own site. Try surfing to www.corelnet.com nowadays and you end up at the corporate Corel home page.

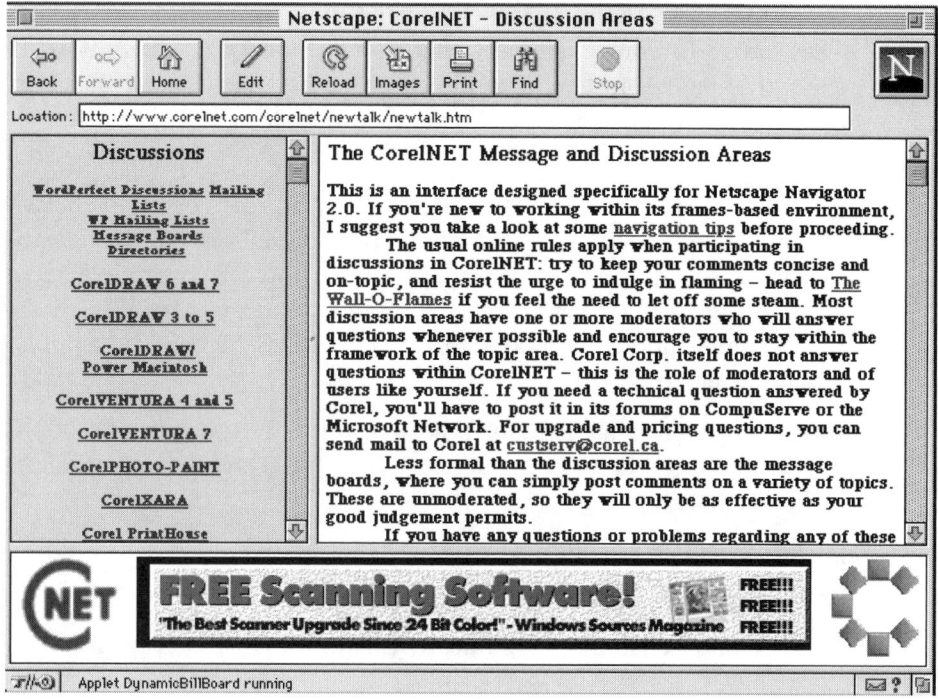

Figure 5.6 CorelNET became such a popular place for discussion, they were able to sell banner ads on the site.

Hosting Your Own Newsgroup

Besides posting purified, disinfected data for the masses, and beyond answering e-mail from individuals, there is tremendous value in getting your clients to talk to each other on your site. Getting them to talk about you and your products can be a very powerful tool for building loyalty. It can also expose you in unpleasant ways.

Marketers have always used testimonials. Now there is a way to get people to express their ongoing love affair with your products and services in their own words, online and in real time.

On the other hand, they will also air your dirty laundry. They will be only too happy to espouse your shortcomings. They will be delighted to take their frustrations out on you in public. Kept them waiting on hold for more than they could tolerate? Didn't offer a refund? Didn't even say "I'm sorry"? Now your customers can tell the world in a instant. Is this really such a good idea?

It's a very good idea. Managed properly, these complaints become a wealth of information for product and service improvement. They become the springboard to people's helping each other and forming a community of customers. They prove to your customers that you value their contribution. They also show that your company is embracing this new technology in order to open the doors between you and your clientele, instead of using it to simply disseminate the company line.

Put a newsgroup on your Web site to drum up conversations between your happy customers. It's nice to have real people telling real stories about how really pleased they are with your products. You can even have separate discussion groups for each product line. But don't get carried away. With too many conversations to choose from, any site visitor may be confused about where to click first.

Dell Computer created a DellTalk area on its site, where 200,000 Dell customers can ask and answer questions in a variety of forums. It begins with a choice of just a few topics:

- I want to talk about Desktops and Mini-Towers.
- I want to talk about Portables/Notebooks.
- I need non-technical assistance with your order or account.

Then they open up a whole range of topics open for discussion (Figure 5.7).

The Giga Information Group, a technology research and consulting company (www.gigaweb.com), figures that it costs a company anywhere from $5 to $50 to answer a customer's phone call and solve a technical question. That spells an enormous return on investment—as long as you have a few people monitoring the action to be sure the information being swapped by customers is good information.

When you add to that the ability for product managers to monitor the discussions in order to learn more about customer use of products, the effort becomes a lot more important than just saving money. It becomes an investment in the future of your products.

The people at eBay know they're running a service that puts people together with other people. They make it as easy as possible for those people to talk to each other (Figure 5.8).

As they put it, "Meet new friends, and chat about that one topic that consumes you, 24 hours a day. Or get help from other enthusiasts."

It's Organic

Ever try to grow your own organic garden? It's not a day at the park. Instead of feeding your plants out of a bottle, weeding them with a spray gun, and killing bugs and fungus from a bag of chemicals, you have to compost, pick,

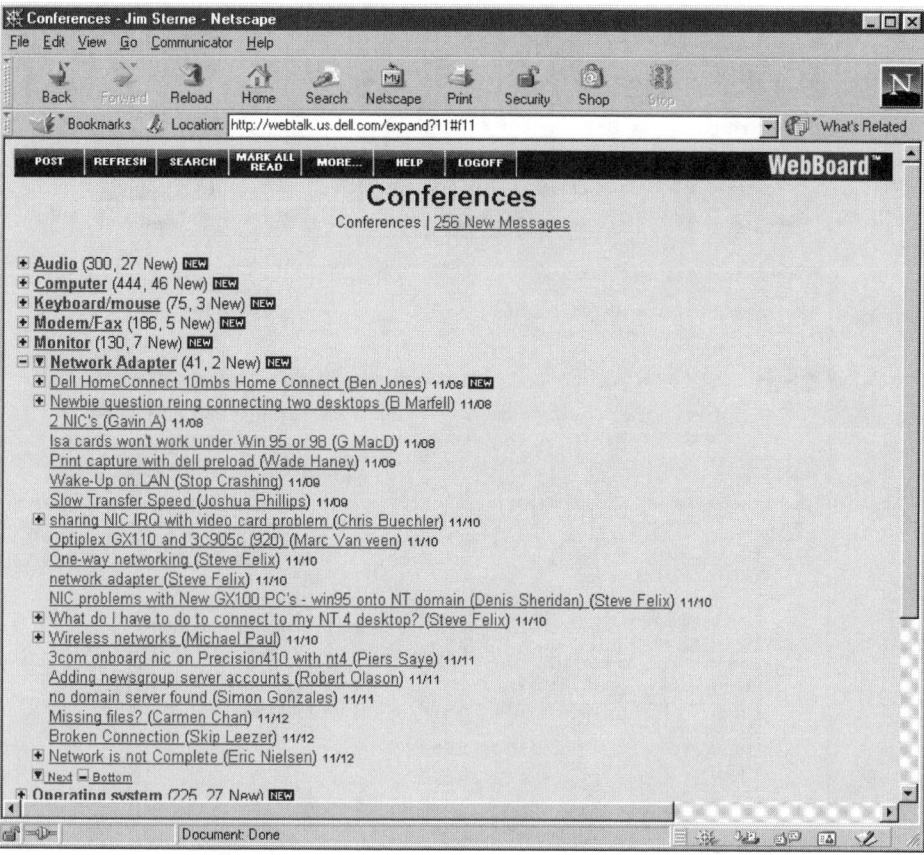

Figure 5.7 DellTalk invites customers to talk to customers.

squash, and wash by hand. Even with all that effort, there's no guarantee that the combination of seed, soil, and sun will result in a healthy plant that will bear fruit.

Getting people to post to a dozen discussions is not a minor task either. You could easily end up with a healthy number of categories suffering from an unhealthy amount of interchange.

The Usenet Newsgroups are out there for all to see. A discussion group on your Web site will only be seen by the people you notify. Plan on some time and budget to get the word out to engender conversation—even if you have to use the telephone to do it.

Wine Spectator magazine (www.winespectator.com) offers a place for people to post their comments (Figure 5.9), but carries it one very useful step further in order to keep people actively talking to each other.

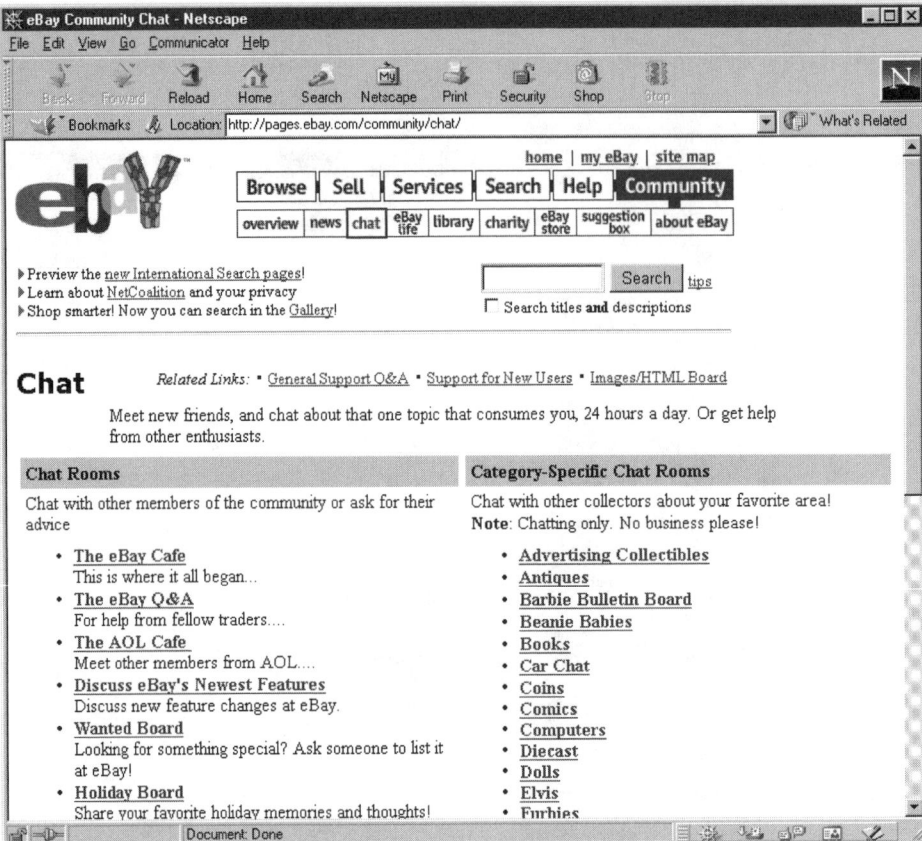

Figure 5.8 eBay offers lots of different areas where people can interact.

In their own words:

> This is where you get to be the wine critic, or the restaurant critic, or the reporter with a scoop. Pick your favorite topic and start contributing your opinions, discoveries, and tips. Please stick to the forum's topic—if your favorite subject isn't included, e-mail us a suggestion and we'll consider creating a new area for it.
>
> You can lurk to your heart's content, but to post a new message or reply you'll need to sign in. Every time you post, you'll have the option of requesting an e-mail notification when someone responds. The message you get will contain a link that you can click on to take you right to the response.

Pay Attention or Pay the Price

Whether public or private, you need to pay attention. It's quite possible to make the Pentium gaffe on your own site. This happens when somebody gets the idea to create a discussion area, but nobody is assigned to manage it.

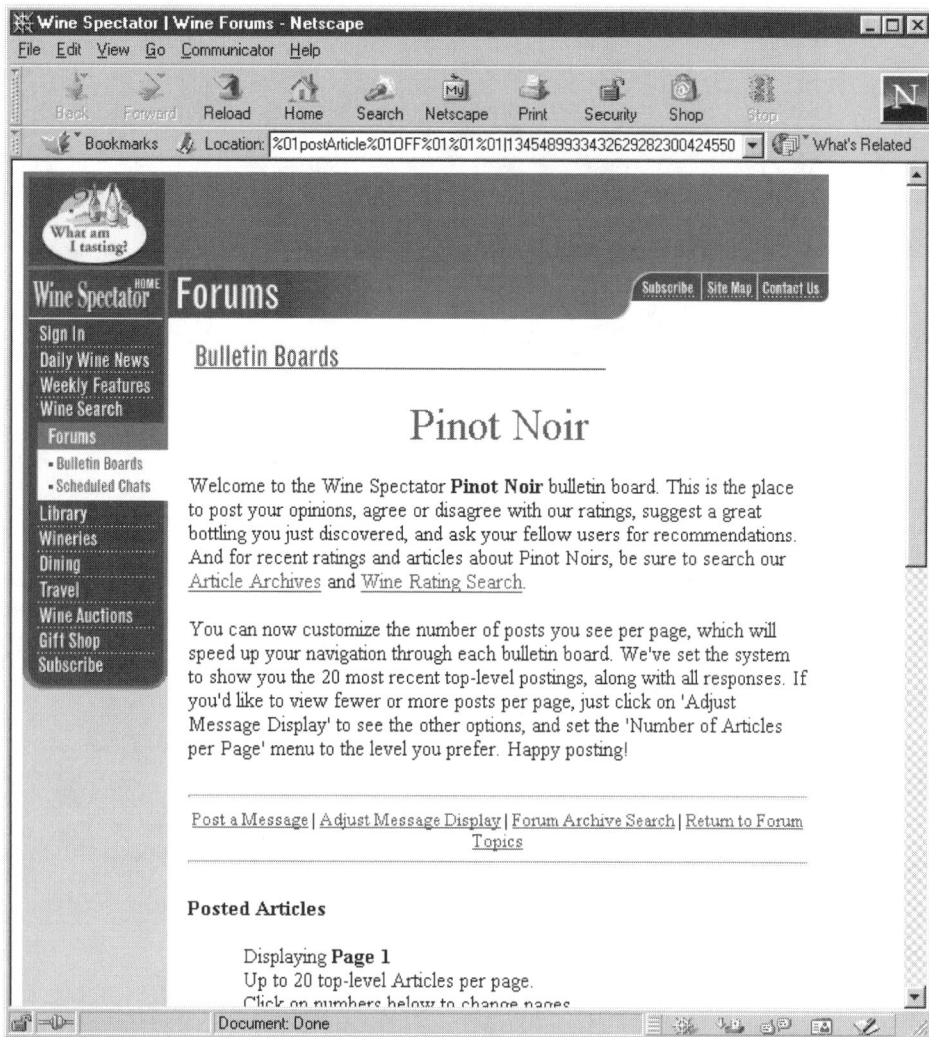

Figure 5.9 *Wine Spectator* posts comments from visitors and lets them know when somebody has an opinion about their opinion.

The names in the following forum exchange have been changed to protect everybody (including yours truly), but the following was taken from a Web site with a private discussion area. *Private* means that a password was necessary to get in.

```
Final Warning

This article submitted by xxx@xxx.com 10/22.

To: YYY Technical Support Re: YYY Technical Support

Okay, let me make this clear. This is not a threat. But if, by
Wednesday, I do not get a call from a Technical Support Technician, or
```

```
replied to me by e-mail, like I was promised LAST WEEK, I am calling the
Better Business Bureau and I'm asking for their help in resolving this
question of so-called support. It might end-up costing me a fortune in
long-distance, but your attitude is appalling. The only response I EVER
got from YYY on this page was the deletion of my previous messages,
because I mentioned the BBB. I've tried EVERYTHING to get in contact
with you people. When I succeed in talking to someone, I get brush-offs
and empty promises. I called the company directly, and got some lame
excuse about tech support being overwhelmed by requests for help with
Win95.. Unfortunately, the situation's been the same for A YEAR!!!! SO
WHERE IS THE HELP WITH YOUR PRODUCT?!?!?!?!?!?!

From a VERY angry customer, XXX
```

This was followed the next day by somebody a bit less perturbed but annoyed nonetheless:

```
Is YYY Monitoring this Forum?

This article submitted by zzz@zzz.com on 10/23.

I've seen all kinds of messages posted about problems with YYY products,
questions of availability, and general concerns about YYY support. But
nowhere do I see that someone from YYY is reading and responding to
them.

If there is no action, why should anyone post messages here? About the
only benefit I see is that user's complaints are voiced "locally" rather
than the more public Usenet. I'm really starting to wonder whether this
was the plan all along!
```

Finally, the original shouter was heard and reported it back to the group:

```
I GOT AN ANSWER!!!!!!!!!

This article submitted by xxx@xxx.com on 10/24.

Well, it took months, many hours on hold, lots of frustration, a long-
distance call to their corporate headquarters, and the mention of the
Better Business Bureau, but I finally got a letter (not even a form-
letter! :) ), from the director of Tech Supp. While it doesn't solve any
of my technical problems, it did address my frustration with the company.
So while their support is still blatantly lacking, I'll give 'em the
benefit of the doubt, and simply stay away from future YYY purchases (at
least until the support has improved). Happy surfing to all :)
```

A quick check back to that particular site revealed the following under "Members Only":

Reconstruction in Progress

The Members Only section is undergoing reconstruction and will be back online shortly. Please review the other active areas of the site, including the Special Offers and Hot Stuff.

Owners will [sic] technical questions can review the FAQs and contact information in the Technical Support section.

Don't be discouraged. There aren't a million cybersurfers planning your demise and posting ASCII art that spells out "Surrender Dorothy." But be forewarned. Keep in mind that this is like having your customer service calls all tied together. Everybody can hear each other's questions and problems. If you put them on hold, they can all talk to each other about how much they hate being on hold. The solution? Never put them on hold.

Printer or Publisher?

If you are a printer, your job is to put words on paper. You are not responsible for the words. You are merely providing a service and offering equal service to all who will pay. The newsgroups are printing presses. The only people responsible for the words that appear in them are the people who write those words.

But a publisher is responsible for the content. A publisher is an editor, deciding which words get published and which don't. A discussion that happens on your Web site is an uncomfortable mixture. It contains words that others have written, but that you are *publishing*. Just like the letters to the editor. That means you are responsible for the content. That means you must exercise some control over what is published and what gets flushed.

If some misguided miscreant decides to lambaste you and yours in a newsgroup using language that would make a sailor blush, the correct response is one of reasoned calm and solicitousness. Unless, of course, the antagonist has no point and is merely trolling for flames. Then the correct response is silence. Just let the other participants straighten out (or ignore) the evil one.

If some misguided miscreant decides to lambaste you and yours in a discussion on your own Web site, you have the editorial authority to simply not post the remarks. This may result in the offending party's becoming offended, running out to the public newsgroups, and becoming offensive. This is called whining. People reading the public newsgroups for serious business purposes can smell a whiner coming and cross the street to avoid him or her.

As an editor, you have saved your audience from having to make that decision. They weren't faced with the whiner in the first place. This is the sign of a good editor. Can you take editorial control too far? Just ask George Orwell. The advice? Be prudent, but don't be so controlling that it's obvious you're only there to blow the company horn.

Iron Fist or Velvet Glove?

A delicate balance is required to maintain an interchange that is healthy, valuable, and not so controlled as to be useless to your customers. You must edit with care.

The role of the editor has been vastly underrated in this world. It is only now that information is so painfully abundant that we have come to realize the need to have human filters to protect us from an onslaught of facts, figures, fashion, and foolishness. When you assume the mantle of editor, you must remember that your customers come first.

A ripping tirade on your company's poor practices posted on your site, or a diatribe outlining your latest atrocities, will make you look bad in the eyes of the public. Your customers may be incensed and send copies to your competitors. They may even decide to feed it directly to the press. But if you hide it, it will grow, Pentium-like in the dark, until it bursts into the public eye on the cover of *The Washington Post.*

And don't underestimate the power of your clients' combined intellect. If you hide, you will be found out. If you skirt an issue, you will be made a laughing stock. If you dissemble, you will be upbraided. If you lie, you will be turned into blackened toast by a furnace of flames.

On the other hand, if you freely disseminate everything and anything that comes your way, you're not providing much of an editorial service. So you must be moderate in your moderation. There is also some insight that can be borrowed from other forms of human interaction, such as the "tragedy of the commons," where all can take without giving.

Moderation in All Things—Social Skills

We turn briefly to the academic world for a look at group dynamics. In January of 1994, while at U.C.L.A., Peter Kollock and Marc Smith wrote "Managing the Virtual Commons: Cooperation and Conflict in Computer Communities." In this paper, they applied to electronic discussion groups the work done by Elinor Ostrom in her *The Logic of Collective Action: Public Goods and the Theory of Groups* (Harvard University Press, 1965).

The paper explains Ostrom's work:

> Ostrom studied a wide range of communities which had a long history of successfully producing and maintaining collective goods. The set of cases she examined include common forest and grazing grounds in Swiss and Japanese villages, fisheries in Canada and Sri Lanka, and irrigation systems in Spain and the Philippines. She identified a set of design principles that are features of communities which have successfully met the challenge of producing and maintaining collective goods despite the temptation to free-ride and without recourse to an external authority. In comparing the communities, Ostrom found that groups which are able to organize and govern themselves are marked by the following design principles:
>
> 1. Group boundaries are clearly defined.
> 2. Rules governing the use of collective goods are well matched to local needs and conditions.

3. Most individuals affected by these rules can participate in modifying the rules.

4. The right of community members to devise their own rules is respected by external authorities.

5. A system for monitoring members' behavior exists; this monitoring is undertaken by the community members themselves.

6. A graduated system of sanctions is used.

7. Community members have access to low-cost conflict resolution mechanisms.

Group Boundaries Are Clearly Defined

Kollock and Smith pointed out that the two main boundaries at work in newsgroups are the stated subject matter and the knowledge that "one will be interacting with others on a continual basis (which) can lead to the creation of reputations and serve as a powerful deterrent to short-run, selfish behavior."

When the topics discussed get too far away from the intended conversation, the solution is to create a new newsgroup and tighten the focus. The power of building a solid reputation is a major responsibility of the moderator. A good moderator wins respect and admiration as a voice of reason. A bad moderator is ignored or ridiculed. All participants know that their reputations are on the line, and that helps establish a social order.

Rules Governing the Use of Collective Goods Are Well Matched to Local Needs and Conditions

Ostrom argued that "this feature results in better designed rules because the individuals with the knowledge of the day-to-day workings of the group and the challenges the group faces could modify the rules over time to better fit local conditions."

As a moderator, you have to do your utmost to let the discussion evolve. If the crowd wants to discuss the same topic for months without complaint, it's not up to you to alter the course of the discussion just because you're tired of it.

If you see that others in the group are unhappy with the structure or the direction of the discussion, the way things are posted, or the time it takes to post, or even the format of the posts, be sure to include them in the process of changing the group, as brought up by items 3 and 4.

Most Individuals Affected by These Rules Can Participate in Modifying the Rules

The Right of Community Members to Devise Their Own Rules Is Respected by External Authorities

A System for Monitoring Members' Behavior Exists; This Monitoring Is Undertaken by the Community Members Themselves

As the host of this forum, you have one foot in the community and one outside of it. You are a participant with valuable information to share, but at the same time, you are stepping outside the discourse by being an external force. You are the mediator. You are the adjudicator. You call the shots. But it's critical that you are also a participant. If there's a question about a service; if there is a complaint about a policy; if there is a problem with a product; you are the one who has to find the answer, ease the procedure, and solve the problem. You will have to know where the answers lie.

If you choose to run multiple discussion areas on different topics, you might consider dividing these roles. One person can be responsible for playing the constabulary force on all of the groups to keep the conversation flowing and the constituents in line. That person furnishes support to the several topic experts who represent the company from a knowledge perspective. This way you can have order without compromising the veracity of your expert.

Overall, a discussion will be self-policing. If somebody complains that your chewing gum loses its flavor on the bedpost overnight, others will step in and either agree, disagree, suggest an alternative to the bedpost, or all of the above. The point is to start a discussion.

Ostrom's final two principles have to do with discipline:

A Graduated System of Sanctions Is Used

Community Members Have Access to Low-Cost Conflict Resolution Mechanisms

The simplest sanction in a group like this is the ridicule of associates. Of course, those who ridicule are setting themselves up for ridicule in return. It falls, then, to the moderator—you—to act as the cop on the beat. Low-cost is a nonissue from the customer perspective. You're there and they don't have to pay you. Cost is an issue on your end because it is a dirty job and somebody has to do it.

So how do you sanction people and resolve conflict? With care.

Slander, Libel, and Litigation

Steven Lieberman, an attorney specializing in First Amendment law, points out that the global reach of the Internet means added liability for U.S. companies that put information up on the Web: The defamation issue "has enormous economic implications for U.S. companies with assets overseas. It is theoretically possible for a company with a Web site accessible in Singapore to be sued in Singapore for defamation if someone puts up a message critical of the Singapore government. The same thing could happen in China, for that matter."

Investor's Business Daily, 27 Feb 96, as reported in EduPage (listproc@educom.unc.edu)

A Few Tips from the Trenches

Marisa Bowe, editor of *WORD* (www.word.com, Figure 5.10), had some words of advice for readers of SIMBA's *Online Tactics* about how to manage the free flow of ideas on a Web site.

Figure 5.10 WORD, a Web-based e-zine with a penchant for the eccentric, does its best to include its audience.

A Primer in Bulletin Board/Forum Management:

Moderator must be an exhibitionist. If the moderator adopts a style that is forthcoming and bold, it will encourage users to do the same.

Praise users when they talk. If the moderator responds regularly and uses language that is positive as reinforcement, participation is likely to increase.

"Be a mommy." Successful BBS (bulletin board) systems have been run by women, who tend to be more nurturing than men. Sometimes it requires coddling to get participation going.

Deliver content up front. Often the discussion content is buried within forum topics. That works against catching and engaging users' attention.

Carefully manage number of discussion threads. Too many topics can overwhelm users, while too little can underwhelm them.

SIMBA *Online Tactics,* January, 1996

People Love to Talk about Themselves

Everybody's favorite subject is themselves. If you want people to talk about your products, good or ill, don't ask them about your products. Ask them about their experience with your product. Ask them about how your products affected them, changed them, helped them, or exasperated them. Get them to participate.

Fishing for Compliments

Think about a product or service that you really like. Something that makes you feel smarter, happier, or just plain better off when you use it. Something you recommend without hesitation to colleagues, family, and the even the woman next to you on the plane.

What if you were surveyed by the company that produced this wonder of modern commerce? What could they ask to get you to say nice things?

What are you able to do now that you couldn't before?

How has your daily life been improved?

Why would you recommend this to your children/coworkers/friends?

Look for another twist on, "Please say something nice we can put in our brochure." Rather than ask for generic flattery and purple-dinosaur type compliments, ask your customer to think about the real value of the product:

If your boss asked you to justify the continued use of this product, what would you say to warrant the investment you've made?

The customer is not being asked to defend the product, but the use of the product. The customer is not being asked to think about what he or she likes about the product, but why it was a wise choice. In fact, the customers are being asked to defend themselves for using the product. This is a much more personal question than asking them to dream up nice things to say.

Begging for Guidance

Your customers will only appreciate your concern for their positive feelings about your products if you exhibit positive feelings about their concerns. But a little subtlety is a valuable tool in this case as well.

My all-time favorite question when interviewing customers for product endorsements puts just enough spin on the old "How do you like it?" to elicit thoughtful answers:

"If you had a magic wand and could make one or two improvements with a wave of the wand, what would they be?"

This is a much easier question to answer than, "What's wrong?" or, "How can we improve it?" This question empowers the customer to think of all the disappointments, all the impositions, and all the drawbacks in a positive light. You haven't asked the customer to complain; you've asked him or her to help. The customer is now free to say, "The best thing would be to get rid of that awful noise it makes," instead of being forced to say, "It's really noisy."

Different people respond in different ways according to the order in which these questions are asked. If you ask somebody to recommend the product to their boss, it makes them think about all of the positives. But if they are genuinely unhappy with it, this may not evoke much of a response at all. It may even cause them to say they should never have purchased it in the first place and come tomorrow morning, they're going to throw it out!

These people need to be given the magic wand first. They need a chance to vent their spleen and simply get their dissatisfaction off their chest. Only then will they be able to think about what commendable traits your product may have.

On the other hand, if they feel that your product was the reason for their meteoric rise in the corporate structure, you want them to focus on their joy and gratitude. Keep them happy as long as possible. *Then* hand them the wet noodle and ask for the forty lashes.

Tools You Can Use

No, it's not necessary to take every post and hand code it in HTML. No, it's not necessary to write a CGI script to do it automatically. You can buy one. They're not expensive. They're worth mentioning simply because features change so fast, that by the time you read this there will be vendors out there with Psychic Inference Engines in Simulated Kilocycle Yak Sessions (PIE in the SKY).

You could follow Dell's lead and use WebBoard from O'Reilly. Here's how O'Reilly describes it on its site (webboard.oreilly.com):

> WebBoard is frequently used to provide online customer service or technical support. Conferences are set up for specific product activities. Customers can then post a question. Other participants can answer or comment from their own experience, or a staff member can provide an official answer. The WebBoard Administrator may choose to moderate some of these conferences to ensure that solutions are proper. Once a solution is posted, it's available to other users who may have similar questions. In fact, rather than repeating the same information over and over, support staff can point users to WebBoard conferences for answers to questions. WebBoard's message searching functions quickly locate information on a given topic, posted by a specific user, or from a specific date.

On the other hand, you might want to head over to CNET (www.cnet.com) to discuss the whole thing (Figure 5.11).

Moving to a List

If you find yourself dealing with unhappy customers, you may want to use a private listserver. A listserver is software that will send the same message to everybody on your e-mail list. It can be engineered to let everybody post to everybody, or for only the moderator to post. A list differs from a newsgroup in its immediacy. People have to go look at a newsgroup. If they subscribe to a list, the posts are delivered directly to their e-mail in-box. Subscribing and unsubscribing are as easy as sending an e-mail message and are usually free.

Lists are easy to set up and make customers feel special. Ask a select group of people to give you advice on your products and services and they'll reward you with their loyalty and their opinion. They pay the bills, so you should take an active interest in how they feel.

Good Moderators Are Essential

In April of 1995 Sara Kim, a graduate student in educational technology at the University of Washington, and Vivian Hon, completing her Ph.D. in economics at the University of North Carolina, wrote and posted a paper on "user-oriented, user-centered listserv operation from the perspective of user feedback, system enhancement, the roles of administrators, organizational dynamics, and monitoring tools."

Writing about a listserv project they managed called PHNLINK at the Department of Population, Health, and Nutrition of the World Bank, Kim and Hon stressed the need for good administration:

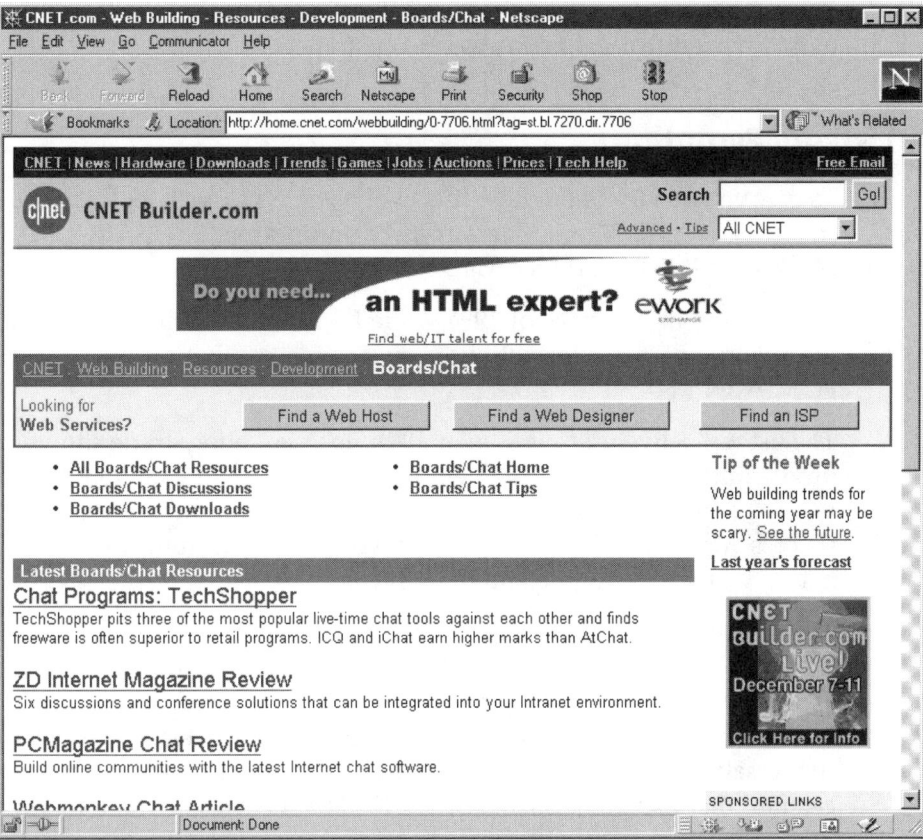

Figure 5.11 CNET is an excellent source of technical information—even from other information seekers.

In order to serve as a vital human link between the user and the system, listserv administrators must go beyond the realm of technical support to actively seek user feedback, negotiate with system developers to improve technical features that reflect user needs, and keep abreast of changing technology that has implications for improving services. Also, the administrators should follow other relevant electronic and non-electronic resources that may present opportunities for collaboration and resource sharing with other information providers. More difficult challenge for the administrator lies in shaping the listserv as a participatory tool that fosters network opportunities among the users themselves for information sharing as well as collaborative initiatives. PHNLINK surveys revealed users' desire to network with other subscribers but the answers to concerns for unsolicited message traffic remain unresolved. One suggestion may be to create a sub listserv forum among PHNLINK subscribers who wish to carry out discussions on topics important in their work without involving the entire subscription base.

The moderator must play chief cook, bottle washer, mommy, and cheerleader to turn a list into a valuable asset for customers.

A Listserv Evolution

To give you an idea about how lists evolve, here's a quick look at three lists I've subscribed to: High Tech Marketing Communicators (HTMARCOM), Internet-Marketing (INET), and Free Market.

It all started in February of 1994 while I was out scouring the landscape and the cyberscape for information on marketing on the Internet. I came across HTMARCOM.

The list was a lively discussion of all things marketing; trade shows, brochure production, product management issues, and a great deal about how to convince the engineer/founder of the company that marketing was critical to his success. Moderated by Kim Bayne of wolfBayne Communications, the subject matter was wide-ranging and of high value.

Kim chose a relaxed moderation approach. Anybody could subscribe (as is true with most lists), and anybody could post. They could post whatever they wanted. Kim would pop up now and again with admonitions about flaming or advertising. She would steer the conversation instead of control it. If the conversation drifted too far afield, she would gently nudge it back with suggestions on other subjects to discuss. Kim Bayne—listserv den mother.

In the summer of 1994, Bayne tried hard in her amiable and humorous way to slow down the number of posts about how to do marketing on the Internet. All anybody wanted to talk about, it seemed, was how to get a server running and where to find the shareware and what techniques could be used to bring in more customers. Delighted with the last subject, but none too thrilled with the technical issues, Bayne finally put her foot down.

She invited anybody on the list to start another. Please. Take this technical discussion off into another corner and go for it. Within two weeks, on July 22, the Internet Marketing List was born. The task was taken up by Glenn Fleishman, one of the principals at the then-nascent Point of Presence Company, a Web presence provider that wasn't quite online yet.

As a result, the conversation on Internet Marketing took a sharp turn and lodged itself firmly at popco.com. Meanwhile, HTMARCOM went back to enjoying its customary traffic and discussions of interest to all in high-tech marketing. Bayne managed to keep things intact without resorting to drastic measures.

The Internet Marketing List (www.i-m.com, Figure 5.12) was designed to be a strictly moderated list from the get-go. This list was set up so that only one person—Fleishman—could post. Instead of suggesting that some posts were ill-suited, inflammatory, redundant, or spiteful, Fleishman simply didn't post them to the list. All messages were sent to him, and he alone was the arbiter of what would go out to subscribers and what would not.

This approach was discussed for a while on the list. Participants all agreed that there was tremendous value in letting everybody have their say. But Fleish-

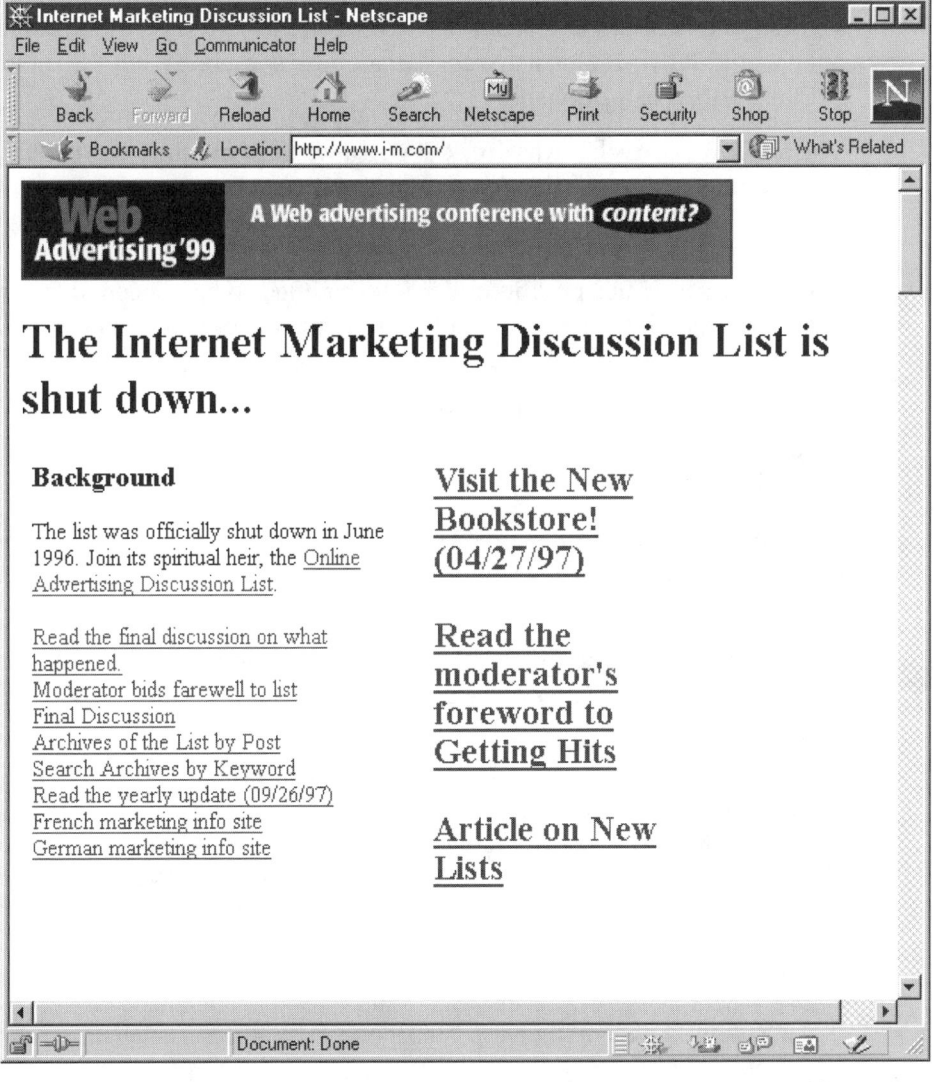

Figure 5.12 The Internet Marketing List was a high-quality, tightly moderated list, and the archives are still available.

man was not moved. He maintained strict control. Most felt that Fleishman was providing a precious service by sifting the wheat from the chaff. But there were some who got downright annoyed.

It was censorship, they said. It was anti-Internet, they said. Information wants to be free, they said. And Fleishman said no. Fleishman said he was running this list and this was the way he wanted to run it and if the annoyees didn't like it they could start their *own* list. And they did.

The Free Market list was born into the world with one rule: no rules. Anybody could post anything and have their place in the sun (except advertising). If you wanted to talk about it, ask about it, argue about it, the Free Market list manager would let you. This list was managed by somebody who wanted to be a printer instead of a publisher.

The traffic was drivel. It was dreck. It was a waste of my time and precious Internet resources. It was a free-for-all. The death-knell sounded when I received over 200 posts in two days about posters' rights to post advertising if they wished. Unbelievably embarrassing rhetoric poured forth about free speech from one earnest and prolific writer who claimed to have been an attorney. He proudly signed his own name and told people to come to his new mall on the Internet which was going to change the way people shopped forever.

I was reminded of the advice that one should hold one's tongue and be thought an idiot, rather that wagging one's tongue and proving it. I unsubscribed.

If you or somebody you assign is going to take on the laboring oar of list moderation, do it with kindness, with firmness, and with your intentions made clear.

Richard Hoy, director of community development for ClickZ (www.clickz .com), started up the ClickZ discussion list in June 1999 and posted this article to kick it off:

> For the last three years, I ran one of the most popular discussion lists in the online advertising industry. Seventy-three-hundred members strong, we shared and debated ideas nearly every business day. When we got together, the collective industry knowledge transcended anything you could find in a textbook or a magazine. Advice was given, business was done, relationships were formed, and knowledge was advanced.
>
> That's the power of a discussion list.
>
> But I have to admit that discussion lists can sometimes suck badly, too. Threads can go on endlessly, debates can degenerate into verbal assaults, and low-value information can quickly become the norm. Moderating for three years taught me a few things about why this is.
>
> First, every group needs a leader. A discussion list moderator has got to take the lead. He or she has to shape the editorial direction and rally members around issues.

Relying on such issues to emerge organically from the group leads to sporadic quality in the discussion.

Secondly, you have to make it easy for members to follow what's going on. That means presenting the discussion and its context, in convenient, digestible, and quickly accessible formats.

Thirdly, every industry has "closet posters" who can offer great information, but won't post because posting to a discussion list takes time. A moderator has to find these people and help them "come out of the closet" by making it both easy and beneficial for them to voice opinions.

And finally, members have to be part of the decisions that affect the evolution of the list. If the moderator isn't in tune with the values of the members, everyone leaves, and there's no more list.

Together with Andy and Ann, my goal at ClickZ is to take the principles I've outlined above and build a new forum for discussing online marketing unlike any other in this industry.

Here are some of my ideas:

1. I've enlisted the help of several industry people across a wide range of disciplines to keep the information content high.

2. The list will come in three versions: digest, post-by-post and weekly summary.

3. We will have a formal topic each week, in addition to topics raised by the list membership.

4. Every post will have links to ancillary information for helping those unfamiliar with the issue come up to speed.

As a real show of his list-craft, Richard created this reply for when new participants subscribe:

```
Hello --

Welcome to the post-by-post version of ClickZ's Discussion list.

KEEP THIS MESSAGE!! It's your guide to using (and getting off of) this
list.

First things first.

You joined this list under the address:

jsterne@targeting.com

You can always remove yourself instantly by clicking on this URL:

http://um5.revnetexpress.net/U/xxxx

If you have trouble unsubscribing using the above method, e-mail me
directly at: richard@clickz.com and I'll fix you up manually.

PURPOSE OF THIS LIST

We founded The ClickZ Discussion List to provide a forum in which
industry professionals can share the good, the bad and the ugly of the
online marketing industry as it stands today.
```

THIS FORUM IS AD SUPPORTED

Understand that we can make this free to you because the costs are underwritten by sponsors. My solemn promise to you is that we will NEVER sell your information to anyone. In fact, no one outside of ClickZ will ever see it. But we will put text ads into the mailings and, from time to time, send messages to this list on behalf of our advertisers.

If you are an online marketer and you are upset about our policy of sending advertisements, you need to find another list and probably another profession.

OTHER VERSIONS OF THIS LIST

There are actually two other versions of this list. The information is identical. The only difference is the way we deliver it.

You're getting the POST-BY-POST version now, meaning you get each individual message as I approve it. It's more e-mail (about eight per day), but there are a couple of advantages. First, you get the information quicker. The digest can lag behind a day. Second, if you can filter your e-mail, you can filter each message into a mailbox and see, all at once, the subject lines of each message. It can make reading and responding a quicker chore.

There is a DIGEST version, which means you get one mailing each business day containing all the e-mails sent into the list for that day.

And finally, there is a WEEKLY SUMMARY version. This one comes once per week and only contains a one sentence summary of each post, with a link to the full post.

If you want to switch, here is what you have to do:

1.) Unjoin the POST-BY-POST version by clicking below

http://um5.revnetexpress.net/U/xxxxx

2.) On the page now in your browser, fill out the form and select the version you want to change to.

It's clumsy, I know. We are working on a better solution.

RULES OF THIS LIST

This is a professional forum. More importantly, it is an advanced professional forum. The topics we discuss here are the kind of things that people who've been in the business a long time discuss. Moreover, it's moderated—which means nothing gets through without my approval. I know it sounds snobbish, but if I don't keep the discussion advanced and concise, all experienced people leave because they are bored. And that lowers the value for everybody on the list.

The rules:

1.) Sign your posts with at least your full name. I don't send through posts from people I can't identify.

2.) Don't send through stuff that is obviously self-serving. By that I mean posts completely lacking of any substantive advice. It is perfectly

OK to push a company or product in which you have a vested interest, as long it is relevant to the discussion and you give good advice—meaning pros and cons. Everyone hates the pushy sales person who promises the world. Don't be that person. Which brings me to rule #3...

3.) If you have an affiliation with a company or product you are praising, state it up front. Finding out after the fact that you get a kickback every time you recommend a company trashes your credibility with everyone.

4.) On the flip side, don't trash your competitors on this list either. It is a clever tactic, used especially in forums like these right before one's competitor goes IPO. It has happened to me once. Now that I know the telltale signs, it ain't going to happen to me again. So don't even try.

5.) Don't send through copyrighted materials—like news articles. It gets me in trouble. Send either a quote, with the source, or the URL.

6.) This is a personal pet peeve of mine—limit your signatures to six lines or less. It's kinda pathetic when your sig file is bigger than your comments.

7.) Remember that this is a public forum. When you put something out there, everyone can see it all—including your e-mail address.

If you have a question about the industry that is entry-level, or you are unsure about a topic you would like to introduce, write me at richard@clickz.com and ask. I know I sound like a bit of a hard-ass based on the rules above, but I'm really a nice guy.

POSTING A QUESTION/RESPONSE TO THIS LIST

Here's how you respond to a message:

1.) Hit "reply" in your e-mail program.

2.) Delete everything except the point(s) in the message to which you are responding. (In other words, don't send me the whole freaking message back as a reply.)

3.) Type in your response(s).

4.) Hit send.

5.) Enjoy.

If you want to send a comment/question directly to the list, send it to: discussion@clickz.com.

IF ALL ELSE FAILS...

Contact me directly at: richard@clickz.com. Or give me a call at: 978.749.3737. I really am a nice guy. And I respond well to Simpsons references and free beer.

best,
richard

This sort of attention to detail makes it possible for people joining the list to know exactly what to expect. They get the benefit of Richard's attention to the process, his attention to the mechanism, and his attention to the social graces necessary to be a good member of the community.

Tracking the Public Lists

Just as you need to track what people are saying about you on the newsgroups, you should be aware of which public lists are singing your praises or decrying your duplicity. Take a look at the Liszt Directory of E-Mail Discussion Groups (www.liszt.com, Figure 5.13). There you can search through what may well be "the world's largest directory of mailing lists (by a long shot!)—90,095 independently managed lists."

Closed Discussion Lists

A Usenet newsgroup might be read by anybody. A public list might be subscribed to by anybody. Access to a bulletin board hosted on your own Web site can be controlled by using passwords. By the same token, a private list can be created by invitation only.

Once a year, I join a very small list for a couple of weeks. As a panel member on the Tenagra Awards for Internet Marketing Excellence jury, I discuss the merits of various Web sites with other Internet marketing mavens. It's a very interesting list while it lasts and is limited to only a handful of participants.

Another private list I belong to includes my father, my brother, his wife and son, my sister, my brother-in-law, my niece, and my uncle. It comes in very handy when trying to decide where we're going to get together for Thanksgiving and Christmas. Clearly this is not a list that should be open to all.

One of the most cost-effective uses for listserv software is a focus group. Instead of flying a cross section of customers to town, putting them up at a hotel, feeding them, and locking them in a small, airless room for hours and hours until they tell you what you want to hear, get them to participate online.

Each individual gets to hear what the others have to say and can comment. Nobody is restricted to a certain place or time. The logistical cost is as close to zero as you can get. You also have the advantage of running as many simultaneous lists as you wish and segmenting them ad infinitum.

Group dynamics change in an online environment. Lee Sproull and Sara Kiesler conducted a series of experiments at Carnegie Mellon University to compare how a group interacts online versus in person. "Using a network induced the participants to talk more frankly and more equally," noted Sproull and Kiesler. "Instead of one or two people doing the talking as happens in

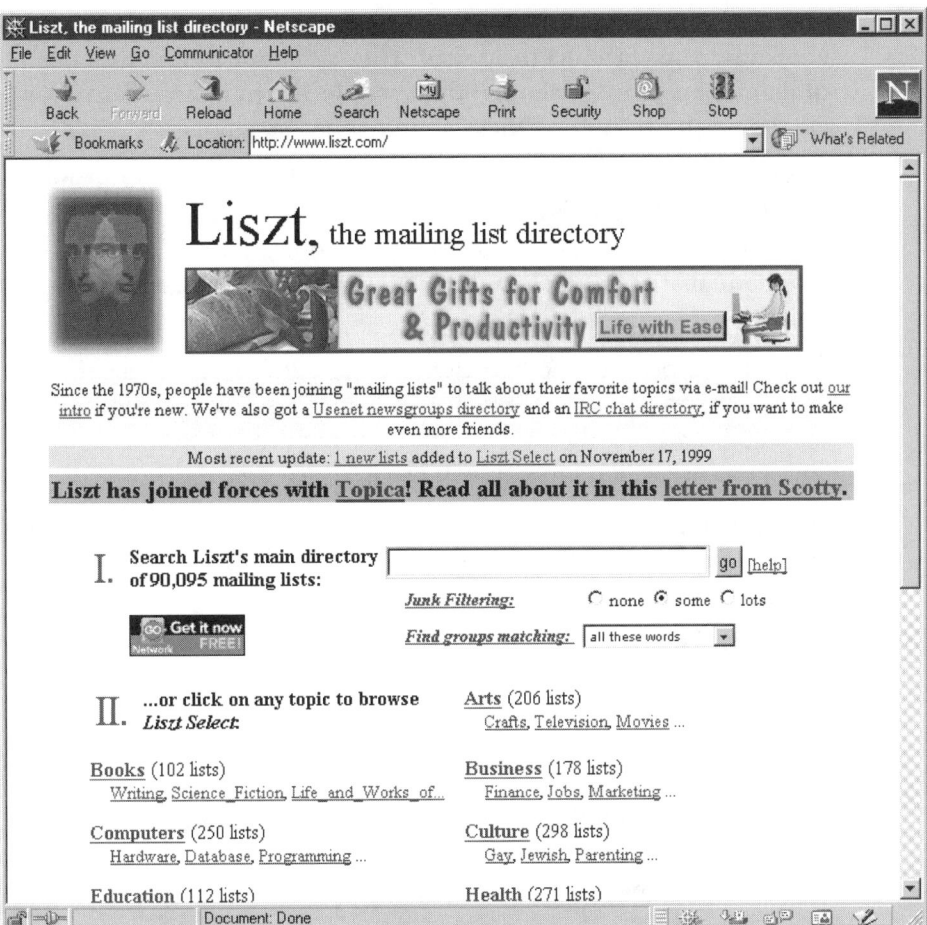

Figure 5.13   The Liszt Directory of E-Mail Discussion Groups enables you to hunt for the lists that may include talk of your company.

many face-to-face groups, everyone had a more equal say. Furthermore, networked groups generated more proposals than did traditional ones."

Sproull and Kiesler also discovered that the electronic medium flattens hierarchies and brings everybody to a universal level of status. Without the extraneous input of clothing, height, weight, age, or accent, people were much more comfortable speaking their minds.

Rational Evangelists

Ron Richards of ResultsLab (www.resultslab.com) describes himself as a persuasion engineer. I've seen him work, and the description is accurate. One of the methods he uses to collect the right information up front is to contact a company's "rational evangelists." According to Richards, these are the people who know your product inside out. They use your product so much that they sometimes know more about it than you do. Getting these particular people in one room is hard. Getting them on the same list is not.

Once on the list, they will brag about how well they've done using your products. They will boast about how they used your product for things it was never intended to do. They'll one-up each other with a list of the suggestions they made that were implemented by your firm. And then they'll get down to business.

These are the people who know what color your merchandise should be. They know how long a customer can wait before a serviceperson shows up. They can tell you with certainty how much is required to keep in stock. Get them talking to each other and you will learn a great deal.

Of course, when you get a group of experts in a "room" together, you have to be ready for the evolution of the social interaction.

From Introductions to All-Out Attack

Your rational evangelists will begin the conversation with introductions, of course. What companies they work for, what jobs they have, how they are using your products, the usual.

Then they'll brag a little bit about how well they've done using your products. How they managed to move up the corporate ladder because of how smart they were implementing your services.

They'll argue a bit about the best ways to make use of your goods and services, but nothing really hostile. At first. Next, you can expect them to take sides and form small cliques around the *right* way to best take advantage of your offerings.

Eventually, one of them will break from the crowd in order to ask a question. They'll rely on the kindness of these former strangers and reach out for help. Now sit back and watch the whole group turn on a dime from a contentious, splintered, alienated set of subgroups into one focused self-help support group.

The very same ego motivation that caused the participants to take sides suddenly prompts them to show off their individual abilities to help the less fortunate with their wisdom. This spawns new discussions about the finer point of getting the most out of what you have to sell. Until the Big Change happens.

Somebody, at some point, is going to post a question. Somebody, at some point, is going to express concern. Somebody, at some point, is going to describe a problem they have that will ring true to everybody involved with harmonic resonance. Now sit back and watch the whole group turn on a dime from a focused self-help support group to a classic mob. A mob out for blood. Yours.

When it is perceived that they are all having the same problem and you are the cause, they will light the torches and storm the castle in the rain.

This is when you know you have won.

If you maintain your composure, wade through the very first round of invective, and welcome their comments with open arms, you will be able to turn this angry mob into the most powerful product development team you've ever worked with.

They are smart. They are motivated. They know more about how to use your products than any other group of people in the world, and they are there to help you make your products better. They are there to help you improve your services so they can get more out of them, use more of them, and recommend them to new customers. This is a win-win.

Special-Interest Groups

Nothing says that your experts all have to be on the same list. You have multiple products? Make multiple lists. You have customers whose needs vary by geography? Different lists. Language? Income? Distribution channel? The only things that will inhibit the apportionment of your lists into tighter and tighter subject matter concentrations are the number of customers willing to talk about such a focused topic and the number of people you have to manage the conversations.

Don't be myopic about the subject matter, either. Bring large-industry-related topics to the floor. Talk about competitors. Discuss your company's methods as well as output. You can learn a lot from your customers, your suppliers, and your business partners.

> Community: a social group sharing common characteristics or interests and perceived or perceiving itself as distinct in some respect from the larger society within which it exists.
> *Webster's Encyclopedic Unabridged Dictionary of the English Language,* 1989

Private Conversations (When to Move Them to E-Mail)

There may come a time in open discussions when it might be wise for a quick sidebar. Just a few words on the q.t. to diffuse a situation, calm a nerve, or avoid an unpleasant scene. Touchy subjects can crop up quickly when you have customers conversing.

Pricing is always a potential powder keg. Whether you price by territory, by volume, or by negotiation, it's sure to be a sticky wicket if customers start comparing notes. Policies in general can vary from customer to customer and should be held out for one of those sideline chats.

Then there are those people who just don't get along well with others. The whiners of the world have to be dealt with gently and those who easily take or give offense need offline counsel. The worst offenders may need to be fired. Fire a customer? Absolutely. When one person is taking up a significant amount of customer service time, it's time to cut your losses.

Live and In Person

The Web is absolutely tops from a company's perspective. You create it, it serves, and all of your customers are happy. You add a few pages, and all of your customers are happier. It's the perfect match, and every time a customer comes to the site, the company saves oodles of money by not answering the phone.

What? It's not happening that way at your company? You say your Web site has caused people to call you for help *more* often? They go to your site, learn a lot, and then call with really *tough* questions? You think it was better in the old days when you could answer a few questions and they'd be satisfied, but now they're more demanding than ever? Welcome to twenty-first century customer service.

If I walk into a store and the clerk ignores me for five minutes, and then knows nothing about the items on offer, I leave, hoping I'll find a smarter clerk there the next time. But hand me a mouse and my whole demeanor changes. I expect every Web site I visit to have a user interface as easy to use, a selection as extensive, and a response time as fast as Amazon.com. Why? Because Amazon didn't just set the standard for online bookstores, it set the standard for the whole Internet.

Customer expectation inflation is growing faster than any Web wrangler can manage. Customers count on their computers to work and they don't tolerate it well when things don't happen exactly as expected and in less than an instant.

The solution, for those of us who cannot convince our board of directors to spend more on Web development and promotion than our total company income like Amazon does, is to offer the customer an alternative. The only alternative that has the best shot at turning a browser into a buyer or at mollifying an unhappy customer is live contact with actual human beings.

Oh sure, you could hire Andrette from Big Science (www.bigscience.com), but that's merely computer-aided-surfing—a database-managed conversation between a customer and your Web site. I'm talking about real people. Operators standing by. Knowledgeable folks to field questions and help customers in their time of need.

The first option that comes to mind is to let customer and company communicate through their computers. Most machines shipping these days have microphones in them. Maybe it's time to take advantage of them.

From the customer's perspective, voice-over-IP is not quite ready for prime time on the Internet yet. Sure, voice-over-IP (using the Internet in place of the phone system) is great for tight budgets looking to stay in touch with the old folks in the old country. We can expect it to be junior's favorite way to reach out and put the touch on Dad from the college dorm. But for serious customer support in a professional environment, consistent bandwidth in the Internet cloud is not quite up to professional standards. The aggravation just isn't worth the choppy value. While we wait for new breakthroughs in voice compression technologies, many people are turning to chat.

Chatting It Up on the Web

One of the first methods of communication on the Internet was via the Unix TALK command. Very simple—you type in the command and your buddy's ID, and an invitation to converse popped up on his screen. Once he "picked up the phone," you could trade sentences back and forth.

Then somebody got wise and figured out how to make it a conference call. They named this new ability Internet Relay Chat (IRC). IRC allows multiple individuals to type a live conversation. Imagine placing a microphone at each table in a crowded bar and having the conversations transcribed in chronological order. Person A may make a comment which person B responds to, while persons C and D intersperse their own line of discussion. To make things more confusing, D, C, and all the way through Z can comment on anybody else's comments. This method of communication can be a lot of fun like a parlor game is fun, but it creates havoc among those wishing to do business this way.

Chats can work well when highly moderated, like a call-in radio show. Somebody screens the calls and forwards the best questions and comments to the discussion leader or the interviewee. A managed conversation ensues.

But the best uses of chat capabilities fall into two categories: letting people post their thoughts about very specific topics, and one-to-one chats. This former type of live interaction with other customers is fine when the topic is narrow and timely. But the latter type of chat—the one-to-one communication—is turning out to be a very powerful customer service tool online.

The customer service page at www.1800flowers.com lists three ways to get in touch with this business:

1. Connect to our Online Customer Service eQ&A Chat.
2. E-mail us a completed Customer Service Inquiry Form.
3. Call us toll-free at 1-800-468-1141.

1-800-flowers' customers are making buying decisions in a matter of minutes—and not many minutes at that. So a quick answer, without having to hang up the modem and pick up the phone and wait on hold, is very attractive. Using software from eShare (www.eshare.com), 1-800-flowers gives customers the ability to get those answers (Figure 5.14).

But the attraction goes both ways. The customer service reps at 1-800-flowers find they can respond to four or five chat sessions at the same time. Just like master chess players in the park, these customer care personnel can read a question, answer it, and go on to the next and the next and the next before the first customer's reply appears. In the long run, they are more efficient than over the phone and serve their customers better.

Chat's a Money Saver and Money Maker

It turns out that customers not only prefer the chat capability; it's less expensive for the company. Peppers and Rogers (the people at www.1to1.com who coined the term *one-to-one marketing*) studied 1-800-flowers and discovered that answering customers' questions via chat was 30 percent less expensive than e-mail. That's a sizable savings, but it's even more sizable when compared to answering the telephone. Not only that, the number of e-mails went down—by 25 percent.

And it's not just for flower buyers making low-cost decisions in a hurry. Hewlett Packard, Gateway computers, and Mail Boxes Etc. have found eShare's tools to be just what the customer ordered. Are they doing it just because it saves them money? No—there's also the fact that almost 50 percent of the people that NFO Interactive (www.nfow.com) surveyed said they would buy more if they could get some simple answers in real time.

Igocorp.com is a Web site for road warriors. The folks there sell personal digital assistants and all that goes with them. They found that adding a live chat capability to their sites didn't just increase the number of sales; it also increased their size. Ken Hawk, chief energizing officer at Igocorp.com, says that the average order size jumped 12 percent after installing a chat package from FaceTime

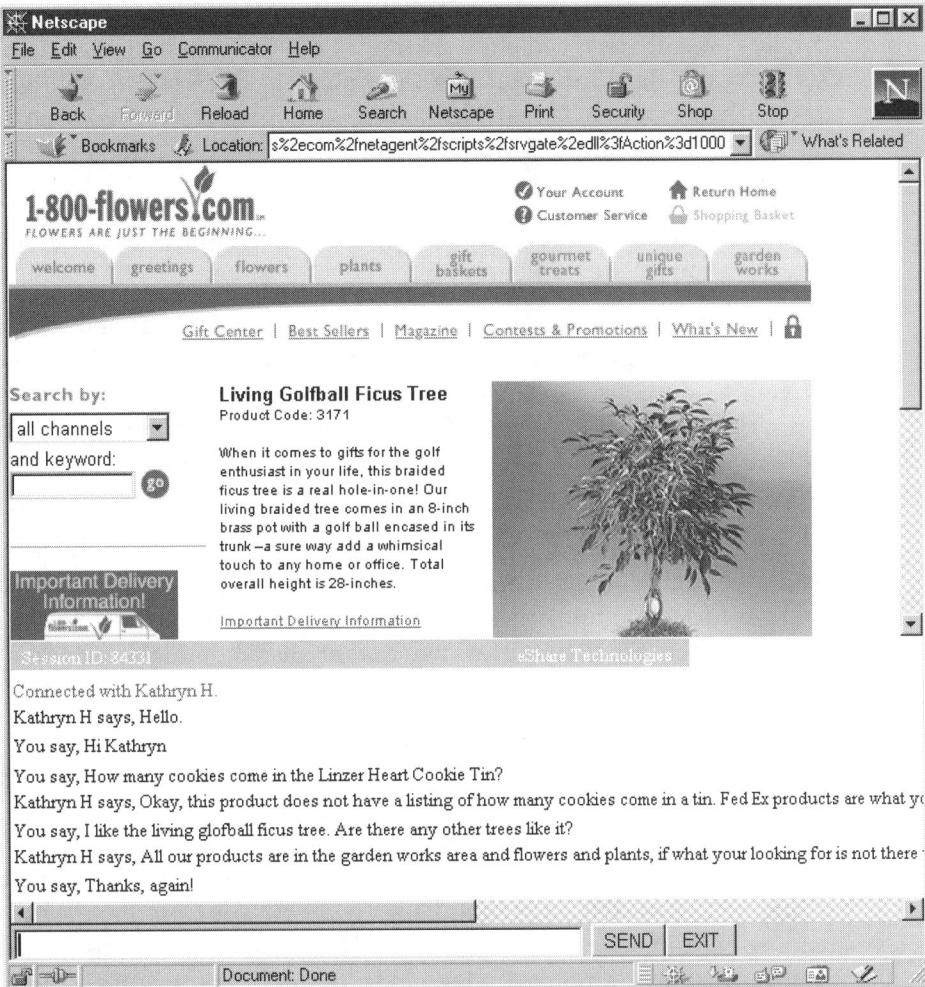

Figure 5.14   1-800-flowers found chat software from eShare lowered their cost of support.

(www.facetime.com). "We try to cater to business travelers," says Hawk, "and they need help when they're on the road. Sitting in a hotel room with a single-line phone means they have to hang up their modem in order to call the 800 number. We decided it was up to us to make it easier for them."

It's true, people still like to talk to people. Yes, I know it said that package would be delivered within three days, but I want reassurance. I want to hear the confidence level in somebody's voice when they say, "It will be there in three days." Do they sound like it happens all the time? Do they sound hopeful? Wistful? Amused?

In the old days you got a phone call asking if you got the fax the caller had just sent. I've actually received a fax asking if I got the e-mail they sent. June 1999 was still early days for e-vendors to implement live chat capability on their sites. Early enough days that *The New York Times* thought it was newsworthy that 911gifts.com, eToys, Furniture.com, and HP had all added live people to their Web strategy.

People want reassurance, and yes, they do have that one last question. Sometimes it's a tough one, sometimes not.

Be prepared, however, for customers who are both dumber and smarter than you'd expected. Many incoming questions will run the low-IQ gamut from navigation questions, "Where do I find your return policy?" to computer questions, "How do I print out your page if I don't have a printer?" Customer service on a Web site looks a lot more like technical support than customer service in the call center.

The other side of the coin sees customers getting smarter at the same time. They are learning all about your products and your company on your Web site. They are self-taught. They know more now than they did a few years ago. "Our customers are better informed, and are asking a higher tier of question when they do write or call in," says Peter Corless, content manager for Cisco Systems' Web site (www.cisco.com).

As a result, customer service reps have to be better informed, and better connected to the systems and people who have the answers. "The Cisco channel and support representatives have to step back from controlling—or bottle-necking—customer transactions," says Corless. "Instead, they must become facilitators and escalation points. They need education on the mechanism the customer is using to obtain self-service. The need to learn it inside and out— from the customer's point of view and the finer details of how the machine operates under the hood. They do not need to be breathing encyclopedia volumes, but rather reference librarians."

Phil Gibson at National Semiconductor was surprised by one aspect of live chat. "People in the call center like it better. Answering the phone is emotionally grueling. People call when they have a tough question or they're upset about something. When agents stay focused and are backed by good tools, they can answer 400 e-mails a day. But answering e-mail is sort of boring. You answer one question after the next and just keep plodding through the list."

But, according to Phil, chat is different. "It's more lively. It's interactive. There's a person on the other side of the screen waiting for an answer. Agents who are bouncing between screens—between conversations—are more animated, they're more upbeat. It's more of a challenge in a way that makes the job more interesting." That's why rotating people from one task to another is important.

"National Semi's people find chat more rewarding, too, because they can solve problems faster," says Phil. When you're on the phone, you can hem and haw only so much while trying to remember or find the right answer in a database. But in a chat session, you can focus all your energy on finding multiple solutions and choosing just the right one. If you are silent for a full minute during a chat session, it's no big deal. Try that on the phone and you have to learn how to search while saying inane things like, "Still checking. Won't be a moment."

When you look at software to handle online chat with your customers, look for features similar to those you'd expect in a phone system, such as the ability to route e-mails based on subject or content or sender (like Caller ID), or the ability to have two people on the line at the same time (conference call).

You want to give people as many ways to interact with the company as there are ways people want to interact. Some like to talk, some like to e-mail, some like to chat. What happens when you get somebody that likes to do all of the above?

Integration Is Critical

One of the major reasons e-mail must be answered promptly is that people have no patience. It's that customer expectation inflation thing again. After writing out a nice, long explanation of their problem and hitting the Send button, customers sometimes take a deep breath, pat themselves on the back for a job well-done, and then realize that they really do need an answer right now. Whatever is bothering them just stays at the top of their minds, so they pick up the phone. While on hold, they surf your Web site hoping the answer really was there all along.

The people at ServiceSoft Technologies (www.servicesoft.com) think they have an answer. A customer's e-mail inquiry can be deleted from the ServiSoft E-mailContact queue if it finds the right answer in the ServiSoft Web Advisor system, which guides customers, step-by-step, to the information they need.

Proactive Can Be Perilous

"Be Proactive" said the banner over the icontact.com Internet World exhibit hall booth. I was skeptical. "Be Uniquely Proactive," said the brochure I was handed. I must have scowled.

"But isn't that the equivalent of snooping and then real-time spamming? Doesn't that fly in the face of netiquette and the fact that people are online to avoid being harangued by salespeople?" I asked.

"Depends on what your site is all about," replied the suited salesman with a voice loaded with the fact that he'd been asked the same thing 23 times an hour, 8 hours a day, for the last 3 days. Nevertheless, he was still persuasive.

What, he asked rhetorically, if you were monitoring current customers and you saw one of your clients you knew really well? What if you see a prospect bouncing between pages, obviously uncertain of the choices being offered? What if you see that somebody is having a problem filling out a form and you can help?

From www.icontact.com:

> Is your customer looking at different brands of the same product and can't seem to make up their mind?
>
> With icontact you can ask your customer if they care to know more about a product's features.
>
> Or maybe your customer appears to be browsing aimlessly throughout your cyberstore?
>
> With icontact you can ask your customer if they are in need of assistance.
>
> Perhaps you customer is ready to check out but seems hesitant to provide their credit card number on your Web site?
>
> With icontact you can explain your Web site's security protection.
>
> Bring the human touch to your Web site today.

From *Net Company* magazine, Fall 1999:

> Diane McGowan is a design consultant who has been trained to use Furniture.com's live-chat software.
>
> She monitors the site, putting out "feelers" to ask users if she can be of assistance. Here's a typical exchange:
>
> "Yes, thanks. I'm looking for a rectangular dining-room table with chairs—possibly Windsor chairs—and maybe a hutch."
>
> "Can you tell me what kind of wood, and what style you are looking for?" McGowan types.
>
> "Hmmmm. I know I don't like oak very much. I know I like cherry and maybe maple. I prefer dark- to medium-colored woods. But harvest tables are sometimes made of pine aren't they? I wonder if they can be stained to a more medium color."
>
> "Yes they can be," McGowan types. "And every manufacturer uses its own stains. On the site, we usually have a thumbnail for a color, which you can click on to get a better idea of how it looks."

The article goes on to describe how McGowan can send out fabric swatches and can review what the customer has in his or her shopping basket at the moment—but only with the buyer's permission.

It sounds just like being able to walk up to somebody in a store and tactfully inquire if they need assistance. But even in a store, people get put off if you ask too soon or too aggressively. The likelihood of that sort of reaction online goes way up.

Be very careful when you get proactive out there. We just don't know what different tolerance levels people have to being surprised by prying eyes.

Only your customers know if being uniquely proactive is the right choice for your site. Don't charge off making assumptions that anybody who is seriously interested in aroma therapy would jump at the chance to chat with somebody looking over their shoulder. Ask them. If you're going to assume anything, assume that they'd rather see a nice big "Got a Question?" button like 1-800-flowers has (Figure 5.15).

There *is* one thing we know for sure. When push comes to shove, people want to talk to people. E-mail may be too slow, chat may be to cumbersome, and voice-over-IP just isn't mature enough at the moment. No matter what you offer your customers in the way of nifty communication tools, make sure that

Figure 5.15   1-800-flowers invites its customers to ask for a chat session at any time.

you post your telephone number of every single page of your Web site. It doesn't cost anything, and the payback is customers who can make buying decisions, get questions answered, and solve problems in a hurry.

Sometimes speaking to another human being is the only communication that satisfies.

The Sound of Your Voice

Being heard as well as seen can add a great deal to your ability to help customers. Since the Web offers a somewhat rocky audio link (more on this later), the telephone seems to be the best way to go for the moment.

The most popular and certainly the easiest way to offer phone contact is by simply posting your toll-free number on every page of your Web site. If you have a complex site and lots of call center operators standing by, you might divide the call-fielding tasks among several operators or groups, by putting different numbers on different pages, based on subject. Accounting questions go to one number, ordering questions to another, and product-use questions to yet another.

But the next step is to be just a little proactive. Call your customer directly.

Geico Insurance was one of the first to try out the Call Me button (Figure 5.16) with a service from AT&T.

That works great if your customer is at the office with multiple phone lines coming to his or her desk and a permanent Internet connection through the local area network. But what about those at home with only one phone line? No problem. They can type in their number, specify a time, and make an appointment for the call.

It seems like the best of both worlds. All the Web pages you can surf plus the helpful, friendly voice of an informed customer service representative. But nothing is easy in life—why should the Web be different?

Pelham Moore, founder of Play Populi, offered up a few valuable insights to the ClickZ Forum (www.clickz.com) about using the phone versus doing it all online:

```
Date: Fri, 19 Nov 1999
FROM: Pelham Moore (APPALS@aol.com com)
Re: CLICKZ FORUM: Pelham Moore: A Live Person is still a problem

Hi Listees:

This one got me off the bench, after being a passive spectator to this
very well coordinated discussion forum. Excellent job to all involved!
```

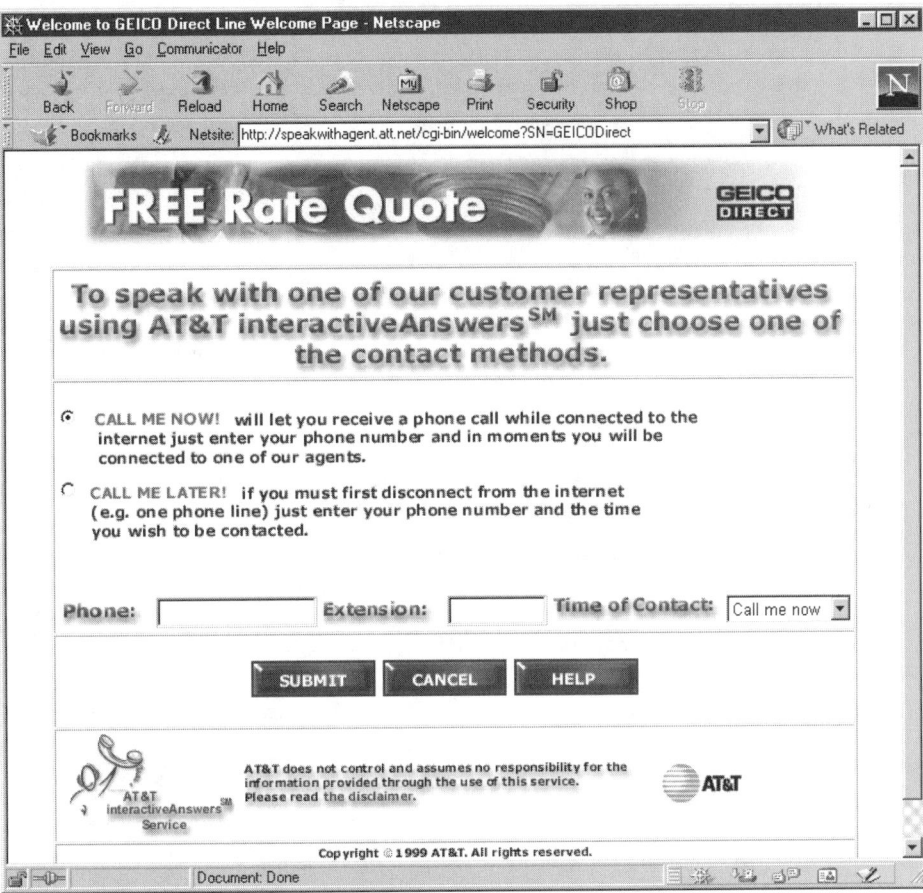

Figure 5.16 Geico insurance will be happy to call you—just give its customer service representative your number.

Having worked as a CSR (service rep.) for a major financial org., several points on the merits and demerits of the live model come to mind, based on the off-line world; first the pros:

1. Potential or existing clients are normally gracious and appreciative of your expert help and reassuring suggestions;

2. When screw-ups occur, they are more inclined to accept your explanations/apologies; their "humanity" comes out in ways that reflect an innate willingness to forgive, forget and go on;

3. Each CSR will "bond" with a select few customers over time, especially where there was occasion for the parties to interact in a noticeable way (a special favor, problem-solving issue, etc.).

```
NOW FOR THE DOWNSIDE:

1. In oral communication (as above) the exchange is spontaneous, smooth
and scalable: a quick compliment/observation; crafted, tone-modulation
techniques; relative control over call duration.

It's logistically impossible without a voice function to achieve above
rapport and clearly much, much more labored typing to each other.

2. Any screw-up occurring would be less likely to relieve the CSR (who
is "naked" without a frame of reference as to the caller's personality,
accent etc.) in her/his task of 1st. spontaneously identifying the
problem let alone immediately attempting to solve it, without putting
the caller on "e-hold" (no music, audio AD etc.) where a minute on-line
could seem a virtual eternity!

3. The probability of "bonding with the customer" is next to zero; in
real (phone) call centers, one can request one's "personal" rep. and
feel comfortable about waiting a few minutes for attention or accept the
promise of a prompt callback.

SUMMARY: The wired-world reality of consumer service must of necessity
reconcile the very nature of this New Medium: it's quick, self
empowering (no baby-sitting available), and pretty much inflexible, if
uniformity of functionality and cost-efficiency are to be maintained.

In the brick-and-mortar world, you can actually cater for a "returns"
counter for underfulfilled orders (usually with near immediate redress)
and a candy or a cup of coffee while-u-wait! No such perks in
cyberspace!

Hope this perspective provides some useful food for e-commercial thought!

Cordially, Pelham Moore, Founder, PLAY POPULI Inc.
```

If you're ready to start verbally helping your Web customers, you don't have to have a sophisticated telephony system or special Web-based voice-over-data telephonic integration. You only need to get a hold of a company like PhoneMe (www.phoneme.com, Figure 5.17).

For less than a thousand dollars to start and a thousand dollars a month (plus a little more than 10 cents a minute), PhoneMe will worry about all the technology on the back end. The visitor enters his or her name, number, and time, and both of your phones ring at the same time.

A warning about this sort of service: Make sure you have operators standing by. There's nothing worse than hitting that Call Me button, having your phone ring, picking it up and being told, "Thank you for contacting us. Your call is very important. Please hold until one of our service representatives is available." It's quite possible that the appointed time happens to crop up when your phone people are busy but think about it from the customer's perspective. You asked them to make an appointment. They did. You said you would call them. You did. Then there was nobody on the other end of the line. How lame can you get?

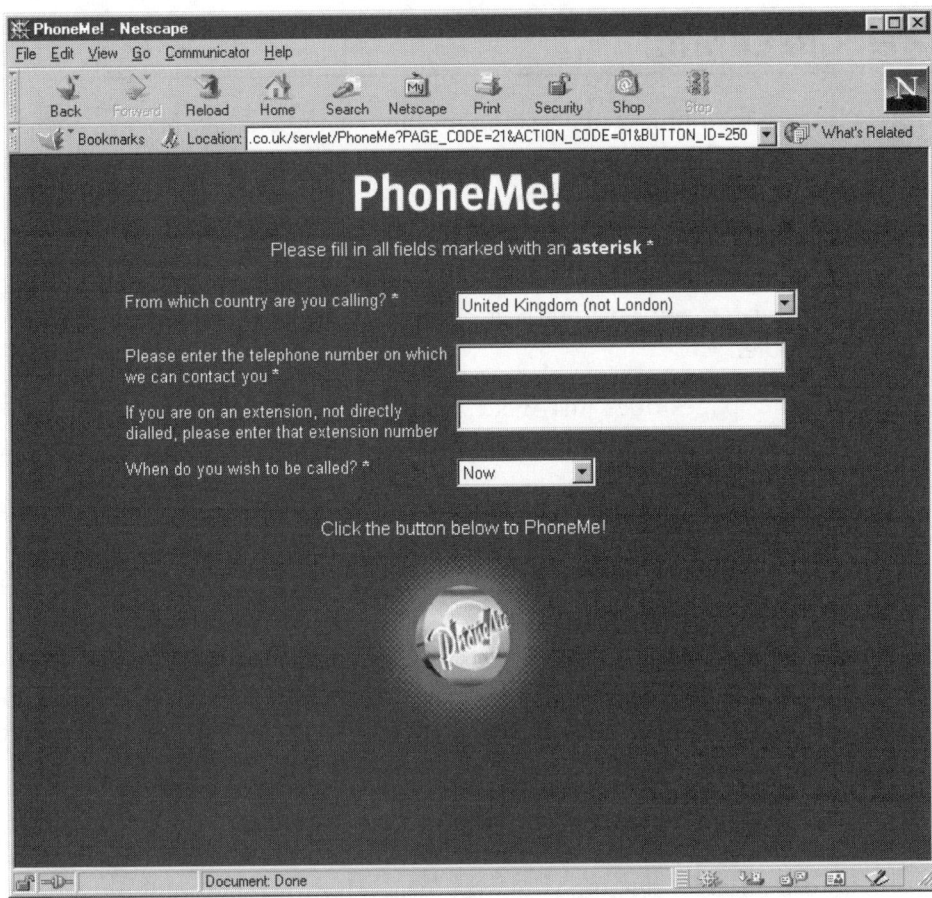

Figure 5.17 PhoneMe offers a service that lets you put a Call Me button on your site without getting software.

But why do you really need to place a call? If the customer is online, they're connected to a phone line. Why not just use the Internet as the single-band voice carrier?

Internet telephone tools like Camelot Corporation's DigiPhone (www.digi-phone.com), and WebPhone from Grace Network (www.gracenetwork.com/webphone/webphone.htm) let you use your computer as a telephone. With a local connection to the Internet you can talk with your customers around the world. When we all get sound cards, this will be great. When bandwidth becomes plentiful, this form of communication will be standard fare. Until then, best to keep the Internet-as-telephone approach on hold.

But if you do have customers on the line, how about showing them where to surf?

Remote Control

In an e-mail or a chat session, guiding customers had always been absurdly easy. Find the right page, copy it, and paste it into your message. E-mail client software turns URLs into live links, ripe for the clicking. Some chat software lets you do the same. But during a phone call? You bet.

There are three levels of remote control you can use to reach out and guide your customers: pushing pages, moving their mouse, and taking over their computer.

Pushing pages does just what it sounds like. The customer service rep can choose the page the customer should look at next and send it down the line.

"If you think you might like that sweater in cashmere, there's this blue one. . . ." Lands' End was not the first company to make use of this new type of communication, but it was the first to build an entire television advertising campaign around it.

Knowing that the Christmas season was fast approaching, Lands' End decided to show America what online shopping could be like. Two young, cheerful, happy, healthy females smiled at each other across a phone line while pages were pushed and just the right sweater was found.

Moving their mouse not only lets you control what page they see, but lets you use the mouse as an accent pointer to direct their attention. Then you can enter information for them in whatever forms show up. This requires a delicate balance of getting their permission. (It's a little disconcerting when you lose control of your computer to a bodiless voice in the Internet.)

If your customer trusts you completely and there is some real reason for it, you can take over their computer altogether and not be limited to just clicking around in the browser. Expertcity.com uses just that sort of technology (Figure 5.18).

Let's say you want to know how to use a special setting in a particular software application. The appropriate expert at Expertcity.com could show you how to do it, one click at a time. But they could also help with system problems by changing any systems settings. They could have the authority to delve deeply into those areas where only help-desk aficionados do not fear to tread.

What if mere page pushing isn't enough? What if you have a particularly complex idea to communicate?

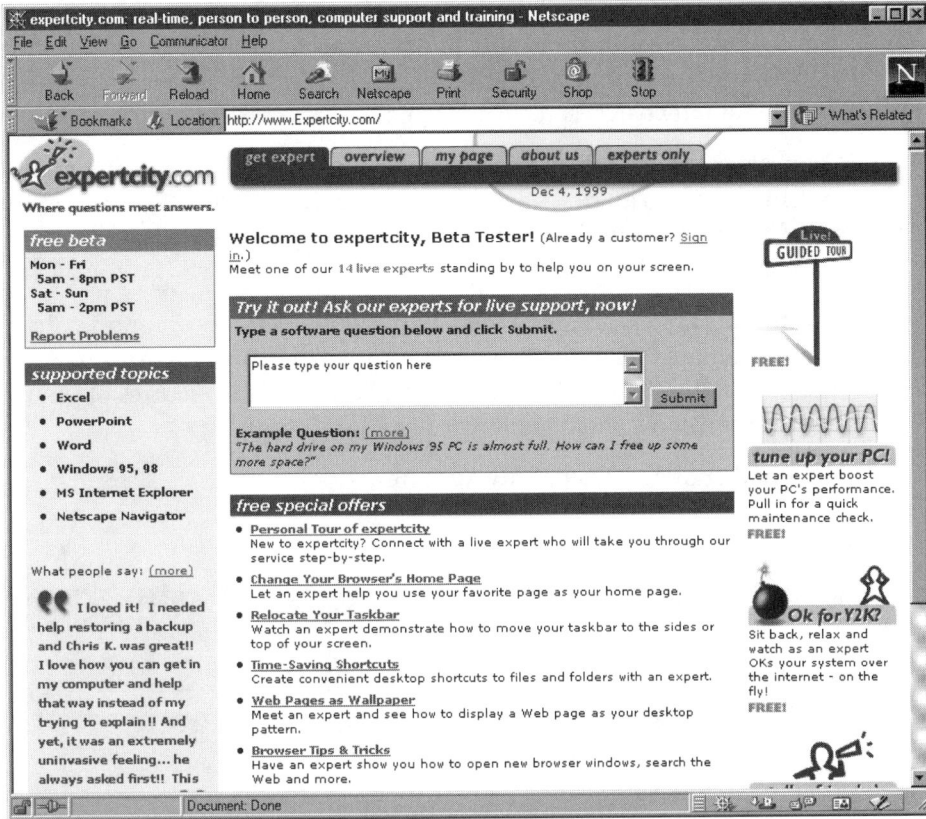

Figure 5.18 Expertcity.com brings together experts and those in need, allowing the experts to reach in and fix things.

Do I Have to Draw You a Picture?

When things get a little too complicated, I often find myself reaching for my pen and a napkin or checking to make sure the marker close at hand is a dry-erase type and not the permanent kind. Some people understand a few squiggles better and faster than a page of text. When they get online, it's nice to have an electronic whiteboard.

Oh, sure, you can show them a PowerPoint presentation. That's very useful for crowds of people in a lecture situation. I've given many "Webshops," as Hewlett Packard likes to call them, to people all over the world who listen in on the conference call and watch as I push slide after PowerPoint slide their way. But what about when dealing one-on-one?

The first electronic whiteboards allowed one to draw and then send. The next round allowed multiple people to draw and then send. Sometimes the results were less than informative, rather like a chat session among a dozen teenagers. But then whiteboards came up to speed.

Groupboard (www.groupboard.com, Figure 5.19) allows many people to use up to 11 colors to all draw at the same time. It's a little like standing in front of a real whiteboard with a handful of ghosts mutually making masterpieces in real time.

This mode of interaction not only allows you to clearly diagram your message; it lets your customers draw a circle around the parts that puzzle them. Combine this ability to simultaneously sketch with a few pictures of your product, and you can show them just what fits where and how.

Not good enough? There's always animation.

Figure 5.19 Groupboard could be useful when dealing with those customers who need to be drawn a map (and face it, there are lots of them).

Cartoon Communication

Cisco Systems won't be worrying the Disney Corporation. The Cisco cartoons do not include a mouse with big ears, or a duck with a speech impediment. Instead, they show how to install and set up Cisco's latest campus switch routers (Figure 5.20).

Macromedia Flash uses vector graphics instead of bit maps. Why should you care? Because it makes the files that store these animations very small. It means you can illustrate quite a bit without all those bits.

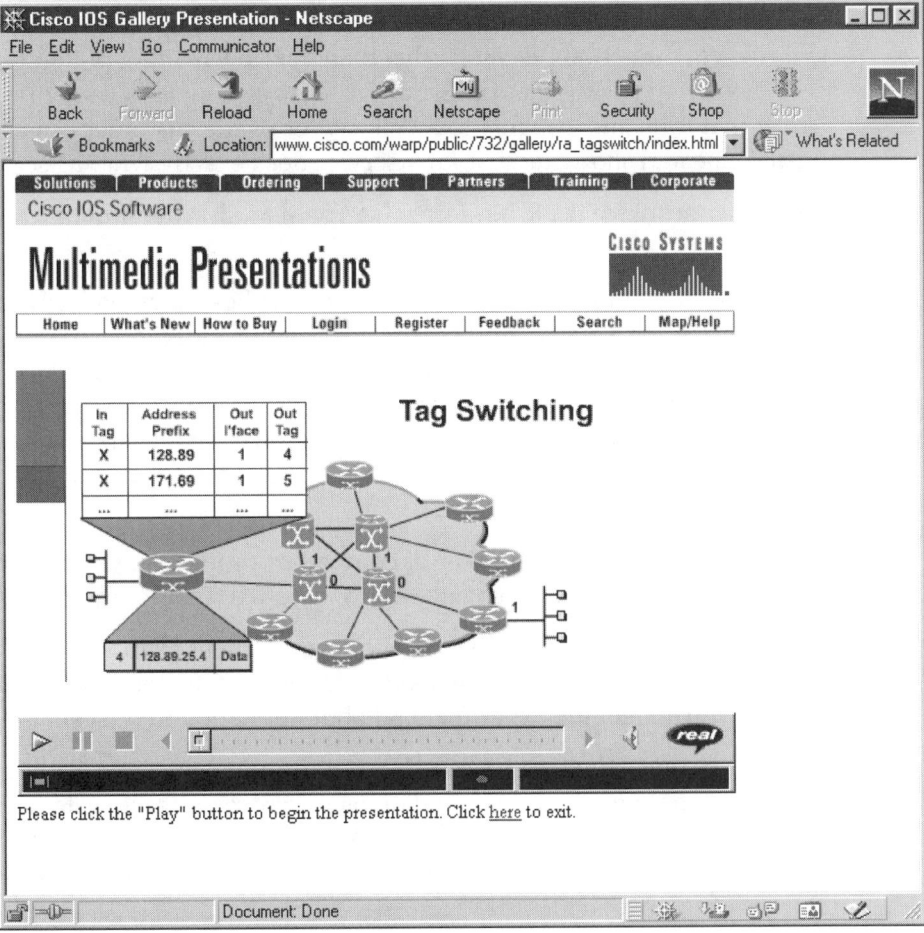

Figure 5.20 Cisco uses Macromedia's Flash to show the benefits of the tag switching feature in its IOS software.

"It's one thing to have a line of text that says, 'You'll need three people to lift this size switch.' It's another thing to show a short movie showing three people doing the heavy lifting," according to Jim Hatlo, Web products manager at Cisco. The next step for Cisco is to make the cartoons customizable. Describe your situation and configuration and then watch a personalized version.

Not good enough? There's always video.

Online Video

Being seen as well as heard can add a great deal to your ability to help customers.

The makers of large factory equipment have been including fixed video cameras in their specifications for years. Remote diagnostics sometimes needs a quick look at the actual process, rather than a simple reading of the speeds and feeds. Some processing plant installations now come with a camera-equipped helmet that transmits a signal to a Web server so the customer can climb into the machine and show the customer service desk exactly what he sees.

Does that mean we'll all be doing Internet-based video-phone calls soon? Nope.

Everything previously described for audio applies to video, only more so. There'd better be a darn good reason for putting video on a Web site these days. These are the days of an average connect speed of 56.6kbps. These are the days when corporate T1 connections are shared by hundreds of people. Video on the local area network (LAN) works great, and it can even service the wide area network (WAN), but when video has to go over the Internet, the medium is just too slow.

Nevertheless, there are a number of companies promoting (a little) video for use in customer service. Videogate.com is just such a company (Figure 5.21).

Just be sure you have the proper level of commitment from your service reps before turning the cameras on them. Just as some are better on the phone than on the keyboard, some are happy to talk but not happy to be seen.

Lisa Stockburger, VP at Vanguard Communications plans, designs and helps companies implement customer relationship processes and systems for their consulting clients. In an article in *Customer Service Management* magazine (September 1999, www.csm-us.com), Lisa spelled out some of the plusses and minuses of two-way video conferencing.

On the plus side, Lisa listed the following benefits of video conferencing:

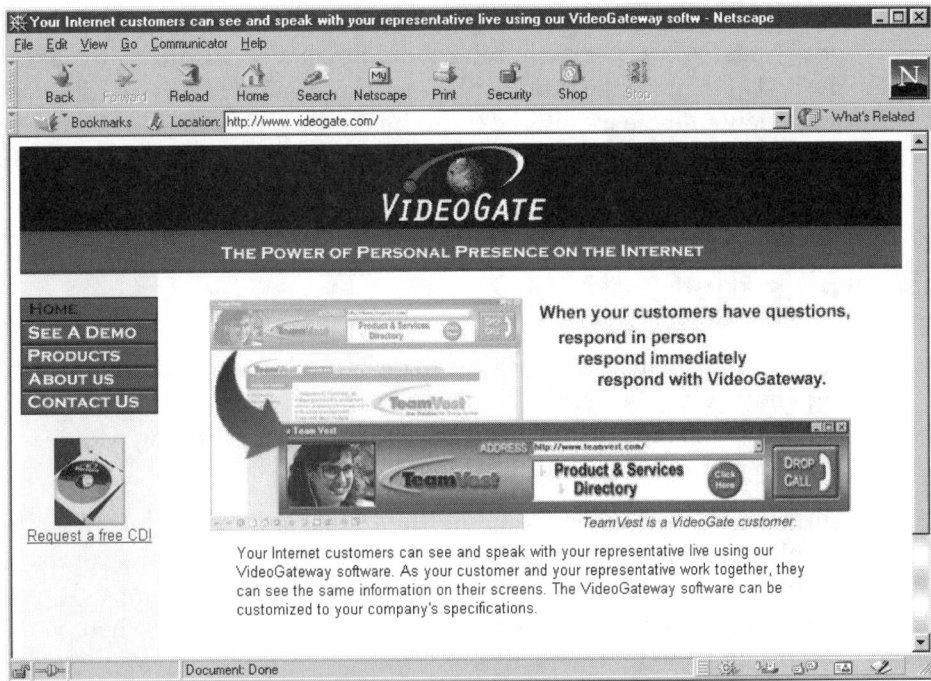

Figure 5.21 Videogate.com suggests that a small, live video feed of your customer service rep will help your customers better understand your level of commitment.

- Eliminates the brick and mortar costs of traditional customer service, through stand-alone service centers.
- Makes customer contact more personal or intimate.
- Allows customer service reps to react to visual cues.
- Extends market reach into underserved areas.

But Stockburger also pointed out a bit of the downside, asking whether video conferencing was a killer app. Her take was that it's interesting, but not compelling. "As a customer I *can* conduct product research on the Web without eyeball-to-eyeball interaction with anyone. I *can* apply for a loan on the Web and e-mail back and forth, or Web chat if I need assistance."

But past the question of whether the technology is ready for prime time (not yet), Lisa hit on a pretty fundamental question. "Do I want them to see *me* at home in front of my monitor in my Doctor Dentons, unshowered and uncoiffed?"

She then extended her concern to the call center itself. "In many call centers, dress code is informal at best. Will stricter dress codes need to be implemented? Will employees with pierced noses be forced to give up their favorite nose rings? What special training should managers institute, to make sure that the body language the staff displays is appropriate? How will compliance with those new rules be monitored? And by the way, how does the average cubicle in the contact center look to the new video-enabled customer with a bird's eye view?

Manning the Effort

Your Web site will take some time to design. Keep in mind that this is an ongoing effort. Your Web site will take some time to construct. Keep in mind that this is an ongoing effort. Your Web site will require training people to support it. Keep in mind that this is an ongoing effort.

There was a time when assigning the proper number of telephone lines and telephone operators was critical to the effective running of a company. When people called and heard a busy signal, they were unhappy. When people called and the phone rang and rang, they were unhappy. When people called and the line was answered instantly, the company was unhappy for having too many operators who weren't optimally deployed.

The ability to respond to newsgroup comments, list postings, and incoming e-mail must be measured and allocated with the same significance as phone operators. Being on hand to field, acknowledge, and reply to electronic communications is no less important than voice communications. Be sure that your budget is sufficient to the task.

At one of the many seminars I give, I asked the audience of about 250 to write down the three biggest problems they had on their site. Along with the expected quandaries, like getting funding from upper management and convincing the design people that customers don't have T3 lines to their laptops, was the dilemma of training people about the finer points of managing e-mail and customer discussions.

So Much to Learn

Your people will be accountable for all the things a customer service department usually handles:

- Product features
- Customer applications
- Company organization
- Problem-reporting procedures

- Listening skills
- Caring for customers
- Determining client value
- Communication skills
- Performance under pressure
- Project management
- Time management

They'll also need some special skills for this cyber-assignment:

- Software training
- Internet introduction
- Utilizing Internet resources (newsgroups, search tools, industry-specific sites)

One of the most important areas that often gets overlooked is writing skills. In the 1999 version of their report "Online Customer Service: Strategies for Improving Satisfaction and Retention," Jupiter Communications (www.jup .com) found a lack of writing skills to be a big red flag. "Almost every site that Jupiter spoke to identified this issue as an early pitfall in transitioning CSRs from verbal to written communications." That leaves you to decide whether you should train 'em yourself, or look to some outside help.

Outsourcing Live Customer Service

If you don't have the time, people, technology, or patience to load one more straw on your camel's back, consider putting that straw on some other camel's back.

PeopleSupport (www.peoplesupport.com) will help you carry the load. This outsource service has eReps who are online 24 by 7. They are expert at using the software, and you train them to specifically help your customers. Use them for overflow, or use them on a permanent basis. Just be sure your ability to train them is in keeping with your customers' needs.

Do it yourself or get help. Either way, in the long run you're going to have to show it was worth the effort. That's what the next chapter is all about.

CHAPTER 6

Measuring Your Success

Think the way the customer thinks, not the way technical people think.
Michael McCadden, The Gap

The customer experience is the next competitive battleground.
Jerry Gregiore, CIO, Dell Computer Corporation

If you're concerned about measuring the return on investment of your Web site's customer service offerings, you're asking the wrong question. If the boss wants to know if using the Web to provide customer service is worth the expense, either your spending is out of control or your boss is.

Sound far-fetched? I don't know your boss very well? The common problem in large companies is your boss. You and the other people at the front line who do the work know the value of the Web. You know the power of the Web. You know how much better the Web can take care of routine tasks and can propel your company to new levels of customer satisfaction and service. And I've got news—so do the people in the executive towers.

Senior level management didn't get there by being dumb. They've read the in-flight magazines and they know something important is happening. They know there's got to be a way to take advantage of all this Web stuff. They just don't know what to do about it. So they turn to your boss and ask. Your boss forms committees and focus groups and task forces and has reports written and benchmarking studies commissioned and spins his wheels (emphasis on the "his").

It will require some funding to get your Web-based customer service up and running. And it is possible to spend more than makes sense. But when was the last time somebody in your firm did a study to determine whether having a telephone was worth the expenditure? What's the ROI on a fax machine?

What's the dollars-and-cents benefit of e-mail? Come to think of it, what's the payback on having a customer service department at all?

Each company faces its own budget in its own way. Your success at securing funds for this endeavor will be related more closely to corporate culture than to spreadsheets and formulas.

Yes, it's possible to take a look at the cost savings on a dollar-by-dollar basis. Sun Microsystems' first calculations were based on the number of literature requests, phone calls, and software patches. They figured the cost of printing, stuffing, and mailing literature; the cost of a warm body answering the phone; and the cost of the call; and they looked up the cost of creating a magnetic tape and shipping it to customers. In the month of January 1995 they came up with a total savings of $1,262,561.

Admittedly there is room for discussion about how many people looked at Sun's online brochures, dipped into their Frequently Asked Questions, and downloaded software, who might not have done so had it not been for the Web. These are the kinds of prickly problems one faces when trying to explain the Internet in terms of hard return. If your boss is still giving you a hard time, just show him what your competition is up to while he's been playing with his spreadsheet.

Perhaps simply mention that in January 1999 Cisco Systems reported saving $550,000,000 per year by offering customer service online. Yes, boys and girls, that was half a *billion* dollars. Remember Danny DeVito in the movie *Twins?* He just loved the sound of the word *billion*. Me too. I also love the sound of Cisco's customer service satisfaction ratings improving by 20 percent. That's payback.

So just what do you measure? The traffic on the marketing side of your Web site, the number of files downloaded, the number of questions asked, and the number of database inquiries on the customer service side are all worth tracking. But the *big* ROI question is: Who is making use of this facility and how can we help them use it better?

Since you can't measure your success until you have people there to measure, we have to get people to your site in the first place. So one of your tasks will be blowing your horn loud enough for people to look your way, and blowing it long enough for them to see that spending some time on the customer service portion of your site will yield some serious benefits to them.

Getting Them There in the First Place

Blowing your own horn about the wonders of customer self-service is expense, pure and simple. You have to advertise that you are providing customers Internet access to your company's customer service function, and advertising isn't cheap.

You thought that was the job of the marketing department. If you have a really good marketing department and it hasn't been downsized, absorbed, outsourced, or merged and purged, it *is* their job. But you had better be ready with some of your own budget to make this a success.

Nobody Calls an Unknown 800 Number

If a shockwave tree falls on a Web site and nobody has their RealAudio player plugged in, does it make a noise? If you set up a contest to give away a million dollars and you don't tell anybody, will anybody win? If you set up a wonderful customer service site full of helpful information and solutions to every customer's problems but you don't tell them, will it have been worthwhile? Nope.

Depending on your business, there are many ways to announce your new electronic support service. You have to use the method that makes the most sense for your customers and your budget. Fortunately, you know who your target audience is: your customers. You know where they live. So send them an engraved invitation.

Bethlehem Steel created a full-color, glossy, trifold brochure that lets customers know the company means e-business. "Introducing the fastest, easiest way to access your order status online," reads the lead, which is accompanied by a cartoon nerd (pocket protector brimming with pens, black glasses with duct tape on the bridge) named e-Charlie (Figure 6.1).

Figure 6.1 Bethlehem Steel decided to tout its online customer services in a brochure/tutorial.

"Hi, I'm e-Charlie. I'm here to help you get fast, real-time order access info right off Bethlehem's Web site at http://www.bethsteel.com."

> It's a Fact . . .
>
> More and more businesses are getting wired to the worldwide web every day—and that includes Bethlehem Steel. We're always looking for ways to better serve our customers. That's why we added "Customer Corner"—your gateway to fast, easy access to order status information 24 hours a day, 7 days a week.
>
> We're no strangers to electronic commerce. We've had Electronic Data Interchange (EDI) for years with many of our customers. EDI is great—but it requires a lot of investment. That's the advantage of Customer Corner. All you need is a PC, Internet access and a password and you're there.

If you expect to save $1,262,561 a month you might want to let people know in every way possible. If you expect your savings to be more modest, you might consider some lower-cost marketing techniques.

Sun Microsystems Saves a Bundle and Wants You to Know about It

Sun saved a lot and can afford to be proactive. The company uses the savings it's enjoyed as a sales tool to convince others to buy its hardware and Internet server solution. Sun boasted about its achievements on its Web site back in 1996 (www.sun.com/960101/feature1, Figure 6.2).

Sun takes out advertisements, hosts seminars, and shows up at trade shows to celebrate the virtues of its success. Others take a more moderate approach.

Consider sending out a postcard to customers after they've contacted the call center, thanking them for helping you improve your goods and services, and reminding them that they might want to check out your Web site next time.

This type of proactive marketing is not expensive and is not wasted. Those customers who have Web access are delighted to learn they have another way of getting help. Those without access recognize that their vendor is a leading-edge kind of company. Besides, they just got a thank-you note for calling up with a problem! It's a nice touch no matter which way you slice it.

Just make sure that you're getting the word out to your customers in a way that doesn't make it look like you don't want to talk to them anymore. From the customer's perspective, that postcard or fax or e-mail could sound like a brush-off. "Thanks for calling . . . just don't do it again."

Get your wording just right so you don't lose the human relationship factor while moving the commodity information out to the Web. Make regular surveys of everyone who is using your Web site to let them know you're watching and listening. Then make any changes they suggest to improve your service.

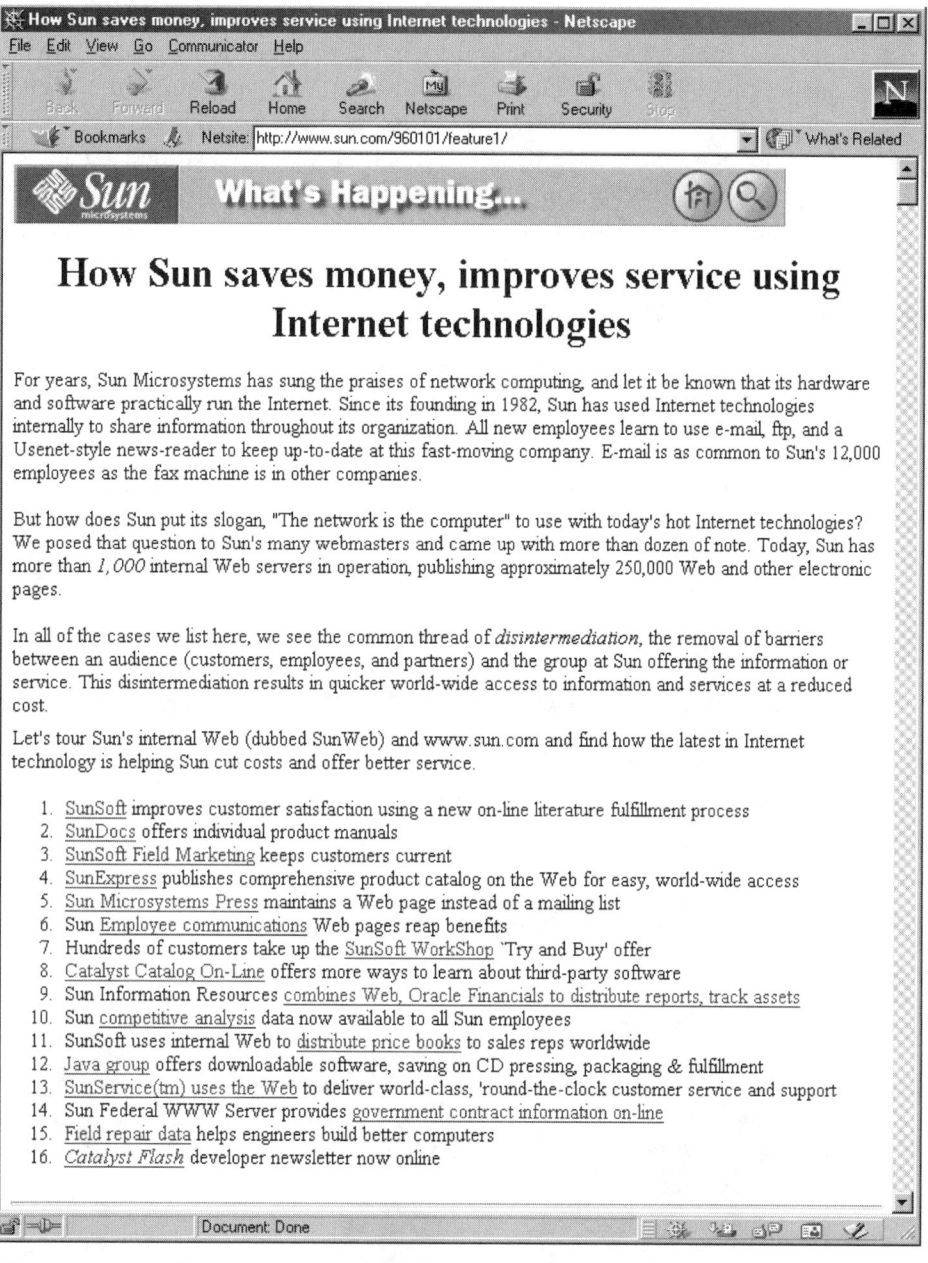

Figure 6.2 Sun likes people to know how wonderful its Web-based customer service has been in order to promote its own products and to draw more people to the site.

This feedback loop is critical. A customer might be benevolent enough to suggest something once. If you implement the suggestion, that customer will take pride and might suggest something else. You can't implement everybody's ideas, but you can express appreciation to them for taking the time. People like to be recognized and they like to have their opinions valued. "Thanks for your impressions, they are an inspiration to us here," will go a long way toward building customer loyalty.

Make It Easy to Get Help

Most of all, you want to make sure that people can find help when they need is. There's plenty of help available at Notebook Computers (www.notebook-computers.com); it's just hard to find (Figure 6.3).

Under the banner ads at the top, in tiny letters, are buttons that let you click to reach your shopping cart, get a personal shopper, or gain account access. But what if you want good, old, plain customer service? You have to be sharp enough to notice that the main menu on the left has an extra tab at the top called *Service* (Figure 6.4).

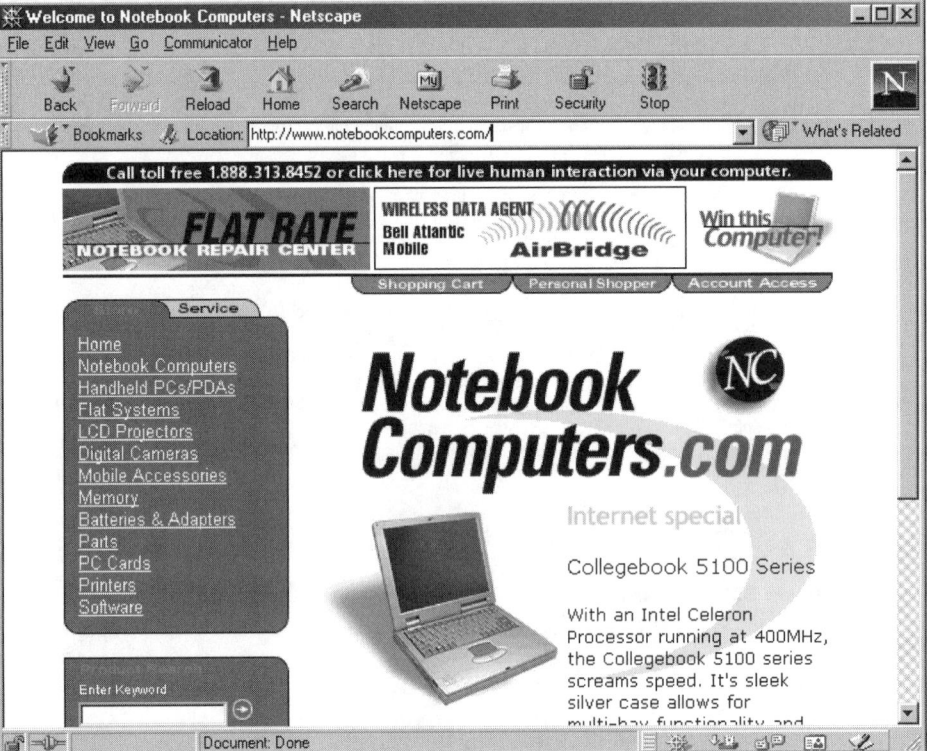

Figure 6.3 Notebook Computers' customer service isn't obvious . . .

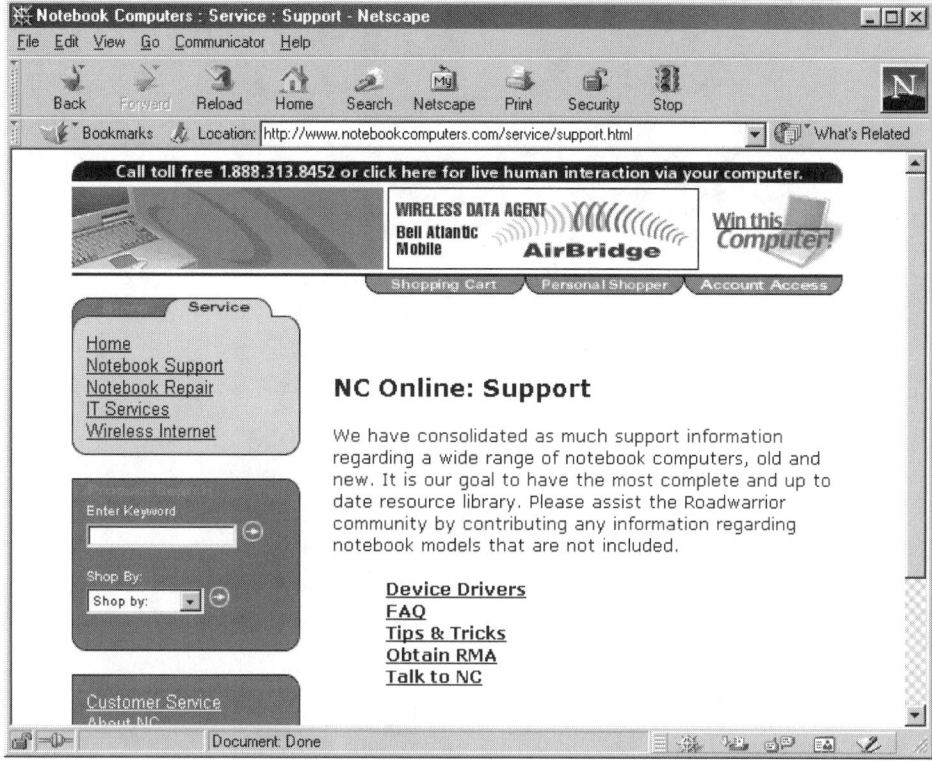

Figure 6.4 . . . unless you know where to look.

DogWatch, on the other hand (www.dogwatch.com), makes it abundantly clear that its people are there to help you (Figure 6.5). This maker of electronic fences to keep Fido out of the street decided the customer service button deserved the very first spot on its home page. Good boy, DogWatch!

Learning from Your List

In the last chapter we talked about online discussion lists. So let's start the measurement process there. How many people are subscribers to your list? Are your promotional efforts paying off? Are you getting lots of new subscribers?

New Subscribers and Unsubscribers

Can you associate separate gaggles of new subscribers with separate promotional events to see which are the most worthwhile ones? If you can, and you can tell what works, do it again. On the other hand, why are people unsub-

Figure 6.5   Looking for help on the DogWatch site? No problem.

scribing in droves? Has the traffic been in a death spiral? Have the postings been too caustic? Or just boring? Did you send out a newsletter that offended people? It's on your shoulders to find out.

Traffic Patterns on a List

Just how much discussion is there? Is there a lot of chatter among a small group of people, or are you attracting some of the best and brightest to participate? Is the discussion a series of questions and answers between people looking for specific information and those in the know, or does it include a more intellectual exchange of ideas?

Where are the people who subscribe to the list coming from? E-mail addresses will yield company names which, in turn, can give you a clue as to the diversity of your list members. A healthy discussion among people from exactly the same background and in the same industry is great for them, but it may be even better if the participants come from a broader base.

Shifting your attention from discussions to your Web site itself, we pull out the magnifying glass and focus on your server logs.

Delving into Your Server Log Files

Every HyperText Transfer Protocol (HTTP) server keeps a log file of every transaction it makes. Some are quite detailed, some are not. If your company is using a freeware server downloaded from off the Internet and modified to the nth degree by your systems people, you might have a problem getting good information out of it. On the other hand, if your systems people are talented and enjoy that sort of tinkering, chances are you can get them to tweak it a bit more on your behalf. So it helps to know just a little bit about them.

Chances are excellent that your Web server is outsourced altogether. In that case, your log files may or may not be useful. They may or may not be saved. They may or may not be backed by industrial-strength log analysis software.

Your Web server logs will tell you which pages people looked at and when. They'll tell you which pages people looked at the most. With this information in hand, you can rethink the organization of those pages, and of your entire Web site. Dave Taylor of Intuitive Systems (www.intuitive.com) points out to his clients that the revision loop is critical. "You need to identify the most popular downloads and most visited pages on the site and then make them super-easy to find online." For whatever reason, people want those files. It's up to you to give them a fast and easy way to access them.

Taylor suggests a number of things to track from your log:

- Number of visitors
- Where they came from (which.com, which.edu, etc.)
- What browser software / computer they used
- How many pages of information they viewed, and how many are viewed on average
- What pages were most popular
- Traffic load by hour of day / day of week

All of these variables are good things to track, and all come right from your logs.

Location and Organization Evaluation

Your server log file stores every page that's sent to every computer that's made a request. If that computer belongs to a company, your log file will record it as coming from company.com. You'll be able to tell if a particular customer is in need of more information. If you then do a reverse-domain name look-up (leave it to your techies to automate this), then you can tell where that company is located.

Why are there more people from the Northeast sales territory utilizing your support pages than from the Southwest? Is there a training problem up there? Why are there so many people from universities (.edu) using this service, and so few from the government (.gov)? Is there an awareness problem in that sector? Answer these questions and you'll know how to spread the word farther and wider to get more and more folks on the Web-based support bandwagon. You'll also be able to see the results of executed promotional activities.

Path Tracking for Usability Measurement

To really help your customers find what they're looking for on your site, take a look at where they've been and how they got there. Follow the clickstream to see how they accessed your customer service area. It's like analyzing the footprints on a freshly vacuumed carpet. Did they look out the windows? Go straight for the bookshelf? Head into the kitchen?

By reviewing the path individuals take through your site, you can better gauge the site's usability. Did people get lost? Did they return to the home page again and again? Did they look at two or three pages and then leave?

The answers to these questions are the starting point of human/computer interface design. That's the science/art of making the screen easy to understand. We used to call it making computers user-friendly, but that's such a daydream we switched to just calling it usability design. For the best information on usability, take a look at Jakob Nielsen's site (www.useit.com). He's the go-to guy on the subject.

Due to the statelessness of HTTP servers (see next section), tracking footprints can be problematic. The log file records which IP address of the computer the visitor used and which files the visitor got. But it doesn't distinguish one visitor from another.

That means if two people come to your site from Microsoft, you'll have conflicting clickstreams. Both people are coming to your site through the Microsoft gateway in their firewall. The log will include two clickstreams but won't show that they came from two people. You're now looking at two pairs of identical footprints on your carpet with no way to tell which is which. Both sets seem to have gone to the back bedroom, but only one went into the den. Which one?

Matters are made much worse by the fact that a lot of people will be visiting your site from www-d4.proxy.aol.com and www-j2.proxy.aol.com, not to mention places like 194.78.15.11. These IP addresses are not very helpful. While you could look up 194.78.15.11 and identify it as living at Silicon Beach Communications in Santa Barbara, you wouldn't know it was me via a dial-up modem. And, of course, the number of people subscribed to America Online goes up daily.

Then we add insult to injury with *cache confusion.* Cache confusion simply says that your home page, having been viewed by one person at www-j2.proxy .aol.com, is stored for a while on www-j2.proxy.aol.com. So when somebody else from American Online clicks on your link, they see your pages as served up by www-j2.proxy.aol.com rather than by your server. Makes it tough to count anything.

Tracking Visits, Not People

As much as we'd like to know exactly who is visiting our Web site, the Internet won't tell us. The World Wide Web is stateless and won't give up information about individuals. There are a couple of technologies that can be used to track each visitor, but none are infallible. This is worth some clarification, as it's important to understand statelessness and how to work around it.

Statelessness, or "Do I Know You?"

When somebody surfs over to your Web site, they are actually copying a few files from your computer (the server) to their computer (the client). The files include your home page text and the different graphics that appear on your home page. The home page text contains links to other documents and graphics on your server. Between the time the visitor has downloaded your home page and the time he or she clicks on a link to request the next one, nothing happens. Nothing at all. There is no connection between the two machines. Your server has served and then falls asleep. It goes dormant, waiting for the next request to come along.

The whole transaction is like getting a book on the history of literature from the library without having to identify yourself or formally check it out. As long as you're at home reading, there is no interaction between you and the library. That literature book is filled with references to other books which can be found at the library and reading it might entice you to go back and get a couple more. In the same way, your server and their client have no relationship until the next click comes along. Except for a brief line in a log file, your server has Alzheimer's.

Because your server maintains no information on the state of the transaction, creating a shopping cart for Web-based catalog sales is a tricky business. Your server has to remember that the shopper wanted the white Blended Pima Pinpoint Oxford (with stripes, for an extra $2), while he's trying to decide between the Machu Picchu, Golden Vertigo, or Bronze Ideals Italian neckties.

So far there are three ways to track individual sessions on your Web site . . . and probably a couple of more by the time you read this:

- Embedding URLs into your links
- Using the Netscape cookie
- Asking them to log in

Each has its own uses and each has its own problems.

Embedding URLs in Your Links

It's possible to serve up your Web pages on the fly—that is, create them as they are being requested instead of having them just sitting around waiting for somebody to ask them to dance. Serving pages on the fly is no simple task, though more and more tools are reaching the street to help. Most Web servers will serve dynamic pages in the future. It's the only logical way to properly manage the content of larger sites.

If you have a dynamic server or somebody who's really good at writing code, you can insert a user ID number into the links on the pages you send out to distinguish one visitor from another. Clear as day, right?

Take a look at Figure 6.6. At the top of the screen is the Netscape location window. The URL shown there (www.amazon.com/exec/obidos/subst/home/ home.html/http://www.amazon.com/exec/obidos/subst/home/home.html/ 103-3843450-9707031) is the result of typing in "www.amazon.com". The Amazon server saw my request and assigned me the number 103-3843450-9707031. As it created the home page for me, it appended that number onto every link on the page.

You can see an example of this technique by looking at the bottom of the Netscape window. The cursor (which you can't see in this screen shot) is hovering over the Home Improvement button at the top. The URL showing at the very bottom already has my user ID in it. If I click on that link, the Amazon server knows that the same person has come back.

The Amazon server then serves up the Home Improvement page the same way, with my ID embedded in the links. The Home Improvement page comes festooned with links which include my number. Looking at the bottom of this page, you can see my number attached to the link for Tools & Equipment (Figure 6.7).

Figure 6.6 Amazon.com embeds user IDs into its URLs.

So does Amazon.com know who I am? Not at first. I am just an anonymous visitor with a brand on my browser so they know where I've been *this time*. Next time, I get a different number. In fact, I get a different number if I simply hit the Reload button. If this were a real bookstore, they would give me a numbered hat when I walk in the front door. The video cameras would track my progress and record my movements as I wander around. If I leave—even for only a second to put more money in the parking meter—I get a new hat with a new number when I come back in the front door.

While this is a workable way to track sessions, or visits, it doesn't help keep track of individuals. Amazon wants to track people. Amazon wants to greet me by name. For that, Netscape created the cookie.

Using Cookies to Track Visitors

Briefly put, the Netscape cookie is a file on your hard drive that stores a user identification number along with some useful information written there by a Web server. If the server doesn't recognize any of the cookies on your machine, it gives you one. It can't read any cookies other than the one it created. If it *does* recognize a cookie, then it knows something about you. It knows that you are

Figure 6.7 The Home Improvement page also has my ID number embedded in it.

the same person who came by three days ago. It can keep track of your every move. It can also look into its database to see what you told it on previous visits. You told it your name? It can greet you personally. Now you know how Amazon knows your name.

More than a Simple How-Do-You-Do

It used to simply be Yahoo! Then those Yahooligans started baking cookies. As a result, now each of us can enjoy our own version of Yahoo! by filling out a profile (Figure 6.8).

The folks at Yahoo! want to know your name, your zip code, your gender, your occupation, what industry you're in, and what your interests are.

In the end, they use a cookie to recognize you when you come back, and they display the news, weather, business, and sports that you care about (Figure 6.9).

Yahoo! uses this technique to keep you coming back, so that it can sell more advertising space. The more you reveal in your profile, the higher the price Yahoo! can charge advertisers. It's rather inexpensive to buy a run-of-site batch of banner ads on Yahoo! But the more you target your audience, the higher the price.

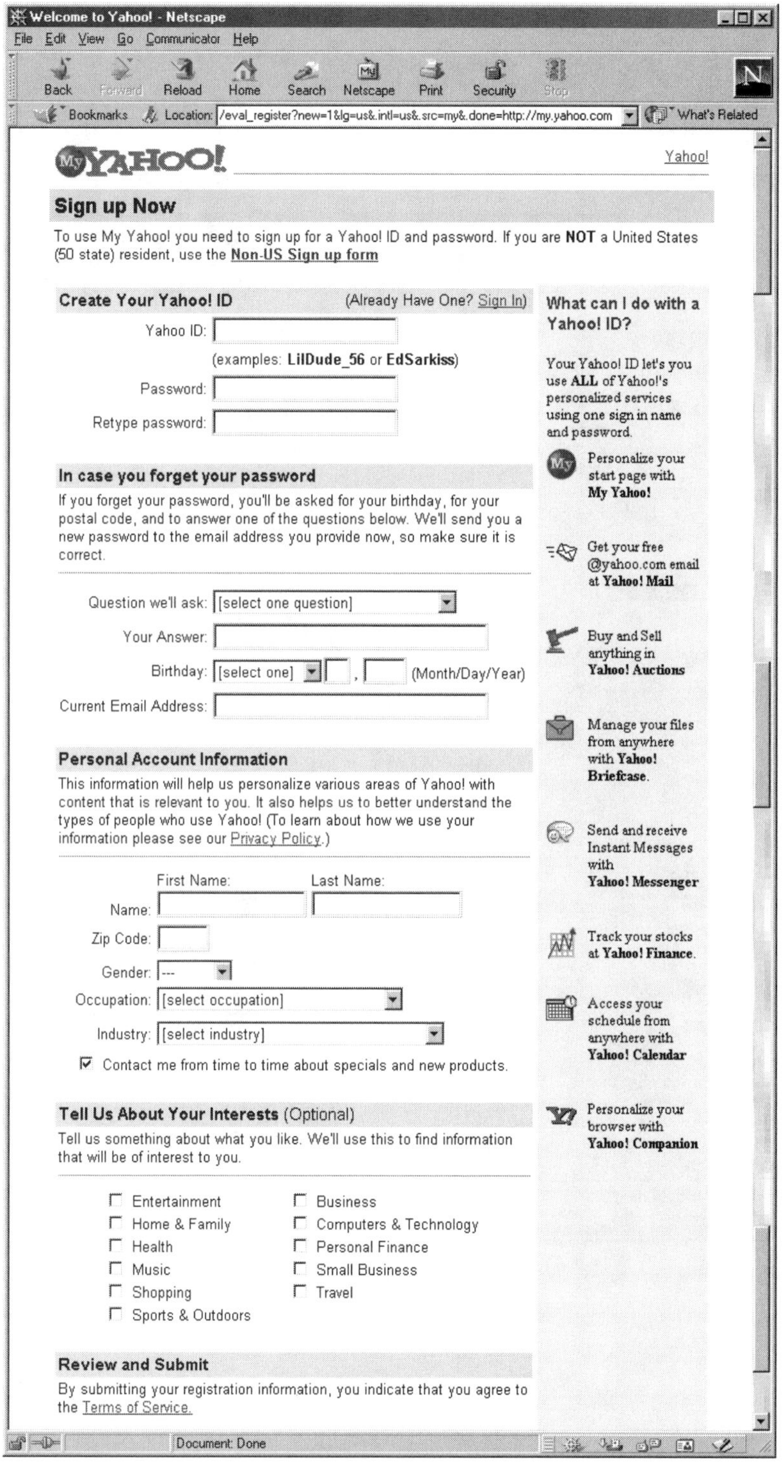

Figure 6.8 The Yahoo! profile asks a lot of questions about your interests.

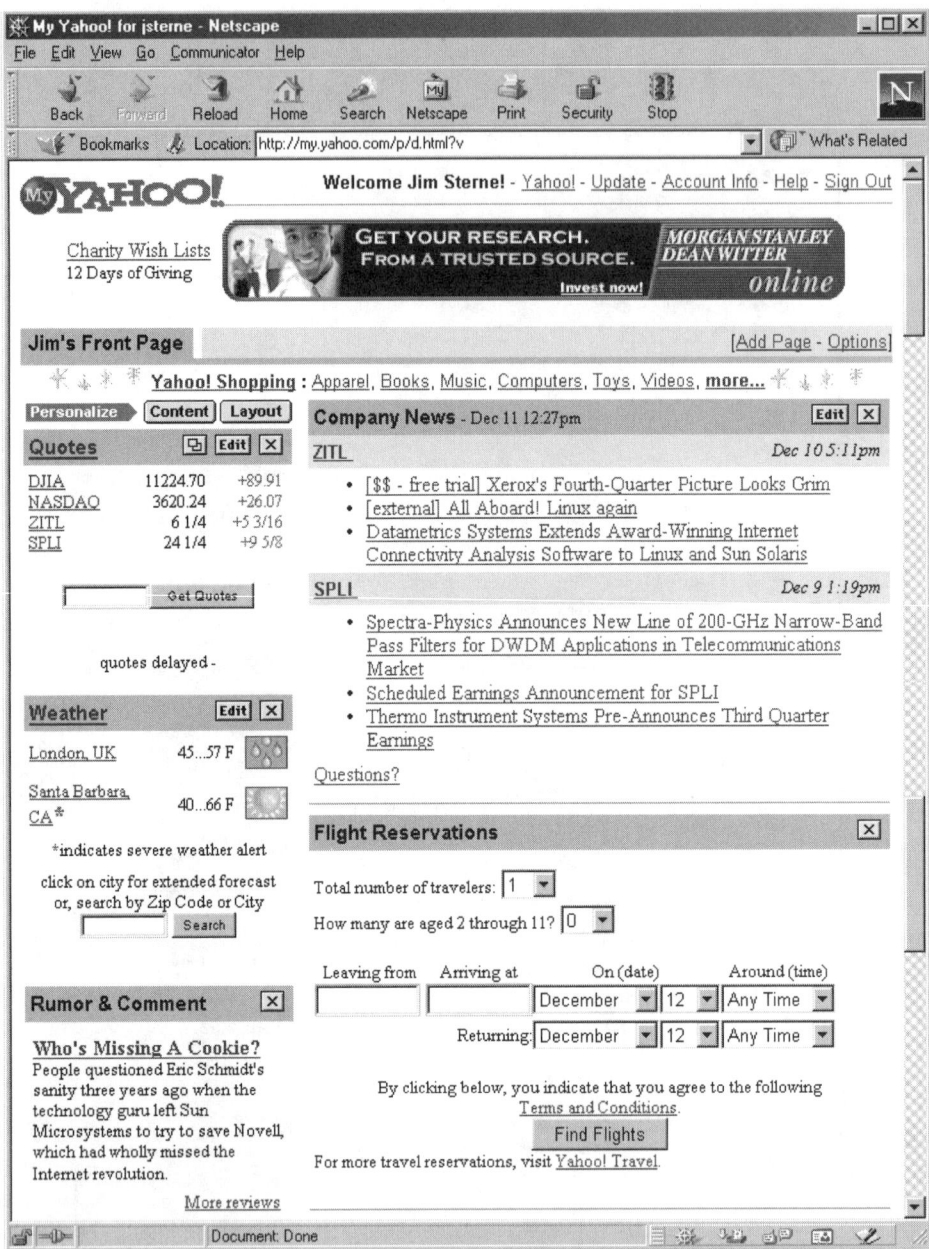

Figure 6.9 You can learn a lot about somebody by looking at their personal myYahoo! page.

But sites that sell advertising are not the only ones using cookies. Cookies are used for personalizing sites such as MyVites.com, Sun Microsystems (http://MySun.sun.com), the Radiology Community site (http://radcom.org), the Greater Fresno Valley Plaza site (www.valleyplaza.com), and Healthwell.com.

Unfortunately, cookies are not foolproof. Cookies have a few problems.

Cookie Drawbacks

As delicious as the first batch of cookies may be, they have a number of problems. To start with, cookies are plain-text files on the client machine, where they can be easily modified or deleted by the user. Don't like the idea of big-brother corporation writing things on your hard drive for later inspection? Don't like the idea that they're collecting information about you? Dump the file.

Even worse—turn them off. Responding to a call for privacy, Netscape and Microsoft both added the ability for each user to choose the Accept No Cookies option in the browser. Want to know if that guy has been here before? Sorry, he's not telling.

Cookies also suffer from being browser-specific. One cookie per browser, only one cookie per browser, and each cookie belongs to only one browser. Once a cookie is written, it belongs to the browser that was in use at the time. If your customers like to surf with Netscape as well as Microsoft's Internet Explorer, they will have a different cookie with each software package.

The next problem is that cookies are fickle. If your customer, Bob, lets his office mate, Fred, use Bob's machine for surfing because it has the LAN connection to the T1, then your server will think that Fred is Bob. When Bob goes home and reaches your site via his home computer, he looks like a completely different Bob to your server. He's using a completely different cookie. Did I mention that Bob travels and takes a laptop on the road with him? Different cookie. Different Bob. So now, your server thinks there are three different Bobs and one of them is sometimes Fred.

All-in-all, the Netscape cookie is an excellent proof of concept. But if you really want to track your customers as individuals, you have to get them to log in.

Asking Them to Log In

Getting people to log in to your Web site is the only way to be certain it's really them. Yes, passwords are crackable, but there has to be a really compelling reason to do it. Remember, no computer system is ever 100 percent safe. For that matter no car, home, airplane, or batch of canned stew can be said to be 100 percent safe either. If you want to get more than your share of information on World Wide Web security, just go to your favorite search engines and be prepared to be overwhelmed. (As a customer service manager, you have to be able to count on your company's supplying sufficient security to serve your purposes. As a Web server security technician, you have your work cut out for you.)

Once a user has logged into your Web site, you can use embedded URLs or cookies to follow them around and see where they go. They've already logged in, so you have a positive ID. A username and password confirm who is Fred and who is Bob, and they'll reset the cookie every time to ensure you don't end up with a Frob in your database. Then you can keep track of the fact that customer Jones likes the search tool and customer Smith likes the index. You can see that customer Brown has been spending some time reading up on a newer model than she owns at present. Time for a sales call?

Offer an Incentive

You may think that people have become accustomed to identifying themselves to computers. You'd be right. We've become used to it because we have to do it so many times a day. Log in at work, log in to databases we use. Log in to online services we use. Enter our PIN numbers at the autoteller and again at the grocery store. The problem lies in there being so many places to log in. It's almost impossible to remember all the codes, numbers, and passwords we each have scattered about the electronic landscape.

The problem with asking people to log in is that it is an immediate barrier to their participation. You have to offer something quite worthwhile to get people to 1. take the time, 2. expose themselves, and 3. remember all those passwords.

BankAmerica Gets Nosy

Take the case of the Bank of Jim Sterne (www.bankamerica.com, Figure 6.10). No, you can't see it, but I can. I signed up, told them a little bit about myself, and now when I log in I get the benefits. What kind of benefits? Articles about money specifically selected because they are of interest to me. How do they know what I'm interested in? They asked me when I signed up.

In addition to creating a newsletter that's geared to my financial tastes, BankAmerica keeps an eye on the calendar. The server knows when I was last in the bank's electronic branch office. BankAmerica wouldn't want me to miss anything, so it tracks What's New since I last checked in. Rather than making me review a What's New page, or sending me annoying e-mail announcing new things I don't care about, B of A simply notes what's happened in my absence.

Knowing that a cookie can crumble, BankAmerica requires a password. BankAmerica wants to be sure it's you logging in, and it wants to know quite a bit about you. Your name, address, and e-mail are required. Then it wants to

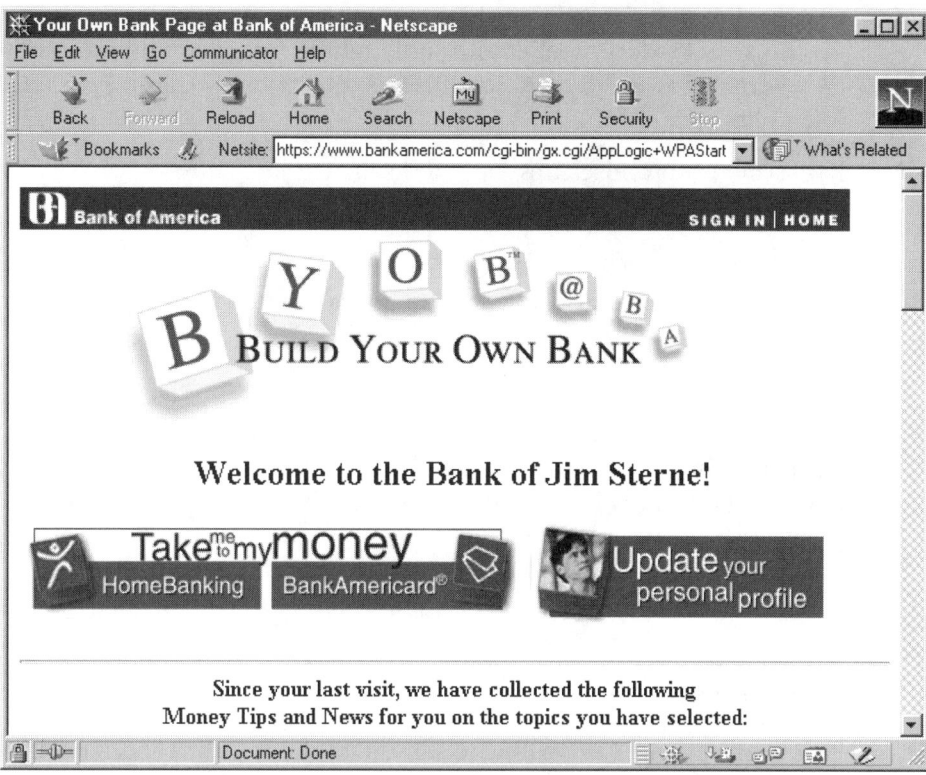

Figure 6.10 The Bank of Jim Sterne acts like a cookie, but at a very high price.

know your phone number, and it wants you to select from a list of topics that might interest you:

- Getting organized financially
- Saving and investing
- Home buying and home improvement
- Building a business
- Retirement
- Economic and financial markets
- Electronic commerce
- The environment

All of this information is fair trade. In return, B of A can create a newsletter home page with topics you're really interested in. Nifty. But wait a minute. It wants to know a little bit more. BankAmerica would like to ask a few questions about your gender, age, occupation, whether you own or rent, *and* your income. Feeling queasy? Suddenly the price of the newsletter just went way up. Most folks don't feel comfortable telling strange computers how much they earn. What will B of A do with this information? Can it be trusted to use it to my benefit only?

BankAmerica promises to keep it to itself:

Bank of America will keep all of your information confidential. It will be used to:

- Identify you on future visits to this site
- Provide you information on topics of special interest to you
- Save you time when you want to fill in forms or applications
- Help us understand who is visiting our site

Even with these assurances, it still feels like more than they need to know to publish a simple personalized newsletter. After all, Amazon.com only wants to know the authors I like and my e-mail address. No Spanish Inquisition from them. And the information B of A provides isn't even interesting enough to make it worth the time to log in. Not only is the bank nosy, but the simple act of remembering my password is too high a price to pay for such a small return.

Quicken Offers Value

On the other hand, I *am* willing to share some juicy tidbits about my investment portfolio with the complete strangers at the Quicken Web site (www.quicken.com, Figure 6.11). Why? Because I get to look at the current status of some of my investments whenever I please (with a 15-minute delay). This information is pretty personal, but the value they offer in return is very high.

If you're running a seriously large Web site, or if your Web site represents a critical part of your company's means of communication with customers, you owe it to yourself to invest in a tool that can glean meaning from your log files.

Industrial Strength Log Analysis Tools

You start out wanting and expecting the most and you end up being happy with almost anything. The fact is, Web site logs are not easy to read, do not accurately reflect what's really happening on your site, and cannot consistently give you the insights you were hoping for. There are several things that upset and bewilder a log file. All of them have to do with how the Internet works.

Cache Files Cause Undercounting

Cache files were a brilliant solution to two pressing Internet problems that stem from the same issue: speed. From the macro view, the designers of the

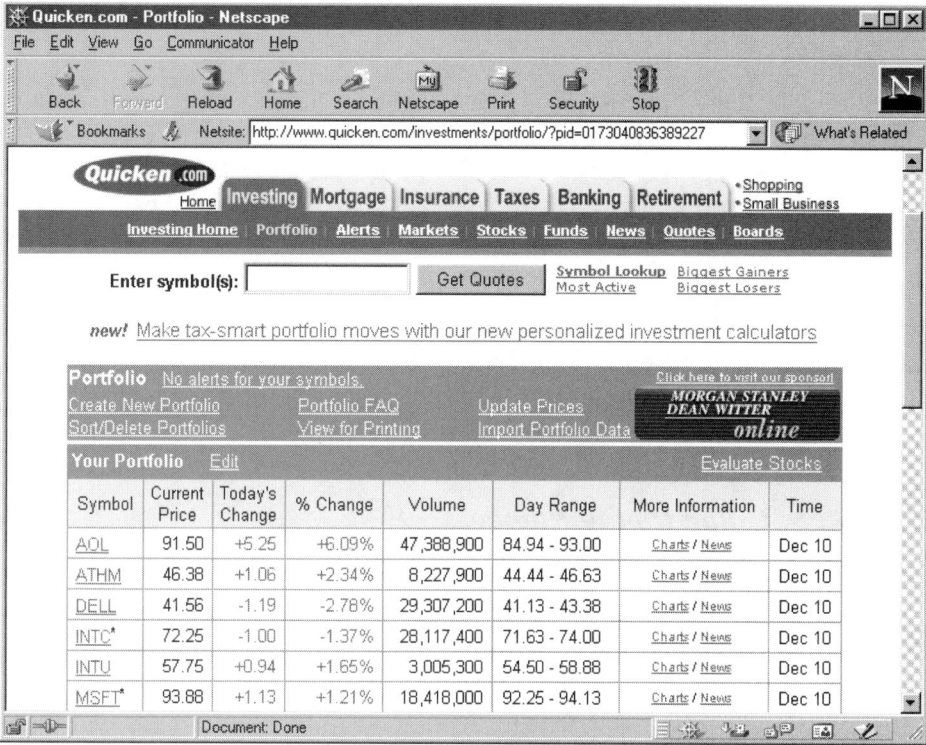

Figure 6.11   Quicken runs an advertising-supported stock quote system.

Internet worried about the whole system's being able to carry the load of all that data going back and forth. From the micro view, waiting for Web pages is as popular and as much fun as waiting in line at the bank.

The solution was to move the information as few times as possible.

When you click on a link and ask for a Web page for the first time, your browser looks in the cache file on your hard disk to see if you've seen that page before. It doesn't find it there, so it looks in the cache file on your Internet service provider's proxy server. It doesn't find it there, so it reaches out across the Web to the host server and asks for the page. The host finds the desired page, sends it to you, and records the event in its log file.

On the way back to you, the file is copied into the cache on your ISP machine and into the cache on your own hard disk. You see the page, find a link you like, and click away.

After several clicks, you feel a need to back up a few pages so you hit the Back button. Your browser looks in your cache file and immediately displays the page. It didn't have to go out on the Net at all. You put no additional strain on your ISP's system and you were instantly served the information you wanted.

Shortly thereafter, somebody else who uses the same ISP as you is interested in seeing that very same page. They click on a link or type in the URL and their browser repeats what yours did. It looks in the local cache file and finds nothing, and then it looks in the ISP's cache file. Since the page was previously recorded when you originally fetched it, it's available for your fellow surfer to grab directly from the ISP. This added no additional traffic to the backbone, and made the retrieval that much faster for the second viewer.

There's only one problem. The hosting server had no idea that you looked at the page again and no idea that somebody else at the same ISP looked at that page. The action is never reported in the log file.

Robots Run Up the Numbers

You track your server logs and you chronicle the access trend over time. One day you send out an e-mail to all of your customers, letting them know about special new service features on your site, and you see an astonishing jump in the number of visits to your site. Time to celebrate? Not yet.

First you have to be sure the additional hits weren't the footprints left by a search spider. The search engines send spiders out across the Web to read and index your site. They follow links from one page to the next to gather the pertinent information for searchers by programmatically clicking on every single link you have. That can make your log file look very full on any given day.

How Many People on One Computer?

Once you've removed the robots from your reports, you now have to sift through and determine how many people are represented by all those clicks. By lumping all of the requests made from the same computer (207.154.137.4, for example), you can assume they all came from the same person. Except for two things: *dynamic assignment of IP addresses* and *gateways*.

When you dial into your local ISP, you are assigned an Internet Protocol address. That number is going to be drawn from a pool of numbers the ISP has on hand, and you can be pretty sure you won't get the same number each time you dial up. Let's say you go to a certain site and then hang up your modem. Somebody else dials in, gets assigned the same IP address you were just using, and goes to the same site. The server logs for that site would think it was only one person.

Another log-baffling situation comes as the result of gateway computers. These are the systems that protect internal corporate networks and control the large number of users on online services such as America Online. Everybody surfing via America Online comes through an AOL gateway to your site. That means 10 different people can look like 1.

Is there somebody from Microsoft who seems to be *very* interested in your Web site? Or is it 200 people from Microsoft who were incorrectly told they could find a funny picture of Bill Gates on your site, found out there wasn't, and left?

Number Crunching—It Takes a Lot of Horsepower

Omar Ahmad manages the servers at Netscape. They have rooms and rooms of servers. They serve millions and millions of pages every day. But the biggest machines they have, the real bruisers, are used exclusively for server log analysis. Why? Because it takes muscle.

If you serve a million pages and each page is made up of 10 files and each file is about 20 kilobytes, then your server has to find, read, and send 200 terabytes of data. It makes a record of each transaction along the lines of:

```
207.77.91.38 - - [06/Dec/1999:09:25:28 -0600] "GET products/
tools/wrenches/left-handeds/crescent.html HTTP/1.0" 200 132
```

That line of text is 120 bytes. Multiply that by a million pages and 10 files and you only have 1.2 terabytes of data. That's much smaller than the 200TB that was served. So what's the problem?

The problem lies in the fact that serving data is one thing, and analyzing it is quite different. To analyze data, the software needs to categorize it, hold it in memory, compare it, and report on the findings. Sifting through a terabyte of data is not something you want to do on the same machine you are using to serve those pages.

So how do the big guys do it? The companies with huge Web sites? The pure Internet companies whose very existence depends on really good information about their site? They either have a room full of very brainy guys who subsist on Jolt Cola and pizza, or they buy some serious software to keep track of everything.

NetGenesis (www.netgen.com) is at the top of the field for keeping an eye on what people do on your site. In their own words:

> NetAnalysis 4.5 and CartSmarts from NetGenesis investigate visitor behavior, dynamic site content, search engine keywords, and advertising clickthroughs.

> Customer data, transaction histories, profiles and marketing campaign data, as well as third-party application data, can be correlated with online behavioral information to give e-business decision makers the most complete view of their online enterprise.

Reports include:

- *Shopping cart activity.* Understand how shoppers are using their carts, which carts they abandon and which purchases they complete.

- *Purchase frequency and recency.* Evaluate how often shoppers have purchased on your site.

- *Acquisition Source.* Understand which sites drive the most engaged shoppers and subsequent buyers to your site.

- *Visitor profile reports.* Create segments of online visitors based on demographic information to precisely target your Web marketing programs.

- *Product category reports.* Identify those products that drive purchases or are candidates for cross-selling or up-selling.

- *ROI reports.* Understand which marketing programs lead to the greatest ROI.

- *Cross channel dynamics reports.* Correlate data from your offline channels to formulate a complete picture of your visitors.

- *Customer lifetime value.* Evaluate which customers contribute the most to your business.

Count the Registrations and Interactions

How many people registered this month? How many people tracked their orders? How many answered a question asked by another customer? There are a myriad of ways of taking the pulse of your site and all of them are revealing.

All of them can also indicate actions you can take to improve the picture. Are registrations dropping? Place a "Customer Service First" ad in the trade journals showing off your dedication to your clients illustrated by your amazing World Wide Web services. Discussion on the threaded newsgroup slowing? Send an e-mail asking a pointed question and indicating that the response should be shared on the Web site. Start giving away tee-shirts. Have a customer appreciation contest. It's your job as ringmaster to keep this circus moving and holding customers' attention.

Count Your Accomplishments

The simplest form of measurement can be quantified in your Web logs. The most sophisticated form will be qualified in the feedback you get from your customers. In between, there is territory that is your core assignment. It's the measurable territory of helping your customers solve their problems, and you can get a handle on it by starting with some questions that seem easy, but take a little time to flesh out:

1. What does your customer service department do?

2. What specific services does it provide?

3. What tasks does it perform to deliver those services?

Here are a couple of quick examples (your mileage may vary):

EXAMPLE 1:

1. What does your customer service department do?
   - Helps customers install/implement products

2. What specific services does it provide?
   - Telephone support

3. What tasks does it perform to deliver those services?
   - Receive calls
   - Log calls
   - Respond to calls
   - Follow up on installations via phone

EXAMPLE 2:

1. What does your customer service department do?
   - Answers questions about deliveries

2. What specific services does it provide?
   - Telephone, fax, and e-mail correspondence

3. What tasks does it perform to deliver those services?
   - Receive calls, faxes, e-mails
   - Investigate the shipment
   - Respond with anticipated delivery dates
   - Resolve customer schedule problems

Given a list of the particular tasks you perform in your daily chores, you can start measuring how much a Web site has improved things for your customers.

You can start to track the number of calls and e-mail messages you receive. You can measure the number of problems resolved. And you can even come up with a formula to calculate how many calls you deferred due to people's getting their own answers for themselves, electronically.

What Are They Looking For?

You do have a search tool on your Web site, don't you? You do want people to be able to quickly find solutions to their problems, right? You did read Chapter 3, didn't you? Good. Just checking.

Search tools can be valuable sources of information on how well your Web site is organized, how well your search tool provides the right answers, and what interests the people who visit your site.

If you study the results of searches at your site, you can learn some interesting things:

- What are people most interested in?
- What terms do they use to find things that are uncommon to the company?
- How do they misuse the search tool?
- Are there any searches that are seasonal? Periodic?
- How are people responding to current events and the issues of the day?

What Are People Most Interested In?

This should be of gigantic interest. This will give you an opportunity to peer directly into the gray matter of people who are looking for answers. What subjects are on their minds? What is it they most want to know about and how can you better dish up this information?

You will also gain some insight into their thinking processes by tracking which pages they were on before they performed their search. Do people hit the Search button as soon as they hit your home page? Or do they roam around for a while?

A good Web server can keep track of *referring pages*. These are the pages that the visitor was on before he or she came to the present one. (This is usually used to tell Webmasters which advertising links out on the net are the most powerful at drawing people to your site.) With this tracking in place, you will get a good idea of where people got stumped before they gave up looking and went for the Search button. If everybody who goes to your Power Supply page looks at it for two minutes and then runs over to the search tool and enters Battery, you know you have to provide some better navigational support.

What Are They Reading?

Keeping tabs on which documents are being downloaded and which ones are most popular will give you some real insight into which areas people feel they need more information and more instruction on. There's no question that people who are *not* accessing your archives are just as troubled by these topics. Knowing which areas are causing consternation gives you the chance to be proactive. Time to beef up that training course, add a new section to your user manual, change the copy in your advertising, or give your salespeople some new ways to describe your products and services.

How Do They Misuse the Search Tool?

Some people are not library scientists. They have not studied the fine arts of relational databases, Boolean logic, concept searches, object-oriented cataloging, or fuzzy logic. Still, they want to look something up on your site. What mistakes are they making? How could you change the search tool or provide additional guidance/training to make it easier for them?

Are There Any Searches that Are Seasonal? Periodic?

Do the same search requests come up in the same frequency day after day, week after week? Or is your business seasonal? Should you be expecting more queries about delivery schedules for your perishable products in the winter? Do they want to know more about volume discounts in the summer and about overnight shipments around Christmas? Plan accordingly. Make sure the equipment is up to the seasonal challenge. A search engine can put a strain on your server, so be sure to monitor it for stress under peak loads.

How Are People Responding to Current Events?

Did the industry news on the front page of *The Wall Street Journal* change the searching habits of your visitors? If everybody is suddenly interested in your earnings, get a button up on the home page that they can click on. Instead of making them search for "financial statement," "gross earnings," or "stock price," give them a big Investor Relations button. Then they can get the story fast without having to play hide-and-seek. You won't be stopping them from searching, you'll just make it easier for people to get at whatever is uppermost in their minds.

Got a new product announcement? A new software release? A new product recall? Remember, your home page is much more like the cover of a magazine combined with the table of contents than like the cover of the annual report. It's not there just for the sake of saying "Hi! We're glad you're here!" It's a communication tool. Put a procedure in place that allows for quick updates to that page to keep pace with the times. You're in the publishing business now.

How Well Do You Compare?

Besides keeping an eye on your log files, Dave Taylor (www.intuitive.com) also reminds his clients to keep an eye on the feedback about their Web efforts from their customers:

- Is the site well-designed and easily understood?

- Are problem reports promptly followed up?

- Are problems quickly resolved?

- Are customers able to get a high priority when they have a real emergency?

- Are customers given training opportunities?

- Are they informed of system and product changes—software upgrades, bug fixes, and so on?

Remember, this second set of questions is different when you ask them of a customer. It's no longer about logs and charts and statistics. It's about perception. If your customers don't feel they're getting the information they need or getting the attention they deserve, it doesn't matter if your logs show more pages read this week than last.

According to *Consumer Reports*, computer owners aren't very happy with the customer service they're getting. Well below half (40 percent) were "completely" or "very" satisfied with the computer manufacturer's support. *Consumer Reports* says this is "one of the lowest satisfaction levels we've ever measured for a service." Thirty-eight percent felt they had suffered on hold for an "unreasonable" amount of time. They complained that the staff they talked to didn't know enough to help, and 34 percent claimed to have problems that had never been resolved.

One can make excuses for the personal computer industry. It's a very complex product in use by all manner of people for all manner of applications. Problems could stem from hardware faults, software faults, communication faults, networking faults, and the all-time favorite: configuration faults. That's where every vendor says that its piece works just fine, but the way the components are all put together must be at fault.

Given that sort of an industry, the only fair way for companies to measure how well they're doing is to compare their service offering against their competitors'. You do keep a watchful eye on your competitors, don't you? Good.

What Are Your Competitors Up To?

Chances are, the players in your industry are in all phases of Web site development:

Under discussion. We're not sure how to do this yet so we'll wait for others to try it first.

Under construction. You can be sure we're doing everything in our power to create a wonderful Web site for our customers and their children's children.

Brochure Stage. We're a wonderful company with wonderful products. Want us to mail this page to you? Just click here.

Sales cycle support. Click here to learn the details you need to make a buying decision without having to listen to an obnoxious salesperson.

Retail Sales. Click here to order and enter your credit card number.

Client Sales. Click here to order and enter your client account number.

Customer Service. Click here to get instant solutions to a myriad of problems.

Take a close look and see how well you stack up.

The Chip Business Is Highly Competitive

National Semiconductor takes its competitive edge seriously. Periodically, it has an independent research company round up 50 design engineers (National Semi's core customers—nerd's nerds) and sit them down in front of National's site and three competitors' sites. Then they watch carefully as they hand each engineer a task: Find a price. Spec out a component. Find the mean time between failure on a part. Get an answer to a tough question.

They measure how long it takes. They measure how many times each engineer furrows his or her eyebrows. They interview each one and ask how user-friendly each site was. Which site did they like best? Why? What features do they think they'll use the most?

As a result, National makes structural changes, cosmetic changes, and adds new features to their Web site on a quarterly basis. There's no such thing as a Web site that's finished.

Plan to Compete

Make sure you have "competitive review" on your calendar every month. Get somebody to check out your biggest rivals to see what they've put in place. They still don't have a feature that *you* implemented weeks ago? Mail another notice to your customers and prospects, letting them know you're a leader in electronic support.

The competition created a whole new support service on their site? Time for a tiger-team meeting to determine the ramifications. Either it's a minor issue or a major formidable challenge to your marketplace superiority. If it's the latter, you'll have to pick it apart and figure out how to do it better. And fast.

Assign somebody to the task of keeping tabs on your competition on a set, periodic basis. Create a matrix of the companies you feel are competitive, plus a few more you feel are front-runners. Across the top, list the different things they are offering on their sites, and keep a record over time. This will tell you at a glance how you stack up, and will give you some insight into how important the competition considers the Web.

Benchmarking for Prudence and Profit

Dr. John Anton specializes in customer service strategies at the Purdue University Center for Customer-Driven Quality. While he focuses on call centers, a lot of what he has to say about benchmarking applies directly to Web-based customer service as well.

1. Identify and document the process, practice, or service to be benchmarked.

    Dr. Anton points out that if you just go into another firm and suck up a lot of information, it may be interesting, but you'll end up with too many conflicting factors. You want to end up with a clear to-do list of action items instead. Make sure your list of processes and so forth is manageable in a small enough time that you can put the results to work immediately.

    While the good doctor is worried about holding the attention of upper management long enough to get the job done, on the Internet things move so fast that a six-month study is not going to help. We live in an age of constant improvement and a world of competitive change. To get the most out of your benchmarking efforts, you have to come up with decisive answers in a hurry. As Dr. Anton says, "Go for the low-hanging fruit."

2. Identify the companies against which you will benchmark.

    Some of the features on your competitors' Web sites are visible and comparable. Some lie behind password protection and, therefore, are invisible to outside observers. Find other companies that are similar but noncompetitive. For example, such companies could be in your industry, but not your segment. Or they could be in manufacturing (or service or distribution) as you are, but not in the same industry.

The further steps are fundamental:

3. Collect and store data about these companies.
4. Analyze the data.
5. Project future performance.
6. Communicate the results and get acceptance within your organization.
7. Establish objectives.
8. Develop an action plan for each objective.
9. Implement and monitor the results.
10. Repeat.

While this list looks straightforward, Dr. Anton warns that there are a few critical success factors that cannot be ignored. Things like upper management support, a clear idea of the goals of your organization, organizational flexibility, a willingness to share operational information with other companies (including some competitors), and protection of the proprietary information you collect from others are all important.

Finally, benchmarking isn't about copying somebody else's process, it's about understanding why that process works better and how it can be adapted to your business. Tom Peters says copying competitors' molded, shaped, and cast-in-iron methods is the slippery slope to stagnation. Study them, yes, but don't copy them. Run circles around them instead.

Hire a Secret Shopper

You really want to know how well you're doing? Hire a spy.

It's a common recommendation that management should call its own company and see how good customer service really is. How quickly is the phone answered? How long on hold? What does the music-on-hold sound like? How friendly are the voices on the other end?

The hard part is knowing what the answers might be, could be, and should be. Better to get an outside service to play secret shopper and test out how well you fare. BuyerTouch (www.buyertouch.com, Figure 6.12) does just that for a living.

Prioritize to Compete

By the time you finish reading this book you'll have accumulated a number of ideas you'd like to implement. With any luck, it will be a large number of ideas. But resources are never plentiful and time is of the essence. Based on

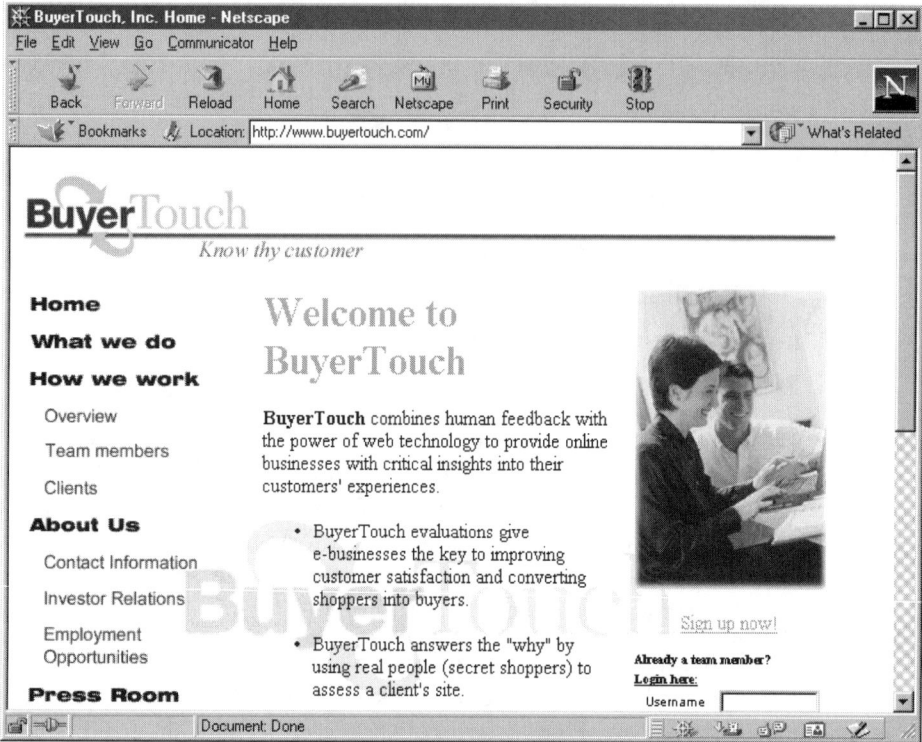

Figure 6.12 BuyerTouch will evaluate your customer service abilities and report back to you.

what you already have on your site . . . based on what the competition is offering . . . based on what the competition could do if they had another three months to work on it . . . what do you absolutely, positively *have* to add to your site in the next three months?

If you look at your Web effort as an ongoing project without end, you have a pretty accurate view. When you've nailed your list down to twice as many items as there is time or money to implement them, you've got a good start and it's time to prioritize. Here's a basic approach to prioritization:

What are the easiest features to add to your site? Rank these on a scale of 1 to 10, with 1 for the easiest and 10 for the hardest.

What are the least expensive features to add? Rank, with 1 for the cheapest and 10 for the most expensive.

Which are the features your customers are asking for the most? Rank, with 1 for the most frequent and 10 for those you only hear about from one or two certified cranks.

Which features will require the least amount of training and/or cultural change? Rank, with 1 for the least disruption and 10 for things that require everybody to adopt a new attitude and learn a foreign language.

Which features will require the least amount of political upset? Rank, with 1 for those that sound good to everybody and 10 for those that threaten the CEO's brother-in-law's empire built up brick by blood-soaked brick over the span of an entire career.

You'll want to add some other measures, of course, but the end result is the same. Add up all the numbers and the lowest scorers get the highest priority. Done.

Open the Door for Customer Comments

If you remember anything, remember that this is your customer's Web site and not yours. How good it is, how well it serves its purpose, and how much of an asset it is to the corporation depends on how it is perceived by your customers.

Ask Them

Often.

They'll help you prioritize your list because they're the ones who have to live with the results. People are happy to share ideas about what you can do to make their lives easier. Just ask them.

Rather than providing a simple Feedback button on each page, ask a specific question. Got a page that allows people to look up products by name or part number? Add a small text box to the bottom of the page: "Were you able to get the information you needed?" At the bottom of every product description, ask if there was something else they'd like to see on your pages to help them.

Don't expect people to answer a 48-page survey of their own free will. Instead, either ask one question here and one there *in direct relation to the page they're on*, or offer some powerful incentive to encourage them to fill out the 48-pager.

United Airlines figured bribery might do the trick. It sure worked on me. I'll do anything for frequent flier miles . . .

```
Delivered-To: jsterne@silcom.com
From: United Airlines Mileage Plus <ual@mileageplus.com>
To: Mr. James B. Sterne <jsterne@targeting.com>
Subject: 1,000 miles for your thoughts
Date: Wed, 14 Jul 1999 12:35:31

Dear Mr. Sterne:

HOW DID WE DO?
YOUR FEEDBACK IS WORTH 1,000 MILES
```

According to our records, you recently contacted the Mileage Plus(R) Service Center to request program information or account data. We have prepared a brief survey to verify that our response was timely and that we addressed your specific request. We would very much appreciate your taking the time to complete this questionnaire by going to:

http://www.uasurvey.com/mpp059

When you respond within 30 days of this e-mail, we will thank you with 1,000 bonus miles. This bonus will be credited to your account four to six weeks after the end of the survey. Your feedback is extremely important, and we look forward to providing you with efficient service and a more hassle-free travel experience in the future.

Respectfully,

Colleen Sanders
Customer Survey Coordinator

+++

TO CONTACT US WITH QUESTIONS OR COMMENTS
Visit our Customer Service Web page at:

http://www.ual.com/CService

TO UNSUBSCRIBE

Please do not respond to this e-mail unless you wish to unsubscribe. Mail sent to this address cannot be answered. To remove your name from the United Airlines Mileage Plus e-mail list, reply to this message and type UNSUBSCRIBE in the subject line.

+++
This e-mail message and its contents are copyrighted and are proprietary products of United Airlines.
Copyright 1999 United Airlines, Inc. All rights reserved.

UAMP 15653 7/99 (MPP 059)

Have Others Ask Them

These days, you can hook up with a third party like BizRate (www.bizrate.com, Figure 6.13) to find out how you're doing.

While search engines, price bots, and portals feature only those stores that pay them most, BizRate.com is free to list every quality store on the Web. In fact, online stores CANNOT pay to be listed or featured on BizRate.com.

Also, because BizRate.com is the only resource continuously collecting direct feedback from millions of actual customers as they buy, we know which Web sites are good, what they are good at, and how their service varies each day. So, BizRate.com is the only site that can take your particular needs and match them with the stores that are best suited to serve you.

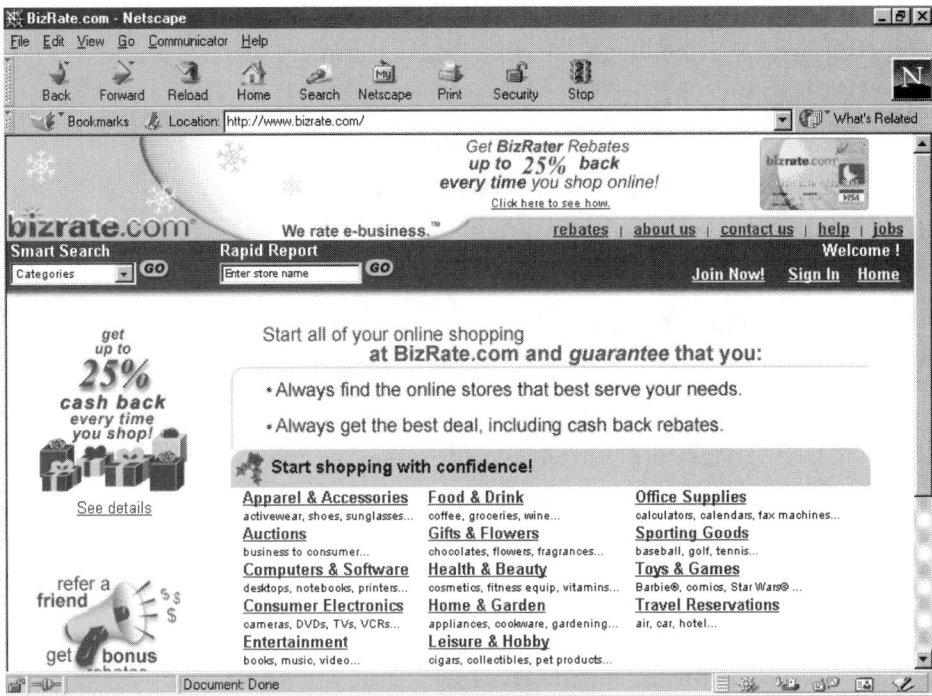

Figure 6.13 Bizrate is a shopping portal/business rating system.

This direct feedback is what retail Web site owners are craving.

> BizRate.com sits on the receipt page of its members' online stores and independently invites buyers to participate in the BizRate.com survey. The aggregation of the merchants' customer surveys is presented to shoppers as Customer Certified ratings listed on www.bizrate.com. This information is also available to merchants in the form of unedited customer feedback and actionable market research.
>
> What benefits do merchant members receive?
> FREE on-demand access to merchants' customers' comments
> FREE listing on the BizRate.com network
> FREE monthly site-specific market research
> FREE use of BizRate.com customer certified medal for marketing
> FREE market research on "hot" e-commerce topics

Process Improvement

Want your customers to think more highly of you? Fix those processes that they see. How quickly and how well you answer your e-mail is far more important than how you actually get it done. We don't care how the restaurant cleans the rest rooms just as long as they do it frequently and properly.

In *Online Customer Care* (ASQ Quality Press, 1998), Michael Cusack lists some of the things you do that your customers watch you do. He calls them *customer-facing processes.* Among them:

Routing inbound customer calls (think e-mail) to appropriate agents

Handling customer account maintenance, such as

    Changing customer address

    Changing pricing plan

    Responding to returned mail

    Renewing or canceling contracts

    Modifying credit limit

    Changing billing responsibility

    Recording customer comments

Resolving presales requests, such as

    Pricing inquiries (noncustomer)

    Feature availability

    Nearest branch/store location

Handling customer orders and reservations, such as

    Inventory location

    Credit approval

    Price negotiation

Resolving general inquiries and problems

Resolving billing inquiries, including

    Pricing inquiries (customer)

    Requests for invoice copy

    Changing billing cycles

    Explaining first bill

    Explaining feature changes

    Creating revised bill

    Explaining taxes

    Producing on-demand bill

Handling collections, including

    Response to late notice

    Response to treatment report

    Response to nonpay deactivation

Handling customer complaints

Handling misdirected calls (think e-mail)

Online escalation of customer calls

Customer agent callback commitment handling

Handling customer-initiated callbacks

Why does Cusack go to such lengths to enumerate the process possibilities? Because most of us start small and don't think much about this stuff as we grow. In a huge customer service organization, there are large binders outlining every task and every anomaly and every set of approval initials required to sneeze. In a small organization, most things are passed along by word of mouth. The result? Those who weren't in the room at the time missed the verbal memo.

Pay attention to how things get done. If the customer can *see* you getting it done, or is part of the process, be sure you do it well.

Strike Up a Relationship

Reach out to your customers every chance you get. If they ask you a question, ask them a question back. Don't just solve their problem and send them on their way. Actually try to engage them in a longer conversation so you can learn more about them.

```
To: Jane "Valued Customer" Doe
From: John "Customer Service" Smith
Re: Your Opinion

Thanks again for taking the time to talk to me last month about
our customer service progress on the Web. You told me that you'd
like to see more case studies about how other customers are using
the 7100 model 15sf in their companies. Well, we added two more at
http://www.ourcompany.com/cases6.html and /cases7.html and I'd like
to get your honest feedback.

Is this the sort of thing that would help you? Is there any additional
information you'd like to see about these two stories? I'd appreciate
your input.

P.S. I'd also_*love* to have you write one for us!
```

Every month, select a handful of customers and (are you sitting down?) call them on the phone! Have a conversation with them and find out what makes this Web site a good place for customer service. Ask them what you could do to improve it. Get to know them as individuals and continue the conversation via e-mail.

In the May 1999 issue of her newsletter, "Marketing Technology," marketing genius and spot-on consultant Kristin Zhivago wrote about a company that she feels deserves recognition for "Instant Market Leadership":

Is it possible to enter an existing marketplace and instantly become a leader? Yes. And we predict that works.com is going to be one of those companies. Why? Because they're doing so many things right. Marketing is a lot like sailboat racing; those who make the fewest mistakes win the races. Works.com is just out of the gate and already way ahead of the pack.

Works.com sells office supplies. But it's more than an online store; it's a buying process facilitator. The company is run by a marketing guy (surprise, surprise), Bo Holland. Other companies could learn a lot from Bo, so we'll go into detail about what he's been doing.

CUSTOMER-CENTRIC MISSION

We'll start with the works.com mission statement. "Works.com's mission is to provide companies with the better way to buy business products. Works.com achieves this mission by offering all companies—regardless of size, location, or purchase history—wholesale direct prices on an extensive selection of office and technology products.

"In addition, with works.com, companies can automate and manage their entire purchasing process—from purchase requests and approval to ordering, tracking, and reporting. This allows companies to organize and streamline purchasing, lower purchasing costs, reduce processing time, and improve spending control."

Even the mission statement, usually a ho-hum series of phrases dripping with egotism, is worth a quick analysis. In the first sentence, they immediately and clearly communicate the unique value they provide ("the better way to buy business products").

Note how there is no mention of "becoming the leading supplier of," which is the most common first phrase included in mission statements.

SHOCKING: COMPANY DOES RESEARCH

How did Bo and his team know what people wanted? Hold on to your chair: They asked them! "I've been in commercial software for the last twelve years," Bo says. "One of the hard parts is getting everybody in the organization to understand what it is that the customer is experiencing, what they need, and why." Getting this right is critical, especially if you're a Web-based company. "The site is the company," Bo says, stating the obvious. "It's not a product that you put in a box, throw over the wall, and then find out how painful it is on the other end. First, you have to find out, real-time, how the product actually works [when being used by a customer]. Second, you've got to automate every function that supports the sale."

Here's what Bo did to make sure that his staff truly understood the total customer experience: "One of the things we started doing early on—and intend to continue forever—are weekly calls to customers. Every week, on Tuesday, at ten o'clock, we get a customer on the speakerphone in a conference room.

"The customer is expecting the call. And we often look for an unhappy customer. This is not intended to be 'happy time.' It's more like, 'Who's upset with us?' And we get that person to agree to come on the phone and tell us what they experienced. And we get the whole company in the meeting around the speakerphone, and we sit there and we listen for thirty to forty-five minutes."

Customers are prepped, just a little, in advance of the call. Either the customer has called in with a problem or a call to the customer has uncovered a problem. "We ask them if they'd be willing to get on the phone and describe the problem to us," Bo says.

He asserts, "The response has been unbelievable. We had a person who printed sixteen pages from the site, annotated them, and faxed them to us. She spent an hour and a half on the phone with us, going through interface changes: 'I want to see this information here. No, you're showing me this too late. I need it up here. . . . This is stupid, you're wasting my time. . . . I don't understand this.' It was amazing."

Satisfaction Formulas

When Cisco Systems set out to track how customers felt about their Web services, they realized there was more to it than, "Please rate our Web site on a scale of 1 to 10." They broke it down into multiple metrics.

How happy are you with our search engine? How happy are you with the completeness of the information we offer? How happy are you with the speed with which your questions are answered? How happy are you with the knowledge base? The FAQ documents? The troubleshooting guides? The remote diagnostic tools?

Then Cisco went one step better. Peter Corless, Content Manager, Software Center, Cisco Connection Online, explains that the happiness level of any feature is important, but doesn't make any difference unless the feature is important.

Sure, they wanted to know if they were saving money. "Did this visit to Cisco's Web site save you a phone call?" They divided that one up between guest users (people who showed up but didn't register) and service customers (people who paid extra in order to get access to more in-depth information). But they also asked how important it was to them that they didn't have to call.

Sure, they asked about overall satisfaction, but they also delved into user opinions about usefulness, completeness, the search facility, speed of response, and ease of use.

Says Peter, "If you were to re-sort by the greatest gap, you can see customers are pretty happy with the completeness and responsiveness of our site. . . . What they want more from us now primarily is better search capabilities. That is by far the biggest challenge for us as a large site. . . . How do we let you find what is important to you? Next are better ease-of-use, and better utility (usefulness) of the services. That might be adding more functionality to existing apps, or adding new apps that don't exist today.

"Each one of these becomes a 'drill-down' series of questions with focus groups and usability studies."

Caroline Fisher, a professor of marketing at Loyola University, offered up a mind-expanding article in *Customer Service Management* magazine (November/December 1999). She starts by lamenting that measuring satisfaction these days is simply looking for the absence of pain. "It does not indicate the presence of anything that would draw and hold customers to your product or service." Or to your Web site.

Fisher proposes that a much better measurement is the value of the product or service as perceived by the customer. "Value is a trade-off between the positive and negative consequences of purchase and use." She outlines the difference between satisfaction and value this way:

SATISFACTION ORIENTATION	VALUE ORIENTATION
Measures only positive consequences	Measures trade-offs
Measures one brand	Compares major competitors
Focuses on the product	Focuses on product use
Focuses on attributes	Uses attributes, consequences, and values
Provides short-term view	Provides more long-term outlook
Encourages incremental change	Encourages radical change

To really understand where Fisher is going with the differences, another table is offered, full of examples.

PRODUCT	ATTRIBUTE	CONSEQUENCE	VALUE
Candy	Sugar	Tastes sweet	Happiness
Chicken	Low in fat	Consume fewer calories	Health
Computer	Low price	Costs less money	Frugal
Fast food	Fast service	Don't have to stand in line	Efficient
Toothpaste	Fluoride	No cavities	Health
Flower delivery	Fresh flowers	Last a long time	Social approval
Flower delivery	Quick delivery	Arrive on time	Social approval
Flower delivery	Good arrangements	Look expensive	Social approval
Flower delivery	Take credit cards	Can charge	Efficient budgeting

Then, says Fisher, gather the voice of the customer and measure the levels of importance as Cisco did. But make sure you take into account the weights of the consequences and the values as well.

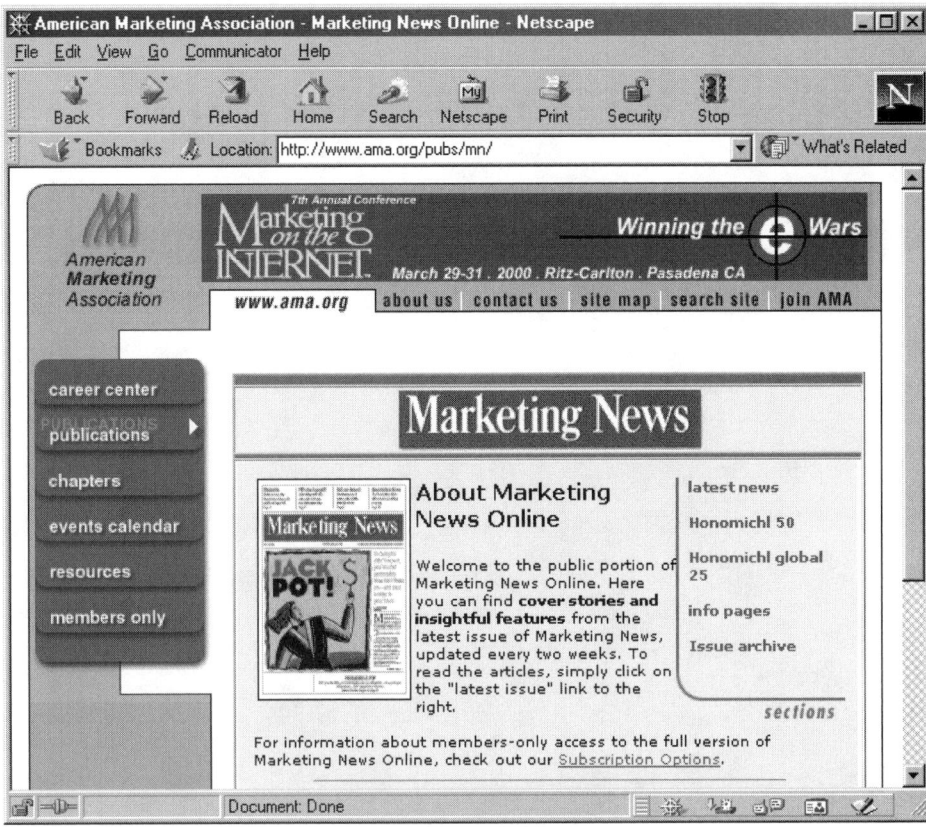

Figure 6.14 *Marketing News,* from the American Marketing Association, published a list of firms that can help you measure customer satisfaction.

If you need some outside help measuring how happy your customers are, the October 25, 1999, issue of *Marketing News* magazine listed close to 100 different companies in its Directory of Customer Satisfaction Measurement Firms (www.ama.org, Figure 6.14).

Making customers happy is about making people happy. Communicating with them personally is the first step. Getting your computer to communicate with them on a personal basis is the next step, and the topic of the next chapter.

Count what you can and track what you count. Once you get a sense of how much people are using your Web-based customer services and how they feel about it, you'll know what you need to make your site better and to turn it into a competitive advantage for your company.

CHAPTER 7

Knowing Your Customers as Individuals—Again

*The battle for customers in the future will be won by marketers who understand how and why their customers **individually** buy their products— and learn how to win them over, one customer at a time.*
**Rob Jackson and Paul Wang, *Strategic Database Marketing*
NTC Business Books, 1994**

In the days before mass transportation and mass communication, Mr. Johnson, the General Store proprietor, knew his clients very well. Mrs. Carson always bought an extra sack of flour and an extra bag of sugar when her brother-in-law's family came to visit. Mr. Johnson could pretty well guess at the maladies suffered by the folks who crossed the street from Doc Sullivan's office by the tonics and elixirs Doc prescribed. He knew when Mrs. Markins was expecting again, and he knew Fred Peterson was seeing somebody on the side because Mrs. Peterson's head was just a tad too large for the pretty new hat Fred selected and had wrapped up.

As a result, when any of the town's folk came into the General Store, Mr. Johnson would have reason to inquire after their family, their health, and their common sense. And when any roving traders rolled into town, Mr. Johnson had an excellent idea about what he would and would not be able to sell in the coming months. He knew who had finally cleared out the back 40 and what they were preparing to plant. He knew who was sick and not likely to last the winter. He knew who would be ordering extra supplies for new a barn and extra provisions for out-of-town visitors.

In Japan, pharmaceutical retailers have been getting very personal with their clients since the mid-1700s. Yes, that's 1700s, as in 300 years ago. Sales representatives visit individual families and review the contents of their company-issued medicine cabinets. Items that have been used are replaced. Items that have not are either removed or replaced, based on expiration dates. They found this method so successful, they continue it to this day.

Things changed in America as we spread out across the country. Things changed when it became possible to talk to a massive number of people over the radio and television. In order to sell into a new, mass-transportation, mass-communication marketplace we resorted to mass marketing. Mass marketing discounted the individual for the statistics. It ignored the man in the street and replaced him with the man in the survey. We no longer knew our customers as people but as integers.

When we started selling things by remote control we lost that intimate knowledge of our customers. We had to rely on demographics, surveys, samples, and surmises. The focus group told us what we wanted to hear so that we could make what we wanted to make. Then we would scratch our heads and point in mystery at a good, solid, scientific study and proclaim, "The numbers said it would fly. I don't know why the market didn't buy."

Our customers didn't buy because we had turned our backs on them. It's because we stopped the dialog and started the monologue. We continued talking to them without getting enough feedback. We told them why our remedy would fix their malady, and if they didn't have that malady we set about convincing them they did. If the manufacturing industry couldn't find a need and fill it, it would invent a need. Nobody ever complained to their local merchant that they needed something to cure house-itosis or ring-around-the-collar. In the process we stopped listening to our customers. We stopped paying attention to individuals on a one-to-one basis.

In the land of the blind, the one-eyed man is king. In the land of the blind-to-the-market, the man with a 2 percent response to a direct mail piece is king.

Bringing Back the Intimacy

The point at which information is captured, stored, and analyzed has been on a march toward the customer. That point has moved from the manufacturer, to the stores, and now because of the Web, directly into the customers' hands. The information itself started from an industrywide perspective, narrowed to a regional perspective, dropped down to the store level, and has finally zeroed in on each customer. This move has come out of the need to get the right product at the right price in front of the right customer at the right time.

The Industry Perspective

Stonyfield Farm in Londonderry, New Hampshire, makes yogurt. The folks at Stonyfield Farm wanted to spot trends and changes in tastes for their product.

The label on each carton of their product asked people to write in and tell them about their favorite flavors and flavors they'd like. This information used to be received on scraps of paper and be filed away to be forgotten. Then the company improved its tracking abilities by implementing a database that could keep track of flavor ideas, and can now react to customers' preferences more quickly. If enough people want sour cherry yogurt, Stoneyfield Farm will produce it.

Unfortunately, the information they are gathering and the actions they are taking are based on market-wide inclinations. They may have moved from buying survey results from data consolidators to polling their own customers themselves, but they're still in the realm of extrapolating the thoughts of the few onto the desires of the many. The information they get is on a one-way street. They listen to a few and hope the rest will agree.

The Store's-Eye-View

Manufacturers have long recognized the power of knowing what is selling in each store. Debbie Field made the news when the Mrs. Field's Cookies story was told. Computers in every store feed daily cookie sales information back to headquarters in Park City, Utah. There they evaluate what is selling where and plan the next day's shipments accordingly. Because the product is manufactured on-site on a just-in-time basis, Park City need only be responsible for the ingredients showing up on time.

Anheuser-Busch knows the weekly sales of Bud 12-packs by store and scrutinizes those numbers by cross-referencing them to the surrounding area's income, ethnicity, population density, and you name it. All in the name of guessing who is buying their product in an attempt to broadcast the right message to the right people at the right time. Joe Patti, senior director of retail planning and category management at Anheuser-Busch, was quoted in *Advertising Age* magazine, pointing out that in the 1980s "you spent the majority of your time trying to get the data to analyze. Today, you spend the majority of your time analyzing what this information means."

The United Colors of Benetton took the same model and applied it to clothing. They only manufacture white clothing. That's it. Why? Because every day they get feeds from all of their stores around the world telling them which items sold that day—in which color.

People are funny animals. Especially young ones. Once they find a chocolate chip cookie they like, they tend to stick with it for years. But clothing? That's a horse of a different color. Benetton caters to the young and the trendy, and trendy is a tough game to play. These customers will follow a trend that is only days old. To compensate, Benetton analyzes retail sales on a daily basis and determines which color to dye the premanufactured clothing for shipment the next day.

Benetton customers vote with their pocketbooks. Then their friends and neighbors and other trend followers rush out and get the same color to keep up with the hippest. Then they'll walk across the mall and buy the same White Chocolate Chunk Macadamia Nut cookie from Debbie that they've been eating since they were twelve. Knowing that their customers are fickle, Benetton has positioned itself to be alert, to be responsive, to be nimble—to the store level.

Seeing Customers Eye to Eye

In January of 1992, a Direct Marketing Association study showed that over 90 percent of business-to-business companies used database marketing techniques to bag new customers and to keep the ones they have. They realized that intimate knowledge of individual customers yields better return sales than simply knowing which days of the week to move the beer display closer to the cash register.

The hotel industry found that out by happy accident. Taking a tip from the airlines, Holiday Inn started the first frequent flyer club for hotel guests in 1983. The move caused a great deal of attention in the hotel business, and soon others were hopping on board.

The goal was simple—get people to come back to your hotel because they could earn points toward free nights, gifts, airline travel, etc. It worked. Marriott Hotels found that the same people spent two and a half times more nights at Marriott once they were Honored Guests than they had prior to signing up, based on a survey of 30,000 members. They used a customer-rewards hook to build the bond between the customer and the company.

Customer Bonding

Getting people to know who you are is the first step in customer bonding. Then you want them to identify with you, establish a relationship, form a sense of community, and, if you're good, become advocates. All of these steps are spelled out in detail in *Customer Bonding: Pathway to Lasting Customer Loyalty* by Richard Cross and Janet Smith (NTC, 1995).

Awareness Bonding

Awareness bonding is going from zero to sixty as soon as possible. You start with people who have never heard of you and you end up with people who understand how you are positioned against your competition. The usual way to accomplish this is with standard broadcast-type marketing—television, magazines, billboards, skywriting—whatever it takes to get your name in front of as many people as possible.

Cross and Smith point out that awareness bonding is fragile, expensive, and a one-way street. It's easy to lose mindshare to a competitor; it requires a whopping budget; and you end up learning nothing about the intended recipient of your message. These map directly to the Internet as well. In fact, it's even easier to lose mindshare to a competitor, because every Web site is competing for your customer's time.

Identity Bonding

Identity bonding refers to a customer identifying with the values and emotions embodied in your product, service, or organization. This means making astute suppositions about your prospective clients before you get to know them. It's what makes people think your product is so cool, environmentally conscientious, socially responsible, or macho that they're willing to wear your tee-shirt, sport your bumper sticker, or put up a link to your Web site.

This level of attachment suffers from the some of the same weaknesses as awareness bonding. It's easy for the next guy to be cooler, hipper, better, or exude just the right lifestyle preferences and attitudes to win over your prospective customer. Like awareness bonding, it's very hard to measure your effectiveness. If you can provide the right appeal to emotions and values, as well as an excellent experience every time the customer comes in contact with your company, they will move into this higher level of connection.

Relationship Bonding

The next level of customer connectivity is relationship bonding. This is where the customer interacts frequently enough with your company to be worth knowing and tracking as an individual. It usually involves database marketing, and rewards the customer for continuing to do business.

Fly a lot with one airline and you get free tickets. Stay enough with one hotel chain and earn free accommodations. You agree to have your transactions tracked, and they promise to make it worth your while. In the hierarchy of customer bonding levels, Cross and Smith explain that this approach makes it harder for the customer to move to a competitor. If I can get free airfare *and* get free car rentals *and* get free hotel nights *and* you'll give me triple miles for each flight, it's going to be hard for a competitor to get me to switch. But it's possible. To strengthen the ties that bind, you have to move into community bonding.

Community Bonding

This step requires the merchant to foster interaction between customers. They also refer to this as lifestyle bonding. One of the most successful examples of this approach has been Harley-Davidson Motorcycles' Harley Owners Groups (H.O.G.), with chapters all over the world (www.harley-davidson.com, Figure 7.1). Harley riders are devoutly dedicated to their brand and meet frequently to share in the camaraderie of riding together. The relationship between manufacturer and customer is exceptionally strong here. Very few other companies can state on their home page, "It's one thing to have people buy your products. It's another thing to have them tattoo your name on their bodies."

> Customers or supporters who form a community bond around your brand, product, service, candidate, cause or organizations are usually extremely loyal. Your competitors will be hard-pressed to shake their allegiance.
>
> Think about it. When people get together to share their use of your product . . . they are really putting their brand loyalty out there for others to see and judge. If they're

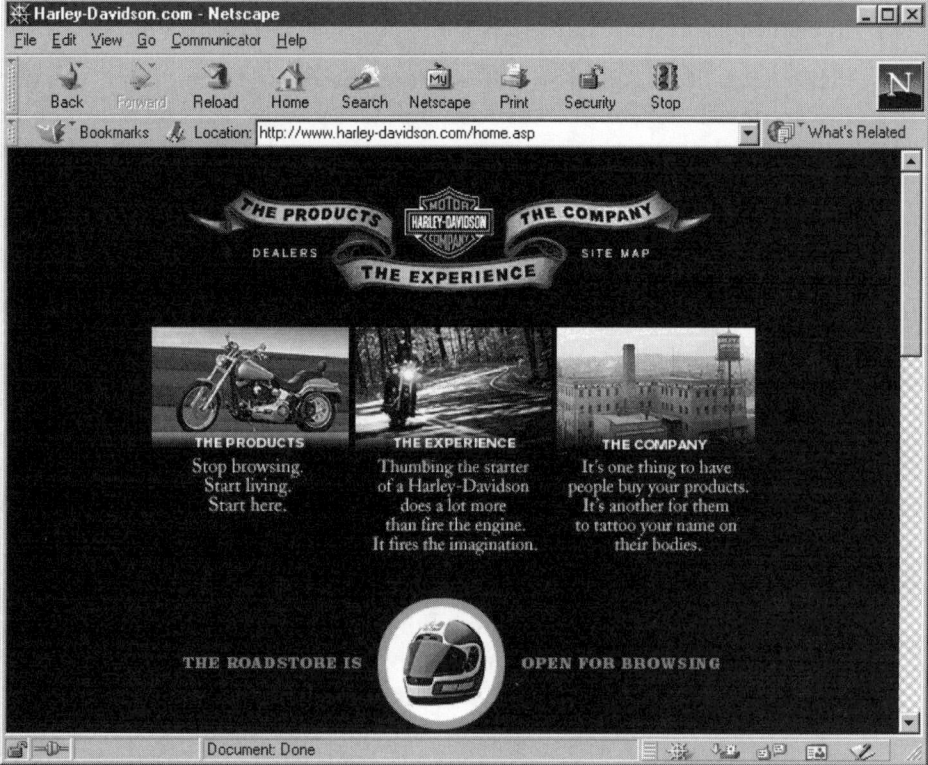

Figure 7.1 Harley-Davidson knows its customers are loyal, and it's not bashful about saying so.

willing to do that, they're often willing to be advocates as well, meaning they will sell others on the benefits of your offering.

Customer Bonding, page 152

Advocacy Bonding

Advocacy bonding, when the customer becomes pitch-man, is the highest form of customer bonding, according to Cross and Smith. Call it word-of-mouth, call it referrals, call it evangelical praise—it's based on a dedication to your product, and it is the most powerful form of advertising.

Don Schultz, professor of integrated marketing at Northwestern University, will happily tell you the difference between people who say they are willing to buy from you again and people who are willing to recommend you to others.

"When we rate customer satisfaction on a scale of 1 to 5, the people we care about are the ones above 4.5," says Professor Schultz. "These are the people who generate the most positive word of mouth. Trying to get customers who rate their satisfaction from a 3 to a 4 is a waste of time. Moving a customer from a 4.4 to a 4.6 is where the action is. This changes people from advocates to apostles."

Customer Bonding on the Web

Awareness and identity bonding fall into the realm of marketing. Relationship and community bonding fall squarely into the realm of customer retention and customer service. Your ability to track customers as individuals and provide a personalized experience is what will stand between you and your competitors from here on out. Providing them with a personal experience on your Web site is the beginning of that competitive edge.

The Value of Customer-Centricity

Storing up information on each customer seems daunting. No more so, however, than the thought that your competitors are doing it. The goal in the long run is to hang on to your customers as well as you can. There's a bit of factor inflation at large regarding the cost of selling to a current customer or making a new one. Twenty years ago people said it was five times more expensive to acquire a new customer than keep an old one. Today the investment seems to be seven times as high.

John Groman is executive vice president at Epsilon, a company that's been collecting customer data for the financial and retail industries for years. According to Groman, you only have three choices for growing your business: get more customers, sell them more stuff, and sell them more profitable stuff. These three choices work hand in hand.

You make a certain amount of profit from all customers—something Groman refers to as the *base profit*. But when you sell more to an existing customer, you save money on reduced operating costs—you don't have to do quite so much data entry or send packages to the wrong address like the first time. You also generate new sales through long-term customers due to referrals. A happy customer is a profitable customer. Treating each customer like the individual he or she is, is more likely to turn that person into a happy customer.

In the May-June 1995 issue of the *Harvard Business Review,* B. Joseph Pine II, Don Peppers, and Martha Rogers wrote an article entitled "Do You Want to Keep Your Customers Forever?" Their answer was a resounding "Yes!" They explained the requirement and the value of obtaining a "customer for life." They described the role of marketing as following each customer through life stages to ensure sending them the right message at the right time. Now they are graduating from college. Now they are entering the business world. Now they are traveling. Now they are creating a family.

In the June-August edition of the same journal, columnist Michael Schrage took exception with the idea of keeping *all* of one's customers for life. Surely, suggested Schrage, there are customers we are economically better off without. Some are cash cows, some are stars, some are question marks, and some are simply dogs. Schrage's advice: "Get rid of them!" Schrage wants us to focus on which customers we learn the most from in order to determine which are worth investing in.

Getting to Know You, Getting to Know All about You

Storing every mouse-click and every e-mail of every customer for on-the-fly analysis is in your future, make no mistake. Computing power, computing storage, and software development will make it possible. After it's possible, it will be profitable. That's worth knowing about and looking into further in the next couple of chapters. Until then . . .

Until then, let's keep it simple. Let's keep track of our customer's recency, frequency, and monetary value (RFM) as they whip through our Web site. How long ago did they buy from us? How often do they buy from us? How much money do they spend when they do?

Recency is a valuable statistic because newer customers are more likely to be repeat customers. Newer customers have not had the chance to be sidetracked by the competition, to move to a new address, or to change their buying patterns. Information about new customers is much more likely to be correct than information that is even just six months old.

In the frequency column, we want to know how often customers buy and how many products they buy. The more they buy (purchasing agent at a large company) or the more often they buy (the dealer or retailer), the lower the cost of the sale. Dealing with them is easier, and the transactions are smoother.

Monetary value refers to the profitability of each sale. If customers only buy the loss-leaders, they score low on the value side. If they stick to the high-margin items, treat them well.

When R, F, and M are combined, you end up with a ranking of customers that can drive your service expenditures. Recognizing and classifying the top partners lets you focus marketing and customer service offers on them and others like them. By the same token, you can identify your worst customers and follow Michael Schrage's advice: Get rid of them! In fact, make sure that you don't do anything in your marketing efforts to attract any more like them.

Even with just a little customer knowledge at your finger tips, your Web site can be responsive to individual customers. Your site can look different depending on the visitors' preferences. It can show them only those areas they are allowed to enter. It can provide greater or lesser on-screen help, depending on how often they visit a particular page and how much time has passed since their last visit.

Barriers to Competitive Entry

Customers teach Web sites about themselves. Giving your measurements to your favorite department store takes time. When that store's Web site keeps coming back with good suggestions, it is worth it. But the thought of typing in shirt, shoe, and sock sizes for twelve stores becomes a little disconcerting. A customer's loyalty is going to be limited to those few stores that serve him or her best.

Similarly, it's going to be more tempting to go to the Web site that knows what computer system you're running and shows you the daily specials for that model. When you ask for a new modem, it knows to ask if it's for your laptop or desktop. It no longer needs to ask what manufacturer, what chip, what operating system, and so forth. It knows. That kind of customer service raises the barriers to competitive entry.

So whether your company is small, medium, or large, you need to get started on the path to customer recognition, recollection, and reverence. And the first step is figuring out how to segment your customers.

Before You Personalize, Group Customers by Their Needs

by Bruce Kasanoff, Accelerating1to1 (published on Personalization.com)

It's nearly impossible for your company to deliver meaningful personalization to a customer unless you have capabilities that are relevant and attractive to that customer. But no sizeable enterprise can develop capabilities by examining one customer at a time. First, you need to develop capabilities around groups. Only then can you profitably customize around individuals.

We have summarized this process as one of our guiding principles of customer-driven firms: Group customers at the finest profitable level of needs.

"Finest" means the tightest, most detailed understanding of customer needs. "Profitable" means that enough valuable customers can be grouped together that the enterprise can profit by fulfilling the needs.

This principle can be applied at any level of an organization: across the enterprise, division, business unit or subgroup. The higher up in the organization you apply it, the more powerful the impact.

Dell Computer, arguably the most advanced practitioner of 1to1 business practices of any major global firm, is the best example of applying this principle.

If you look at Dell back in 1994 when it had about $3.5 billion in sales, it divided its customers into two groups. One was called large customers, and the other group was called small business and consumer. Large customers obviously have different needs than small businesses/consumers. At first, this approach was largely a sales and marketing strategy in which Dell used different tactics to market to the two groups.

By 1996, Dell had divided its customers into four groups (Large companies; Medium companies; Government & Education; Small customers). By 1998, when they had $12 billion in sales, Dell had created eight groups in all.

Every time a group gets too big, Dell divides the group into parts in order to get closer and to stay closer to the customers. Here is what Michael Dell said about this practice in his book, *Direct from Dell*, "Segmentation takes the closed feedback loop and makes it even smaller and more intimate."

Dell also said that "while some have expressed concern that as we grow, we'll lose touch with them, we have found that the opposite happens. Each time we segment, we learn a little more about a customer's unique set of needs."

Think about what Dell has learned: The faster it grows, the more finely it can group its customers by needs, and the closer it can align each of its units to the needs of the customers upon which that unit focuses.

Dell's pivotal moment—and the first pivotal moment for any firm seeking to become a 1to1 enterprise—was to realize that organizing around customer needs is not just a sales and marketing strategy, but rather, an enterprise-wide strategy.

Each division of Dell has its own sales, marketing, operation, and manufacturing activities. As a result, Dell can tailor its products and its services to meet the needs of the types of customers who are served by that business unit.

Here's an obvious question: Why is the first step in building 1to1 relationships to group customers? The answer is simple: It's not practical or efficient for growth-oriented firms to build capabilities around individual customers. Rather, it makes sense to design capabilities around groups that share common needs, such as small businesses. As soon as the firm can do so profitably, it should then seek to divide each group into a more finely tuned assembly of customer needs.

For example, a firm that tries to develop capabilities for Joe's Pizza Shop will never be able to invest sufficient funds to develop new services. But a firm that identifies small local businesses as an important group can afford to develop innovative services that it can then tailor to meet the individual needs of each customer.

Personalization Levels

Do you know me? That great line from old American Express ads has come to be the dividing line between Web sites that are brochures offering 800 numbers for service and sites that are serious about their competitive position. Recognizing people who come to your site is as easy as using a cookie. What's their cookie-stored user I.D. number—look it up in the database—boom, it's "Hello Jim."

But what do you remember about me? Do you remember that I'm interested in the weather in Santa Barbara, California as well as in London, England? And how much does that memory affect my experience on your site? Here's a quick ranking of levels of Web site personalization.

Recognition

Greetings, Jim Sterne. (If you're not Jim Sterne, click here.)

That's what I see when I wander over to Amazon.com. The site's the same to all and sundry, but that home page is watching for people it knows. If my wife uses my desktop computer while I'm on the road, she can hit the "not Jim Sterne" link and let them know who she is.

If the site's the same to all surfers, what's the point? First, it's a nice gesture. It makes you feel warm and fuzzy that they care enough to remember you. More important, the site is watching to see what you do. It does that so it can give you advice.

Making Recommendations

A startup called Firefly, out of the MIT Media Lab, started the whole thing with a site that recommended music. Microsoft bought them early on. But Amazon.com seems to have made excellent use of what is now referred to as *collaborative filtering*.

In a nutshell, the software watches what I click on and what I buy and makes a profile of me. Then it compares my profile to other people in their database to see who has the same, or at least a similar profile. It then looks to see what everybody else bought that I have not yet purchased, and recommends it. The results are pretty good (Figure 7.2).

Figure 7.2 Amazon does a good job of finding books I might like.

How do you generate Instant Recommendations?

We determine your interests from your previous purchases, your Top Sellers ratings, and the titles that you rated on any recommendations product page. Additionally, we compare your interests with the interests of other customers to generate titles for you.

How often do my recommendations change?

Your recommendations change immediately when you purchase or rate a title. Changes in the interests of other customers may also change your recommendations. Because your list will fluctuate, we suggest you bookmark the page of any recommended title that interests you, or add it to your Wish List. We wouldn't want you to miss a title you might enjoy!

These books, *Customers.Com* by Patricia B. Seybold, *World Wide Web Marketing* by yours truly, *Hosting Web Communities* by Cliff Figallo, *Digital Darwinism* by Evan I. Schwartz, *The Vest-Pocket Guide to Business Ratios* by Michael R. Tyran, and so forth, are all right on topic. But they're not great recommendations.

Amazon didn't know that I got an early edition of Patty Seybold's book. They didn't set up their database to see that *I* wrote *World Wide Web Marketing*. They couldn't have known that *Digital Darwinism* was given to me as a gift—purchased elsewhere. So what's a bookworm to do? "Rate these items."

While Amazon will continue to claim that it has "Earth's Biggest Selection of Products," it knows that it's not the sole purveyor of books, CDs, toys, and so on to the planet. Therefore, there must be other places people might get stuff that Amazon's database doesn't see. So it gave us the ability to rate its recommendations (Figure 7.3).

Once the recommendations are rated, a whole new set of books pops up, based on your latest input. Amazon even lets you rate your previous purchases. I've been shopping there since the beginning of 1996, so that one took me a while. The result? Brand new recommendations.

Making Customer Service Recommendations

Now put on your thinking cap and come up with some ways to use collaborative filtering. If the system can come up with recommendations for things to buy, it can surely come up with recommendations for solutions to problems.

A quick look in the database should determine that most people with a profile that reads, "Pentium II, 28.8 modem, 250MB disk space," usually are also suffering from an old version of the operation system and not quite enough random access memory to do much of anything but click around the FAQ documents.

If the database says that this person has had nothing but trouble with his or her washing machine, as have others in the neighborhood, it can suggest that the person look into installing a water softener.

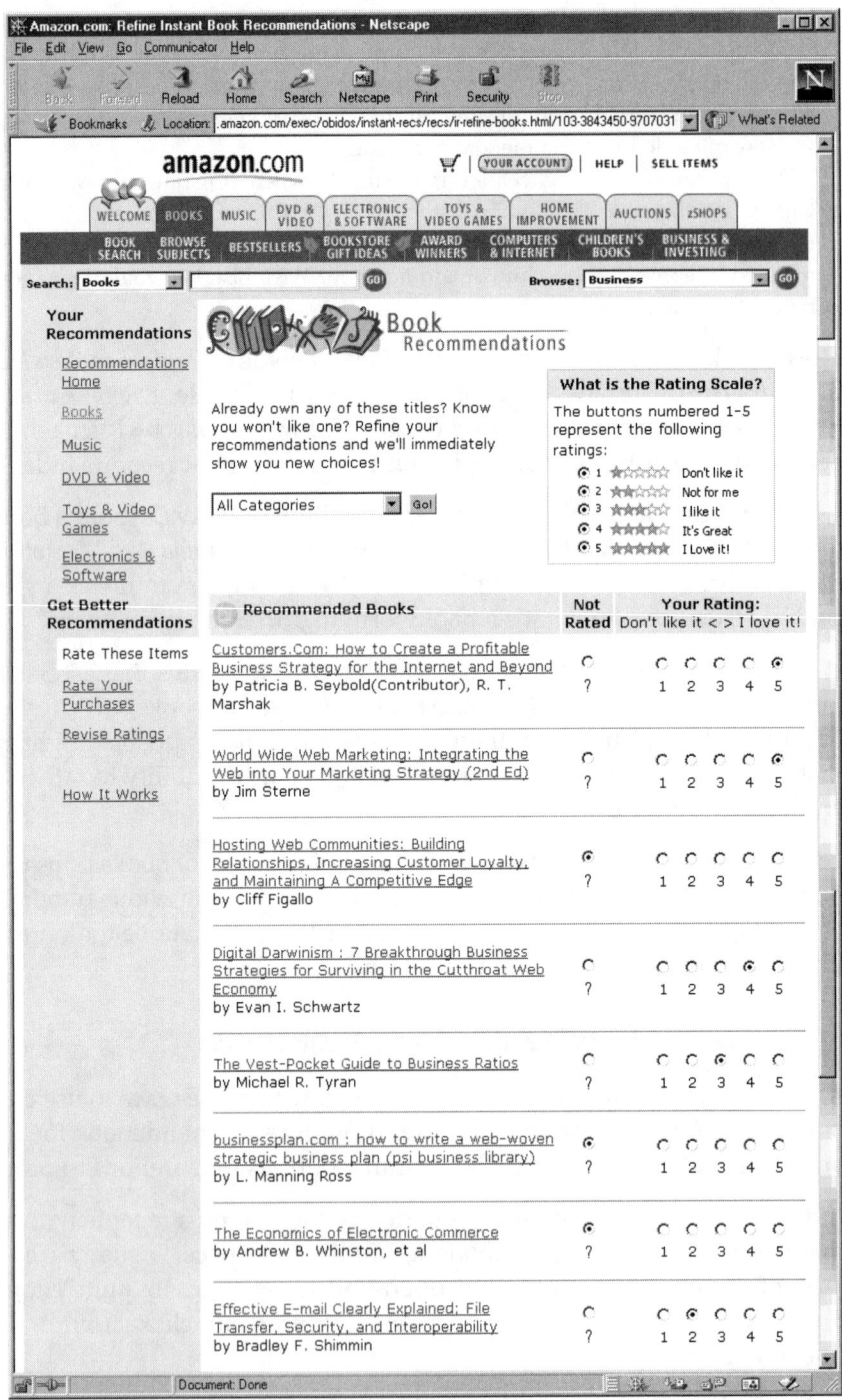

Figure 7.3 Ranking Amazon's suggestions is quick and painless and makes for better recommendations.

Profile Access—Password Required

In order to customize what I see on your site, you'll have to store a profile of me and let me reach in and twiddle with it. MyCNN, MyNetscape, and MyYahoo! all provide a way for me to select the news, traffic, weather, and sports I care about, but that only gets me so far. I don't do business with these sites, I just read and search there.

Customer-modifiable profiles come into play where the rubber meets the road. Or, if you prefer, or where the wings hit the air.

From Personal Profile to Profiling Your Personality at UAL

United Airlines (www.ual.com) has long kept profiles of its customers. Now its customers can keep their own profiles up to date (Figure 7.4).

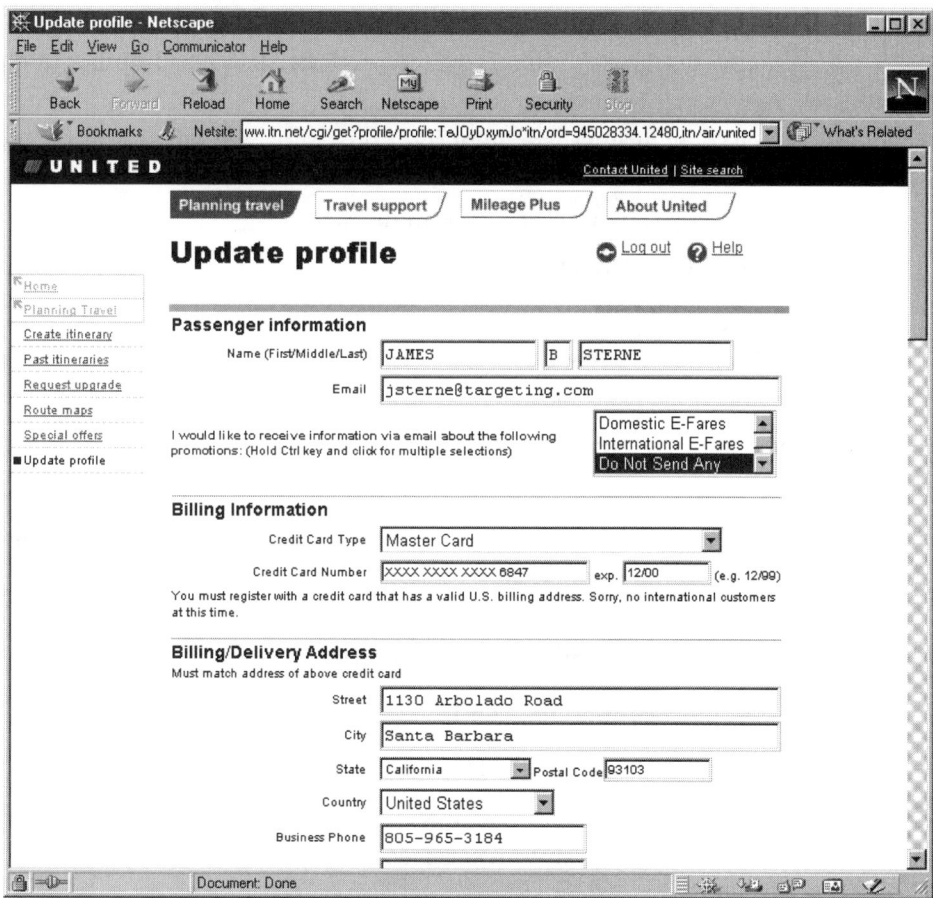

Figure 7.4   United Airlines gives frequent flyers lots of control over their mid-air persona.

United Airlines will let you enter and change:

- Your name and address
- Your billing address
- The credit card you like to use
- Several e-mail addresses for your reservation statement
- Whether you need a wheelchair
- How you'd like information displayed (eg., airport abbreviations or full names)
- Which airport you call home
- Which service class you usually fly
- Your seat preference (window or aisle)
- Your meal preference (vegetarian, kosher, etc.)
- How many flight segments to display at once
- Whether you like the flights sorted by price, distance, number of connections, etc.
- Which other airlines' frequent flyer programs you belong to (for proper credit)
- Corporate frequent flyer program number
- Your car rental preferences
- Your car preference sorting
- Your car rental agency preferences
- Car rental agency membership program numbers
- Your hotel preferences (room type, distance from airport)
- Your hotel membership program numbers

With this information, the United Airlines reservation system can speed the process of making travel plans.

Trading Personal Information for Software

Microsoft invites you to register to:

- Download free Microsoft software
- Subscribe to free newsletters about Microsoft products and services
- Access Microsoft premium services

Frequent visitors to microsoft.com find they are asked to register in several circumstances, including the aforementioned free software, premium sites or e-mail newsletters. However, once you've registered, we know who you are the next time you visit us. So rather than fill in an entire registration form, all you need to type in is your Registration ID and password. We fill in the rest, speeding you on your way.

Dynamic Content Based on Profiles

American Airlines is included in the list of customer success stories at the Broadvision site (www.broadvision.com):

> To provide a valuable, personal experience for each member, the site integrates three databases—travel preferences, AAdvantage information, and customer-provided information—into a single customer profile database. Using BroadVision One-To-One, the individual visitor receives content based on customer profile and American's business objectives.
>
> American's offerings are composed dynamically based on this specific customer's profile to reflect information such as home airport and preferred destinations. In this case, a member from New York has requested information on vacation specials in California and Hawaii for a family vacation that is over a month away. His first login to www.AA.com shows the following offer:

> San Francisco Wine Country
> San Francisco, every breath you take will make you
> fall more in love with the "City by the Bay."

> In the meantime, a business manager at American Airlines has finalized a vacation package that offers a fantastic deal on a trip to Hawaii. She opens up the BroadVision One-To-One Dynamic Control Center and targets a rule that will display this special to the group of visitors who will find it of interest. "We use the BroadVision Dynamic Command Center to manage the business rules for when the content will be displayed, allowing for easy cross-selling, special offers and a compelling return on investment"—Sandy Herndon, manager, AA Interactive Marketing at American Airlines.
>
> The member's profile indicates that this trip may be of interest as the Waikiki resort provides many of the activities and preferences of his family. When the visitor logs on to AA.com and checks specials again, he is informed of the new special. With vacation still a month away, the vacationing family has plenty of time to finalize their plans.

Explicit versus Implicit Information

The top registration sites are those that started life as controlled-subscription trade journals. One information industry magazine/Web site I subscribe to wants to know a great deal about me and my information technology department, including:

- What is your primary job title?
- What is the primary business activity performed at this location? What is the annual dollar value of computing/networking/communications

equipment and software which you are currently or will be involved in purchasing at this location?

- What is the annual dollar value of computing/networking/communications equipment and software which you are currently or will be involved in purchasing for other locations?

- Which of the following products, services, and/or technologies do you currently or plan to approve, specify, recommend purchase, or influence the purchase of?

Why so snoopy? Because then they can slice and dice their database of subscribers, the better to attract advertisers. Naturally, I'm a little disinclined to tell them that I purchase one PC every two or three years. They'd rightly imagine those advertisers would not be very impressed with me as a reader if they knew I ran a corporation consisting of one human and a couple of canines.

So I lie.

I tell them I'm responsible for recommending the purchase of millions of dollars of software and Internet connectivity. I am, actually, just not within my own office.

That, then, is the real problem with explicit information. People will tell you what they think you want to hear in order to get their hands on what you're offering. They will tell you whatever they want you to think of them. They'll tell you things to the best of their recollection. And *that's* why implicit information is so much more valuable.

Tracking the Wild Customer

It starts very simply: remembering where the customer left off the last time they were there. PKWARE (www.pkware.com) created the almost-everybody-uses-it PKZip utility. They offer downloads from their site, and their system remembers how many bits reached you before the backhoe cut your transmission and power lines.

> Downloading software which was electronically wrapped with Sm@rtCert is an easy two-step process.
> Step 1: Transfer the Sm@rtCert Download Manager to your desktop or other folder. The Sm@rtCert Download Manager is the wrapper that contains all the files associated with your new software. Sm@rtCert Download Manager is smart and easy to use. If, for any reason, your download is interrupted, Sm@rtCert Download Manager remembers where you left off. This saves you time and effort.

That's a good start, but it's purely technical. What if you remember what pages each customer saw the last time they were there? What if your site keeps a running commentary in its head about how deeply this customer delved into the

Frequently Asked Questions, or how often they did a search on Flooding at your dishwasher Web site?

You can *say* you like reading biographies and you want Amazon to e-mail you notifications, but if you *buy* books about dogs, Amazon knows what to put on your recommendation list.

Watching what you actually *do* is far more revealing than reading what you *say* interests you. And it's revealing in ways that don't necessarily make sense.

Men who are shopping for electric razors are also buying personal CD players. Is that the sort of thing marketing mavens are going to come up with in a virtual smoke-filled room? Nope. It doesn't make any sense. But it's true. So now the marketing mavens have a new datapoint to work with, and the systems behind the scenes have the ability to act on that sort of information in real time. Customer service systems can (and will) do the same.

Getting Proactive—Anticipation Engines

Quick & Reilly (www.quick-reilly.com) lets you create your own personal space, your own personal pages. But then they go a step further and let you choose to have personal pages that dynamically respond to your portfolio, research, and news. Button options can change by themselves, depending on what sort of investments you make.

In March 1999, eMarketer (a Web site well worth watching) interviewed J. G. Sandom, head of Ogilvy Interactive (www.ogilvy.com/o_interactive). In that interview (www.emarketer.com/enews/enews_sandom.html), Sandom described the power of forecasting what somebody might need on a Web site and how to make the most of it:

> If we're trying to reach women between the ages of 35 and 45 with x income level, we go back and look at their pattern through the site. You can actually go and say, "Hmm, it looks as though there are about six or so OSPs (Optimal Site Paths) that really worked for this particular target segment, for this particular objective."
>
> Having done that, our next job is determining how we drive these individuals through the correct OSPs. We use any number of techniques, but I'll give you three of them.
>
> One is we use outbound e-mail. For example, I'll use my generic example again, you go to the home page, go to the car configurator, finance configurator, dealer locator, and then you go to the e-mail center and tell the dealer you want to buy. But what if a user goes to the home page, goes to the car configurator, but he never goes and figures out the financing terms? We can do an outbound e-mail. And the e-mail says, "Ford Credit is doing a special this month." There would be a link in that e-mail where, if she clicks on that link, it takes her automatically into the financing configurator. So now we've got her to step three.
>
> Using the outbound e-mail we've persuaded them that there was an offer, and made it compelling enough so that they clicked and went to the next step of the OSP.

Outbound e-mail is one great technique. Another technique would be personalization; that's the ability for the end user to create a personalized home page. That personalized home page may have any number of things on it.

It's not about layout—it's about what is on that home page. It may include things like user defined best picks. I've gone in as an end user and said of all the thousands of possible links in the site, these are the six sections I go to all the time. I select them with radial buttons. Boom! They now appear on my home page. We also do what we call ECRM-defined best pick, CRM being customer relationship management. So, as I said before, we track user behavior. So even if someone says I want to have these six links on my home page, we know that he goes to these two other sections all the time. And we have business rules behind our site which say if we track this guy's behavior and he goes to these other things that are not on his personalized home page to find, you know, through his form, and he goes there more than x times during this period of time, then automatically post those other sections to his personal home page. Another thing that a personalized home page might include is an archive of personal searches. If you're like me I never remember what searches I did. So it's nice to have all the searches you've done of a site. The last thing, and the most important thing— the reason I brought this stupid thing up in the first place—is we always make sure that we auto-rotate on people's personalized home pages the next step on the OSP.

If a guy comes in and he goes to the home page, he goes to the car configuration, maybe now he's even gone to the financing configurator—but he hasn't gone to the dealer locator, we would rotate OSPs on his personal home page, including, of course, a link to the new groovy little dealer locator that we've got now. And guess what? There's a little editorial comment on that link that says, "If you go in now and check out our new dealer locator you get a coupon for $20 off your next oil change at the dealer nearest you." We give them an incentive to go there.

Another way of driving them along the OSP is to pop open a daughter window—it's got a little messaging, a little promotional information, to move them to the next step.

Yes, the example is from the marketing perspective. But it only takes a small turn of your head to get the customer service viewpoint.

What if you could tell that people who complained about delayed shipments also seemed to have problems assembling the bicycle they ordered? What if your site had a deep enough database to make the connection between people who always complained about getting the wrong products shipped to them and the speed with which they were placing their online orders?

What could you do about it? You could get proactive. Send them an e-mail. Personalize their version of the standard newsletter. Add a button to your home page that only they can see.

The Prickly Privacy Puzzle

There comes a point at which everybody who looks into the power of the Internet begins to wonder about the sanctity of personal information.

Lots of research companies ask a bunch of Joe Surfers if they're worried about privacy, and the cumulative concern numbers are very high. At the end of 1999, Forrester Research asked a bunch of new-media executives about the biggest challenges they faced when personalizing a Web site. Some had trouble figuring out what to track (6 percent). Some were worried that the technology wasn't there yet or that their sites wouldn't handle the growing load (both scored 14 percent). Figuring out which content to deliver bothered 16 percent, and not having the resources was the bane of 20 percent of those queried. But "visitor privacy concerns" topped the chart, with 32 percent furrowing their brows and rubbing their necks in consternation.

Do you want some computer watching every click you make? Do you want some company to make wild guesses about your interests and needs and shortcomings based on which FAQ you clicked? Eventually, if you're dealing with a reputable organization, the answer is yes.

Protecting Privacy and Making a Bundle

by Jim Sterne, Target Marketing (published on Personalization.com)

For those who like to get right to the point, here's the payoff:

Give me a reason
to give you information
and you can use it
to sell me more stuff.

That is so 1995. As in Pepper and Rodgers's book, *The One to One Future* (Bantam Doubleday, 1995). It's cheaper to sell to a current client than to drum up a new one.

If you know my preferences and my habits, then you can treat me like the individual I am. Your offers will be more interesting. I won't have to waste time filling in forms and explaining myself to you again.

So now that you know the punch line, here's the philosophy that should inform every step you take along the path to Web site personalization. Here's the reason that your corporate data security systems should be hardened against corporate raiders: It's all about respect.

R-E-S-P-E-C-T: Find Out What It Means to Me

What started out as your friendly grocer asking about your health and then remembering you the next time you come in, has turned into a international, over-intrusive, oh-my-god-what-happens-if-it-gets-into-the-wrong-hands, multi-mega-database.

You get that sinking feeling that some insidious individual is watching you for some nefarious purpose. Your innermost thoughts might be sold to other merchants who will flood your mailbox with offers you can't refuse.

What kind of mail and phone calls would you get if the Christian Coalition should get their hands on your opinions, attitudes, beliefs and buying preferences? What if the Pacifists for Animal Rights knew every time you looked at www.nra.org? What if your boss signs up with a service that lets him know that you went to Career Mosaic three times last week?

Just where, as a card-carrying member of the data-hungry marketing industry, do you stand on the issue of privacy?

Rules, Laws, and Good Marketing

The European Union Data Protection Directive, which was supposed to bring down all of American international marketing data management, was supposed to go into effect in October 1998. It would have forced American companies to be a bit more careful than we're used to.

There are four basic rules:

1. You have to tell people you are collecting information about them and what you're using it for.
2. You have to allow people to decline to be tracked.
3. You have to allow people access to their data so they can correct it.
4. You have to ensure their data is safe from others' prying eyes.

That first one means you're not allowed to use personal data for anything except for which it was specifically acquired, unless you have explicit consent. In a nutshell, if you sell somebody a teapot, you're not allowed to turn around and try to sell them tea, unless they've signed a waiver.

If you're heavy into rules and regulations, you can feed your jones with help from Peter Swire, Associate Professor of Law at the Ohio State University College of Law (www.osu.edu/units/law/swire.htm).

But if you're simply into good marketing, you're going to follow these rules anyway. The fact is, if you treat people with respect, you can sell them more stuff. If you don't, you will be designated a data-nazi.

Jason Catlett runs a company called Junkbusters (www.junkbusters.com) that covers personal privacy and the Web. He e-mailed me the following example of target marketing run amuck:

Dear Mr. Jones:

Our research indicates that you have not bought condoms at SpiffyMart recently. (Your last purchase was 8 weeks ago.) Further, you have stopped buying feminine hygiene products, but have sharply increased your frozen pizza and dinners usage in the same time frame.

It's clear that Ms. Jody Sanders and you are no longer "an item." (It's probably for the best—she consistently buys inexpensive shampoo, and it was obvious that the two of you were not economically compatible.) The Postal Service database confirms that she filed a change of address form.

We at Hotflicks International offer our condolences.

As the number-one vender of hot XXX-rated videos, we want you to know that our products can help you through this difficult period. When you're feeling lonely, check out our unmatched catalog, there is guaranteed to be something that you'll want to purchase!

Order from this catalog and we'll throw in an extra tape FREE!

Yours Truly, Hotflicks Marketing Management

Convince me my privacy is important to you. If you collect all sorts of information about me, then your offerings can be more interesting to me. If you treat information about me with respect, I'm going to feel much better about our relationship.

The question that should be running around in your head at this point is whether all of this data gathering and protection is worth the trouble.

ROI?

Can you really make money after investing in systems that accommodate true opt-in and true access to all customers? Will it make that much difference in their buying patterns? Yes it will. It will because the focus is on time rather than money.

Oh, money's great, don't get me wrong. I love the smell of profits in the morning. Absolutely. And as much as your customers love to save a dollar here and get 20 percent off there, we're all out of time.

It's about Time & Trust

Barnsandnoble.com may be a wonderful book store. It may have a fantastic collection of books. It may have lower prices than I've ever seen before. But I'm never going to find out.

I'm never going to take the time to tell them where I live, what kind of wrapping paper I like on the gifts I send or what books my uncle likes. I already went through all that with Amazon. We have a relationship. The barrier to switching is way over my toleration threshold and I'm a one-book-site kinda guy.

All through my relationship with Amazon, they have tracked me like a bloodhound. They have memorized every book I bought and everything I looked at and every bit of information about me. They have also come through on the promise of their brand and not abused this information—only used it to make my shopping experience more enjoyable.

So it's not just that I don't want to train another store in my buying habits, it's that I already know I can trust Amazon with my innermost book desires—and they won't sell me down the river. Because they know the instant they compromise my privacy, I'm going to tell all my friends at The Motley Fool and CNNfn and Quote.com. It wouldn't be pretty.

Capture and control information about your customers and use it to sell them smarter, and they will reward you by buying more stuff. But only if you show them the proper level of respect.

There are lots of privacy statements on the Web and they're well worth a look. Because chances are, your customers are looking at yours. Check out the carefully crafted Microsoft Statement of Privacy (www.microsoft.com/info/privacy.htm, Figure 7.5).

Microsoft tells you why it wants your information (identification, navigation, relevancy, and to create alerts and reminders). It makes it clear that you don't have to fork over your hard-earned privacy if you don't want to. Of course, "you will not be able to access areas that require registration." The company is right up front that it might share some of your information with third parties, but that you can opt out.

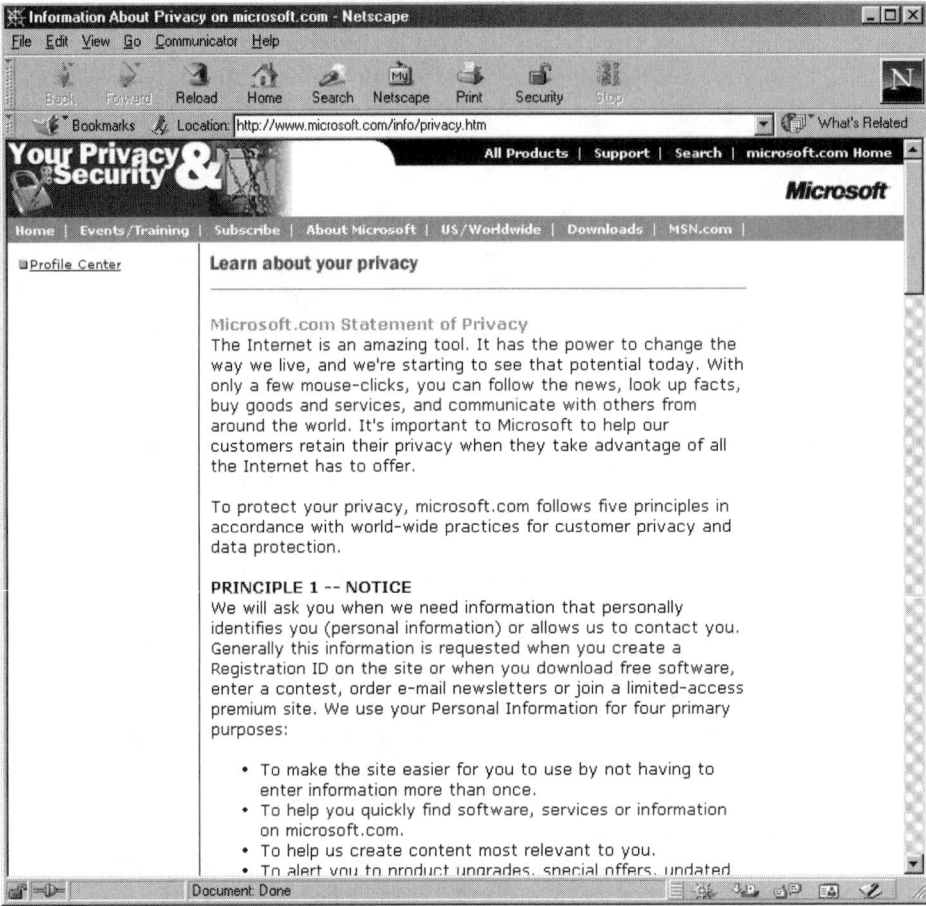

Figure 7.5 You'd be right if you figured Microsoft would take extra care when posting its Statement of Privacy.

The folks at Microsoft let you know you can view and edit personal information, and assure you that your information will be kept secure. They also want to raise parents' awareness. "Parents or guardians: we want to help you guard your children's privacy. We encourage you to talk to your children about safe and responsible use of their Personal Information while using the Internet. You can find a wealth of information at the microsoft.com Internet Safety site." They answer questions about cookies and make sure you understand the benefits of profiling.

You could do worse.

The whole point is to build trust and loyalty. These are not things you can simply go out and buy; you have to earn them.

Trust and Loyalty

Can your customers trust your site to deliver the goods? Will the goods be good? When you boil it all down, it's a matter of brand. With limited time and limited knowledge, I'm going to trust a brand. I'm going to put my faith in the millions who went before me and made that vendor the giant it is today.

People all begin at the same point: They've never heard of you. You try to move them along the relationship path as quickly as possible.

- Aware
- Familiar
- Comfortable
- Secure
- Trusting
- Depending
- Advocating

Trusting is required to get customers to buy, and depending is built when they discover that you quickly and consistently give them the right answers. They lean on you for help because they know they can count on you. Then they recommend you to their friends and colleagues.

And once you have your customers' trust, once you've secured their loyalty, you can plumb the depths of their most private information to learn things about their likes and dislikes, hopes and fears, dreams and schemes that you could only have guessed at before. Now you know why it was worth spending a little time on the importance of privacy.

Data Mining for Fun and Profit

It doesn't take a genius to figure out that you're going to sell more ice cream in Florida in the summer than you are in Wisconsin in the winter. But learning why profits are down in response to a promotional contest is a different story.

A grocery store in Brazil spent a good deal of money promoting a big contest. Every time you come into the store and buy something, you get another chance to win a color TV, a stereo, a microwave oven, and so forth. They carefully selected these products because they would appeal to the majority of their customers. But halfway through the contest, although store visits were up, profits were down. Why? They turned to data mining for the answer.

In the long run, data mining is the art of asking interesting questions of giant databases which are intended to know everything about your company. Every transaction, every customer, every cost, and then some.

There's a fairly wide gap between the rich and the poor in Brazil. Somebody at the grocery store decided to ask a very important question. What is the profile of our most profitable customers?

In order to compete, the store sold most staples at competitive prices and earned the highest margins from the relatively few luxury items they had on hand. The increase in store traffic was indeed made up of those who would be most interested in the types of prizes offered, and that was the problem. Low-income families came more and more, buying items that were on sale as loss leaders and not buying other items with higher margins. How then, do you run a profitable contest? You change the prizes.

The latter half of the contest offered prizes like diamond jewelry, mink coats, and a Rolls Royce. Profits improved immediately.

Peapod, the online grocery store (www.peapod.com, Figure 7.6), has also discovered the value of data mining.

Peapod keeps a shopping preference list for everybody who shops there. Cholesterol worriers, calorie counters, vegetarians, and others with special diet considerations are all accounted for, and that information is combined with purchase histories to serve up special aisles where each customer's special type of consumable is available.

The Peapod site mixes the above with seasonal offerings and special, personalized discount coupon offers, all selected based on the past, the profile, and the path the customer is taking through the store at the moment. Then, they can report back to their suppliers in order to improve merchandizing collaboration.

"Procter and Gamble might want to know what their category share is in the e-commerce space, versus the in-store environment," says John Furton, Peapod's chief information officer. "They can easily see that in the regular grocery world, Tide might have 45 percent of the laundry powder aisle. At Peapod, Tide might have that same 45 percent, but it could also be responsible for 80 percent of laundry powder sales to college-educated women with more than two children, who work outside the home." Time for a special coupon offer?

> Data mining, in a nutshell, is inductive data analysis. When data is too large and complex to be examined by humans, a summation in the form of a ratio or a formula can often reveal a pattern. The voluminous amounts of data generated from a Web site, for example, often hide patterns that reveal conditions when visitors are likely to make purchases or click on certain ads or banners.

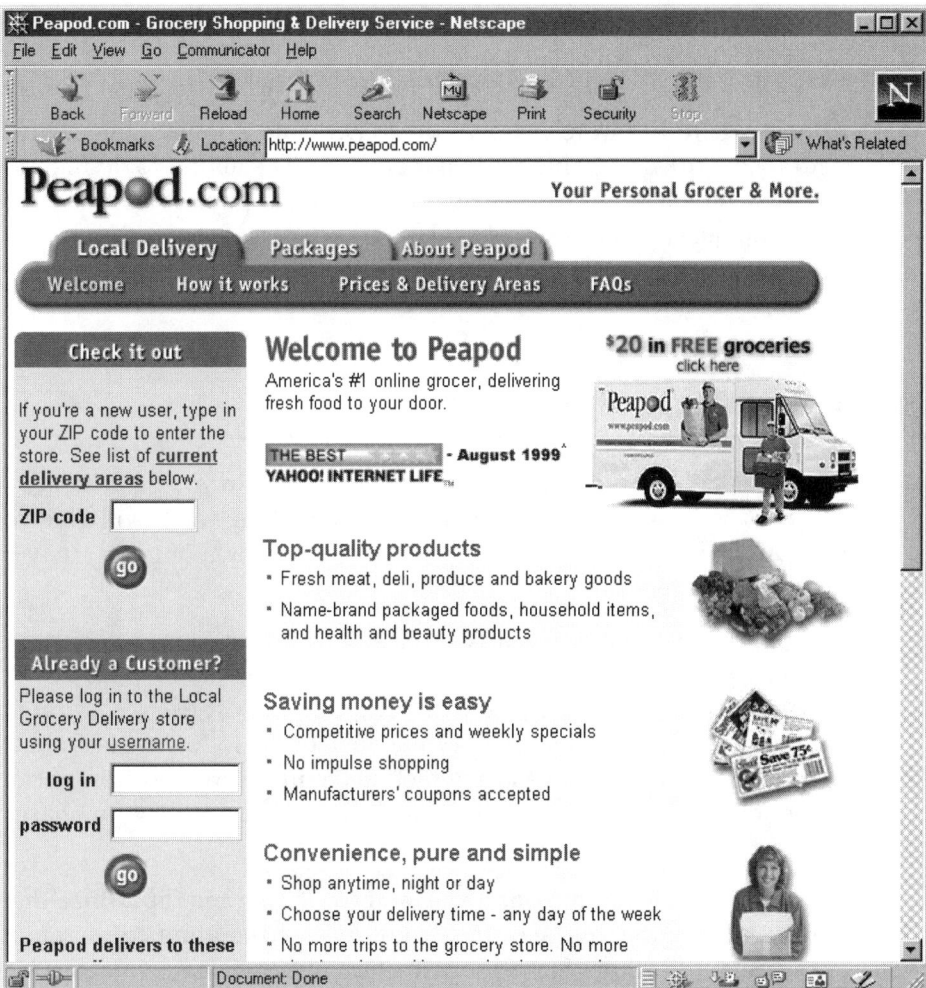

Figure 7.6   Peapod tracks what you like, what you buy, and which aisles you walk down.

IF	domain	AOL	
AND	keyword	broncos	
AND	gender	male	
AND	age	18–49	
THEN	ad	ESPN	68 percent
		AUTOBYTEL	18 percent
		Amazon	9 percent
		Microsoft	5 percent

Data mining software can reveal how the value of one field in a database is affected by other fields. For example, a field such as "total purchases" may be affected by other values or fields in your logs or forms database, such as the visitor's age, gender, referral engine, or keywords he or she used. . . . Data mining, then, can be defined as the iterative process of detecting and extracting these patterns from large databases: it's pattern recognition.

Data Mining Your Web Site, Jesus Mena, Digital Press, 1999

This is where big iron, massive databases, and sophisticated software like neural networks are going to earn their keep. The ability to do high-level pattern matching based on low-level data is being applied to customer purchases today. But just as Web sites themselves were first devoted only to the sales side of things, it didn't take long for people to see the need for online customer care.

Tools That Make It Happen

A number of interesting tools on the market can help you get a handle on all of this personalization stuff. Understanding how they work will give you some clues about what they can do now and some insight about what may be possible in the future.

Because the marketplace changes so fast, and fortunes on the Internet seem to be won and lost overnight, I selected the following list of tools for their illustrative powers only. Some are without question best-of-breed, and some are simply the ones I was aware of. While none of the following is intended as an endorsement (aside from those which make up a large portion of my investment portfolio), each of the following deserves to be on any purchaser's short list.

I owe a tip of the hat to Bruce Kasanoff for letting me reproduce these short snippets from the Accelerating1to1 (www.accelerating.com) report about software applications for personalization, "Advanced Strategies for Differentiating Customers and Partners: Software That Enables 1to1 Relationships."

Tracking Tools

These are the products that read your server log files and watch what people do on your site. They tell you where people are coming from, what they look at on your site, and where they go when they leave. They started life as log analysis tools but have now grown through their second and third generations. These tools were once the work of individual Webmasters, anxious to get *any* sort of metrics from their servers. Now, they are a collaboration between fast-paced technology companies and large Web sites in the heat of battle.

NetGenesis

NetGenesis helps you, through information gathered from visits to your Web site, understand customer behavior and create and test business rules that will drive personalization. Sophisticated reports provided by the software can help your firm understand what each individual customer needs. Through its net.Instrument module, NetGenesis blends customer online behavior data with other third party databases and applications you may have available, to provide a broader view of your online visitors. For example, if a customer registers at your site and also has bought from you through traditional channels, net.Instrument can correlate the online data with information in your other databases to illustrate how your customers may behave differently online.

Web sites have the potential to provide exponentially more insight regarding customer behavior than marketers have ever had access to before. If your company can capture this information and make integrated use of it, you will be far more successful at developing 1to1 relationships than companies that rush forward with personalization programs without validating the assumptions that underpin their business rules.

(Accelerating1to1)

Smart Dynamic Servers

Dynamic servers have been around since about day three of the Web. Instead of static pages shown to each person who clicks by, dynamic servers reach down into a database of content and a database of design templates to create pages on the fly. Personalizing those pages just seemed like the right thing to do.

Smart servers choose their content based on what the surfer is up to on the site at the moment, coupled with personal profile information.

Broadvision

I was sorry that Accelerating1to1 had not yet written about Broadvision, because it's hard to write about. Aside from the generic description above, this tool set is difficult to describe.

Broadvision's One-to-One line of products was built for large sites massaging lots of transactions in real time to determine the right content to serve. It chooses content to serve based on business rules that can be change on the fly. People who like green sweaters also like brown hats? Set up a business rule that will show these customers those products, and *shazam!* the very next person to look at a green sweater will be offered a brown hat.

To make all this magic, Broadvision makes use of alerts, attribute search, collaborative filtering, community rating, e-mail targeting, entitlements, event-based matching, full-text search, matching agents, observation, rule-based matching, and user profiling. Say *that* 10 times fast.

Collaborative Filtering

This is the technology that compares your habits with everybody else in order to figure out what to offer you.

Net Perceptions

Net Perceptions' collaborative filtering software turns size into an advantage in the delivery of personalized service. It allows big companies to tailor their services to meet individual needs better than a small competitor can, even one that knows its customers personally.

This is one of the most fundamental shifts to occur in business this century, and the implications are enormous. Net Perceptions' software enables you to harness the power of "community knowledge," which is the combined tastes and preferences of all the members of your customer base.

The more customers a firm has, the more likely it is that it has customers who share tastes and needs. A firm that uses Net Perceptions can gather insights from other customers and use them to deliver more useful, tailored services to individuals.

(Accelerating1to1)

Profile-Directed Answerbots

Remember Andrette from Big Science? Big Science put a good face on it, but lots of companies are trying to find ways to interact on a real-time basis with customers. Some, like Big Science and Ask Jeeves, are building databases of frequently asked questions. Others, like eHNC with SelectResponse and Inference, are building systems that sift through a knowledge base to build the right answer on the fly.

Inference

Inference k-Commerce software enables you to maintain more natural and personalized interactions with your customers to increase e-commerce sales and create superior service and support interactions. The company has two product lines—k-Commerce Sales, and k-Commerce Support, each of which address a key point in the e-commerce customer lifecycle.

Inference's k-Commerce Sales application creates a detailed profile on each user who visits your site, and enables you to deliver advice, assistance, promotions, and content that is personalized to meet the needs of that user. The firm's k-Commerce Support application uses a conversational approach that seeks to get people the answers to questions or solutions to problems they need, quickly and easily, across the customer contact center.

This software applies both rule-based and case-based technologies to provide service that feels like old-fashioned personal service than is common on the Web today. Inference's goals for k-Commerce Sales are to enable companies to sell additional products and services to more customers on the Web, to convert more browsers into buyers, and to help build long-term, loyal customer relationships.

(Accelerating1to1)

Transaction Visibility

Getting a handle on everything that's going on inside a dynamically generated Web site is a major challenge. Half the battle is getting the information out; the other half is displaying it in a useful way.

E.piphany

E.piphany's various software modules—there are 16 in all—serve as information "dashboards" for customer relationships. You can sit at your desk and get instant information about your customers using an easy-to-manipulate Web browser.

Now, imagine that car dashboards had never been invented. All these years, there was no speedometer, oil warning light, fuel gauge, tachometer, headlight indicator, or music console. You'd have a completely different set of habits, and you'd be a much less informed driver. In the same manner, many business managers are accustomed to operating with little or no access to valuable information about their customers.

So, when you acquire flexible software that gives you access to all this information through your desktop PC, you may have to learn the questions you could—and should—be asking. Here is a tiny sampling of questions E.piphany software can answer for you:

- How much revenue was generated for this product by each customer segment?
- Which products does this customer segment prefer?
- What is the lifetime value (LTV) of a customer?
- What percentage of customers who purchased this product were not targeted by the campaign/promotion?
- If customers receive personalized Web-site content, are they more likely to make a purchase?
- What other products (and how many) are purchased by customers who buy this product?
- Do customers who receive a thank-you mailing tend to place their next order sooner? What is the difference in subsequent order size?
- Which customer segments are most profitable?
- How many customers cancelled while their orders were pending?
- Are customers whose shipments were delayed more likely to churn?
- Are customers who register at our Web site more likely to make purchases?
- Are our most valuable customers more or less likely to pay their bills online?
  (Accelerating1to1)

Personalization on a Shoe String

Jim Sterne
Inc. Technology magazine, March 2000

Come In. I've Been Expecting You.

Cheap personalization tools make every site visitor feel like an audience of one. When I go to the football stadium, I am one of tens of thousands of sports fans. When I go to the theater, I am one of hundreds of arts patrons. When I watch television I am one of three or four family members. When I surf the Internet I am alone.

The fact that each surfer is an island plays straight to the Internet's strengths. Dozens of software packages promise to personalize online customers' experiences so that the world revolves around them—so long as they remain on your site, anyway. Install Broadvision (www.broadvision.com) and you can track your visitors' every move, learn their interests, and serve them the ads and special offers most likely to make their hearts go pitty-pat. GroupLens from Netperceptions (www.netperceptions.com) lets you perform the Amazonian feat of recommending products based on the purchases of customers with similar tastes and buying histories. Want an artificial intelligence package that understands incoming e-mail and responds to customers' specific questions? SelectResponse from eHNC (www.ehnc.com) is there for you.

Of course, these products require that you shell out somewhere between $5 and $10 million for software, training, integration, and the personnel to run it all. I'm sorry, is that a problem?

Well, you might be able to do it yourself. Perhaps you already know how to use cookies to recognize your visitors and greet them by name. You might even be able to hook up a database that remembers customers' preferences and a dynamic server that creates Web pages for them on the fly. But watch out: You're likely to find yourself leading a team of learning-on-the-job developers who are macrameing together a seriously complex Web site with no documentation. That's not exactly a stable foundation for your e-commerce empire.

Fortunately, you can still achieve a little pampering on the cheap. The trick is to approach your customers as segments: ones small enough to suggest customization but not so minuscule that you need a bunch of software to manage them.

Mirror, Mirror on the Web

Visitors consider a Web site "personalized" when they see themselves there. That means you must avoid the broad brush when addressing your audience. Say you're the owner of a dental-supply company and Algernon K. Floom visits your site looking for a drill. You can't afford the software that would give him a form to fill out with the Algernon K. Floom story and henceforth greet him by name ("Hello there, ALGERNON K. FLOOM!") and show him only Algernon K. Floom–tailored offers. But suppose you present him with these options:

- If you're in private practice, click here.
- If you're part of a dental co-op, click here.
- If you're a hospital purchasing agent, click here.
- If you're the materiel director of an HMO, click here.

This shows Algernon K. Floom you understand that all drill buyers are not cut from the same cloth; that he has specific needs, and that you've made an effort to address those needs by offering information, pricing, or services tailored for his market segment. You may not be drilling down far, but at least you're drilling.

Another way to show customers you're trying to do something just for them is to walk them through a series of questions about their requirements. Suppose your company sells just one product: an extra-quiet, high-speed drill that can be used equally well by right- and left-handed dentists and is bundled with a disposable spittoon. You could describe the drill just that way on your home page and invite dentists of all stripes to click to buy. Or you could lead them through the following questions:

- Do you use your cavity drill on a *daily* basis or only a *couple of times a week*?

- Do you use your drill with your *right hand* or your *left*?

- Do you have your patients *wear headphones* or *not*?

- Do you prefer your high-speed drill to *include* the wrist-mounted spittoon, or *not*?

Instead of offering a single product description, you would then write several different product descriptions, with each emphasizing some combination of drill features identified as desirable by the customer's responses. A right-handed dentist would arrive at a page describing the drill as right-handed (the fact that it is equally well-suited for lefties is unimportant). Dentists with their own, stationary spittoons read a product description that doesn't even nod to the wrist-mounted accessory, which you simply don't ship. Suddenly it seems as though you have eight products instead of just one, and that your sole interest in life is making sure customers choose the product that is best for them.

Asking questions accomplishes two things. First, as customers click away at their options they produce data-rich server logs that you can squeeze for market research. Second, when customers shape their requirements they generally feel better about their purchases. If someone goes into a store looking for a digital camera and the clerk immediately recommends the RX7-11, the customer suspects that that model produces the biggest commission. But if the sales clerk asks questions about why the customer wants the camera and how he plans to use it and then recommends the RX7-11, the customer believes him or her and is comfortable with the choice.

You've Got Mail (from Me)

My last column explained the value of creating personal pages for your best customers. (See "A Fine and Private Page," *Inc. Technology*, November 1999). That strategy works great for sites serving a handful of corporate accounts, but if you sell to hundreds or thousands of customers it becomes unmanageable. An alternative is to send those hundreds or thousands of customers newsletters that address them, if not as individuals, at least as members of discrete and cherished groups. This is a case where a little technology—specifically the software customers use to sign up for the newsletter on your site and the software that manages the mailing list—goes a long way.

Like most personalization efforts, newsletters require segmentation. Identify the ways that various customers use your goods and services. Think about the different problems they're solving, the different industries they're in, and the different reasons they do business with you. Use those distinctions to divide them into groups—then keep your eyes peeled for news and ideas pertinent to those groups. Your basic newsletter will probably comprise information of value to everyone. But if you can include some advice on finding prime office space in the letters that go out to dentists in private practice, and notices of institutional discounts on x-ray film for hospital procurement staff, they'll know you're thinking about them.

Does that mean you have to send out 4 or 8 or 32 full-fledged newsletters a month? No. Sometimes it's more effective to shoot off snippets as you stumble across them. Just make sure anything you direct toward your customers' mailboxes is really interesting, or you risk becoming a pest. How do you know when you're hurting, not helping? When customers unsubscribe.

If this sounds like more than your Web-hosting service can handle, you might consider some products and services that allow you to get personal without going personally bankrupt.

MessageMedia's UnityMail (www.unitymail.com) for example, is a Web site that assumes the burden of newsletter mailings and other customer segmentation tasks. Customers still go to your site to sign up for your newsletter and select the subjects they want to hear about. But you construct the sign-up form on MessageMedia's digital turf, and MediaMessage handles addressing and distribution for about $200 a month.

Entice!, a software product from MultiActive (www.multiactive.com), lets you drag and drop your way to answer-dependent paths, so if visitors express interest in the bagels and the jam rather than the croissants and the jam, your site can also recommend the cream cheese. In addition, Entice! sends your customers different e-mail messages based on where on your site they touched down. (Someone landing on the bagel page, for example, might find in her mailbox an announcement of a sale on slicers.) And you can use the product's nifty dashboard to observe customers' real-time peregrinations around your site. Entice! costs about $25,000, which isn't bad when you consider that it also includes an e-commerce engine. If that's still too rich, you might try the combination of GuestTrack and GT/Mail (www.guesttrack.com), which together offer many of the same personalization features as MultiActive for only $6,000. What's the catch? GuestTrack and GT/Mail are developers' tools, so you have to be ready, willing, and able to build your own SQL databases and e-commerce applications.

Of course, all of these tools merely give function to the form that you provide. And that form derives from an intimate understanding of your customers as individuals, rather than as some some undifferentiated, money-waving mass. No, you may not be able to afford to treat each customer like a king. But if you treat him like an archduke, chances are that he'll go away satisfied.

Personalization Is Leaking Offline

The first I heard of the idea of personalization in the real world I realized just how powerful a marketing tool it is. The first time was a cross-over from the Web at a Web-savvy company, IBM.

IBM offered its customers a choice. Which brochures, notices, news updates, and general *postal* information did they wish to never see again? Deep behind a customer password on the IBM Web site was a lengthy list of paper epistles IBM was wont to send to customers in a flurry of marketing madness. IBM marketing magistrates were surprised at the response. People unsubscribed in droves.

First the e-mail came in. "Thank you so much for letting me control the flood of junk that pours into my office." Next came the budget figures. IBM was saving millions and millions of dollars by not sending things its customers didn't want to receive.

The Viking Office Products direct mail team in England figured out a great way to make their customers happy. They combined their database of customer purchase history with a high-speed, color digital printer. The result was an individual catalog for each recipient. The first time they tried it, they sent out just a few thousand to see what sort of response they might get.

In an all-out effort to get the very best response they possibly could, they programmed what they were now calling their database canon to print the customer's name on the cover, along with a deep discount offered on a product that customer usually buys, and was due to purchase again any day.

They hit their goal. They got the very best response they possibly could. Everybody ordered. *Everybody.*

Business-to-Business Personalization

All this personalization wizardry seems, well, personal. What about the world of B-2-B? What sort of personal preferences does somebody have about buying paperclips and silicon chips?

There are two answers to that question. The first is that even business people are people. Everybody does their job a little differently. The purchase agent at one desk might be a morning person and the one at the next might prefer doing everything via e-mail instead of clicking on Web sites. All of the tools and techniques you use for a consumer marketplace applies to the individuals inside a company.

The second answer takes a little more time to answer than that. In fact, it deserves its own chapter. The second answer is that each company you sell to deserves its very own Web site. It's what we've taken to calling an *extranet.*

Extranets—Access to Live Information

Once large firms move their purchasing online—as, say, GE [General Electric] has done with its Trading Process Network, on which suppliers can bid electronically for components contracts—business partners and suppliers will have to do the same. It will become progressively harder for firms that cannot or do not want to trade online to survive.
The Economist (June 26, 1999)

Here's the quick definition: An extranet is when you hook up two intranets. Got that? OK, let me do that again. When Company A is using Web technology for internal consumption only, that's an intranet. When Company A then offers to let Company B poke around in special places in their intranet to place orders and such, that's an extranet. Just think of it as electronic data interchange (EDI) all grown up and running rampant through the fields of commerce.

Whatever your definition or metaphor of choice, extranets are where the competitive battle lines are being drawn in several industries today and all of them tomorrow. In a memo written in the fall of 1998, the Ford Motor Company told suppliers that said suppliers would allow Ford to place purchases online within six months (spring, 1999), or Ford would buy elsewhere. That's not a fad. It's a fact.

Every time you check, there are more and more people on the Internet. Every time you check, Dell is selling more and more computers from its Web site. It's become an unspoken measure of how current the reporter or speaker is when they say Dell is selling $15 million, $19 million, $25 million of computers from its Web site every day. What's the latest number? Do you know?

How do they do it? By creating personal pages for each of their business customers, regardless of the size of the business. More about Dell later. First, it's important to understand why this sort of connection is causing such a commotion.

If you could pick just one thing that would improve your business from top to bottom—one thing that would guarantee your success—what would it be? More customers? They can leave you in a heartbeat. Cheaper raw materials? Buy them too cheaply and your quality plummets. Better cash flow? That's good for this month, but there's no assurance because the flow of true cash never did run smooth.

This is not intended to be an impossible question. There is an answer. There is one thing that would ensure your success in these times of e-commerce: access to accurate, live information.

What if you could tell exactly how much of your goods and services your customers were going to need in the coming year? What if you could see the precise inventory levels of your suppliers and up the chain to their suppliers so that you knew exactly when you could expect delivery? That's live information.

If you had the ability to see the warp and weft of the pattern of orders, deliveries, and payments, you could buy only what you needed only when you needed it. You could manufacture only what was necessary. You could ship into your distribution chain in anticipation of orders to ensure your products were on the shelves when the demand was at its peak. You could remove about 70 percent of the fat from the whole supply chain. You'd be invincible.

And what would it take to make all that happen? You'd have to be in business with only the best suppliers who could give you the most visibility. *That's the sort of vendor you should be to your customers.* That's the sort of business partner people will flock to. This is not a spare-time, petty-cash, lets-ask-for-volunteers sort of task. This requires being a change agent, altering the course of corporate history, and forever changing the rules.

If you sat in on a Steve Covey presentation in 1999, you probably heard the author of *The 7 Habits of Highly Effective People* (Simon & Schuster) talk about trim tabs.

A trim tab is a rudder's rudder. It's very hard to turn a very large rudder when you want to turn a very large ship. So they put a little movable rudderette at the bottom of the rudder: a trim tab. The trim tab can be moved with much less effort, but it provides the leverage that moves the big rudder that moves the ship. Your job, should you choose to accept it, is to be the trim tab that moves the executives that move the company.

It takes a bit of doing. You're approaching a massive, old, bureaucratic institution with deeply felt and widely held beliefs that everything they've done is right and should continue to be done that way. Your job is to tell them that everything they know is wrong. This is a challenge that may take some time.

You may feel it's an impossible task and that your company simply moves too slowly for anything productive to come from trim-tabbing within your lifetime. If you were looking to be an independent consultant anyway, then simply e-mail the following memo to your chief executive:

```
Good morning Mr. Van Winkle,

While you were dozing, the world took a few turns around the sun—in the
other direction. While you were calculating your portfolio's net present
value on your abacus while listening to various toadies telling you only
what you want to hear and insisting that your secretary print out your
e-mail and leave it in your in-box, the business landscape became a
business cyberscape. It's a 3-D World After All.

While you thought you were safe behind your walls with a phalanx of
defensive administrati keeping the rabble at bay, the walls have turned
translucent and are quickly becoming transparent. The rabble can see you
now. They can see you prevaricate. They watch you vacillate. They see
your attention fluctuate. They know if you've been bad or good.

Those little people, waaay down there, that you dismiss as mere
customers are now eye-level with you and yours through their computers.
They are taking their purchase orders to other companies with open-door,
open-window, and open-system policies. Other companies that are letting
information flow like water between trading partners.

Customers are voting with their wallets and the results are starting to
pour in: it's a rout. Our traditional competitors are figuring it out
and are doing their best to keep up with the new kids on the block who
are ignoring fifty years of business tradition and simply serving
customers online.

Where's the problem Mr. Van Winkle? The problem is somewhere between you
and me. You didn't get where you are by sticking your head in the sand
for lo these many years. You read in-flight magazines. You know which
end of the pencil has an eraser. But those guys in the middle, who have
spent decades building their fiefdoms brick-by-brick on the backs of us
worker-bees, are terrified of change. They think if they let this Web
stuff grow to its full potential they might be out of a job. The funny
part is - they're right! And there's nothing they can do to stop it.

So it's time to open your kimono, Rip. Time to wake up and smell the
customers. Time to admit that this old, cranky organization is not made
up of the best and the brightest. It's just made up of good, old-
fashioned people. People who will do their best to help their customers
in every way they can *including* turning this stodgy old dust trap into
the Visible Corporation.

Make it possible for customers to see when they're likely to receive
their orders. Let them see how we go about doing our best for them. Stop
hiding behind press releases and memoranda and go meet people face-to-
face and monitor-to-monitor.
```

```
I have a few ideas about how we can do that down here in the customer
service department. If you'd like to chat, you can *click here* to see
my calendar which includes doctor appointments for company-induced
stress attacks and interviews with venture capitalists about a little
Internet start-up idea I've been thinking about. My schedule is an open
book. See how well that works?

I hope to hear from you soon, because that really *is* an iceberg dead
ahead and it has your name on it.
```

So? Did that get you a meeting or a pink slip? Pink slip? Well, it's high time you were out of there. Meeting? Great—here are some of the issues you want to go over with old Rip.

Order Processing

When a customer wants to give you their money, it's only right that you should take it. And the easier you make it for people to give you money, the happier they are doing so.

Too many studies have shown that 60 percent, 70 percent, and in some cases even 90 percent of electronic shopping carts are abandoned by surfers who never pushed that last Submit button. Why? You only need to do a little online shopping to find out.

You have to get all the way to the end of the checkout process to find out how much the shipping is. Or if there's a quantity discount. Or what the tax is going to be. You want to serve your customers? Make it as easy as can be to buy from you.

Fellow Internet speaker Philippa Gamse (www.CyberSpeaker.com) recently told me this story and it's right on the mark. "I received a $10-off offer from CD Now—if I bought goods over $19.99. So I headed over there to get the Santana and David Bowie stuff that's missing from my collection—not exactly obscure choices.

And the shopping cart informed me that, unfortunately, it so happens that those two CDs are stored in different locations, so I have to pay two lots of shipping charges . . .

Perhaps they should give us an online guide to their warehouses, so that we can know what's stored with what before we're misguided enough to try to buy seemingly straightforward CDs . . . meanwhile, back to Amazon."

It can't really be said that Amazon provides extranet services, but it *does* provide that wonderful 1-click shopping experience (Figure 8.1).

Figure 8.1 Amazon was the first to figure out how to make it as easy as can be to buy something.

With 1-click in place, I am much more likely to buy a book. It's so simple. If a friend e-mails me about a book I should read, I click on the link to Amazon they sent me, then hit the 1-click button, and I've bought a book in about 30 seconds. They've earned my loyalty with that one.

What happens when you apply that concept to a company, rather than an individual? You get an extranet that's specifically designed to meet the needs of different corporate buyers. Office Depot (www.officedepot.com) was thinking along these lines when it picked its Web site tag line: "Ba da bing, ba da boom."

Office Depot creates a separate buying environment for each customer by letting them set up their own online account (Figure 8.2). In February 1999, it was said to have 40,000 users across 5,800 companies and to be adding 200 new companies (between 700 and 1,000 new users) every week.

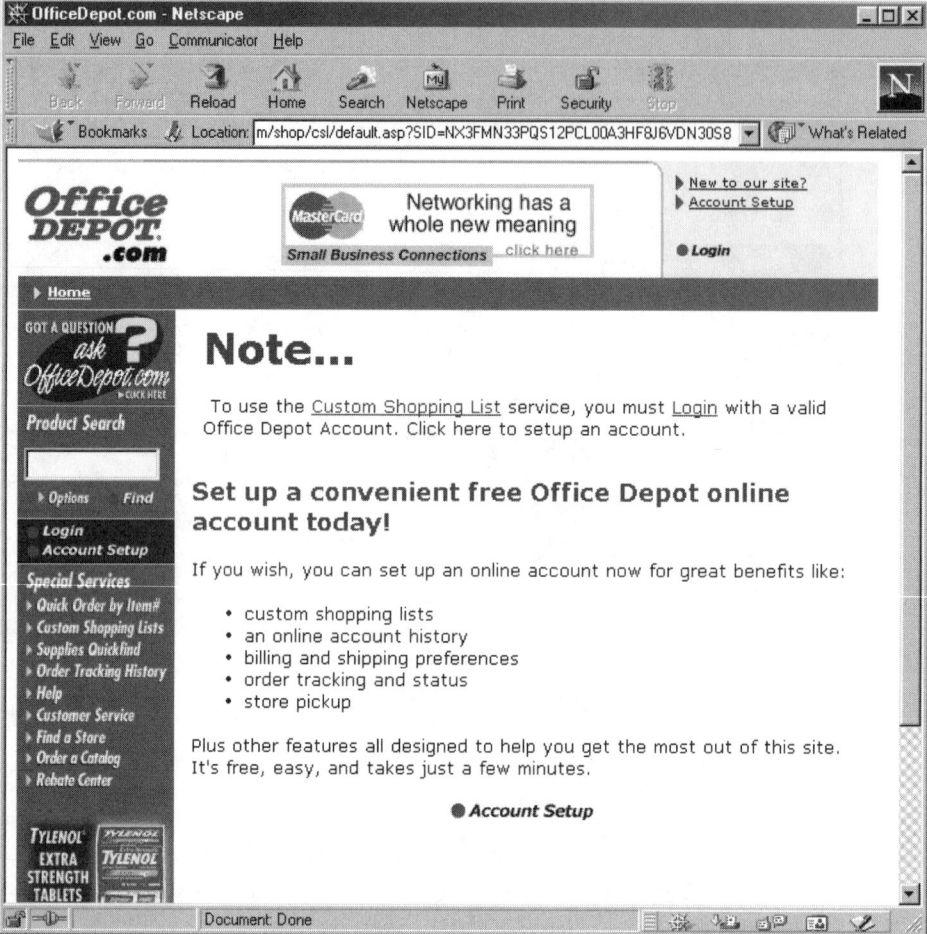

Figure 8.2 Custom shopping lists, account history, personal preferences, order tracking and status, and store pickup are all part of a private account at Office Depot.

Product Configuration

Let's say that you run a company with 10,000 people. Let's say that 6,000 of them need a new computer every three years. That makes for 2,000 PC purchases each year, which equates to a gazillion person-hours wasted over catalogs, brochures, in computer stores, and talking to friends in the IT department, and another thousand hours each, doing online research. What if you standardized the choices?

Ford decided to do just that when it signed up with Dell. Dell created five different configurations of PC to Ford's specifications, and a Ford-specific extranet where the orders could be placed. As a Ford employee, you head over to that page, make your selection, and hit the Buy button.

Michael Bulkeley manages the Raytheon Systems electronic catalog. An article in the October 26, 1998, *Computerworld* described Michael's situation this way:

> Raytheon is one of the companies that has built a site on its intranet for employees to buy supplies, ranging from electrical and computer parts to maintenance and office supplies. The site was developed with the help of Trade'ex Electronic Commerce Systems Inc. in Tampa, Fla. It incorporates catalogs from about 50 suppliers and gives them a consistent and intuitive look and feel to save Bulkeley's users—who range from scientists and lab technicians to maintenance people and secretaries—from having to learn 50 ways of navigating.

Making it easier for customers is what it's all about. At Dell, your service tag number reveals all of the updates and downloads and service memos about the particular computer you own. It also shows what other hardware and accessories are compatible with your system.

The improvements in productivity alone were enough to make the whole thing worth Ford's signing on the dotted line. But that was only one piece of it. As the previous article puts it:

> The site includes products that only Raytheon employees are authorized to buy, with pricing and terms as negotiated with Raytheon.

Negotiated Pricing

Ford also saved a bundle because it promised Dell most-favored vendor status. Ford would buy all of its PCs from Dell and, in return, Dell would drop its prices. The benefit to the seller is as obvious as low price is to the buyer: a locked-in customer and a locked-out field of competitors.

The manager of process development for the sourcing organization at Steelcase in Grand Rapids, Michigan, is Rob Heitmeier. Rob's job is to negotiate better prices with suppliers. When he and his people spend all their time writing purchase orders and solving problems between the vendors and those who requisitioned the goods, there's no time left for negotiating. "By setting up on the Internet," said Rob in the same *Computerworld* article just quoted, "we can move toward select suppliers, reduce our over-all number, and negotiate better terms."

If you promise low prices, you get invited to negotiate. If you then promise online convenience and productivity savings, you clinch the sale based on improved customer service.

Cost of P.O.

Why did Ford decide to force suppliers into moving online? Because of the amazing savings they realized by Ford's calculations, online processing took $2 million off the cost of buying computers from Dell. This had nothing to do with the negotiated price; this was just the money spent moving paperwork between companies.

Dell had automated the process to the point where one of their customers cut the number of people involved in the purchase cycle from 16 to 4. Microsoft boasted that buying office supplies using most-favored vendor extranets let them shrink the 19 people involved in paper pushing to buy paper to 2.

The National Purchasing Association has long estimated the average cost of a purchase order at $150. Texas Instruments used to shell out $100 per purchase just to get the paper through the system—even on items costing $10. Now, with extranet purchasing with its most frequent suppliers, TI has knocked that number down to $3.50 per order. When you add up hundreds of thousands of orders in a year, the savings become significant.

MasterCard was so proud of its success that it even let Microsoft make a magazine ad out of it. "Mei Morin saves MasterCard up to $85 every time she places an online order using their new Microsoft-based corporate purchasing system. By the way, MasterCard employees place over 6,000 online orders every year." The implied math? Annual savings of up to half a million dollars.

Inventory in Real Time

If your customers can see what you have and where you have it, they can make better decisions about what to order and when.

Phil Gibson, director of interactive marketing at National Semiconductor, has been the change agent there, pushing through initiative after initiative. Phil and his team were delighted to give their design engineer customers access to product information online. But their sales team pointed out that they were ignoring half their clientele. So, National Semi went to work building a purchasing portal for the purchase agents who have to execute the engineers' requisitions (Figure 8.3).

My Bill of Materials

What is My Bill of Materials?

It is a personalized table for National's registered users that allows you to build a personalized website for the parts you specify (containing Part Numbers, Package

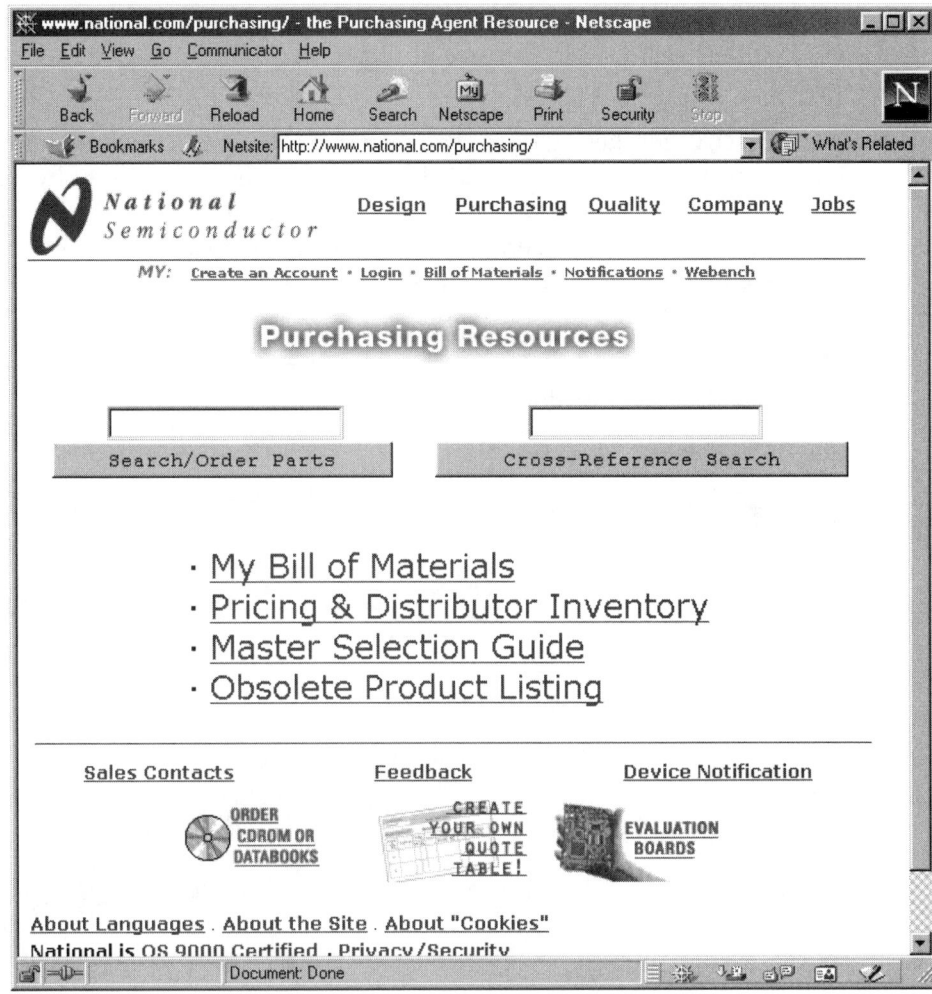

Figure 8.3 National Semiconductor built a special area just for purchasing agents, and built instant loyalty at the same time.

Type, Part Status, Pricing & Distributor Inventory, Standard Pack Method and list of user selected distributors with on hand available inventory to sell along with hot links into their order forms). You can create multiple projects and select the information that you would care to see. Each project will become an additional link on your private website.

All attributes in these selection criteria are updated daily, so you can get the latest information available for the parts you want, when you want them.

Pricing and Distributor Inventory

Buyers using My Bill of Materials thought it was great. It showed the part numbers, then quantities used in packaging, and even the distributors who carried each particular part. The only problem, they told Phil and his people, was that they then had to traverse multiple distributors' Web sites in order to get availability. They needed availability figures as part of their negotiations.

The interactive marketing team scratched their heads and came up with one of those solutions that is a giant stride in innovation, but just seems obvious after the fact. When a buyer looks at the My Bill of Materials page, the National Semi Web site instantly queries a handful of their distributors' online inventory systems and displays the results (Figure 8.4).

National Semi shows what the downhill supply chain looks like. Do their distributors object? Some do. And chance are, they get fewer orders than those who are willing to play along.

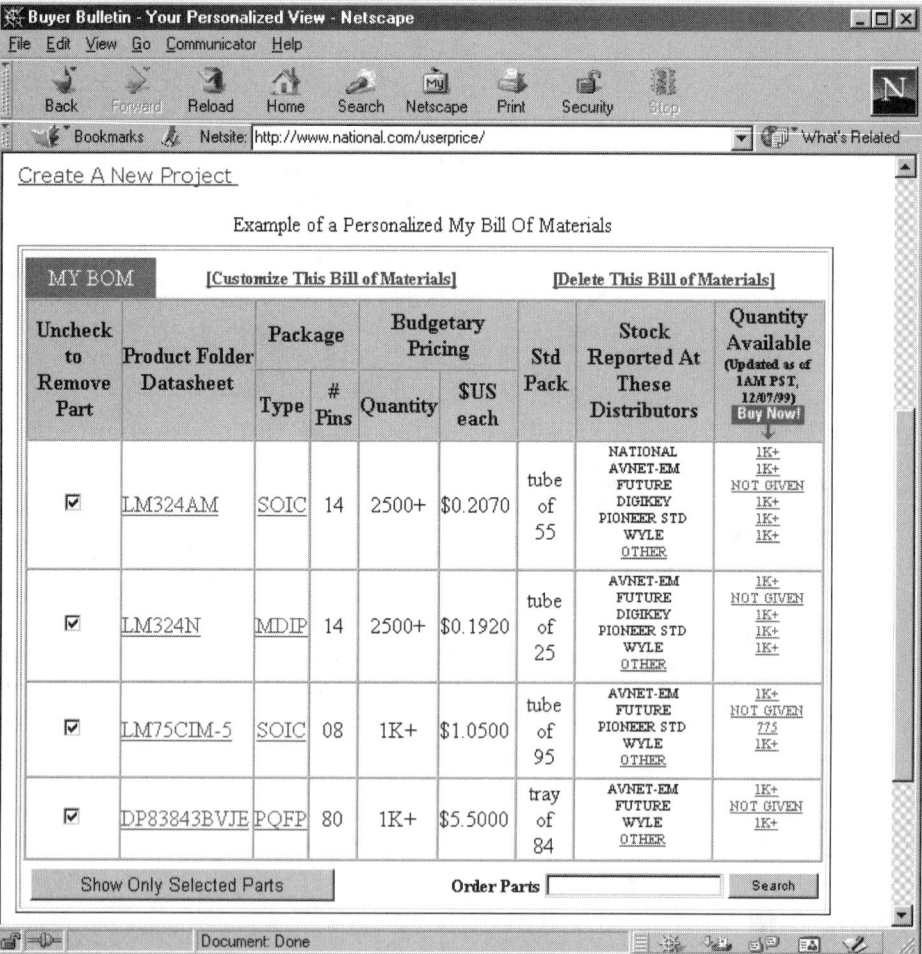

Figure 8.4 National Semi customers know at a glance which distributor might cut them the best deal.

Dell's Master Selection Guide shows all of the available products, and the Obsolete Product Listing shows all the unavailable products. That's the sort of functionality you get when you listen to your customers. *All* of your customers.

If your suppliers can see what you have and where you have it, they can make better decisions about what to send you and when. Thompson Consumer Electronics is a case in point.

Thompson makes RCA and GE televisions and VCRs. Their customers, like Circuit City and Kmart, were complaining about the same thing *their* customers were complaining about: product availability. Anybody heading into a store with a purchase in their heart and money in their wallet is bound to be disappointed when the just-out-of-high-schooler tells them the item is out of stock. Anybody running a retail facility with inventory turnover in their heart and a customer in the hand is bound to be disappointed when the inventory system tells them the item is out of stock.

Nowadays, Thompson posts their inventory levels and their forecasts on their extranet site and lets suppliers worry about order fulfillment.

Order Tracking

Now that the proper products have been configured and the orders placed, what happened to them? I know the items are in stock. I know you have access to Federal Express. So where's my order?!? Dell takes order tracking very seriously and lets you follow every step (Figure 8.5).

Here's the process as described on the Dell site:

Dell Order Processing

Your order is currently being processed for release to the manufacturing floor. Release is generally dependent upon approval of your designated form of payment. Credit card orders move faster while orders paid by other methods generally take longer. Once payment is confirmed, your order will be released for production.

Dell Preproduction

We are awaiting the arrival of component parts into inventory before we can schedule your order for production.

Preproduction time varies based on the system ordered and is dependent largely on the availability of parts. An estimated "lead time" reflecting the anticipated time it will take to get parts on hand and build your order should have been communicated to you at the time of order confirmation. Order confirmation may have been provided over the phone by your sales representative, or via e-mail for electronic orders.

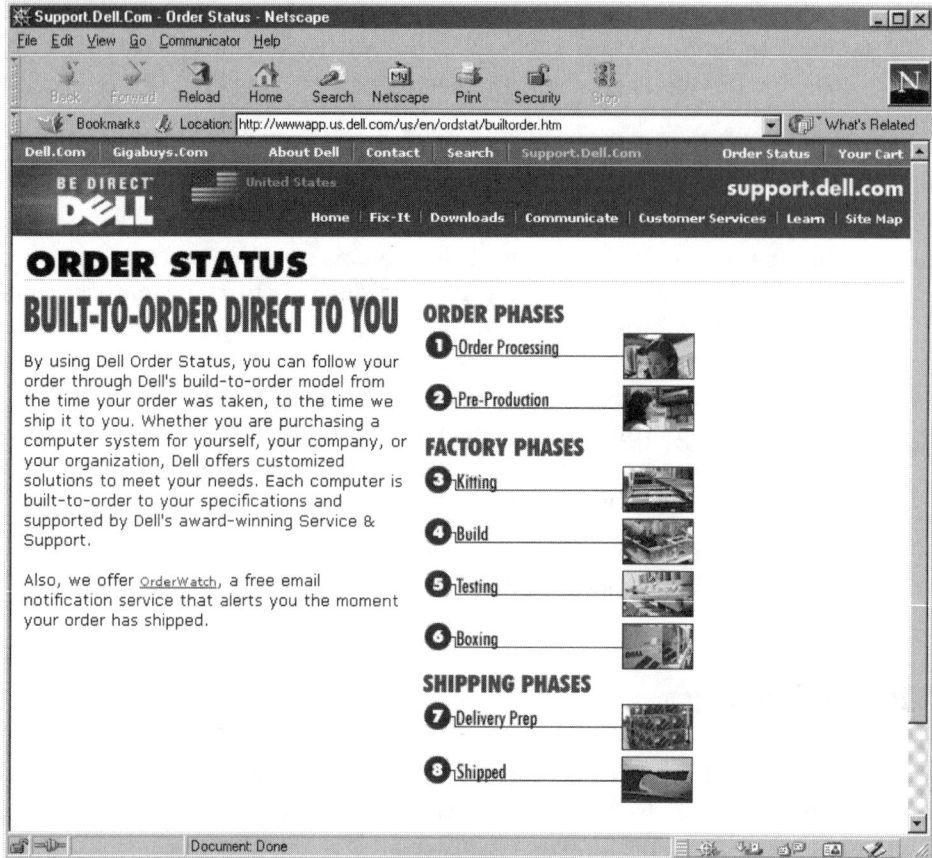

Figure 8.5 Dell offers customers a window into the entire order processing process.

Kitting

When a system order is released to manufacturing, the material availability is confirmed and all parts needed to complete the system are placed into a tote. The completed tote is mated with the systems chassis [and] placed on a conveyor which takes it through to build.

Build

An assembly team takes the tote and assembles those parts in a system. This team is responsible for the entire build of the system, which promotes accountability for quality and pride of ownership. The system then goes through testing.

Testing

Systems are received into testing for Dell-designed diagnostic testing and software download. This includes 200+ titles available in Dell's software library, as well as proprietary and commercial packages, as requested by DellPlus Customers. Upon successful completion of Testing, the system moves to the boxing phase.

Boxing

Completed systems are placed in boxes along with the mouse, keyboard, powercords, documentation and manuals as requested by the customer.

Once the boxing is complete, the system box is sealed and placed on the appropriate truck for shipment to our customer.

Delivery Prep

Delivery prep is normally completed within one day of the date production is complete. However, larger orders and orders requiring special handling may take longer.

Shipped

Your order has been shipped and was en route to its ship-to destination as of the "Ship Date" indicated. Delivery time varies based on the shipping option chosen at the time of order entry. Your order will generally reach its intended destination within 2–5 business days of the "Ship Date" noted. Please fill in your Order Number, your name and your email address. Click on the "Register Your Order" button to receive an e-mail when your new Dell computer ships.

Then, of course, it's a simple matter of checking with FedEx or UPS to see if your order is in the air, on the van, or delivered, and who signed for it. What's next? Paying the bill, of course.

Bill Presentment

Banks started it. They let you check your account balances at ATM machines and then online. Then they let you transfer money between accounts. Then they moved to online bill payment, except that it was online *manual* bill payment.

Wells Fargo (www.wellsfargo.com) has yet to master the art of electronic payments with its Bill Pay service (Figure 8.6). Sometimes the payment is electronic, but sometimes it's still on paper.

Q: Who can I pay?

A: You can pay any merchant, institution or individual in the U.S. including credit cards, utilities, relatives and even your baby sitter.

Q: Are all payments sent to payees on the Merchant Directory List electronic?

A: Most of the payees on the Merchant Directory List are set up to receive electronic payments. We are always updating and improving this list to make as many payments electronic as possible.

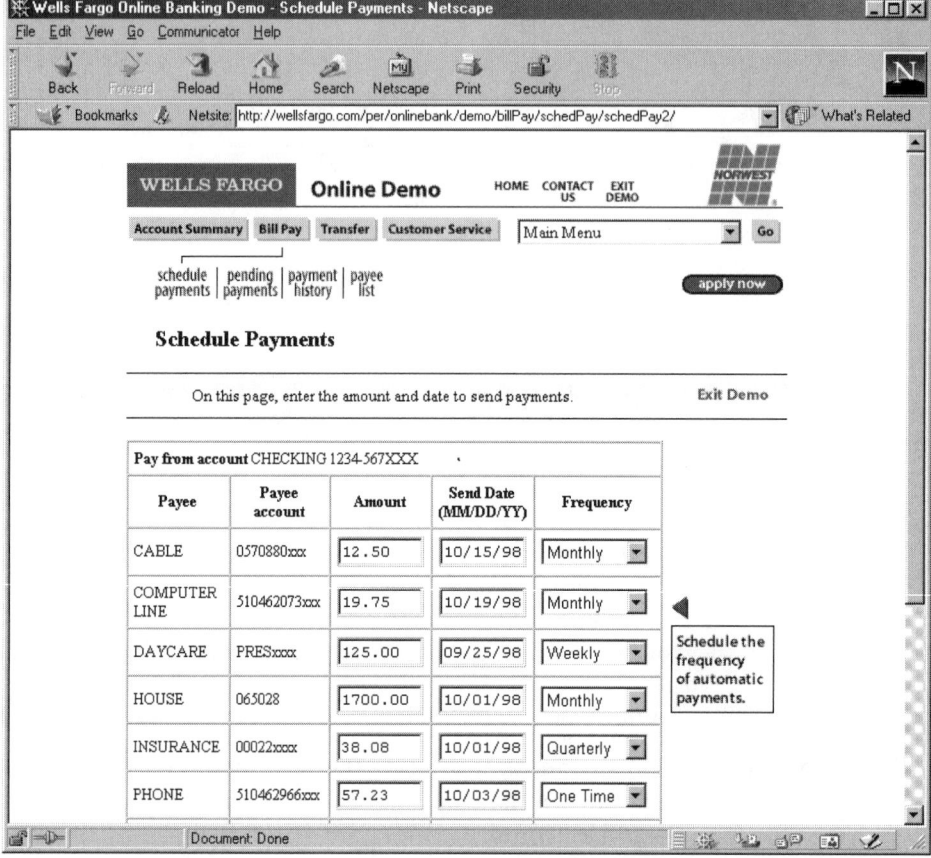

Figure 8.6 Make a payment through Wells Fargo, and they might mail a letter with a printed check in it.

Q: How do I know whether a merchant will receive electronic payment or a check?

A: Unfortunately, we do not have a process to communicate which billers receive electronic payments. Therefore, regardless of the payment method, you should schedule your payments at least 5 business days before the due date on your bill.

Q: What do payees receive?

A: Electronic payees receive payment information in an electronic format that automatically updates their accounts payable system. Non-electronic merchants or individual payees receive a laser printed paper check sent through the U.S. Postal Service.

On the flip side, at First USA (www.firstusa.com), you can ask that your credit card be paid electronically from Wells Fargo (Figure 8.7).

The "You Will" people at AT&T let their customers check their bills online (Figure 8.8).

Figure 8.7 Just tell First USA where to get the money and they'll reach out and put the touch on you.

Manage Your AT&T Business Account Online

Perform powerful account management transactions within a secure online environment:

- Make account balance inquiries
- View your monthly AT&T bill
- Get real-time credit adjustments
- Download itemized call details from your AT&T bill to your PC
- Check telephone listings of unfamiliar calls

When this sort of technology gets applied to extranets, the cycle of billing and payment changes. If we can negotiate the amount, then we can negotiate the interval. With electronic bill presentment and payment, a sliding scale of dis-

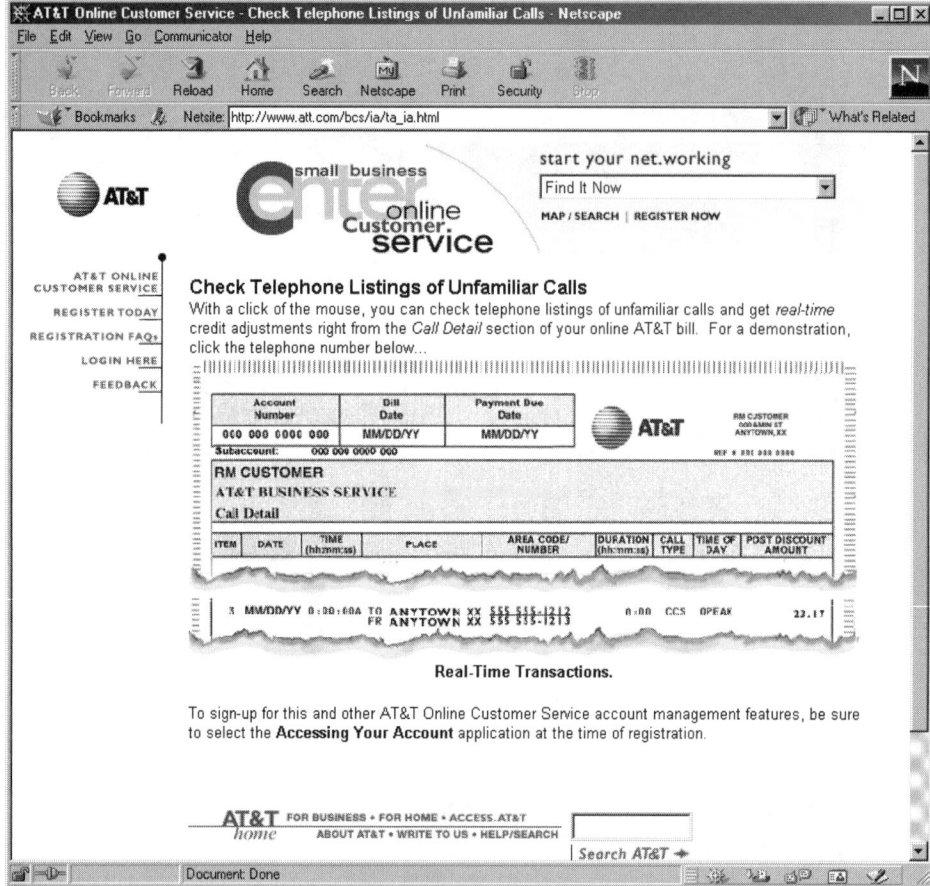

Figure 8.8 Checking unfamiliar phone numbers is as easy as clicking on the number you're wondering about.

counts can be agreed. You could give your customers a 5 percent discount for paying within 3 days, a 3 percent discount for paying within 5 days, and a 2 percent discount for paying within 10 days. Further, you can negotiate a 2 percent fee for paying over 30 days, a 5 percent fee for paying over 45 days, and a 10 percent fee for paying over 60 days.

Customers would be delighted with this sort of setup, because of the control we all have now on precisely when payments are made. Customers could manage their cash flow much more aggressively, taking advantage of discounts when they could and pushing out payments when necessary.

While controlling money is a key component of companies' doing business with other companies, allowing customers to control their time is quickly becoming the biggest draw of all. That's where access to real-time information comes into its own.

Real Time: It's Not Just for Order Tracking Anymore

When you start publishing information online in real time, you give your customers the ability to run their companies differently. Knowing how much you have on order is one thing. Knowing how much you owe and when it's due is another. But there are a wide variety of data that could be useful to your customers. What are they? It depends.

If you're a software company, letting people access the progress of their customer support requests might be just the ticket.

Oracle's Visible Trouble Tickets

Arnold Wong is the manager for customer care & quality in the Asia Pacific region of Oracle Support Services. He is a customer champion who believes very strongly in obtaining feedback from customers and employees to discover how the company can best fulfill their requirements.

"Oracle MetaLink was developed by Oracle Support Services to provide access to our support analysts and 24×7 access to our technical service information," says Arnold. "While using these services, customers will be able to obtain the latest product information and installation instructions and do text searches against Support's internal databases technical bulletins, problem/solution articles, online documentation questions and share ideas in our technical forums." Sometimes Arnold takes a breath between sentences, but usually he is very excited about how Oracle uses the Web to benefit its customers.

Through OracleMetaLink, customers can interact with the technical support repositories used by Oracle Support Services (OSS), including troubleshooting systems, problem-tracking systems, and technical libraries. They can also log and check the status of technical assistance requests (TARs), which you may refer to as trouble tickets, incident reports, or problem reports.

MetaLink allows customers to customize their home pages to display the information they care about and sign up to be notified by e-mail of product availability, bugs, patches, and TAR changes.

The user profiling system also displays information on all software licenses customers are holding, including the level of support you've signed up for, support contract expiration dates, and de-support dates. "De-support" is the Oracle euphemism for pulling the plug on a software product they're no longer going to upgrade. That qualifies as information that's important to know about. And, while the content is all in English, you can change your profile to show the user interface in the language of your choice.

The technical library is organized by product and computer operating system and includes installation and product documentation, white papers, problem/solution articles, bug information, release notes, and information on Oracle's latest supported versions.

Oracle offers a support knowledge base for full-text queries against all of the content contained in MetaLink's repositories, including the technical forum postings and the bug database. The forums allow customers to post questions to technical analysts and receive responses within two business days, as well as to share information and ideas with other Oracle customers.

Aside from MetaLink, Oracle offers the kind of advanced support that only hardware and software companies can provide, like ExpertONLINE that Oracle introduced in October of 1998. ExpertONLINE consists of ExpertDETECT, a monitoring, diagnostic, and recommendation service, and Expert DBA, an end-to-end online database administration service

Dell's Visible Forecast

Dell lets suppliers see Dell's forecasts for upcoming orders. The is *very* sensitive information. You can see why Mr. Van Winkle might lose a few more gray hairs over this sort of open-handed information flow.

Dell has several numbers that it uses to make predictions. There are the number of orders that came in during this period last year. There are those orders multiplied by the rate of increase experienced last month. There are the orders received so far in this period. There is the rate of growth of online orders.

Dell used to use these numbers to divine the right number of components and parts to order to mesh with the company's just-in-time manufacturing process. But Dell's suppliers kept asking for more detailed prognostications so they could plan *their* inventory accordingly. Dell finally woke up and began giving the suppliers the information they needed. It wouldn't serve Dell's purposes if its suppliers were caught empty-handed when big orders started coming in at the beginning of the school year or the beginning of the government budget year.

Penske's Visible Trucks

While FedEx will tell you where your package is, Penske Truck Leasing will tell you:

- Vehicle location tracking and routing
- Exception-based reporting for vehicle, driver, and/or on-time performance
- Vehicle and engine performance reports
- Driver performance reports
- Electronic trip planning
- Electronic fuel tax reporting
- On-board fleet incentives
- Fuel economy management
- Customer site accounting (delivery times, rates, locations)
- Vehicle dispatch software
- Vehicle tracking and routing

Home Depot's Visible Projects

Home Depot (www.homedepot.com) knows a good customer category when it sees one. In its eyes, small building contractors are the company's most valuable customers, since they're too small to get big discounts directly from manufacturers and too big to ignore.

Each contractor signs on with a password and enters information about each job they're running, and the Home Depot site lists the materials needed, what the work schedule might look like, and what sort of obstacles the contractor can expect along the way.

The company provides up-to-the-minute inventory availability, of course, but it also offers scheduled and split deliveries to the job sites. Home Depot will also let contractors post requisitions for subcontractors like framers or electricians and give contractors access to expert advice. Due to just-in-time delivery, contractors can order less material, and therefore, be more competitive on bids.

Chlor-Alkali's Visible Tanks

Chlor-Alkali & Derivatives tracks inventory with ultrasonic sensors that use telemetry to notify customers about how full their tanks are. Sharon Picainac-chio, Chlor-Alkali's customer service manager, says the company knows how much inventory customers have, how much they ordered recently, how much they use every day, and can guess when they're going to need more.

The goal is to remove the barriers between the customer and the information you're keeping about the customer. If you enter into partnerships with your customers, rather than the typical adversarial relationships that develop, then trust can grow to where responsibility rests in the hands of those with the most power to fulfil the need.

Retailers have the responsibility to report on sales trends. The only control they have is to cut purchase orders or threaten to stop ordering altogether. Distributors have the responsibility to get the goods from here to there on time. Manufacturers have the responsibility to get the goods shipped on time. That turns them into retail buyers of raw materials—and the cycle begins again.

If the extended chain is visible to all of the players, then the mining company can dig out more raw materials for the three manufacturing companies to process in sequence in enough time for the assembly team to get the finished product boxed in time for the distributor to get the items to the proper locations in time for the Christmas rush.

That takes a lot of teamwork. It takes more than simply opening up the doors to the data warehouse. It takes opening up the doors to the buying process. That's called *workflow.*

Workflow

When you automate a business process, you have to look at how the data flows from one task to the next. When you automate how and when that data flows, you're now into workflow. Now that the Internet has come between us, workflow means more than getting a performance review signed off on so your assistant can get his raise—it means automating the approval of a purchase order through the supply chain.

You start by asking, What gets done? Then you ask, How does it get done? Then, How can it be automated? Finally, What does all this have to do with extranets?

Both Office Depot and Staples have created unique online catalogs for each large customer. Companies buying office supplies can lock in set prices and lock out employees from buying expensive office equipment without management approval. Where there are business rules, there is workflow.

Business rules are those often-spoken, seldom-written steps:

"Didn't you know you have to get Jane's signature on there before Mrs. Plotsky will even look at it?"

"Adding new staff members is a division-level decision. Everybody knows that."

"We have to get the green copy back from the vendor before we can pay that."

"If that puts them within 10 percent of their maximum credit allowance, then Bernie needs to approve it."

Vendors are building these rules into the extranet services they offer:

Everybody with a classification of X may order no more than $500 per order or $5,000 per month.

If a classification X person clicks on the Exception button, an e-mail is sent to that person's designated manager Y.

If the designated manager approves the purchase, and it is above $10,000 per order or $100,000 per month, an e-mail is sent to their designated director Z.

Workflow comes into the picture when X and or Z can click through those e-mails to the approval page, put in their access password, and the work flows through. Business rules can also be applied to the customer support desk. They can be defined by type of user. They can be set up to determine when somebody's boss gets notification that their underling needs training. They can be set up so people asking really tough questions get sent to the right peopled or customers with really ugly problems get bumped up in the queue.

It gets more interesting when you create business rules and workflow processes for your customers and from your suppliers. The results are an open communication that, in the long run, includes the sharing of business goals.

Whole New Worlds

What's the supplier's business goal? To sell more stuff. Likely. But sometimes those goals change. Maybe this supplier's goal for this month is to even out the spikes in shipments. Maybe erratic ordering on the manufacturer's part makes life hard for the supplier. If that goal is shared with the manufacturer, who shares it with the distributor, who shares it with the retailer, maybe some rearranging can be done within the supply chain to smooth things out.

What if the retailer were willing to place the order a little more in advance to ensure the proper level of inventory at Christmas? And if the distributor were willing to store some of the goods a little longer? What if that could allow the manufacturer to not have to hire a third shift, lowering costs and allowing those savings to be passed along? That's the sort of value that comes from sharing goals as well as rules.

Definition of Value Chain Integration

A process of collaboration that optimizes all internal and external activities involved in delivering greater perceived value to the ultimate customer.
John Dobbs, Cambridge Technology Partners

You may think you sell stuff, but it's time to realize that you have to surround that stuff with information to stay in the game. Then you need to create a service out of that information to get ahead of the game.

Beyond Parts

Mazda North American Operations has been selling parts to Mazda dealers for years and years. But just knowing how many parts a dealer buys doesn't help make that dealer more profitable. What makes Mazda more profitable is if that dealer can sell more cars. What makes the dealer more profitable is if he can service more cars.

So Mazda went one step beyond serving up parts. It serves parts and information for each individual car. When an automotive technician punches a vehicle identification number into the Mazda extranet, he or she gets the service bulletins that apply not just to that particular model, but to that particular car. Warranty information, policy changes, service updates, all of that critical information that used to live in file cabinets behind the bookkeeper is now in front of the one person who's going to get his hands dirty.

Personal Extranet

National Semiconductor allows online ordering. In fact, the goal of its staff has been to make online ordering "as easy as Amazon.com." For example, they confirm the order on the screen. They e-mail confirmations. When these features became routine, they decided to take a few more risks and try a few more new things.

The first additional step was to create private account pages. The idea was to take an extranet and make it available from both sides. Sure, each customer had their own page; now National Semi made that page viewable and *changeable* by the salespeople.

Take just a moment to catch your breath and let that thought seep into your psyche. Salespeople were given the authority to muck about with their customers' private extranet connections to the company.

Each and every salesperson was given the standard template and a set of easy-to-use modification tools. Each and every salesperson was given access and authority to post proprietary information about products, schedules, shipments, whatever the sales rep thought the customer would want. Even contracts are posted online. What? Secret contractual agreements between companies available for those operating under the terms of those contracts? Unheard of! Scandalous! Brilliant.

Trust the salespeople to know what the customer might want in the way of information or transactions? Bizarre. Strange. Outlandish! Right on the money. Who else has a vested interest in keeping the customer happy? Who else will profit directly from having the customer be able and willing to order more? It works.

Application Service Provider

Time to go to the next step. The fundamental question was, How can we sell more stuff? The answer was to get more design engineers to the National Semi-conductor Web site. So what could they offer design engineers? Their customers already had a steady diet of Dilbert cartoons. That wasn't going to help.

We're talking about a Web site that half of the design engineers in the world visit at least once a month. They download 400,000 datasheets per month. There are 220,000 registered users. National sends out 48,000 biweekly newsletters, and processes 21,000 orders per month. They had to go one better.

So they asked a question that should be engraved on your plastic terminal casing with a hot soldering gun where you can look at it every day and have to explain it to the various facilities management people and fire marshals who roam your building:

> What do our customers do, how do they do it, and how can we make it easier for them to get it done?

In the case of National Semi, they saw that a lot of their customers were spending a lot of time using various slow and annoying simulation systems to design power supplies so they could tell what components they wanted to buy from National Semi. The fastest of these simulation software packages National could find was from a company called Transim (www.transim.com). Here's how Transim described its product:

> The Simplis family of simulators are powerful tools developed specifically to deal with the issues inherent in switched mode power supply (SMPS) design: rapidly slewing signals, disparate time constants, and a periodic rather than a DC operating point. The Simplis simulators are based on unique algorithms; they are not Spice derivatives. Instead, they take advantage of the repetitive nature of switching power supplies by "learning" the switching behavior of the circuit being simulated and storing that information for later reuse. Simplis typically simulates a SMPS circuit more than forty times faster than other analog simulation engines. That speed advantage, plus fewer convergence problems, makes Simplis the preferred simulator for SMPS design.

I don't claim to be able to recognize a rapidly slewing signal from rabbit stew, but I do know a brilliant Internet move when I see one. National licensed the Transim software for use by many. And I do mean many. National Semi customers can go to the National site and simulate power supplies to their hearts' content (Figure 8.9).

Instead of getting their companies to evaluate and approve the software, buy the software, install the software, and support the software, National's customers pay from $5 to $10 to run it on the National site. After five or six simulations, the customer knows if the design is going to meet the need. Then comes the good part.

The simulator identifies the generic components you need to turn the inputs you have into the outputs you want. The National Web site then displays the specific National Semi parts you might choose from to build what you have just simulated (Figure 8.10).

This is Web magic. Forget thinking outside the box, this is getting all the way out of town. So ask yourself: What do your customers do, how do they do it, and how can you make it easier for them to get it done?

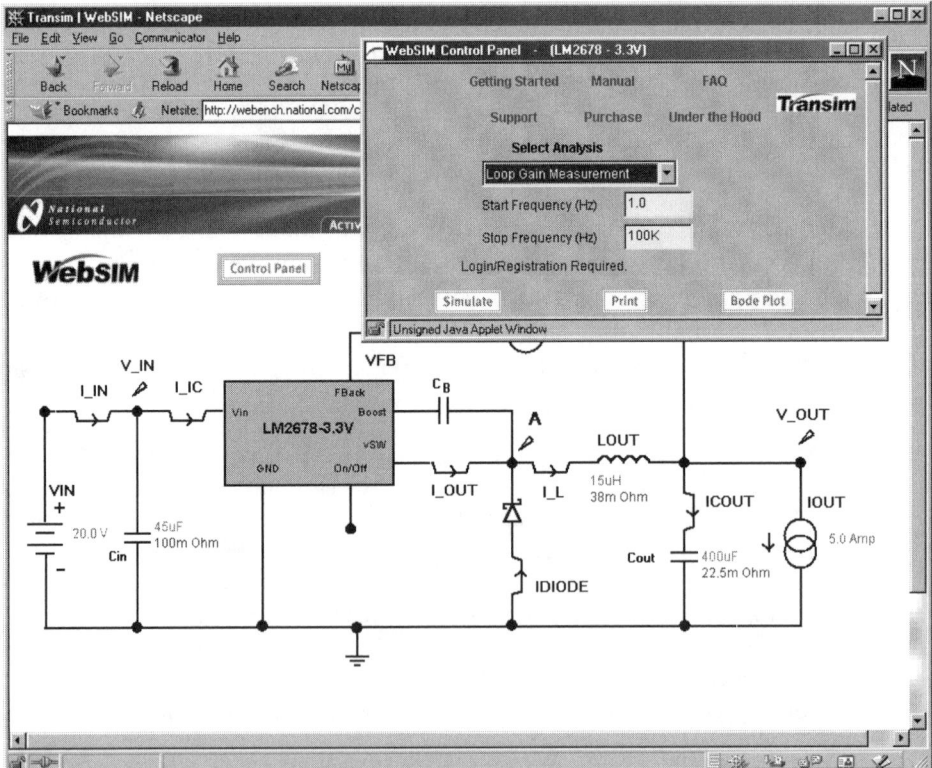

Figure 8.9 National Semiconductor makes simulation software available to its customers for a modest fee.

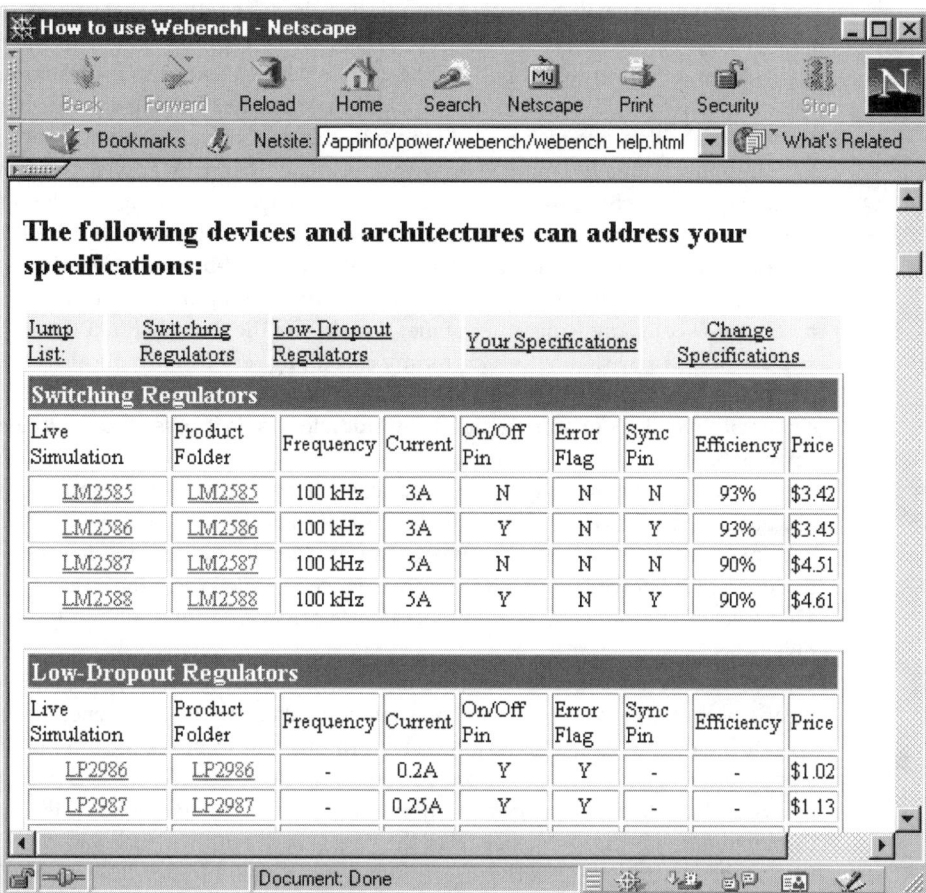

Figure 8.10 After the simulation comes the order form. You know it'll work; all that's left is to buy the parts and build the prototype.

You don't even have to have a gazillion-dollar budget to make something that's useful to your customer and a cut above the rest.

Extranet on a Budget

Jim Sterne
Inc. Magazine, November 15, 1999

A Fine and Private Page

You don't need to book an expensive extranet to give site visitors rooms of their own. For many, the words extranet and E-commerce conjure visions of highly paid Java programmers melding complex enterprise-wide systems with state-of-the-art, gazillion-page Web sites. That's the sort of project you try to avoid if you don't have an IT department the size of a small country.

Does that mean small companies should steer clear of anything that smacks of back-office integration? Absolutely not. Web technology is ideal for any organization that wants to improve communications with business partners but lacks the resources for a full-blown marriage between its network and customer-relationship-management systems. Those with shallowish pockets can take this as consolation: Sometimes technological sophistication has more to do with appearance than with application. Consider extranets, a relatively straightforward customer-management concept that has become freighted with the jargon of intranets and virtual private networks. If building an extranet sounds too involved, think instead of creating Web pages that only specified parties can see. Such pages may not even require password protection. I am the head of a very small company (consisting of me, myself, and the recently hired I) with a Web site that acts as a marketing vehicle for my consulting services. My site also contains a discreet page with photos of my dog Puck, a schipperke, that my wife and I wanted to share with members of a discussion list for dog lovers. Is it password protected? No. Private? Sure.

The Puck page is private in the same sense that an unlisted telephone number is private. It is known to, and therefore used by, only a designated few. Puck's photos are not linked to any other page anywhere. Family, friends, and the dog fanciers on my discussion list know how to find it because we've E-mailed them the specific address. That level of security suffices to protect Puck's privacy, and it's enough for many of my clients as well.

I also use private pages for business-related purposes. I use them, for example, as a means of making my PowerPoint presentations available to conference hosts who wish to hand out the material to attendees. Printing and shipping the presentations is a pain, and I've had consistently bad luck sending 2MB or 3MB files as E-mail attachments. So I create private pages on my site that people can download instead. I send the conference producers the URLs of the pages; they can then click and capture the files without worrying about viruses, gateways, or e-mail in-box limitations. Again, the information on those pages isn't something that everyone who visits my site needs to see, but if it gets out, it's not going to do any damage.

Of course, much information needs ironclad security. I discuss Internet strategies, potential markets, products, services, and business models with my clients. For that kind of information, an unpublished address isn't good enough. It calls for both private pages and passwords. Creating a password-protected page isn't done at a trivial cost, but it's not a budget-buster either. Password-protection routines are described in most online HTML tutorials. (The company hosting your site will have to handle the server-side software. If it doesn't know how to do that, then stop reading this article and start looking for another provider.)

Once the technology is in place, your employees can exploit password-protected pages in ways your customers will love. Sales representatives at National Semiconductor Corp. create and maintain private Web pages for each customer, for example. When a customer calls and asks about a product, the rep can add the requested information to that customer's page. Or the rep can create a new page for things like customized pricing quotes, specials, or specifics on whatever configuration of the product in question works with the customer's system. The sales reps can do all of the above in a number of ways, including authoring new material, cutting and pasting information from other Web pages, or simply adding links. Whatever the mechanism, the result is far more helpful than telling the customer "Oh, I'm pretty sure you can find that on our Web site." (If your sales force is unwilling or unable to assume that kind of responsibility, consider having your Webmaster do it for important customers.)

The Tenagra Corp., a 20-plus-employee Internet marketing agency in Houston, used private Web pages to beat out some of the largest players in the industry in a bid to design and build the top-level Web pages at Unisys Corp. Cliff Kurtzman, Tenagra's president, had his team build a password-protected area on Tenagra's own Web site that contained a clear, concise description of how the vendor planned to handle the Unisys contract. Instead of handing out reports 200 pages in length on 24-pound letterhead bond, Tenagra simply gave a URL and a password to Unisys committee members. The members thus gained access to the protected site and checked out first-hand the quality they could expect from the company. The proposal was also easy for members to discuss by e-mail: instead of quoting vast tracts from a paper document or having to cite page and paragraph numbers, they just forwarded the URLs of specific passages, which the recipient then called up for review.

Building customer-specific pages or protected areas works well for companies that serve only a small number of clients. If you're in the consumer market, however, you may need the kinds of personalization afforded by tools like GuestTrack and Broad-Vision, which can track thousands of individual customers. Such tools serve up customized Web pages on the fly based on database-driven customer profiles or profiles created as site visitors click on some links and not on others. Unfortunately, such applications can be pricey, ranging from $5,000 for GuestTrack to $350,000 to $1 million-plus for BroadVision.

The Commerce Compromise

What is true for extranets is also true for e-commerce: A lack of sophisticated data integration needn't keep you from taking orders over the Web. Yes, in the ideal world, online purchasing information would be sucked into your back-office order processing system, which would check it for accuracy and validate the credit card; the system would then print out a label in your warehouse for use in packing and shipping. But scratch the surface of all but the most Webcentric companies and you'll find that they are only putting a good face on their e-commerce capabilities. The information collected by those wonderful online order forms is merely e-mailed to someone for data entry.

Of course, you can save a bundle on order processing and fulfillment if you automate everything. But first you'll have to spend a bundle: anywhere from $250,000 to $1 million or more, depending on how hard it is to take and process orders in your line of work. Such an investment may be pointless if you don't expect a significant number of online orders. If your projections for Web commerce are modest, focus your energy instead on your site's look and feel: how it appears to the customer. Put up that order form, by all means. Just make sure your visitors can't see the man behind the curtain who's printing out the e-mail orders, hand-entering them into a 1978 Commodore PET, and sending out confirmation e-mails one by one.

As long as you can keep up with the flow of orders, it doesn't matter how you get the job done. All that matters is that customers have a positive experience, get the information they need when they need it, and feel confident that the system is working. The Web can do all that, even if your budget barely covers kite string and duct tape.

Yes, there's value to an extranet, even when you do it on the cheap. But what happens when you look through the other end of the telescope? What happens when you bring together the power of personalization, the convenience of customer communication, the depth of data mining, and the expediency of an extranet?

You get customer relationship management.

CHAPTER 9

Customer Relationship Management

The Evolution of a Web site:

1. *Brochureware.* Also known as *shovelware.* This is when you wander into the literature room with a snow shovel, scoop up as many brochures as you can, fling them onto the scanner, and voila!—a Web site is born. It contains product information, company information, press releases, and maybe some investor relations stuff. Yawnsville.

2. *Customer-considerate.* Somebody in customer service realizes they can post information on the Web that might actually be useful to customers. Up go the frequently asked questions pages and the troubleshooting guides.

3. *E-mail overload.* Once customers realize there are things you *could* have put up on your site, they start the barrage of questions. Where's my order? Do you have an alternative? Whom do I talk to about that? The Webmaster tries to handle it but soon turns it over to the call center. The call center realizes that e-mail is a different animal and tries to get the IT department to help out with some automation.

4. *Extranet.* Now fully focused on the customer, the IT department gets into the swing of things. Order processing, order status, business rules. You read the last chapter. You know.

5. *Customer relationship management (CRM).* The brass ring on the merry-go-round. The Holy Grail. The pot of gold at the end of the rainbow. The Omega to the Web's Alpha. The hope of every marketing and customer

service person who's ever tried to make Microsoft Excel work as a data-base.

CRM was born when people started dreaming of a system that would apply some computer intelligence to customer acquisition, customer satisfaction, and customer retention. What if, asked the dreamers, we could merge together all this information we have about each of our customers? What if we could give all that information to our customer service representatives on one screen? What if we could feed that information into a software application that could analyze it and figure out how to treat each individual customer better?

Bringing the Customer All the Way into the Picture

When the MIS department at any company of any size sits down to write a five-year plan, they know in reality it's only going to last for about six months. The changes that take place in technology, business, management methods, and budgets make a five-year plan an exercise in conjecture.

Presented with the infrastructure as it stands and the technology that is right around the corner, what can we do—what *must* we do—to stay competitive? Building an electronic dialog that brings the customer all the way into the organization requires much deeper thought than putting up a home page and offering up product data sheets.

The tide of customer expectations is rising faster than ever. Once the masses get it into their heads that something technical is possible, they assume it's a done deal.

What? You mean you don't have a virtual reality Web presence where I can hand-select the components for my next home entertainment system, get a readout of the sound quality based on the configuration I'm considering, and follow the picking, packing, and shipping process so I'll be home to receive it when it's delivered? Well, why not!?

Why can't I participate in an online discussion your managers are having about whether to extend my firm more credit? Why can't I track that software bug through your development and testing process while I discuss how I'm going to implement it with 20 of your other customers? I can do that at half a dozen other vendor sites! What's the matter with you?

Did you even bother to give all your employees e-mail? No? Well, that's it for me! I'm taking my business where I'm treated as part of the business and not just a number!

Stanley Marcus of Neiman Marcus said it best, "Consumers are statistics. Customers are people." The consumer is dead. Long live the customer! It's time to stop thinking about how nice the world would be if we could just get rid of those pesky customers. It's time to take out those customer-colored glasses and start seeing the world a little differently.

Tomorrow, the effort now being spent on improving the grocery store aisles will go into answering questions and solving problems. Then we'll see customer profiles that cover more than the usual acquisition-only data:

- Gender
- Zip code
- Number of site visits
- Length of stay per visit
- Purchase volume per visit
- Types of products bought
- Preference profile

Customer profiles will include information on how much the customer knows and how they like to communicate:

- Questions per month
- Problems per month
- Company training courses attended
- Industry lexicon knowledge
- Alerts delivered (via phone, fax, e-mail, what's new Web page, pager, mail)
- Reminders delivered (via phone, fax, e-mail, what's new Web page, pager, mail)
- Personality quotient (chatty, friendly, terse, gruff, demanding)

These are the sort of data that enable customer service representatives (be they human or android) to be better attuned to each customer's needs and, therefore, more helpful. In addition, they spell serious profits—both from the sales end of things, as one would assume, and also from the cost savings side of the street.

Heed the advice of Bruce Kasanoff from Accelerating1to1 and segment your customers into finer and finer groups. Start by dividing your customer base into different market segments—say, small, medium, and large. Then divide those up into vertical markets (manufacturing, distribution, health, etc.). Then break up the people who work at those companies by function (executive, management, accounting, front line). Subdivide those into groups according to their breadth of responsibility (corporate, division, department, individual). Now you're ready for the one-to-one challenge.

Once your Web site starts tracking individual people, you are approaching customer relationship management. In the end it's all about access. Access to information and people. It's no longer enough to be the low price leader. If you can make your company easier to do business with, people will do business with you.

To provide the highest level of customer access to internal information, the world is turning to customer relationship management.

The CRM Promise

The term has become such a strong buzzword in such a short time that it's almost unavoidable. So what's the payoff?

Faster Service

If customers wander into the customer service area on your Web site and they have to click here, there, and everywhere to get their questions answered, it's inefficient. But if they show up and the site knows them and can make an educated guess as to why they're there, they get their answers faster.

It's all about anticipation. Collaborative filtering comes in handy here to sift through your database to make those educated guesses. The majority of other customers who ordered that product from us two days ago wanted to know about when it was going to be delivered. So display the UPS tracking information without being asked. Other customers who ordered this product from us between one and four weeks ago wanted to know about installation procedures. So display a big Installation button right where they're going to see it.

Lower Costs

While reducing costs has been the general driver for putting customer service online to begin with, CRM takes it to a new extreme. Every preempted phone call means another service rep available to take another call instead. Phone calls, faxes, datasheets in the mail—they all add up.

When you have your customers eating out of your hand because your service is so good, they're also doing their own data entry. They'll place their own orders, and they'll be very careful about how they spell their name and what they see before they hit that final Submit button. They will also be a whole lot more inclined to check that they ordered 800 boxes instead of 8,000.

Internally, productivity is greatly improved when service reps, managers, and field support personnel are all singing off the same sheet. The CRM system knows the answers to most of the answers, keeping the interoffice pestering to a minimum.

Bigger Profits

While sales is not a traditional aspect of customer service today, expect it to be so tomorrow. Current customers are more likely to buy than prospective customers. Current customers are easier to reach than prospective customers. Upselling and cross-selling to customers is much more successful in the hands of the customer service department because customers know you're there to help them and not to earn commissions.

But you should certainly expect that the systems you put in place to track and manage relationships will create information of great interest to your sales force. You may not be asked to sell to customers, but the sales department will want to tap into statistics about questions their customers have and plans their customers are making. The result? More sales.

Team Coordination

Victoria Monica, Siebel customer and manager of her company's customer response center, needed to coordinate the people in the support center with the people in the field. Cymer, Inc., headquartered in San Diego, California, is a major supplier of illumination sources for ultraviolet photolithography systems, so it has a lot of engineering to coordinate.

"We wanted to improve customer response times by giving our global support staff direct access to the data, information, and knowledge resident in San Diego," says Monica. That's a critical problem because of the amount of information they need to disseminate and the type of customers they have.

"Security at semiconductor fabrication facilities is extremely tight. Field service engineers can't walk in with a laptop, dial up San Diego, and get online access to our latest laser information. With Siebel, our people can sync with headquarters to get up-to-the-minute product and customer information. So when they arrive on site, they can work at the facility in tetherless mode. All the relevant technical information we have in San Diego, they have now on their laptops at the customer site."

That sort of coordination is critical inside an organization. It can also be very powerful when coordinating channel partners. Siebel Systems has initiated the concept of *partner portals* in its CRM software. You determine which customer data is visible to which partners. Originally designed for sales lead dissemination, this capability lets service companies, manufacturers, and other business partners share information that benefits the customer.

Higher Customer Satisfaction

Remember those Cisco customers who were happier when they could find their own answers online and didn't have to call? They were happier that the information was at their beck and call 24 by 7. When the service is personalized, and personalized to more than just to an industry, market segment, or company level, satisfaction goes straight up.

Improved Retention

> Companies can boost profits by almost 100 percent by retaining just 5 percent more of their customers.
> Harvard Business Review

> The average company loses half its customers every five years, a 13 percent annual loss of customers.
> Fredrich Reaichheld in *The Loyalty Effect* (Harvard Business School Press, 1996)

International Data Corporation (www.idc.com) says it costs online merchants anywhere from ninety cents to $2.67 to get a visitor to their Web site for the first time. When it's that expensive just to get them to show up, you better believe it's worthwhile getting them to stay.

It's that old one-to-one adage that you want to increase your share of customer wallet. If you can identify your most profitable customers and get them to stick around longer and buy more, your ROI is going to look very good.

I buy more from Amazon because they know me. I feel better about buying computers from Dell because its site feels like it was made for me. I don't see lots of extraneous information—only what works with my laptop. The fact that I am much more likely to buy from these companies again is expressed as a rising spiral.

Their sites are easy to use. That's good. When I need help, the information is readily available. That's great. I know how to get around their sites and how to find the things that make life easier for me, and at the same time, they are making changes to their sites in response to each of my visits. That's the clincher. Familiarity breeds retention.

Loyalty

In the white paper called "The Key To Customer Loyalty," Applix (www.applix.com) defines a loyal customer:

Put simply, "loyal" customers are those who are so pleased with your organization's products and services that they do not consider purchasing comparable products elsewhere. Customer loyalty is almost never founded solely on price of goods, and in fact is rarely founded on just a single aspect of your organization, such as just the quality of your products. Instead, a customer's loyalty is usually founded on his/her satisfaction with the "package" that your organization represents—products, services, and price. You can identify a loyal customer based on three common criteria:

1. The desire to purchase incremental products and/or services from you, often without exploring the comparable products offered by your competition.
2. The willingness either to be a reference for your organization and products, and/or to provide frequent word-of-mouth recommendations for your organization and products.
3. The proactive offering of product and/or service improvement suggestions to your organization.

Applix defines loyalty as "a feeling that results from an organization's ability to deliver three things to their customers: knowledge, anticipation of future requirements, and superior communication."

You're going to make me feel that I'm getting the information I need; that you're watching out for me and anticipating my needs down the line; and that you're going to stay in touch with me better than your competitors will. It's a *feeling*.

Loyalty goes one step beyond retention. Loyalty is when customers are so happy with your service they tell others. So how do you create it?

Convey a Sense of Knowledge

So let's start with the challenge of convincing your customers that you are more knowledgeable than your competition. Knowledgeable in what way? When a customer contacts your organization, there are four types of knowledge that they expect from you:

1. Corporate knowledge: Information about your organization, its history, and positioning in the market.
2. Industry knowledge: Information about market trends and practices.
3. Product knowledge: Information about the products and/or services that your organization offers; how the products can, should, and have been used.
4. Customer knowledge: Information about the customer's dealings with your organization.

Anticipate the Customer's Needs

The second factor that helps an organization create a sense of loyalty within a customer is the ability to anticipate the customer's needs. This anticipation can be divided into three areas:

1. Anticipation of additional products that would be of value to the customer.

2. Anticipation of technical services that would help prevent the occurrence of a customer's problem or question.

3. Anticipation (and delivery) of product improvements based on the feedback that is received from customers.

Provide Exceptional Communication

The third contributing factor to engendering loyalty within customers is in no small part due to the recent technological improvements to communications. The Internet, World Wide Web, and Java technologies have all opened up organizations to provide their customers with alternate means of communication. From accessing product specifications to diagnosing one's own technical problems, these new technologies are definitely a contributing factor to making your organization more appealing to customers.

But let's not confuse quality of communication with quantity of communication. Just because an organization is offering e-mail, Web, and Java communications for its customers doesn't necessarily mean that it is providing superior communications. The real test of the quality of an organization's communications with its customers is how appropriate each communication is to the customer's current situation.

Keeping everything in line with the customer's *current situation* is the key. That's why all that technology is necessary. What does each individual customer need at any given point in time?

CRM Roadblocks

All is not blooming rose buds in the garden of customer relationship management. Each blossom comes complete with its own set of thorns. These thorns are not small and they cannot be ignored.

The information you want to pour into the blender to create a rich, smooth, silky relationship is scattered all over your company in places you've never heard of before. There is an avalanche of products out there that claim to *be* and *do* CRM—and oh, yes, it can be very expensive.

Data Silos

Back in prehistoric times, there were mainframes. When minicomputers first showed their under-a-million-dollar heads, companies immediately created islands of automation. Each lived in its own little world, with inputs and outputs that had nothing to do with all of the other division or department-level machines. Engineering had computers. The warehouse needed its own. The folks in accounting didn't care. They still had their monstrous mainframes.

Each of these systems was busy champing away at large pile of its own data. Each of these systems knew a lot about a small portion of the company's interaction with its customers. But they didn't talk to each other.

When client-server technology came along, many companies spent untold bundles of hard-earned cash to get systems to interact. PCs would act as clients to minis, which could sometimes share information with mainframes. And then came the Web.

It became economically feasible to have machines talk to each other across long distances for pennies. All that was needed was the ability to figure out how each software package stored information and which of that information was valid and which was important. That's where we are today. Getting the systems to talk to each other has become a problem of massive proportions.

What's required is the ability to access the data about your customers from the myriad of systems scattered around the company. These systems have evolved over time using different languages, different tools, and different programming methodologies and paradigms. All of which are at different degrees of maturity and provide different degrees of value to the end user. Some of which should have been retired years ago.

And we haven't started looking at the data yet—data that is stored in a dozen formats in as many places. It's pretty easy to identify at least five different databases in your company that house information about your customers. You have several databases which do not talk to each other. Databases which were set up to accommodate each individual department, not each customer.

When a customer calls to inquire about your products, he or she talks to a receptionist, a data entry clerk, or a marketing communications operator. If it's done right, the first round of information gets entered into the marketing database. Here it is hopefully matched up with lead-source information so you'll know the value of your advertising and marketing expenditures.

The next point of contact for this customer is the sales department. Sales notes, names and phone numbers, literature sent, and sales cycle notes go into a contact management system. This helps the sales representative stay on top of numerous accounts and produce forecasts.

When the customer wants to place an order, it's time to set up an account for them in the credit department. Bank and trade references get fed in to establish a credit amount for each customer.

Next, sales order processing needs to know whom to ship the product to, who is going to be the end user, whose name goes on the invoice, and exactly what it is they are ordering.

Manufacturing needs to know the specifications of this special order. Customer service keeps a database to keep track of problems and resolutions. The accounting department wants to take ownership of the invoice after shipping to stay on top of receivables.

In some companies, all of the above is replicated over multiple product lines, departments, and divisions. Kevin Nix, product marketing director at Siebel Systems, says the number of databases sprinkled throughout an average organization is closer to 10.

Simply coordinating that information across the different databases is the subject for a whole bookshelf. Just mention to your data processing managers that you want a system that lets one person at one terminal review all the customer information on one screen, and the term ashen-gray will come to mind as you watch their eyes go up and to the left. It's either that or maniacal laughter.

The conversation will go something like this:

"That's right, Jack. We really do want to be able to see all customer information on one screen."

"Umm." (How to tell this poor soul that her vision is technically preposterous?) "Let me see if I can understand why you need this, Jill, and then I can figure out if it can be done."

"Our customers are our most important asset, Jack. When they call in, we want every point of contact to be able to help them." (It's not so much a matter of *if*, it's *when*. And if *he* won't do it . . .)

"That's why we spent so much time and money on that customer service system." (Don't tell me they want to rewrite that one already!)

"But, Jack, the customers aren't calling just one number. They talk to sales, they talk to shipping, they call accounting." (Jack doesn't have a clue about how the real world works—he only knows what can be flow-charted.) "They call operations, they talk to our designers . . ."

"Well, gosh, Jill, it sounds like the marketing communications people need to beef up their efforts getting the word out to our customers that there's a one-stop-shop for them to call." (We thought about this one long and hard and came up with a good solution.)

(Why that arrogant . . .)

"Just kidding, Jill . . . just kidding. Look, the intention was to allow the call center to answer 80 percent of the frequently asked questions by looking into the customer database. Customers have one handy number to call and that system is saving our customer service people quite a bit of runaround."

"Eighty percent of the calls that come to customer service, yes. You and your team put together a great system, Jack, and it's been very beneficial. If we can just figure out a way to tie in the accounting system to what you've done already, as well as the shipping department, the manufacturing, and the other places customer information is stored, then all we have to do is roll out access to that system to all the people that talk to customers."

(Maniacal laughter) "I see. Well, Jill, give me some time to mull this over. I'm going to want to talk to my engineers and, of course, run this by Fred." (As in Fred, the CEO. He'll have a fit when I outline the kind of effort this is going to take. That'll put a stop to this daydream.)

(Jack's doing the old end-run. Time to pull the ace out of my hat.) "Good, please do, Jack. I spoke to Fred this morning and he understands where we're headed with this thing."

"Oh? How did you convince him this expenditure is going to be worth the investment?"

"I showed him how XYZ Corp is doing it and how they're going to eat our lunch if we don't catch up in a hurry."

"Fred's worried about XYZ? They're a startup. They're not even five percent of our size."

"That's what has Fred so worried, Jack." (Gottcha!)

(Ashen gray.)

Tools Galore

With so much at stake and so much effort required, the natural thing to do is turn to the software industry and see what they've cooked up for us. You won't have any trouble finding vendors that sell CRM software. You'll just have trouble figuring out how to compare them.

Peggy Manconi, research director of CRM at AMR Research (www.amr-research.com), puts it this way: "The way the CRM market is defined today, there are four components: (1) marketing automation, (2) technologically assisted selling, (3) customer support, and (4) field service. I don't include internal help desks in enterprise-wide CRM, which by definition, deals with external customers."

Gary Lemke of Real Market Research (www.realmarket.com) doesn't think it's that easy. He defines CRM software as "integrated applications that help organizations find, get, and keep customers." But that's not helpful, says Lemke, because it's just too vague. "Everything an organization does should revolve around finding, getting, and keeping customers. There're a lot of bloated marketing messages."

This field is a moving target, and the players will certainly change by the time this book hits the printing press, much less when it arrives at your desk. Nevertheless, here's a stab at some broad categories of tools and some of the vendors selling software into them. While these classifications are artificial in your time reference, they do indicate where these companies got their start. Siebel Systems, for example, started in sales force automation but has clearly led the field in customer support, field service, and Web service.

CHATTERBOTS:
- Big Science Company (www.bigscience.com)
- Neuromedia (www.neuromedia.com)

CUSTOMER SERVICE CRM:
- Chordiant (www.chordiant.com)
- Edify (www.edify.com)
- Remedy (www.remedy.com)
- Silknet (www.silknet.com)

E-MAIL CRM:
- E-Gain (www.egain.com)
- Kana Communications (www.kana.com)
- Mustang Software (www.mustang.com)

FIELD SERVICE:
- Astea (www.astea.com)
- Metrix (www.metrix.com)
- Foresight (www.foresight.com)

KNOWLEDGE MANAGEMENT:
- Inference (www.inference.com)
- ServiceWare (www.serviceware.com)
- Primus (www.primus.com)

PRODUCT CONFIGURATORS/CATALOGS:
- Cincom (www.cincom.com)
- Saqqara (www.saqqara.com)
- Trilogy (www.trilogy.com)

SALES FORCE AUTOMATION:
- Baan (www.baan.com)
- Multiactive Technologies (www.multiactive.com)
- Siebel Systems (www.siebel.com)
- Symantec Corporation (www.symantec.com)

WEB SITE TRAFFIC ANALYSIS:

- Accrue (www.accrue.com)
- net.Genesis (www.netgen.com)
- WebTrends (www.webtrends.com)

For some insight into what these tools can do, take a look at www.accelerating1to1.com.

ROI

Is it worth it?

Seems like a simple enough question, doesn't it? A reasonable inquiry from the people upstairs who are trying to decide on how many dollars to spend on all of the toys just listed. A normal, expected exploration of the subject you brought up in your e-mail to Mr. Van Winkle.

In October, 1999, Cap Gemini and IDC surveyed 100 U.S. companies and 200 in Europe about their CRM spending and returns. The average total investment was $3.1 million. Sixty-nine percent spent less than $5 million, and 13 percent went over $10 million. Where did the money go?

The lion's share (34 percent) went to technology (hardware and software). Twenty-three percent was spent on consulting, 20 percent went into training, and they invested 17 percent in integrating it with their legacy systems. The average time to recoup their expenditures was 28 months, but IDC reported skepticism. They felt the answers were far too conservative and underestimated. That—even though 61 percent said they got their money back in less that two years.

Nobody would reveal what their financial return on investment was—too sensitive. CRM, after all, really is a competitive edge.

Keep in mind that these are returns on CRM projects that were implemented by the sales and marketing people. Customer service departments have not yet reported how their CRM projects are going (assuming that's what they call them). Federal Express will proudly tell you that doing offline what they do online would merely require hiring 20,000 more customer service employees. How many reps do you have? How much do you pay them? Do the math. Your mileage may vary.

Customers as Members of the Team

But what about long-term monetary returns? Obviously we're hoping for an extended, improved, augmented lifetime value, but there's more. There's the ideal of making your customers an integral part of your company's planning process. Bring that customer all the way into the organization and give them a chair in the product development meetings, the process planning meetings, and the long-range strategy meetings.

You start with surveys; you graduate to advisory councils; and then you hit the top of the mark through actual customer integration.

Survey your customers to your heart's content and they will tell you pretty much what you want to hear. That doesn't mean I'm against it; it simply means you can't count on surveys to give you real answers.

Advisory councils are often created with the best of intentions, and some are valuable. Some, however, devolve into a game of Placate the Customer. Advisory councils become a place to stick the loudest and more obnoxious customers to give them a feeling that you are hearing their plight and feeling their pain. In fact, you are merely keeping them out of the service reps' hair.

But if you take your customers' input seriously, you make them a part of your daily process. You imitate the people at Works.com, who engage a customer in an hour-long conference call each week.

DHL counts on customer input as a normal way of doing business. That company found out that its nifty Web-based package tracking system wasn't working for mail room clerks in far-flung corners of the world who have trouble maintaining an Internet connection or simply don't want to pay for being online that much. For them, DHL created the E-Track system.

> Just send an e-mail message to track@dhl.com and enter up to 10 airwaybill numbers in the body of the message, separated by a return (press Enter). Within a few minutes, you will receive a return e-mail message with the exact same results shown on our Web site. You may also automatically send the results to anyone else you choose by copying them on the e-mail request as well.

WingspanBank.com decided to create an "i-board of directors" made up of six handpicked customers. A jewelry designer, a television producer, a New York housewife, a convenience-store owner, a software engineer, and an investment manager comprise this august team.

WingspanBank.com published a newspaper ad inviting customers to apply for the posts, resulting in 500 applicants. After a careful selection of people who were demographically and geographically dispersed, the bank chose those who expressed an interest in managing their personal financial lives on the Web. The i-board meets online every month, and its members send e-mail comments in whenever the thought strikes them. They are part of the team.

Whither CRM?

On a more somber note, Forrester Research (www.forrester.com) released a report in June 1999 entitled "The Demise of CRM." Why the gloom and doom? While everybody Forrester interviewed said having a single view of the customer was critical, only 2 percent said they had it. That sounds more like a premature birth announcement than a death knell.

Then Forrester took its tongue out of cheek to announce a whole new buzz-acronym: eRM. The dramatic title of its report was a setup to focus on what they're calling erelationship management. "Dynamic trade will push the traditional model of customer relationship management beyond its limits."

And just what is this magical eRM? Forrester defines it this way: "A Web-centric approach to synchronizing customer relationships across communication channels, business functions, and audiences."

Forrester's general theme in this report was that current tools were not enough, and even more dynamic and more integrated efforts were necessary. In the great game of semantics, they're right. The declaration that CRM is here and well-defined and working is wrong. So, rather than say CRM has a way to go to fulfill its promise, Forrester plants another flag, sets a new goal, and points to eRM as the next peak to scale. But it raises one very interesting issue: the extended enterprise.

The extended enterprise means the whole chain—not the supply chain, or even the value chain, but the information chain. The information chain that allows companies to exchange information about their customers in order to care for those customers better.

No, we're not there just yet, but we will be. And that's why it's worth a few more pages to see where all of this is headed, and a few pointers on how to get there. If, however, you're interested in a lot more on CRM, check out www.crmcommunity.com.

CHAPTER 10

Getting Started

L ots to do. No time to do it. No money to do it. No staff to do it. No surprise. So where do you start? Easy—you start with a solid set of goals in mind.

Setting Goals

If you can decide what you want the outcome to be, you can work backwards through the required steps to the starting point. But the goals are critical.

This next part may sound familiar. You may believe me to be a broken record about this stuff. But I'm willing to take that chance.

You start setting your goals by asking your customers about their goals.

There, that wasn't so hard, was it?

Convincing the Brass

As for the money, staff, and other resources, you'll have to go to those folks upstairs and beg for money.

One of the best ways to convince the brass that this is a good idea is to show them that you're willing to be measured by some strict metrics.

In its December 6, 1999, issue, *Network World* ran a report card on networking hardware manufacturers and service providers. Who won doesn't matter. The interesting part was how they were measured. Number of boxes shipped? No. Revenue brought in? Nope. Number of new customers? Not even close. *Network World* was interested in customer satisfaction. Here are the categories *Network World* asked customers to use to rate their vendors:

- Telephone technical support
- Web-based technical support
- On-site support
- Follow-ups to check on satisfaction
- Time to respond to problems
- Time to resolve problems
- Escalation procedures
- Representative's familiarity with customer company
- Representative's competency/knowledge
- Representative's attitude
- Availability of required parts
- Product line integration
- Ease of submitting trouble tickets
- Price

All of these categories could get higher satisfaction scores from customers if Web technology were put to better use inside the company, and especially when communicating with customers. When upper management finally understands that your goal is not to play with cool, new technology, but to actually help customers, they'll understand and appreciate your level of commitment.

For an example of what sort of commitment it takes, let's look at what it means to build a customer service department from scratch in these online times.

Getting Down to Business—A Woman's Work Is Never Done

We take the case of Ms. Christian Booher, who took it upon herself to seek my advice about setting up a brand-new customer service department. The conversation went like this:

```
From: "Christian K. Booher" <cbooher@imworth.com>
To: jsterne@targeting.com
Subject: Need your wisdom,
Date: Mon, 30 Aug 1999 08:46:23
```

Dear Mr. Sterne,

My name is Christian Booher, and I have recently been tapped to develop the customer service division of a Web-based financial utility. So, I have a rather daunting task in front of me, and am determined to get it right the first time rather than correct costly mistakes along the way.

I have seen your presentations at Thunderlizard conferences, and purchased your books. If it wouldn't be too much trouble, could you recommend other Web sites and or books that would help me hit the ground running when I begin with this company in two weeks? I literally have to do everything from pick the phone system, find e-mail utilities that I want to perform the way we do, hire the people... in short, I have a big job ahead of me. From your lectures and writings, I have come to really respect the way that you approach customer service on the Web, and that's why you have received this e-mail.

I appreciate that you are a busy person, and welcome any sage advice that you can dispense.

Sincerely,

Ms. Christian K. Booher

(Hints to those of you who may also seek advice from me: Flattery works wonders, as do phrases like "daunting task," and "sage advice.")

```
Date: Wed, 01 Sep 1999 08:44:12 -0700
To: Christian Booher
From: Jim Sterne
```

At 06:46 AM 8/30/99, Christian Booher wrote:

>So, I have a rather daunting task in front of me, and am
>determined to get it right the
>first time rather than correct costly mistakes along the way.

Step One: Buy a large bottle of aspirin.

>I appreciate that you are a busy person, and welcome any sage advice that
>you can dispense.

Oh - you wanted *sage* advice... yikes.

Well, I just bought, but have not yet opened "Online Customer Care, Strategies for Call Center Excellence" by Michael Cusack. It has a chapter about e-mail and another about the Web. I wouldn't mention it, but you did say you were looking at phone systems as well. I got it because I'm just about to start the rewrite of my "Customer Service on the Internet" book.

How'd you like to be in it?

If you're willing to e-mail me your thoughts on how you go about putting this whole thing together, I'll respond with my opinions.

I never said I worked for free. And, as a sign of respect to you, who have been bludgeoned with my sage advice page after page after page, I'll limit publishing my responses. Besides, Christian's right on the money.

Date: Wed, 1 Sep 1999 14:53:58

It's really ironic that I have been lucky enough to find this opportunity.

The company is called IMworth (www.imworth.com), a place for online banking customers to go and get all their financial information in one place. I don't know all the details, since I haven't started yet and don't have access to customer profiles, projections ... all the scintillating stuff that makes marketers tick but bores the rest of the free world, it's hard for me to accurately portray the kind of customers I'm going to be providing service to. Additionally, since we will be contracting with banks, brokers, etc., I'm not too sure how much I'll be dealing with their existing CS departments or if we will be providing that service as well.

However, my initial approach is going to be as much Web-based help, question answering, etc. as technically possible. Since we will be dealing with predominately private users, travelers, etc., immediacy is my biggest issue. I know most home users only have one line going into their setup (although that number is steadily decreasing, it's still a major factor to consider when we are relying on tens of thousands of customers), and getting off the phone to make a call for information they most likely won't have in front of them at that point is a hassle and totally inconvenient. I would really like to make use of Instant messaging, but without knowing our programming limits, I don't know how capable we will be to make this seamless. I do know that any phone-based work I do implement will be as far away from "touch-tone hell" as I can find. For instance, I deal with Airtouch for my paging, and I cringe at the thought of having to call them, knowing I will easily punch 20+ numbers for the express pleasure of talking to some chick in Sacramento who knows absolutely nothing about the Missouri plan I am on, but she happily gives me another number (this time NOT toll-free). I also currently work for a company, PonyExpress.net, which is an ISP that has the dubious distinction of being referred to in the community as "PunyExcuse.net" (my heart sings with pride!). Management won't allow access to information so our customer service reps can provide it to the customers, and more often than not, issues fall through the cracks waiting for items to flow through the antiquated chain of command. Both of these companies just don't understand where their revenue comes from and how quickly bad pr proliferates when you add customers with easy access to e-mail, billboards, hell -- the wherewithal to publish their own Web sites!

I guess a brief summary of my initial plans is to make sure that we can answer as many questions or issues as possible via the Web, but when we can't, make sure they talk to a carbon-based life form who will have the capability to resolve an issue immediately if not sooner. And those carbon-based life forms will be able to access what information they need, preferably while they have the customer on the phone, so the customer gets the answers they are looking for at that time, not days, sometimes weeks later.

That being said, my whole plan may fall through the cracks once I begin there and get with the Marketing guy and see whom I'm dealing with, but if I am dealing with customers who are already doing a portion of their banking online (which they will be doing if they are using this service) and are computer-savvy enough to make this work, then I am reasonably sure I'm on the right track.

I would be more than happy to give you a better picture once I'm there, and I've had a chance to review the Web site development and customer profiles, etc.

Thanks so much for your input!

Christian Booher

P.S. Being in a Jim Sterne book would be cool, as long as you make sure I get the appropriate gender credit of Ms. and not Mr. (which is very common among junk mailers and salesmen). All of my Internet friends would envy me and I could rub it in the face of my high school counselors who swore I'd be assistant manager of a Gap by now!

If the Gap only knew what they were missing. All I learned from *my* high school guidance counselor was that I would not enjoy farming.

Date: Thu, 9 Sep 1999 10:42:14 EDT

1.) http://www.balisoft.com

This is the application I am STRONGLY leaning towards for us. It has everything I want, and once I locate and talk to current users for their experience with this product/company, I will most likely begin the process of demo-ing this (barring any horror stories from clients) next week.

2.) Technically, I start Monday the 13th, but the team is already deluging me with e-mail asking for opinions, insights, etc.

3.) Since I'm in charge of also creating and managing the CS department, my overall philosophy for training is this: "The Customer's Time is our most valuable resource." The one thing I hate when I'm shopping, e-mailing, anything, is when the chatty clerk at the counter proceeds to tell either 1.) the customer in front of me his/her life story from DNA up to that afternoon while I wait, or 2.) whoever is on the phone at the other end about the harrowing experience of stubbing a toe on their Barcalounger the night before, and how it threw their whole universe into chaos. Both of these waste my time and don't allow me to conduct the brief business I need to with whatever company I deal with.

What I want to hire and train for is the concept of respecting our customers' busy lifestyle and a monumental appreciation for any nuggets (or creamy caramel nougat, if you prefer) of information they can give us in their brief contact with us. This revolves mostly around listening, which I find an incomprehensible lack of in a lot of CS departments I deal with. Listening seems to be the mostly valuable and least utilized aspect of Customer Service I've encountered, and this simple act can alleviate time and energy wasted from the customer's standpoint. So I'm cross-stitching a sampler for my call center that says "Time is the most valuable payment our customers send us." (You think I'm kidding). It's cheesy, but it's true.

I advised Christian to show it off in an official unveiling ceremony.

Date: Wed, 15 Sep 1999 16:25:43

>> 1.) http://www.balisoft.com...
>
>Haven't heard of it. How did you find it and what
>makes it such an obvious standout?

I found out about it simply through research. Originally, my coworkers had heard of a product called "liveperson.com." Although Liveperson had the Web-based customer service features I wanted, their product line left much to be desired. When you are dealing with any type of customer service, there are several guidelines that you should have, but overall, you have to be available for any type of response that suits the customer: not just your idea of what you want to do. Servicesoft had everything from the chat-based customer service, to e-mail utilities, knowledge-base builders, etc. Basically, they had everything I wanted right now, and many things that I knew I would need in the future, since this is an ever-changing aspect of business. Also, since I am starting a relationship with them at this stage, with a varied product line such as theirs, they will have a good idea of my past needs, and have the necessary background to recommend effective future solutions. That would be the bulk of my advice: Make sure you deal with someone you can grow with. It will help you out in the long run when you don't have to change relationships in midstream and make sure different companies' products are compatible.

We still aren't live yet -- holdups in the Web development arena. Also, we don't have a true customer profile, since we have no way to distinguish between dummy accounts currently set up to beta test, and people who have stumbled upon our site and registered. I'm in the process of adding questions to our sign-up area, so we can get more comprehensive information for future use and development.

I was also getting somewhat ambitious, but have since decided to carefully use autoresponders to some degree in answering our mail questions. As much as I hate the thought of a reply that sounds automated (and I can't tell you how furious I get when I get mail generated to Mr. Christian Booher: I realize it's an honest mistake, but if I've purchased from them or registered information, gender-misidentification is sloppy), and I'm afraid autoresponders are opening us up to that. But, if I partition the message out carefully, and use the first name in the greeting (although that's informal, the Web is also a highly selfish and personal medium, so maybe that transgression will be overlooked?), that could avoid many of the missteps I'm afraid of making.

As for staffing: It would help a great deal if I knew the initial client-base size. But, since we don't have any official clients yet, it's pretty hard to know what kind of ratio I should plan for. Ideally, I would like to have any possible information they might ask for on the Web, and add new information as questions are asked. But I know we will still get phone calls, and making sure there are enough reps to handle that incoming volume is my top priority. Nothing is more irritating to anyone than having to wait on hold for information about yourself...let alone information or questions about information you want about your own finances!

So, that's where I stand at this point: WHHEEE...I know a little more than before, but now I'm actually in the thick of it and can't dodge questions so easily like I could when it was e-mail only accessibility!

Date: Wed, 22 Sep 1999 08:57:51

Web Development is still churning along, but our target date is Oct. 1. The true demo site is at http://---.net. This will actually allow you to enter in your information and it will be displayed as it will be once it is live, etc. I know that we will find many more service issues once we go live, but I guess that's why most websites should be viewed as a work in progress, because things change and you will get mowed down unless you roll with it (or preferably keep ahead of it).

I have a conference call with my Service Soft rep next Tuesday, and I will start with the e-mail section, and see if we can get a demo of the web/chat assistance. E-mail will definitely be my first priority with CS Utilities, because we will most likely get those inquiries before anything else.

Now, I'm wrestling with the issue of where and how we draw the line on what to service. Say Client of XYZ Bank calls in and has a question about how a total is being displayed. We can answer the technicalities of this, but if it comes to a discrepancy between John Doe's written statement and what's on-screen, and we've determined that there is no problem with our server or the way he has entered it, then he is going to have to contact his bank. I would prefer that the Rep he is dealing with directly connect him to his bank, rather than run off a phone number and politely thank this person (who will probably be very concerned, and more than a little frantic, that his numbers don't match. Not a good way to leave a customer) for calling IMWorth.

Are there systems available that will allow you to directly transfer to another company, or should we arrange a conference calling situation so that we can assist the rep on the other end (who may know nothing about our system and not even care)? This is my biggest issue right now to solve and get a protocol in place, because if we are going live next week (depending on if the Web guys get their stuff together), this is an issue that will definitely rear its head, and I can't afford lagging on this. Since the customer will be dealing with their bank and their personal information, would the inclusion of a third party just confuse them?

Christian K. Booher wrote:

>And I know that we will find many more once we go live, but I
>guess that's why most Web sites should be viewed as a work in progress

Jim replied:

Always a work is progress. You'll create a list of things you want to do, a list of things your customers want you to do, a list of things your executives want you to do ("management by in-flight magazine"), and the *real* list which is made up of stuff that's broken. Is the aspirin ready?

>Since the customer will be dealing with their bank and
>their personal information, would the inclusion of a third party just
>confuse them?

Interesting choices:

1) Sorry, it's not our fault.
2) Sorry, it's not our fault but we'll look into it and get back to you.
3) Gee, that's not very good, is it? Let's try to get your bank on the phone right now.

If I'm a customer, and I have the time, #3 makes you look like the Customer Service Goddess. The problem is, how many customers are going to have problems and how many banks are you going to have to educate before it's a money drain?

>Also, I'm sure I'm overlooking something painfully obvious,
>so if there is something you could give me a heads-up on,
>I would be eternally grateful!

I think your signature is too long. It's got the right information, but it goes on and on and on...

Here are two versions; yours and a new one. Whaddaya think?

>Christian K. Booher
>Director of Customer Service
>IMWorth, Inc.
>313 Lawrence Avenue
>Kansas City, MO 64111
>
>Ph: (816) 561-9000
>Fax: (816) 561-5304
>Email: Cbooher@imworth.com
>www.imworth.com
>

>This email may contain confidential and privileged material for the
>sole use of the intended recipient. Any review by or distribution to
>others is strictly prohibited. If you are not the intended recipient,
>please contact the sender and delete all copies.

Christian K. Booher, Director of Customer Service
IMWorth, Inc., 313 Lawrence Avenue, Kansas City, MO 64111

Ph: (816) 561-9000 Fax: (816) 561-5304 http://www.imworth.com

This email may contain confidential and privileged material for the sole
use of the intended recipient. Any review by or distribution to others
is strictly prohibited. If you are not the intended recipient, please
contact the sender and delete all copies.

I added the http:// because some e-mail readers still don't assume that
when they see "www." I'd also love to see you drop that warning
paragraph. It's somehow disquieting....

Date: Thu, 23 Sep 1999 08:21:01

I just got a message from my boss that I have to have my preliminary
budget worked out today. I have been told I have $1,000,000 budgeted
for service utilities, staff, etc. I am basing initial projections on
a customer base of 100,000, and a rep/user ratio of 7500/1. I know it's
a little high, but I averaged the ratio from bank CS (5000/1) and
Brokerage/Investment (10,000/1), since we should be having a good mix
of the two.

And I agree about the signatures. I like your version better, but can't
drop the tag. It's something our investors are dead set on.

Date: Thu, 23 Sep 1999 15:30:58

The bank & broker ratio is derived from conversation I have had with
other MF companies/Banks in the KC area (American Century Investors,
Kemper Financial, DST Systems), and their various departments are using
those with Phone reps only.

The Service Soft package that I am looking at has a very good self-
service e-mail auto response, which pulls information out of a database
and responds with a VERY well-written e-mail detailing the issue and
presenting the problem resolution. But they do have a great knowledge-
base program that integrates well with Web site applications. The cost
is reportedly about .25 per user. Samples came out almost the exact
opposite of what I was expecting. Of course, I understand that Service
Soft was simply trying to put their best foot forward.

Date: Thu, 07 Oct 1999 10:17:14

Things are churning along here. The site is now live, but in Beta Test
mode. I'm putting it through the paces and trying to determine what
doesn't fit with a customer-friendly site.

Also, I stumbled upon another application from a company called Webline,
who provides a program for Java-based customer service, which is perfect
for what I need.

As I was entering information last week, one of the red flags that went up was that, as a user is setting up their account, there are a lot of screens that pop up, and, although the information should be obvious to someone using IMWorth's utility, it's too important a subject to take for granted. Webline allows for the user to click the help button, a CS Rep is notified about the user's name AND the page that they are on and the page is subsequently produced on the Rep's screen, so they see exactly what the user is seeing, and using Chat and this dual-visual capability, the CS Rep can guide the customer through the information-entering process, even taking over the entering session themselves if the customer gets too bogged down.

This takes chat one step further, and I was bowled over by the utility it could provide us. Lands' End and Cisco currently use it (I think Dell does as well), and I tried it through Lands' End and was absolutely, hands-down sold on the product. Another thing I like is that you buy the program outright, and pay licensing fees for the CS reps, and you're done with the company. No monthly fees, no reporting or trying to be sold reports on what your customers are doing. It almost sounds too good to be true! I'm still looking at Service Soft for the E-mail and Knowledge-base utilities, but Webline has got it goin' on!

Also, here's the first draft of my autoresponse e-mail, which will be sent to a user once they set up an account with our system. I KNOW IT'S WORDY-- I am a pathologically un-brief writer in my early stages (No, really-- I can hear you say...), but I am not sure if I am leaving out critical information. Let me know what you think or if you have suggestions on how to make it better.

That is all for now. Oh, BTW...had a FABULOUS experience with Victoria's Secret online ordering. I had a question about an order I placed, and reconsidered a decision about a back-order that they clearly told me was not available before I finalized my order, but changed my mind from placing it to confirmation. I e-mailed to ask if I could change the color to an item that was available, and whether I would have to re-enter the information or modify an existing order.

Rather than play e-mail tag with them, the only response I received from them was from Elise, who told me that they couldn't change the item that was in question since the order had already been placed, but that they would not charge me for the replacement in the color I wanted. Excuse me...it was MY fault and they were taking the responsibility?!?

Needless to say, for the low, low, price of a $15-dollar item, Victoria's Secret has gained a lifelong customer, and one who is intent on giving them the best, cheapest advertising possible: Word of Mouth! I can't say enough good things about them, and I've already detailed my overwhelming pleasure with this transaction and the CS Rep involved in a letter to the CS manager.

It's my goal to make the IMWorth experience as good for our customers as mine with Victoria's Secret was. (Although I doubt our Web site is as

... actively surfed ... as theirs is!) Oh ... and all of this took place in the span of about 3 hours! They are obviously bucking for a slot in the Jim Sterne Hall of Fame!

The sample Welcome e-mail:

Date: Thu, 07 Oct 1999 10:22:32

Welcome to IMWorth, your trusted personal financial manager. We are pleased that you have selected us to assist you with your financial planning, and are committed to providing you with the best service possible.

If you have questions about your account, please contact our Customer Care Representatives at 816-561-900, x 12, or e-mail us at *xxxxx@imworth.com*. We are eager to assist you so that you can get the most out of IMWorth. Please note, IMWorth cannot provide information about specific financial accounts you list in your IMWorth portfolio, and you will need to contact the financial service provider for your account (i.e. checking, savings, brokerage) to resolve issues or questions with amounts, transactions, etc.

If you would like to sign up for monthly newsletters, service enhancement updates, or special announcements, click here. IMWorth strives to bring practical information direct to you without compromising your privacy, and without spamming. We do not sell our lists. Occasionally, we may mail on behalf of vendors who want to contact you with relevant news and product information you have indicated you would like, which you indicated when you activated your IMWorth account. Please note that IMWorth-generated messages will contain this header:

```
------------------------------------------------------------
This is not a spam. This is an IMWorth voluntary targeted list!
TO UNSUB: forward this entire message to deleteme@imworth.com
MAIL TO LISTS: http://www.Imworth.com/ XXX.cgi 100%OPT-IN(tm)
------------------------------------------------------------
```

To review your subscription and preferences, please visit *http://www.imworth.com/review*

If you are interested in MAILING your product or service information to any of thousands of topical lists, please contact pstry@imworth.com.

If you forget your user name and password, please send an e-mail to *xxx@inworth.com*. In order to protect your information, passwords are encrypted and cannot be accessed by your Customer Care Representative. Our system will generate a new, temporary password so that you can access your customer information and input your own password.

For any other questions or comments, please contact our Customer Care at 816-561-9000, xt.12 (between the hours of 8 a.m. 5 p.m., CST) or e-mail us at *xxx@imworth.com*. You can also fax your comments, questions or concerns to 816-561-5304.

Thank you again for choosing IMWorth.

Sincerely,

IMWorth Customer Care

Jim's review:

At 08:22 AM 10/7/99 , Christian K. Booher wrote:

>Welcome to IMWorth, your trusted personal financial manager.
>We are pleased that you have selected us to assist you with
>your financial planning, and are committed to providing you
>with the best service possible.

I'd feel better about your actually *giving* me great customer service, rather than telling me you hope to.

>If you have questions about your account, please contact our
>Customer Care Representatives at 816-561-9000, x 12, or e-mail
>us at xxxxx@imworth.com. We are eager to assist you so that
>you can get the most out of IMWorth.

Good.

>Please note, IMWorth cannot provide information about specific
>financial accounts you list in your IMWorth portfolio, and you
>will need to contact the financial service provider for your
>account (i.e. checking, savings, brokerage) to resolve issues
>or questions with amounts, transactions, etc.

Disclaimers are always too annoying. This language should be on the "Agreement" page rather than in a message trying to greet people.

This way, it says, "Hi! Welcome to our shop! If you have a problem, please go bother the manufacturer - we can't help you."

>If you would like to sign up for monthly newsletters, service
>enhancement updates, or special announcements, click here.

Be a little more forceful - sell me on it! "If you sign up for the newsletters, you'll get all this neat stuff:..."

>IMWorth strives to bring practical information direct to you
>without compromising your privacy, and without spamming.

You'd better not strive - you'd better deliver -- you'd better *promise*!

>We do not sell our lists. Occasionally, we may mail on behalf of
>vendors who want to contact you with relevant news and product
>information you have indicated you would like, which you indicated
>when you activated your IMWorth account.

You've scared me off completely with this. Instead, let me clickthrough to the sign-up page where there are multiple options: The IMWorth Weekly Bulletin, The IMWorth New Features Announcement List, The Coop Marketing Partners Specials List. And tell me why each one is great and I should sign up for it.

>Please note that IMWorth-generated messages will contain this header:

>--
>This is not a spam. This is an IMWorth voluntary targeted list!
>TO UNSUB: forward this entire message to deleteme@imworth.com
>MAIL TO LISTS: http://www.Imworth.com/ XXX.cgi 100%OPT-IN(tm)
>--

MUCH more than I need to know. Put that on the sign-up page - fine. But here, it has stopped me from reading the rest of the message.

>To review your subscription and preferences, please visit
>http://www.imworth.com/review.

To sign up, please visit...

>If you are interested in MAILING your product or service information
>to any of thousands of topical lists, please contact pstry@imworth.com.

Oops. Don't mix customers and advertisers. People who want to participate will seek you out. You can seek them out. But soliciting customers for advertisers who will advertize to those customers is not good form.

>If you forget your user name and password, please send an e-mail
>to xxx@inworth.com. In order to protect your information, passwords
>are encrypted and cannot be accessed by your Customer Care
>Representative. Our system will generate a new, temporary password
>so that you can access your customer information and input your own
>password.

Very good.

>For any other questions or comments, please contact our Customer
>Care at 816-561-9000, xt.12 (between the hours of 8 a.m. 5 p.m.,
>CST) or e-mail us at xxx@imworth.com. You can also fax your comments,
>questions or concerns to 816-561-5304.

Repetitious.

>Thank you again for choosing IMWorth.
>
>Sincerely,
>
>IMWorth Customer Care

Yep - that's verbose all right. If you are overcome by the urge to include more, just write a short description and drop in a link. If I want to know more, I'll click.

E-mail is a black hole of time and if you make your messages too long, with no content of value to the customer, they'll never read another. The most important things for new customers are: Whom do I call? How do I get more information about X, Y, and Z?

If you do that, then you can advise them to save this welcoming message for future reference. Then set up your site to ensure that there's no information in the e-mail that is not also easily found online.

(Hey - you asked me to take a look... ;-)

All-in-all: a good start!

Date: Fri, 08 Oct 1999 10:23:51

Thanks so much for the comments on the e-mail. I'm perfectly aware that I am wordy (my husband is a newspaper editor: imagine the fun at holidays when we start sending cards!), so I always appreciate it when I can get outside eyes to glance at something and smack my hand when I flagrantly misuse the English language. I've cut out a lot and have a revised copy.

The Webline product: Yes, I went through a demo with a company rep, and used it at Lands' End as "Jane Everyday Customer" to see what it was like from a customer's perspective. The demo was VERY thorough, and had some sweet features. The Customer asks for help by clicking on a help icon and typing in their name, and a pleasant "One Moment Please" comes up (I'm partial to that).

While the customer is looking at that, the Rep is getting a notification about the customer's name, account and the screen they are on. The customer has all that information, and the customer doesn't have to repeat everything, or tell the rep where they are. The Rep's screen looks like it is in four sections: Chat, Library (to do a quick search to see if this issue has been encountered before), User Screen and history. So the Rep has what they need, the customer doesn't have to recite account numbers or information (very nice if they aren't somewhere private), and we can immediately catalogue anything new. I do believe there is a choice where the customer can choose the option to call or chat, but I didn't use that, so I'll be honest, I'm not as familiar with that. It's $10,000 for the programming, and $2,000 for each rep's licensing, so for $30,000 or so, it's going to kill many birds with very few stones. It's not the only option I'm looking at, but it will be very high on my list of things to get.

I had asked Christian about vendors selling their software as a service on the Web—an application service provider (ASP)—rather than selling the package outright.

My reservations on ASP: I have gotten a right good screwing in the past with many be-all, end-all providers in the past, and don't mind admitting that I have a bias when it comes to that. Case in point, [an Internet access provider] provided our T-3 connectivity at my previous

job with PonyExpress.net. We signed an ironclad two-year contract
for tech reps, connectivity, hardware, etc., and early into it, the
company experienced internal difficulties. We were so far behind on our
equipment upgrades, and getting our representative on the phone was akin
to asking for Linda Tripp to keep a secret: Good freakin' luck! To top
it off, they were shaving our bandwidth and we found out nine months
into the contract that two other companies were getting the same T-1
we were, so what we thought was full bandwidth was 1/3 of what we were
getting. We were slow as molasses in January, upgrades and patches we
didn't get made us the darlings of the hacking world, and we couldn't
do squat about it because Global was experiencing so much turnover that
I literally never spoke to the same person twice in a six-month period.
And customers hated us for it! We were stuck, with no decent service and
no hope for answers, with only the knowledge that our customers didn't
give a damn about what our problems were: They didn't know the Global
group from Adam, and they were writing checks to us, not them...we'd
better have the answers they wanted. You've never seen a group of people
so mean as "Net Hounds" getting a busy signal 15 minutes before a
cyberdate!

This isn't my only experience, but it has led me to the conclusion
that, although I do believe it is best in the long run to deal with one
person/group, put all your eggs in one basket and you will soon wind up
with egg all over your face! So the Service Soft applications are still
high on my wish-list as well, and will serve my primary CS utility base
for e-mail, database, etc., but it would be nice that, should something
go catastrophically wrong with the Service Soft end, Webline can help to
pick up the slack.

Jim offers 2 cents:

Good point. Having a backup in hand is *very* wise. Checking with
references is good advice, but any company can get bought, sold, merged,
[or land] a giant contract with some other customer, who gets their
attention.

On the other hand, I don't think you can say installing software and
running it yourself is foolproof either. Lots can (and will) go wrong.
Your back-up approach sounds prudent. I'll just keep my fingers crossed
you can do that within your budget.

Christian continues:

Now, one of the things I'm in the preliminary stages of is how to foster
a community with our site. I'm firmly convinced that, in this day of
rapid-fire, humanless communication, this is crucial to maintaining the
connection that people need (whether they recognize it or not). This is
going to be tricky, because the majority of our business will be through
private labeling service, and my thinking is that this could cause
confusion with the consumer, and might serve to tick off the bank/broker
who is doing the private labeling.

But I want some form of branding and community, so that, say consumer A switched to a bank/broker who isn't with IMWorth, they will still use the service. What suggestions do you have? I'm reading a book by Byron Reeves and Clifford Nass, "The Media Equation: How People Treat Computers, Television, and New Media Like Real People and Places." Trying to see how we can best humanize the site/service to make people want to identify with it and trust it. Oh yeah, and keep coming back to it.

That is the latest. Oh, but I do have one weird question. What kind of hold music do you think is most palatable? I'm shopping some local providers for this service, and can get everything from local radio (strongly against: What if they are touting the Chiefs and a Denver Broncos fan is on the line? Not too friendly, but I must say!) to Muzak, to, my personal favorite: news. I know this is a minor detail, but it's going to have direct customer contact, and I can't treat it as an afterthought.

Jim replies:

I agree that it's not an afterthought, it's an important branding issue. I agree with your dislike about the radio, but I'm also against the news-- it's too local.

I would choose a combination of music (classical or soft jazz - it's a branding question) and information- on-hold. "Your call is very important to us" is ghastly. Instead, call Charles Schwab and listen to their own (2 minute? 3 minute) repeating stock reports. It actually adds value.

Christian continues:

Here's the revised Welcome letter:

Welcome to IMWorth, your trusted personal financial manager. We appreciate that you have selected us to assist you with your financial planning, and are committed to giving you the best service possible.

If you have questions about your account, please contact our Customer Care Representatives at 816-561-9000, x 12 (we're available weekdays, 8 a.m. 5 p.m. CST) or e-mail us at *xxxxx@imworth.com*. You can also fax your comments, questions or concerns to 816-561-5304.

Get the most from your IMWorth experience: Sign up for your FREE IMWorth monthly newsletter! You get up-to-the-minute advice, news and tips on making your money work for you! We'll also keep you on top of the latest features of IMWorth, and we WILL NOT sell or rent our mailing lists! *Click here* to choose the IMWorth e-mail features you want.

If you forget your user name and password, please send e-mail to xxx@imworth.com. In order to protect your information, passwords are encrypted and cannot be accessed by your Customer Care Representative. Our system will generate a new, temporary password so that you can access your customer information and input your own password. Your privacy is our top priority!

Thank you again for choosing IMWorth.

Sincerely,

IMWorth Customer Care

P.S. You can save this message, but you can also find all of this information (and more) at *http://www.imworth.com/help.*

Date: Thu, 21 Oct 1999 17:02:55

We just got the list back of folks who want to sign up for a newsletter....and whaddya know...there's 150 of 'em, so far. Not bad for a site that has had no promotion outside of search engine listings.

Problem is...I don't have a newsletter yet and I know that, although the numbers are small, I still need to send them something.

Jim replies:

Not only that, but you need to send them something very special. As the charter members of this rare group, they need to receive something that will make them boast to their friends that they were in on the ground floor. Send them a free membership in the Insiders' Club. Send them a gift certificate good for one _. Send them your personal thanks. But whatever you do, be sure you do it soon and that what you send has immediate value - has them begging for more.

Christian continues:

My thought is, since we are still in beta-testing, to send a message thanking them for signing up, contact info if they want to submit something, general stuff.

Jim replies:

Ouch! "Thanks for signing up! We have no ideas on this end, so let's make this a discussion!" Uhhh... no. You are in control. They are looking to you to lead them. A leader does not start out the day by asking the throngs where they'd like to go (Microsoft ads notwithstanding).

Christian:

Or should I actually have some sparse content relating to security, since that is a big issue with us, and I feel it could go a long way in helping to establish trust between IMWorth and her clients?

Jim:

If you know something about security that's a big issue *to them* then go for it. Otherwise...

So make sure your first foray into customer communication is something they'll like. If you must, entice them to ask a question. So far, you promised something in return for their e-mail address. You have to deliver on that before you can start asking them to contribute, or even to suggest.

Christian:

I just was hoping that I would get a little warning about when I would need to start sending mass mailings. I guess I did -- they are wanting it tomorrow.

Jim:

If you hold an image in your mind of a nest full of starving chicks, screeching for food with their mouths stretched wide, you'll have a clear picture of the effort it takes to keep them happy.

Christian:

Although I would prefer (and not for chicken's sake, either,) to wait until the first of November. We are at the tail end of beta testing, and I think it would be more of a sensible connection to send out the e-mail with the official launch of the service.

Jim:

In the meantime, show those few, those proud, those early adopters, that you love them. Send them a nice, little, personal message that makes them feel they're on the inside with you.

"Here's what wonderful things we're doing during the beta testing process!" "This feature is up and running and if you'll try it and give us your feedback, we'll send you a t-shirt!" Hey - there's only 150 of them. What the heck - send them a polo shirt.

Christian:

I'll try throwing a fit to get it extended, and, in the words of the immortal Corky St. Clair, "Not deliver a stinky product, but a beautifully wrapped, sweet-smelling package."

Jim:

Always a good idea. But you can't delay forever. "Perfect is the enemy of good enough," said Albert Einstein and he wasn't dumb.

Christian:

So, in essence, my questions are 1.) Content: Practical and Short while asking for input (and I think I just answered my own question), and 2) Time newsletter publication with finish of the beta-test and actual live launch of the site?

Jim:

Yes - the Formal, Official, Corporate, Cleansed, Institutional
newsletter should go out with the launch. For now, it's just you and 150
of your friends. Be friendly.

Christian:

The bad part is, now I have to emerge from the shadows and they will
have a name and phone number to put with the complaint! And I am going
to try leaving off that legal disclaimer you mentioned was pretty off-
putting...at least until I'm told otherwise. My husband said he always
feels like he needs to eat the message after he reads it.

That is all for now. I need to go put the finishing touches on my Blair
Witch costume. (This basically amounts to tying up bundles of sticks to
leave for my coworkers on their desks so I can film their horrified
reactions...but since we work with the Internet, I should probably
bundle up AOL disks.)

Date: Fri, 12 Nov 1999 09:01:22

We have begun to figure out some things, and my role is starting to take
shape somewhat. Here's what appears to be happening.

REALLY GOOD NEWS -- beta testers and early users are having NO
difficulties -- or at least none they are bringing to our attention.
Questions thus far have revolved around where to enter information or if
this asset should go under this category, etc. This is very encouraging
in terms of our intentions with site design. I attribute this to one of
several factors,

a.) The FAQ sections are providing the necessary information users can
get to easily and succinctly,

b.) The entry process is logical enough (it can be somewhat cumbersome,
I admit, when you're dealing with all the financial info entry) that it
is easy to follow

c.) My experience with beta testers has been that they tend to be much
more high-end users, and would subsequently not need much assistance and
be more inclined to try to work through problems on their own.

Jim:

A good point, so don't get comfy. When you open the doors, those in need
of Internet for Dummies will be knocking on your windows and ringing
your light switches.

Christian:

However, feedback that we have gotten from them thus far hasn't
specifically laid out problems and has been more along the lines of "How
do I get my bank to sign up for this!" So I'm not basing initial optimism

on this lack of feedback, because I understand the nature of beta testing, but they would also be more inclined to bring out the big problems they encounter. So I am breathing an extremely cautious sigh of relief.

Jim:

Maybe it's time to hand out some wet noodles and ask some beta testers to lash freely. First time, early adopters want you to succeed so much, they turn into cheerleaders. Give away some t-shirts to those who would be so kind as to let you have it.

Christian:

My role, initially, will be first contact with Big Clients, who will handle Cust. Service in their existing customer service departments. I will visit them to train them on the system, but they will handle the day-to-day operations themselves, contacting me when a major problem or issue presents itself.

And for smaller clients that either don't have existing CS departments or just don't have the manpower to handle any extra calls, our in-house reps will take over for them. I am still projecting a ratio of 1/7500. If beta testing is any indication, this should be about right. And the only questions we've gotten thus far have been e-mail only questions which I (pat myself on the back) correctly anticipated and had pre-drafted responses for, which I then tailored to the individual, and have managed to respond within a hour - two hours to most requests.

Again, I am not getting too overconfident that this will be the M.O. of IMWorth future daily operations (if I've learned anything from Customer Service, it's to expect the unexpected! :-O), but I am encouraged that we have managed to start off on the right foot.

So, that's where we stand right now. We are shaping up to take on some mammoth clients, who are mainly concerned with our size, but staffing concerns aside, we should be giving Amazon a run for their money in no time in terms of people being sick of hearing how great we are.

Date: Mon, 15 Nov 1999 10:54:26

Is my face red!

Yes, I have egg all over my face! It seems that a router of ours went down some time during early/late Friday evening (when our staff left for the weekend and no one was here to figure out we didn't work) and our host, which had told us that we had a ping process set up, apparently is red-faced, too. Had they been pinging us as we expected them to, they would have seen this Friday, and not given us a weekend with no service! To say tempers are flaring around here right now is a gross understatement!

Date: Mon, 29 Nov 1999 11:05:00

We're as ready to go live as we can be without clients. We aren't trying to garner a huge client base from the general population, per se. We want the bulk of our clients to come from the currently active users of the financial institutions that use our service. IMWorth will ideally only be used when we look like someone else's site.

Jim:

Is there a process for getting those (suggestions) from the eSuggestion Box into the hands of the right people? And more important, do they understand that these suggestions are the hearts pumping life into your site's future?

Christian:

Good point, and when my in-house Web guys come into our fold next week, I will have them insert some information into our help section regarding that. We are at the end of our good graces with the development team currently building our site, and a moratorium has been put on other changes until we get an in-house development team.

As nuts as this sounds, I wish I was getting some negative feedback. As much of a double-edged sword as I find it, I recognize that this is the best way to make yourself better, and I don't have squat to go on yet. The closest thing I've gotten to negative feedback is that people are ticked that their banks don't offer this. Great for our sales staff, but doesn't help me to streamline our existing site to its most efficient.

Jim:

Do you have one ratio for the big clients and a different one for the rest?

Christian:

No, because it appears that big clients will only need training on our system with their existing customer-service reps. So I may be totally changing my staff structure to more "client service reps" liaisoning with a few very large banks and a small, in-house staff of phone reps for smaller banks.

All in all, I'd say IMWorth is off to a strong start with a very perceptive customer service manager in charge.

Lots to do. No time to do it. No money to do it. No staff to do it. No surprise.

The other thing that helps pry upper management's cold, gnarled, old fingers off the latch of the corporate spending purse is a look into the future. Why? Because the future is ripe for the picking—it's there for whoever has the temerity to reach out and grasp it. It's theirs for the taking, if only they will.

CHAPTER 11

Planning for Tomorrow

T he future of the Web? Tough call. If you can guess what Amazon will be worth at the end of the week you can retire as a day trader of infinite wisdom. If you can look ahead a couple of years and see what will be the next big thing, then it's time to polish up a business plan in expectation of the next eye-popping IPO. Look out five years? Science fiction. Pure and simple.

Arthur C. Clark was interviewed at the end of 1999 at his home in Sri Lanka on his view of the next millennium. After correcting the interviewer that the next millennium wouldn't start until January 1, 2001, Clark expressed his hopes for more space exploration and a manned mission to Mars. As interesting as his statement was about man evolving into computers, the way he said it was riveting. It was offhand. It was casual. As if he were saying, "And, of course, we'll all be driving electric cars in the next hundred years." He takes the cyborging of the human race as a matter of fact.

Somewhere between stock market clairvoyance and all-computers-all-the-time are some interesting technologies and business practices that you should keep your eye on, and tell your boss about.

Multiple Browsers

The idea of creating multiple formats of Web content is not new. There was a time (about 10 minutes ago) when Mosaic was the only graphical Web browser. During those ten minutes, it was wise to create your content so that it could be read by both Mosaic and Lynx, the text-based browser. Since then, it's been a constant battle to make your Web site readable by Mosaic, various versions of Netscape, Internet Explorers, and a dozen other browsers.

It's about to get much worse.

It's not just Mac or PC anymore. It's not just three versions of Netscape and Internet Explorer. Soon, more people will be surfing our sites from:

Television sets	www.webtv.com
Desk telephones	www.hightech-store.com/unidenp200.html
Mobile phones	www.nokia.com/phones/9110/index.html
	www.phone.com
Pagers	www.wolfetech.com
Personal digital assistants	www.palm.com/products/palmvii
And yes, even refrigerators	www.electrolux.com/screenfridge

As time goes on, we *will* have systems wired to our heads. In the meantime, make sure your restaurant guide, stock price, inventory availability, delivery schedule, registration confirmation, and any other time-sensitive information is available via a multitude of devices and formats.

Everything Connected

Get ready for the World Wide Web to touch everything. No matter what business you're in, accept the fact that anything with a battery will have its own Web address and will be smart.

Your wristwatch will tell you when it needs a new battery and, in exchange for a discount, it'll tell the Energizer Bunny as well. If the Energizer Bunny knows when you need the batteries replaced on the majority of tools, toys, appliances, and devices in your home, it can start sending you advice on how to get the most out of your batteries. How can you advise your customers?

This Christmas, I got a TIVO television system (www.tivo.com) that calls up the mother ship once in a while and downloads the upcoming TV schedule so I can review it on the screen and choose what I want to record (on disk—not tape). It also sends info back to the mother ship about the shows I recorded since its last phone call and uses collaborative filtering to prerecord things it thinks I might want to watch. What recommendations can you make for your customers?

If Sears took a look at my refrigerator's, oven's, dishwasher's, and washing machine/dryer's performance every now and then, it could dramatically lower the occurrence of emergency come-and-fix-it calls and the overall cost of maintenance.

I know you don't work for Tivo, Sears, or Energizer. I know your business is very different. But think about ubiquitous connectivity for just a minute. What things do your customers have that could tell stories if they only had sensors on them?

- Light sensors
- Temperature sensors
- Pressure sensors
- Location sensors
- Duration sensors
- Size sensors
- Weight sensors
- Speed sensors
- Quantity sensors
- Frequency sensors

One progressive auto insurance company was offering a discount if you'd allow them to wire your car to report back to them. How far do you drive? How fast do you go? Do you make sudden starts and stops? What if that sort of technology were applied to fleets of delivery trucks? What if your pizza delivery guy had a GPS system so you'd know when to put the dogs in the bedroom?

What if you could watch how your customers use your products? What if every time your company performed a service, that information were entered into an intranet database and available to one and all inside the company? What if, after every service, your customers could punch a few buttons on their wristwatch and rate their satisfaction in real time? What would happen if everything were connected and you could have real information instead of surmised extrapolations?

And what if you started sharing that information with others?

The Third-Party Infomediary

Vertical portals are doing it already. They are aggregating the buyers and the sellers and taking a little piece of the pie from every transaction. They are the connection point between multiple interests and they are managing the information. Not only do these vertical portals make those one-to-one connections, they accumulate industry data for analysis of trends. But it's that individual profile shared among trading partners that's so interesting.

Wouldn't it be interesting to share customer profiles with other companies in order to serve those customers better on a one-to-one basis? (Before Jason Catlett from www.junkbusters.com climbs all over me, let me hasten to add this all *must* be on an opt-in basis.)

We know some things about customers, and our co-op partners know some things about them. If we pool our resources . . .

Yes, there are e-wallets coming out of the woodwork, but I'm talking about real, in-depth kind of information. The kind that would allow my local electrician to recommend the installation of a new circuit breaker because of the new DVD player and HDTV you bought at Shopping.com. Or would allow HP to e-mail you a new printer driver so you could use the business office printer at the Hyatt hotel you checked into 10 minutes ago.

Image a competitive landscape where data cartels roam the earth. It would make sense for big players in the computer industry, for example, to form close ties with big partners. It's not hard to picture the databases of noncompetitive corporations getting chummy. The result might be as in Table 11.1.

In the meantime, the means to make it happen are being created.

> The Customer Profile Exchange (CPEX) Network is a volunteer organization dedicated to developing an open standard to facilitate the exchange of privacy-enabled customer information across enterprise applications.

CPEX (www.cpex.org) wants to create the communication standards to let vendors talk to each other about you. How? More from its Web site:

> The CPEX standard integrates online and offline customer data in an XML-based data model for use within various enterprise applications both on and off the Web. The result is a networked, customer-focused environment that allows e-businesses to leverage a unified view of their customers into more compelling e-relationships. More than simply a DTD or XML tag set, CPEX will include a data model, transport and query definitions, and a framework for enabling privacy safeguards.

Table 11.1 The Big-Three Data Conglomerates

	DATA CONGLOM 1	DATA CONGLOM 2	DATA CONGLOM 3
Software	Oracle	Siebel	Microsoft
Hardware	Sun	IBM	Intel
Network Gear	Cisco	Nortel	3Com
Telco	AT&T	Nortel	MCI

Why?

> Few of today's supply-and-demand chains share a unified image of the customer, leaving customer support, order management, lead sharing and other primary business functions working independently to grasp a customer's identity, behavior and needs. Customer service capability is severely reduced by this lack of shared information, creating significant and redundant short- and long-term IT integration costs. Businesses will be able to apply CPEX across a disparate range of back-office applications, front-office applications and Web customer automation applications. While the benefits of a singular customer view are growing increasingly apparent within an enterprise, CPEX solutions will prove vital in tomorrow's world of connected enterprises.

We know that a single, integrated view of the customer will give us a competitive edge. But how much better if the whole supply chain could share a single customer image?

The CPEX data model would include:

- Descriptive information about a customer
- Deterministic information (name, address, phone)
- Demographic information (age, gender, family)
- Transactional information (interactions, declared preferences, behaviors, purchases)
- Relative information (relationship to others, groups)
- Inferred information (affinity groups, category scores, lifetime value)

Start looking around to see whom you might like as your data partner. Is it Big Brother? Or is it one who can help you serve your customer better? Your customer will decide.

Weird Tech

In the May 1999 issue of *CIO* magazine, author Don Tapscott talks about personalization and television:

> Take Volvo for example. The best person to sell a Volvo to is someone in the Volvo demographic looking for a car. I want permission marketing. I want to define myself as a market.
>
> I say, "I'm looking for a car. Here's how much I've got to spend. Here's what I care about." And have Volvo there to respond to me. This can happen in subtle ways like Simon Templer drives on the screen in a Volvo in the movie The Saint. I stop the action, and I say, "Cool car! What's that?" He says, "It's a Volvo." But he doesn't see Volvo as a safety car because Volvo is the "anything" car. He says, "What's important to you?"
>
> I say, "Performance."

He says, "Good! Volvo is the performance car! Here's how a Volvo Turbo does against a BMW 318i. And you live in Denver, that's even more important because of the oxygen level in the air."

Back in May 1999 that sounded far-fetched. Today, it sounds like just a couple of days away.

Other technology is further off, but well worth thinking about in terms of where it might lead your industry, your products, and your customers' expectations.

We Know How You Feel

Using video cameras and microphones, BlueEyes (www.almaden.ibm.com/cs/blueeyes) from IBM records where a computer user is looking and what the user is saying verbally and "gesturely." Then it's a matter of analysis to figure out the associated physical, emotional, or informational state.

> For example, a BlueEyes-enabled television could become active when the user makes eye contact, at which point the user could then tell the television to "turn on CNN." The television would respond to the user's request by changing the channel to CNN. If the television then "sees" the user smile or nod, it would know that it had satisfied the request. If the television "sees" the user frown and complain, it would explain that it didn't understand the request and ask for clarification in which you could explain you meant CNN Headline News.

IBM is investigating these technologies:

Affect Detection

The cameras and real-time analysis detect your emotional state from the expression on your face and head gestures. Are your eyebrows up or down? How about the corners of your mouth?

Emotion Mouse

Let's try the same thing as affect detection, only this time using pulse, temperature, general somatic activity (GSA), and galvanic skin response (GSR) to read somebody's emotions from their mouse. Hard to believe? Sometimes it's easier to swallow when they overwhelm you with the technical side.

> Sensors in the mouse sense the physiological attributes, which are correlated to emotions using a correlation model. The correlation model is derived from a calibration process in which a baseline attribute-to-emotion correlation is rendered based on statistical analysis of calibration signals generated by users having emotions that are measured or otherwise known at calibration time. A vector in N dimensions, representative of a subject user's emotions, is output or subsequent subject users whose emotions are sought to be known, with the baseline being the reference in the N-dimensional space of the vector.

Heart rate is taken by IR on the thumb, temperature is taken using a thermosistor chip, GSA is taken through the mouse device driver, and GSR is taken through fingertips. These values are input into a series of discriminate function analyses and correlated to an emotional state (we are doing 6). Specifically, for the mouse, discriminate function analysis is used in accordance with basic principles to determine a baseline relationship, that is, the relationship between each set of calibration physiological signals and the associated emotion.

To be included in the discriminate function analysis, the proportion of each signal's emotion-specific variance (that is not accounted for by other nonexcluded signals) to total variance must exceed a criterion proportion, which for the mouse is 0.001 (or one part per every thousand). After any signals are excluded from the analysis, all signals are analyzed simultaneously to describe the baseline relationship by a number of discriminate functions equal to one less than the number of emotions sought ($N - 1$) or the number of physiological signals, whichever is less.

Makes you wonder what the proper emotion-specific variance is for "Huh?"

Simple User Interest Tracker (Suitor)

So what *is* an "informational state"?

It's a measurement of whether the person on the other side of the screen is still looking for something, or is happy with what he or she found. It's not based so much on their emotions as it is on keeping track of what is holding their interest.

By paying constant attention to what a computer user does, Suitor can infer what sorts of information that will likely be most interesting at any moment and can then deliver that information on the spot. For example, by watching what Web page the user is browsing, Suitor can find additional information on the same topic. By watching where on the screen the user is actually reading, Suitor can more precisely determine the current topic of interest. To provide the user with additional information, Suitor can display text in a scrolling news ticker display, create a personalized Web page, or deliver the information to a hand-held device such as a PalmPilot.

The key is that a user simply interacts with the computer as usual—reading, typing, clicking—and the computer infers user interest based on what it sees the user do.

Now apply that to chatterbots and other Web-based customer service tools. Just how upset *is* the customer? How much apologizing is enough for this customer? Did the answer satisfy him or her? Is the customer still confused?

Have Your Agent Call My Agent

My office is completely overrun with stuff. Mostly paper. So, after one last, longing gaze, I am throwing out my last copy of an ad from 1996 by Lucent Technology. It shows a sharp old invoice spindle—a needle set into an ornate, square cast-iron base with one pink telephone message on it. The headline reads, "While you were out: your communications system called us, told us about a glitch and we fixed it."

Now apply that sort of prescience to human interaction. In time we will all own our own cyberagents that will do our bidding—literally.

"I'd like an international cell phone (*mobile* in the U.K., *handy* in Germany) that will let me have one phone number, and be the most economical given the places I travel to, without sacrificing quality, and I want to be able to pick up my e-mail with it."

Given those instructions, my personal agent will go looking for phones and services that meet my needs, then it will compare features and negotiate pricing. It will pick the best one and make the best deal. Which is all well and good for e-commerce. Now it's time to talk about e-customer service.

I want my agent to monitor the quality of my calls, my calling pattern, the places where I cannot get reception, and the latest developments in phone technology—without pestering me about it. The result?

- My agent will send me a voice mail reminding me to recharge my batteries.
- Based on the frequency of those reminders, my agent will order a spare battery and a charger.
- My agent will continue negotiations with service providers and send me an e-mail every time a new provider has been selected, approve their invoices for payment, and watch over the bills from the previous provider to ensure there are no extra charges.
- My agent will send the service company updates on the status of my phone and download and install software upgrades to it.
- When the phone simply does not work, my agent will contact the service company and the manufacturer and work out how to fix the problem or where to send a replacement.

Why do you need to be thinking about what my agent is doing for me? Because you're going to need an agent on your end that will respond in a timely manner.

The first personal agents that get put to use will be treated like human assistants. Human service representatives will receive a-mail (agent e-mail) and respond as if it were coming from an administrative assistant. At first this will be because they won't know it's an automated agent, and later because they figure that's good enough. It won't be. Two agents can get more done in 10 minutes than two people can get done in 10 days.

How do you prepare? It will require turning up the heat under the people who feed rules into the artificial intelligence engines we already have today. At what point does the customer need a human to get involved? At what point do we send a replacement? Under what circumstances do we send a refund?

In practice, the AI system will continually ask questions from customers of the appointed experts. In time, it will learn about frequently asked questions, frequently experienced problems, and frequently offered solutions.

It's Still about Making People Feel Cared For

Technology is great as long as it helps people. It helps people as long as people think it helps. When the goal is to cut down the amount of time you spend on the phone with your customers, you've missed the boat.

Whether you do it by phone, fax, Web site, or through collaborative filtering or vector-based dynamic reckoning, or by simply hiring more people to hold your customers' hands, the bottom line hasn't changed since people started conducting business: You're going to have to do whatever it takes to make people happy—and people are getting harder and harder to please.

Falling Behind in Real Time

You know you have to e-mail and you know you have to chat
Customer satisfaction's not a thing to dabble at
Customer expectations are doubling fast as mice
It's insufficient to be merely friendly, kind and nice.

We cannot make a promise and not come through with action
Customers would bomb us, a blow to satisfaction
You know you need a knowledge base, a chatterbot and more
Access to the production process down on the fact'ry floor.

You have to give them information, don't ever make them wait
You need to earn their admiration, so give it to them straight
If things aren't what they should be, you've got to let them know
Proactive's what you could be if aloofness you'd forego.

Say every step along the way from order to receipt
Were visible throughout the day in phases quite discrete
Your customers would know the score, they'd love you for your candor
Your competitors they would abhor and in newsgroups they would slander.

You can gain more wallet share ahead of all the masses
If you see your Web site through customer-colored glasses
You can hold your head high if you just get reflective
And build yourself a Web site from the customer's perspective.